SOCIALISM AND COMMUNISM
IN INDIA

Socialism and Communism in India

SANKAR GHOSE

ALLIED PUBLISHERS

BOMBAY CALCUTTA NEW DELHI MADRAS BANGALORE

First Published 1971

ALLIED PUBLISHERS PRIVATE LIMITED
15 Graham Road, Ballard Estate, Bombay 1
17 Chittaranjan Avenue, Calcutta 13
13/14 Asaf Ali Road, New Delhi 1
38-C Mount Road, Madras 6
39/1 J. C. Road, Bangalore 2

PRINTED IN INDIA
BY P. K. GHOSH AT EASTEND PRINTERS, 3 DR SURESH SARKAR ROAD,
CALCUTTA-14, AND PUBLISHED BY R. N. SACHDEV FOR ALLIED
PUBLISHERS PRIVATE LTD, 17 CHITTARANJAN AVENUE, CALCUTTA-13

To Shipra

Preface

In this book an attempt has been made to bring together in one place the main ideas which shaped and moulded the socialist and communist movements of India, to trace these ideas to their historical roots and to present them against their economic background.

The reaction of the early nationalists of the constitutional as also of the militant variety to socialism has first been considered and then the impact of the Russian Revolution on the socialist and communist movements in India. In the early stages of the Indian nationalist movement political freedom was regarded as the primary objective, but later socialist and communist parties and groups began to emphasize the social and economic content that the freedom struggle should have. They introduced the class question and thus contraposed themselves against the Gandhian theory of trusteeship and class collaboration.

Gandhi's faith in trusteeship, class collaboration, and decentralization of political power, and his critique of the communist theory of revolution have been considered, as also Nehru's espousal of scientific socialism, the divergent pulls of Gandhism, Western liberalism and Marxist communism over him, his approach towards fascism and his differences with Subhas Bose with regard thereto, and the policy of pragmatic socialism or empirical gradualism that he sought to pursue in post-independent India during the years of power. The crisis inside the Congress in the post–Nehru era, the polarization within it over the question of bank nationalization and during the presidential election, and, finally, the split inside the Congress and the part that the divergent approaches towards socialism had to play in this regard have been analysed.

The policy and programme of the Indian socialists belonging to divers political parties and their varying approaches towards class struggle, Marxism, Gandhism, and democracy have been considered as also the attempts at the consolidation of socialist forces to form a broad front opposed at once to the forces of capitalism as also to those of communism. The Indian socialists emphasized that political democracy was integral to socialism and many of them explored revisionist statements of Marxism. Some of the early socialist leaders later renounced socialism for *sarvodaya* or even for liberalism, as some of the early communists, pre-eminent among whom was M. N. Roy, forsook Marxism for some kind of twentieth-century Radical Humanism. Roy's role as a communist revolutionary, his crusade against fascism, his denunciation of Indian spirituality and, finally, his radical humanist critique of Marxism have been discussed.

The communist movement in India from its early stages, through the days of the Meerut Conspiracy Case, the period of the left militant phase, the succeeding period involving the pursuit of the policy of the United Front, the phase of the people's war, the insurrectionary phase during the Telengana movement, the espousal of Mao's doctrine of new democracy by the Andhra communists, and, later, the abandonment of adventurism and the pursuit of the Leninist policy of the combination of extra-parliamentary with parliamentary methods, and, finally, the communist split of 1964 have been analysed.

There had always existed two dominating and yet conflicting trends in communist strategy: one, the anti-imperialist strategy, and the other, the anti-capitalist strategy. According to the anti-imperialist strategy there has to be a combination of four classes, namely, the industrial workers, the peasants, the petty bourgeoisie and the bourgeoisie in order to fight foreign imperialism and its allies, the forces of feudalism and monopoly capitalism. According to the anti-capitalist strategy there has to be a combination of three classes, namely, the industrial workers, the peasants, and the petty bourgeoisie, in order to overthrow domestic capitalism. Though with the enunciation of the concepts of people's democracy and new democracy and their concomitant of the four-class alliance the sharp distinction between these two strategies has been somewhat blurred, the divergences over the relative importance of these two strategies none the less remained a source of grave dissension within the ranks of the Indian communists. In the end, the Sino–Indian border conflict and the Sino–Soviet ideological dispute interacting on the pre-existing complex pattern of differences within the Indian communist movement brought about its split in 1964.

The programmatic and tactical differences between the CPI and CPI(M), their respective attitudes towards Marxism and Maoism, national democracy and people's democracy, revisionism and left-sectarianism have been examined. These and other differences brought about a further split in the communist movement when in 1967 the Maoists broke off from the CPI(M). Maoism in India dates back to the days of the Telengana movement in 1948, when the Andhra communists had sought to contrapose Mao's doctrine of new democracy against the teachings of Marx, Engels, Lenin, and Stalin. The impact of Maoism on the present-day Naxalites have been considered in this connection.

The socialist and communist movements in India have brought to the forefront the problems relating to food and freedom. But in presenting the ideas of the leaders of these movements, too often the approach has been purely adulatory or wholly pejorative. Though it is not possible, nor even desirable, to be dispassionate in respect of these great issues, it is none the less necessary that the history of these movements should be presented fully, fairly, and in their many-sided complexity.

I have indicated in appropriate places my indebtedness to others where I have benefited from the written word. Friends by discussion with whom I profited are legion but they would prefer anonymity. My indebtedness is particularly great to my wife and children to whom belonged much of the time devoted to the writing of this book.

SANKAR GHOSE

2F Camac Street
Calcutta
2 January 1971

Contents

Chapter One : THE FIRST CONTACT WITH SOCIALIST
THOUGHT

I. The Early Nationalists and Socialism *1*
II. India and the Russian Revolution *8*
III. Socialist Technique of Nationalist Revolution *16*
IV. Socialism and Indian Tradition *24*

Chapter Two : THE ECONOMIC BACKGROUND

I. Rise of Modern Industries *35*
II. The Growth of Labour Movement in India *45*
III. Landed Aristocrats and Peasant Movements *73*

Chapter Three : GANDHI ON SOCIALISM AND
COMMUNISM

I. Gandhian Socialism *92*
II. The Theory of Trusteeship *95*
III. Gandhi and Modern Industrialism *101*
IV. Gandhian Non-violence and Communism *108*
V. Gandhian Decentralism, Nehru and Socialism *115*
VI. The Communist Critique of Gandhi *120*

Chapter Four : M. N. ROY AND COMMUNISM

I. Roy as a Communist Revolutionary *143*
II. Roy as a Crusader against Fascism *163*
III. Roy's Denunciation of Indian Spirituality *167*
IV. Radical Humanist Critique of Marxism *169*

Chapter Five : NEHRU ON SOCIALISM

    I. Nehru's Faith in Scientific Socialism *181*
    II. The 1936 Congress Crisis over Nehru's Socialism *185*
    III. Conflicting Pulls of Gandhism and Communism *187*
    IV. Divergent Approaches of Nehru and Bose
        to Communism and Fascism *195*
    V. Post-Independence Planning and Socialism *202*
    VI. The Years of Power and Pragmatic Socialism *209*

Chapter Six : THE CONGRESS SPLIT AND SOCIALISM

    I. Polarization Inside the Congress *216*
    II. Indira Gandhi, Bank Nationalization
        and the Presidential Election *224*
    III. The CPI, the CPI(M) and the Congress Split *248*

Chapter Seven : THE INDIAN SOCIALISTS

    I. The Socialists, Class Struggle and
        Nationalization *260*
    II. The Socialists, Marxism and Democracy *268*
    III. The Socialists, Gandhism and Liberalism *276*
    IV. Fragmentation of Social Forces in India *283*

Chapter Eight : THE INDIAN COMMUNISTS

    I. The Early Years *293*
    II. The Meerut Conspiracy Case *301*
    III. The Left Militant Phase *304*
    IV. The Policy of United Front *308*
    V. The People's War *314*
    VI. The Multi-National Theory and Pakistan *317*
    VII. Ranadive and the Insurrectionary Method *320*
    VIII. Mao's New Democracy and the Andhra
         Communists *324*
    IX. The Rejection of Adventurism *328*

X. The Communists and Parliamentary Institutions *334*
XI. The Communist Split of 1964 *347*

Chapter Nine : THE UNITED FRONTS OF BENGAL
                AND KERALA

I. The Emergence of the United Fronts *362*
II. Inter-Party Clashes *370*

Chapter Ten : THE IDEOLOGY OF THE CPI

I. The CPI on Marxism and Maoism *395*
II. The CPI Concept of National Democracy *403*

Chapter Eleven : THE IDEOLOGY OF THE CPI(M)

I. The CPI(M) Critique of Revisionism *414*
II. The CPI(M) Critique of the Russian
     Communist Party *419*
III. The CPI(M) Critique of the Chinese
     Communist Party *431*

Chapter Twelve : MAOISM AND THE NAXALITES *439*

Bibliography *445*

Index *465*

List of Tables

Large industrial establishments in British India (1935) *42*

Population growth in India since 1891 *44*

Indian population highlights during 1951 and 1961 *44*

Index numbers of industrial production since 1951 *45*

Growth in the number of registered trade unions
between 1936 and 1939 *63*

Registered trade unions and their membership
from 1947 to 1958 *69*

Number of strikes in India since 1921 *73*

Communist position in the state assemblies and parliament
in 1952 and 1957 *337*

1957 election results—Lok Sabha *337*

Percentage of communist votes in the states
in 1962 election *339*

1962 election results—Lok Sabha *339*

1967 election results—Lok Sabha *340*

1967 election results—state assemblies *341*

Kerala assembly mid-term elections : 1970 *376*

CHAPTER ONE

The First Contact with Socialist Thought

I. THE EARLY NATIONALISTS AND SOCIALISM

The first contact of resurgent India with socialist thought was through Raja Rammohan Roy, the father of modern India. When Rammohan was in England many of the religious and economic reformers of the time were guests of Dr. Arnot, and there Rammohan met Robert Owen, the socialist leader. Owen sought to convert Rammohan to socialism and the discussion that ensued was not only animated but somewhat heated. Rammohan's biographer, Sophia Collet, recorded that Owen lost his temper in the course of the discussion.[1]

Indian nationalists have always found some support for their cause from the labour leaders of Europe. At first this association of Indian political leaders with the labour and socialist leaders of the West gave rise to criticism. In 1897 it caused some uneasiness to the friends and admirers of Dadabhai Naoroji, the moderate leader, to find him seeking the support of socialists in his political crusade for the liberalization of British rule in India. The *Hindu Patriot,* an organ of the British Indian Association, an association of landlords, considered it a dangerous policy. But Dadabhai answered such criticism saying: "Do not be prejudiced that it is the socialists who are helping us ... it is an unexpected good fortune that the Indian cause has been taken up by a powerful and advancing organization to whom the future largely belongs."[2] Dadabhai, the grand old man of India, had come into contact with socialist thought through Hyndman with whom he had developed a friendship. But the socialist Hyndman always regarded Dadabhai as being too moderate in his politics.

The early Congressmen or moderates were generally immune from the influence of socialist thought. At a time when the moderates were criticizing British Indian policy, Robertus and Marx had completed their writings and had laid the foundations of what is called "scientific socialism," and the evolutionary socialism of the Fabians had emerged, while in the world of practical politics Hyndman and Keir Hardie had begun their socialistic agitation. The moderates, however, were not so much concerned with the problems or inner contradictions of a capitalist society as with the economic problem that India faced as a result of the impact of an industrially advanced imperial power on a traditional economy.

The moderates, such as Romesh Dutt and Dadabhai Naoroji, referred to the phenomenon as to how the traditional Indian economy was disintegrating under the influence of British imperial policy, how the old agro-industrial balance was being shattered and how the poverty of the masses was increasing. On this economic diagnosis the moderates built up a powerful critique of British policy in India and made it the basis of their indictment of British rule. They pleaded for the liberalization of the administration, also advocating that the state should play a positive role in effecting the economic growth of India's underdeveloped economy. The moderates were thus the forerunners of the modern advocates of welfare economics.

Socialists in Britain criticized British imperialism and said that imperialism was bound to lead to exploitation. Indians who were struggling to end British rule in India also traced the poverty of the people to British imperialism and exploitation. The attack of the Indian nationalists on British imperialism was in a sense the same as the socialistic attack. This criticism, imperceptibly and gradually, led some Indian nationalists to a vague socialistic approach. "You have been regularly draining and bleeding us of millions of money ... these millions do not go to make you any better off, they go into the pockets of the capitalists," declared the moderate Dadabhai in 1901 before a British audience,[3] but yet Dadabhai was by no means a socialist.

Dadabhai attributed the poverty of India primarily to the drain of the wealth of India to Britain. He asserted that "not till this disastrous drain was duly checked and not till the people of India were restored to their natural rights in their own country was there any hope of the material amelioration of India."[4] Dadabhai's views were published in the form of a book entitled *Poverty and Un-British Rule in India*, wherein he claimed that the drain prevented India from retaining any capital, that the British, by bringing back the capital which they had drained from India, secured almost a monopoly of all trade and important industries, thereby further exploiting and draining India.[5] According to Dadabhai, by the year 1871 the amount drained out had exceeded £500,000,000 (a figure considered excessive by William Digby and Professor Furber,[6] an American investigator). Dadabhai asserted that it was no wonder "that the great mass of the poor people have hardly 2*d* a day and a few rags, or a scanty subsistence."[7]

The drain theory of Dadabhai was subsequently hailed by many socialists and communists of India. Asoka Mehta, a later socialist of India, claimed that, "sociologically speaking, the Drain Theory alone enables one to understand the havoc that was being wrought in India by the working of imperialism. The working of the laws of imperialism can be uncovered by the Drain Theory alone, as the law of capitalism can be uncovered by the Labour Theory of Value."[8] Mehta did not attribute any analytical significance to either the Drain Theory of Dadabhai or the Labour Theory of Value of Marx. He asserted that both these theories could be proved wrong but claimed that they had "sociological significance" in rousing Indian nationalists and the working class of the world respectively.[9]

The drain theory of Dadabhai, though much criticized, was the first attempt of Indian liberals to examine the nature of imperialism. Like Dadabhai, Romesh Dutt, the first distinguished economic historian of India, also attributed the poverty of India to the exploitation that the country was being subjected to under a foreign rule. But whereas Dadabhai laid greater emphasis on the "drain" through Home Charges, Romesh Dutt emphasized the role of land revenue settlements as an impoverishing factor. But both Romesh Dutt and Dadabhai referred to certain aspects of British imperial rule in explaining the "deep and deepening poverty" of the country.

The criticism by the moderates of British imperial rule in India was virtually the same as the socialistic criticism. In support of such criticism the Indian moderates or liberals, however, did not refer to Karl Marx but to John Stuart Mill. Mill had written: "The government of a people by itself has a meaning and a reality, but such a thing as government of one people by another does not, and cannot, exist. One people may keep another for its own use, a place to make money in, a human cattle-farm to be worked for the profits of its own inhabitants." Romesh Dutt said that there was more truth in this strongly worded statement than appeared at first sight.[10]

No socialist could improve upon the criticisms that Dadabhai Naoroji or Romesh Dutt made of the economic policies pursued by Britain in India. Referring to early British rule Romesh Dutt wrote that "in many ways, the sources of national wealth in India have been narrowed under British rule. India in the eighteenth century was a great manufacturing as well as a great agricultural country, and the products of the Indian loom supplied the markets of Asia and of Europe. It is, unfortunately, true that the East Indian Company and the British Parliament, following the selfish commercial policy of a hundred years ago, discouraged Indian manufacturers in the early years of British rule in order to encourage the rising manufacturers of England. Their fixed policy, pursued during the last decades of the nineteenth century, was to make India subservient to the industries of Great Britain, and to make the Indian people grow raw produce only, in order to supply material for the looms and manufactories of Great Britain. This policy was pursued with unwavering resolution and with fatal success; orders were sent out, to force Indian artisans to work in the Company's factories; commercial residents were legally vested with extensive powers over villages and communities of Indian weavers; prohibitive tariffs excluded Indian silk and cotton goods from England; English goods were admitted into India free of duty or on payment of nominal duty."[11]

Apart from criticizing British imperialism, which the socialists criticized, the early Indian liberals also attacked the doctrine of *laissez-faire*, a doctrine wholly opposed to socialistic theory which relies on state power to effect social and economic changes. Among the first Indian nationalists who attacked this theory of *laissez-faire* were K. T. Telang and M. G. Ranade. In 1877 Telang argued that while Indians were denied the benefit of the British political theory that a people should not be taxed unless their representatives consented to such taxation, there was no reason why the economic theory of *laissez-faire*, which prevailed in Britain, should be adopted in India.[12] He referred to John Stuart Mill who, though a believer in the *laissez-faire* doctrine, had conceded that in countries where the people were poor, ignorant, unenterprising, and lacked the spirit of cooperation it might be necessary and desirable that a progressive government should take an active part in the development of the national economy by building roads, works of irrigation, hospitals, schools, printing presses, etc.[13] Telang similarly asserted that in a backward country like India there could not be any great industrial development without state aid and assistance, and that the adoption of a *laissez-faire* policy would prove as harmful in India as it had proved beneficial in Britain.[14]

In 1892 in his essay on "Indian Political Economy" M. G. Ranade also pointed out that the theory of *laissez-faire* could not be applied indiscriminately to all countries. He drew particular attention to the fact that this theory had been challenged by new economic schools and especially by the German Historical school.[15] He championed state interference for improving the economy of the country. Ranade may be said to have thus laid the foundations of a policy whose fruition one sees in the subsequent five-year plans of India.

From a résumé of the history of the growth of economic science in England, France, Germany, Italy, and America, Ranade established that modern European thought did not at all countenance the view of the English writers of the Ricardian School, that the principles of the science as enunciated in their text-books or the doctrine of *laissez-faire* were universally true or were valid at all stages of advancement. Whatever may be the position in an advanced country, in a backward country like India the state had to play an active role in the development of the economy. Towards the end of the last century the meddlesomeness of the mercantile system had provoked in Europe a reaction against all kinds of state control and guidance. This negative approach led to the development of the theory of *laissez-faire*. But later there was a reaction even in Europe against this doctrine so that "the province of state interference and control," wrote Ranade, "is particularly being extended so as to restore the good points of the mercantile system without its absurdities."[16]

But though the early Indian moderates or nationalists would have joined hands with the socialists in their denunciation of imperialism and *laissez-faire*, they were not advocates of socialism, an ideology with which they were only imperfectly acquainted, if at all. So far as the extremists or militant nationalists are concerned they repeated the criticisms that the moderates had made of British imperialism and the doctrine of *laissez-faire*, but they were also not socialists by any means. Aurobindo Ghose, the extremist leader, sometimes referred to "the proletariat" and, again, the strike of the Bombay mill-workers in 1908 in protest against the arrest and imprisonment of Tilak, the extremist leader, was hailed by Lenin,[17] but the proletariat was yet to become a force in Indian politics.

Among the extremist leaders, Lajpat Rai and Bepin Pal, to some extent, came in contact with socialistic thought. Lajpat Rai, the Punjab nationalist leader, and Bepin Pal, the extremist leader from Bengal, when in Europe met many socialist intellectuals and labour leaders. Lajpat Rai, without troubling himself with the theories about capitalistic economy, was drawn almost instinctively to the labour leaders of the Western world. In England it was among the members of the British Labour Party that he felt at home. In the USA the group that attracted him most was the group associated with the Rand School of Social Science and the Civic Club in New York, both centres of socialistic intellectuals.

At the end of World War I Lajpat Rai came to believe that the nationalist movement in India should adopt the aims of the British Labour Party. He condemned the prevailing social order of Europe as vicious and immoral, and wrote: "It is based on injustice, tyranny, oppression and class-rule, certain phases of it are inherent in our own system. Certain others we are borrowing from our masters in order to make a complete mess."[18] He warned his countrymen that what was needed in India was "not the power to implant in full force and in full vigour the expiring European system." Lajpat claimed that Marx's diagnosis of the ills of capitalist society had turned out to be so true "that there is now practical unanimity among western thinkers about the indescribable evils of the capitalist system."[19] But Lajpat was not a Marxist. "I am neither a communist nor have I a great deal of sympathy for the doctrine of communism," he

wrote in *The People* in 1928.[20] Further, Lajpat did not think
that the Marxist appeal that the workers of the world should
unite could ever be translated into reality inasmuch as the interests
of the British labourers were different from the interests of the
Indian labourers, who were suffering under British rule. "To
talk of the solidarity of the Labour Movement all the world over,
to the Indian workers is simply bunkum...what the Indian
workers need," wrote Lajpat, "is not dogma but help in organizing and in the redress of his grievances against the government
and the employers. To feed him on the doctrines of communism
or any other ism, to talk to him of international solidarity as if
it had already been achieved, to ask him to throw himself into
international controversies for international affiliation is to lead
him [astray]."[21]

In 1919 Lajpat declared that many Indian nationalists were
afraid of attacking the privileges of the territorial aristocrats and
the industrial magnates and were willing to maintain an economic
system in which a small minority of the people possessed the greater
part of the national wealth.[22] He felt that it was not enough to
fight against the domination of foreign rulers, it was also necessary to fight against the privileges which the Indian capitalists
and landlords enjoyed.[23] He declared that India needed leaders
like Keir Hardie and Lansbury who would not be afraid of
attacking the privileges of the men of property and who would
fight for the establishment of a real democracy in order to provide equality of opportunity for all.[24]

Lajpat and Bepin Pal were both impressed by the achievements
of the Russian revolution. Pal said that he had fought shy of the
word "Bolshevism" at first, but after a visit to Europe, where he
could study the literature of Bolshevism, he came to realize that
the aim of Bolshevism, a powerful and growing force in Europe,
was to emancipate the working men from the rule of the capitalists.

In 1913 Pal drew attention to the fact that there had arisen a
powerful group of thinkers in Europe who had realized that so
long as there existed grave economic inequalities the establishment
of a political democracy alone would not secure the freedom of
the common people.[25] He claimed that though representative
government had theoretically transferred all political power from
kings and aristocrats to the common masses, as a matter of fact

the real rulers in modern political democracies were the wealthy
capitalists, who with the help of the educated middle class,
controlled the democratic parliaments.[26]

Pal believed that in democratic countries such as Britain,
France, and the United States of America, class conflict might
be ended peacefully and constitutionally by the adoption of some
form of State Socialism, but he doubted whether this class conflict
could be ended peacefully and constitutionally in countries such
as Germany and Austria-Hungary where there did not exist any
democratic political structure.[27] In Russia, where there existed
no political democracy, the Bolsheviks came to power by pursuing
revolutionary methods. In 1919 Pal asked the rulers of India to
consider whether in India, where the people were very poor and
where there existed no political democracy, there might not
break out a violent Bolshevik revolution if vigorous and timely
measures were not taken to increase the political liberties and to
improve the economic condition of the masses.[28]

Lajpat and Pal criticized various features of the capitalist system
but they were not socialists. They wanted to reform the capitalistic system by the development of a strong trade union movement and by various other means.[29] Lajpat said that he wanted
to avoid class struggle but in order to ameliorate the condition
of the masses socially beneficent legislation would have to be
introduced and for this India needed Home Rule.[30] In 1919
Lajpat wrote: "We know we cannot fly the flag of Socialism.
We do not understand Socialism. We have never studied it."[31]
In fact till the Russian revolution not many educated Indians had
come into contact with socialistic thought. Lajpat and Pal were
attracted to socialism in a vague humanitarian way but their
ideas on socialism were neither very clear nor consistent. In fact,
at certain stages Pal even toyed with the idea of "Hindu Socialism" and "Pagan Socialism."

II. INDIA AND THE RUSSIAN REVOLUTION

In the twenties and thirties of this century India presented a
problem which in some respects was similar to that faced by pre-
revolutionary Russia—the problem of agriculture and a peasantry
unadjusted to the economic forces which had been let loose

upon them by modern industrialism. In both, despite universal illiteracy, an élite or a highly trained intellectual class had developed throughout the nineteenth century which had entered into a struggle with the efficient but unimaginative bureaucracy which controlled the governmental machinery of these countries. The principle of autocracy on which the Russian and Indian systems of government was based was constantly challenged by this intellectual class. Some leaders of this class rebelled against the Western influence and the tendency to modernization, such as Tolstoy in Russia and Gandhi in India. The Russian *slavophil* and the Indian peasant saw in the ancient religious doctrines of their respective countries a means by which rapid Westernization and modernization might be arrested.

Within a few years of the revolution Russia industrialized herself. Education spread among the ignorant masses, internal racial antagonisms were reduced and peoples as varied as those in India were brought into greater social cohesion. This was a tremendous achievement and a surprising revolution. The great and fascinating unfolding of a new order in Russia is the most promising feature of our dismal age, proclaimed Jawaharlal Nehru in his Congress presidential address of 1936.[32]

Immediately after the Russian revolution many articles appeared in various Indian newspapers and periodicals, such as the *Kesari* of Tilak, the *Bombay Chronicle*, edited by B. G. Horniman, and the *Modern Review*, edited by Ramananda Chatterjee, hailing the Russian revolution and claiming that the Bolsheviks stood for the down-trodden and that they were opposed to imperialism.

On 29 January 1918 in an editorial on Lenin, the *Kesari* stated: "We are publishing the main facts of Lenin's life since mischievous propaganda is being carried on that the popular Russian leader Lenin is the son of a German Jew and has been bribed by the German government. Lenin is being accused of creating disaffection among the Russian people who are claimed to be loyal to the Allied powers." On 20 July 1920 the *Kesari* wrote that the foreign policy of the Soviet government was "not to annex foreign territory or to impose the principles of its economics on foreign countries by force" inasmuch as it believed that "the social and political institutions in each country arise out of the historical traditions and economic conditions of the country concerned."

B. G. Horniman writing in the *Bombay Chronicle* on 24 December 1917 stated: "Our ideas about the Bolsheviks are very vague ... [but] we recognize the fact that they could never have met with the present success had there not been something in their programme that was attractive and of promise to serve the present. ... The Bolsheviks came with a definite scheme which took into consideration the necessities of the peasants and promised immediate confiscation of lands for the people." Again on 11 January 1918 another editorial in the *Bombay Chronicle* claimed that the victory of the Bolsheviks would mean the victory of the common people. It said: "If Lenin is successful the March revolution will sink into insignificance before the November revolution, for its success is nothing less than the end of the upper-middle class and the final triumph of the common people."

Ramananda Chatterjee, editor of the *Modern Review*, also welcomed the Russian revolution. In its issue of February 1919 the *Modern Review* stated: "It is refreshing to turn from the chorus of abuses and mis-representation directed against the Russian Soviets by the capitalist press to the illuminating sketch of the frame-work of the Soviet state. ... We are, at last, given an insight into the mighty efforts of revolutionary Russia to organize herself and work out her communist ideals. ... In fact, the Bolshevik is striving to make Russia better and nobler than anything she has ever been."

Before the Russian revolution there was very great admiration in India for America and for the American people's vitality, energy, and optimistic attitude towards life. In 1917 Tagore had said in *Nationalism* that America was destined to justify Western civilization to the East. Europe had her great traditions but also her imperial possessions. The relationship between the Eastern peoples and the European powers was not free and easy because the European powers came as conquerors in Asia. America was a country untrammelled by traditions and the foundation of her glory was more in the future than in the past. "Europe," said Tagore, "has gradually grown hardened in her pride in all her outer and inner habits. ... In America national habits and traditions have not had the time to spread their clutching roots round your hearts. ... this very freedom of detachment will enable you ... to achieve the goal for which Europe began her journey but lost herself in other parts of the world. . . . The freedom of your history from all unclean entanglements . . . carries all the responsibility of a great future because you are untrammelled by the grasping miserliness of the past."[33] At first Vivekananda had also been much impressed by American power, wealth, and vitality. But later he developed doubts whether America had any significant spiritual message to give to the world and he prophesied that the next awakening would come either from Russia or China.

While, before the Russian revolution, America was a great source of inspiration to Indian nationalists, after the Russian revolution many Indians began to turn to Russia for light. The Russian revolution had also its impact on Tagore, who had once admired the dynamism and vitality of the American people. In 1930 when Tagore went to Russia he said that he had come on a pilgrimage. Wherever he looked he saw only workers. "Where are the so-called gentlemen? The masses of Russia live no more in the dark shadows of the so-called gentlemen," wrote Tagore.

Furthermore, the Soviet Republic was in Indian, and indeed in Asian, minds regarded as somewhat of an Asian rather than a Western country and Russia was thought to be the precursor of the new Asia. Before Western civilization, so triumphant in the power of wealth, Russia had raised the dispossessed to the seat of power, said Tagore. The colonial peoples of Asia had anxiously watched the intervention of certain powers in Russia on behalf of the vested interests of the old régime but their sympathies were with Russia, where the poor were not despised for their poverty. The polish of luxury was altogether absent from Moscow. "Why should we be afraid of that," asked Tagore, "we the hungry and helpless underdogs of the world?"

What impressed Tagore most in Russia was the absence of luxury. Tagore said that he was familiar with the ostentation of wealth in various European countries, but it was so Olympian "that, poor as we are, even our envy fails to reach its height. In Russia, the display of luxury is wholly absent. . . . There I saw mighty efforts being made to provide universally everything of which India is deprived."[34]

It is not abstract or dogmatic regard for socialism or Marxism that attracted Tagore. For what filled Tagore's heart with delight was the spread of education in Russia, and he wondered how literacy could spread so quickly there. "Again and again I have

asked myself: How has such a great miracle been possible? The
answer that I have received in my mind is that here there is no
barrier of greed."[35]

Russia was ruled by a dictator. But to perpetuate such rule,
Tagore said, Russia had not chosen the path of the Tsars, namely,
"the subduing of the people's mind by ignorance and religious
superstition, the impairing of their manliness by the lash of the
Cossacks." The punitive rod was not inactive in Russia, yet the
Russian rulers were diligent in spreading education among the
people.

Tagore said that Bolshevism sprang from a hatred of injustice
and from a desire to remove inequality and poverty. But Tagore
was distressed by the excesses of the Russian experiment, its
scant regard for individualism, and its great belief in violence as
a means of social transformation. He said: "Bolshevism ... is like
the storm which rushes in all fury flashing its lightning teeth. ...
This unnatural revolution has broken out because human society
has lost its balance. It is because the individual's apathy for the
community had been growing that the suicidal proposal of
sacrificing the individual in the name of collectivity has
arisen."[36]

Tagore conceded that Russia was engaged in the task of building the road to a new age, of tearing up the roots of ancient
beliefs and customs, and "of penalizing the luxury of time-
honoured habits." Tagore even conceded that it may be that the
ills from which the world suffered required drastic remedies like
Bolshevism. "It is not improbable that in this age Bolshevism is
the treatment," said Tagore, "but medical treatment cannot be
permanent; indeed the day on which the doctor's régime comes
to an end must be hailed as the red-letter day for the patient."[37]
Tagore was distressed by the fact that a violent effort was being
made to cast public opinion in Soviet Russia into the mould of
Marxian economics and that, accordingly, free discussion was
being deliberately stifled.[38]

Tagore, the poet and individualist, could not approve of the
suppression of individuality or liberty, though he could understand it, and in the case of the Soviet experiment he could even
sympathize with it. He said: "Where the temptation for quick
results is too strong, the political leaders are loth to respect man's
right to liberty of opinion. They are wont to say: 'Let us attain

our objectives first: We shall attend to other things later.' The situation in Russia resembles wartime conditions. She is beset with enemies at home and abroad. There is ceaseless manoeuvring all round to wreck the entire experiment. The foundations of their structure therefore must be strengthened as quickly as possible; hence they have no qualms about using force. Nevertheless, however insistent the necessity may be, force is one-sided. It destroys, it does not create."[39]

The communists in Russia were in a hurry to create a new social order and for this they had established a dictatorship. Tagore was not prepared to support dictatorial rule in any sphere or in any country. During the first non-cooperation movement Tagore had publicly opposed some of the views of Gandhi and had warned his countrymen against accepting what Gandhi said as gospel truth or allowing Gandhi to control the nationalist movement as a dictator. Tagore recalled: "When Mahatmaji called foreign cloth impure, I protested and said that it might be economically harmful but could on no account be impure. But our blind scripture-led mind must be bewitched or else nothing gets done. What can be more eternally humiliating to one's manhood than this? Thus is a dictator-led country hypnotized; one magician takes leave to be replaced by another with a different formula."[40] Tagore, therefore, cautioned his countrymen against accepting Marxism as a dogma or as the absolute truth. He was afraid, however, that in a scripture-ridden and priest-led country like India the temptation to regard Marxism as a dogma would not be inconsiderable.[41]

Iqbal, the other great poet of India, was at first antagonistic to Russia and socialism. He believed socialism to be materialistic. In a poem written in 1922 he put Lenin along with Kaiser in Hell, but gradually Iqbal's ideas changed and, later, Iqbal wrote many poems in praise of socialism and used the name, and sometimes the ideas, of Marx in his condemnation of the West. In a poem composed in 1935 he even canonized Lenin. Iqbal said that the USSR was to some extent, though only unconsciously, doing God's work. He attributed the anti-religiousness of Russia primarily to the history of corrupt practices of the old orthodox Church of Russia. Iqbal declared that if he was made the dictator of a Muslim State he would first make it a socialist state. Though Iqbal made no clear analysis of the capitalist system he was emotionally attracted to socialism. His views on socialism were not, however, always consistent and in spite of all his admiration for socialism, Iqbal throughout remained a firm believer in Pan-Islamism.

Though after the Russian revolution Indians also sought inspiration from the Russian experiment, it is undeniable that Russia and America remained the two great sources of inspiration for Indians. Both these countries in their different ways had achieved greatness, and their vitality appealed to Indian nationalists who wanted to energize and activate a stagnant people. "The USA and USSR both had a dynamic outlook and vast resources, a social fluidity and an absence of medieval background, a faith in science and its application, and a widespread education and opportunities for the people. In America in spite of vast differences of income there were no fixed classes as in most other countries and there was a sense of equality. Both America and Russia did not carry that heavy burden of the past which had oppressed Asia and Europe," observed Nehru in *The Discovery of India*.[42]

Since the Russian revolution socialist and communist thought have increasingly spread throughout the world. The growth of trade unions, in particular, helped in the development of the socialist movement in India. In 1920 the All India Trade Union Congress was formed. In inaugurating the All India Trade Union Congress Lajpat Rai, its president, said: "Imperialism and militarism are twin children of capitalism; they are one in three and three in one. It is only lately that an antidote has been discovered and that antidote is organized labour. . . . The workers of Europe and America have now discovered that the cause of the workers is one and the same all the world over, and that there can be no salvation for them until and unless the workers of Asia were organized, and then internationally affiliated. . . . The movement we are inaugurating today is thus of more than national importance. It is a matter of international significance. The workers of India are joining hands and brains not only to solidify the interests of Indian labour, but also to forge a link in the chain of international brotherhood. . . . My own experience of Europe and America leads me to think that socialistic, even Bolshevik, truth is any day better, more reliable and more humane than capitalist and imperialist truth." The idea of the international solidarity of labour which Lajpat proclaimed in 1920 was, however, later rejected by him, for in 1927 he declared that the idea that the interests of British labourers, who exploited India, were the same as that of Indian labourers was "simply bunkum."[43]

Ever since the Russian revolution Indian labour had been pulled in two different directions. The moderate trade unions were attached to the Second International. The more extreme section was attracted to Soviet Russia and the Third International. In India the conflict between the Second and Third International led to a split in the trade union movement in 1929. The moderates walked out of the All India Trade Union Congress and set up the Indian Trade Union Federation on the ground *inter alia* that the All India Trade Union Congress had affiliated itself to the League Against Imperialism and the Pan Pacific Trade Union Secretariat, both of which were dominated by communists.

Industrial labour, particularly in Bombay and Calcutta, have since the 1920s been influenced by Russian propaganda and by the English and Indian agents of the Third International. The Communist International set up a special branch for the dissemination of communism in India, and communist literature advocating the development of a revolutionary mentality was circulated. The red flag and the device of the hammer and sickle became increasingly evident in labour meetings in India and in the processions of workers the cry of *Inquilab Zindabad* (Long live the revolution) began to be heard. Further, Calcutta, Bombay and even some small towns began to have their May Days and November Days.

Since the 1920s vague socialistic and communistic ideas began to spread among the young intelligentsia of India. The young welcomed these ideas with energy, enthusiasm, and even recklessness. They read Karl Marx as eagerly as an earlier generation had read Mazzini. Everywhere there was a new spirit of inquiry and growing discontent with the older ideologies. Those who were inclined towards the left asserted that Gandhi and the Congress represented a bourgeois policy.

One of the most important contributions of the Russian revolution and the Russian experiment in planning was to make planning popular among Indian nationalists. Many had looked at socialism only as a theory of distribution, but the revolution in Russia gave rise to the idea that through socialism and state planning production could be raised. Socialist agitators had preached equality and had emphasized the need for equitable distribution. In academic circles, however, greater production was thought a much more pressing need in the peculiar backward conditions of India. After the Russian revolution the chief attraction of socialism to some academic economists lay in the idea of planning and not in the idea of class war or of economic equality. A National Planning Committee was set up by the Congress in 1938 with the support of Jawaharlal Nehru and Subhas Bose, both of whom declared themselves to be socialists, to inquire into the possibility of a planned development of India's resources.

Nehru believed that in a country of arrested economic growth, such as India, planning was essential. "I am all for tractors and big machinery and I am convinced," wrote Nehru, "that the rapid industrialization of India is essential to relieve the pressure on the land, to combat poverty and to raise standards of living, for defence, and a variety of other purposes. But I am equally convinced that the most careful planning and adjustment are necessary if we are to reap the full benefit of industrialization and avoid many of its dangers. This planning is necessary today in all countries of arrested growth, like China and India, which have strong traditions of their own."[44] Subhas Bose in *The Indian Struggle* had also visualized the emergence of a left party which "will build up a new belief in a sound system of state-planning for the reorganization of agricultural and industrial life of the country."[45]

III. SOCIALIST TECHNIQUE OF NATIONALIST REVOLUTION

During the freedom movement in India the communists called for a proletarian revolution in order to destroy imperialism. They summoned the workers to organize themselves for overthrowing British rule. To them the Indian national struggle appeared to be a stage in the longer journey towards socialism. The question arose whether India would be able to attain economic freedom along with political independence or would have to attain political freedom first and then build upon its foundations a structure of economic liberty and equality.

The end of the Indian nationalist movement was *Swaraj*, but *swaraj* was never defined positively. Negatively, it implied the elimination of alien rule. But what form of government and what type of economic structure were to follow the disappearance of the alien rule was never adequately discussed. Did *swaraj* mean the establishment of a parliamentary form of government in India on the British model as the moderates envisaged, or the establishment of village self-government and *Ram Raj* as Gandhi proclaimed? The communists argued that it was dangerous to fight for freedom or *swaraj* without knowing the kind of freedom that was desired. They said that freedom was not very much worth having if it meant the replacement of the exploitation of foreign capitalists by a similar exploitation at the hands of Indian capitalists, and that freedom could not mean the freedom of the capitalist and the worker at one and at the same time. They urged that it must be stated categorically as to whose freedom it was desired, for the freedom of the capitalist might be tantamount to slavery for the workers. M. N. Roy, one of the early communists of India, felt that a vague nationalism which sought to combine the interests of all classes, such as of labour and capital and of the peasant and the landlord, was a snare and a delusion and he asserted that a true socialist movement could not combine the interests of all classes. M. N. Roy elaborated his views in *India in Transition*[46] (1922), *India's Problem And Its Solution, One Year of Non-Cooperation*[47] (1923), and in other books and tracts.

Marxists said that theories which asserted that capital and labour were interdependent, that class struggle was harmful, that revolution was destructive and that a synthesis of all the social forces was a higher ideal than class war, were the commonest ideas of the West preached by bourgeois apologists of the existing order, but that a true revolutionary must rely on the strength of the workers, peasants, and the petty bourgeoisie and should not seek assistance from other classes in society, such as the landlords and the capitalists. Developing this line of thought R. P. Dutt, the Marxist theoretician, stated in *Modern India* (1926) that the Indian bourgeoisie was a counter-revolutionary force and only the workers, peasants, and the petty bourgeoisie could organize a truly nationalist movement.[48]

Most nationalists opposed these theories on the ground that

the preaching of class war would split the nationalist movement. They said that *charka* and *khaddar*, which constituted the economic ideology of Gandhi, might be a backward ideology but it would not break up the *swaraj* front, whereas the division of the people on the basis of capitalists and workers or of the haves and have-nots would break up the unity of the national will and thereby strengthen the forces of imperialism. Only after national liberation was attained, it was argued, could people be divided on the basis of class and economic ideology, but during the period of political dependence class antagonism in the economic sphere should be overshadowed by the community of interests of the workers and capitalists in the political sphere.

The Congress was not a proletarian organization and it did not exclude the capitalists or landlords from its ranks, though, being a mass organization in a poor country, it could not be a purely bourgeois or rightist organization. "If the Congress," claimed Nehru in *The Unity of India* (1944), "is looked upon from the Right and Left point of view it might be said that there is a small Rightist fringe, a left minority, and a huge intermediate group or groups which approximate to Left-Centre. The Gandhian group would be considered to belong to this intermediate Left-Centre group. Politically the Congress is overwhelmingly Left; socially, it has Leftist leanings, but is predominantly Centre. In matters affecting the peasantry it is pro-peasant."[49]

National democratic movements the world over showed how all classes of the people could combine together against an alien rule. In many European countries in times of national crisis the whole nation rose as one man to throw off the foreign yoke or to resist the imposition of a foreign rule. In England, in critical times, or in times of national calamity, the political genius of the British evolved the system of a national government. Even in the first revolution, that overthrew the Tsar, the Bolsheviks did not stand apart from others but joined hands with all those who worked for supplanting the old order.

In his presidential address at the third session of the All India Trade Union Congress in 1923, C. R. Das, the nationalist leader, said that there could be no conflict between the national movement and the labour movement because *swaraj* was for the masses.[50] In the previous year in his presidential address to the Indian National Congress, C. R. Das had asked the Congress to take up the cause of the working class and the peasants and had warned that if this was not done others would take up their cause.

Expressing the views of most of the Indian nationalists at a meeting at Poona on 3 May 1928, Subhas Bose said: "Another attack is being made on nationalism from the point of view of international labour or international communism. This attack is not only ill-advised but unconsciously serves the interests of our alien rulers. It would be clear to the man in the street that before we can endeavour to reconstruct Indian society on a new basis, whether socialistic or otherwise, we should first secure the right to shape our own destiny. As long as India lies prostrate at the feet of Britain, that right will be denied us. It is, therefore, the paramount duty not only of nationalists but anti-nationalistic communists to bring about the political emancipation of India as early as possible.... I have already hinted that I plead for a coalition between labour and nationalism (I am using 'labour' here in a wider sense to include the peasant as well)."[51]

So far as those Muslims who belonged to the Muslim League are concerned, they also believed, like Congressmen, that for the attainment of political independence the cooperation of all classes of people would be necessary. Jinnah, who dominated the Muslim League and who eventually founded Pakistan, said in 1938: "When you think you will be able to destroy the British Government, the Zamindars, the Capitalists, with one stroke, refer to the conditions of Europe. In Germany Hitlerism came into existence because of socialistic and communistic activities. So did Fascism rise in Italy. What is the fight in Spain about? It is the same issue."[52]

Till communism came to China, socialists and communists in India were largely nurtured on the literature dealing with the industrial proletariat of Europe. In the West the grand cause of social upheaval has been urban labour. The Indian labour movement was a growing and powerful movement but it was confined to the cities, whereas India was primarily agricultural and its vast peasant population lived mainly in the villages. European socialism hardly dealt with the peasant. Gandhi, on the other hand, had always emphasized the peasant's point of view. And it was partly to safeguard the interests of the peasants and partly because of Gandhi's belief in the ideal of economic simplicity, that Gandhi defended the cottage industries as against the big machines and thereby he endeared himself to the peasants.

In economic ideology Gandhi was sometimes amazingly backward. Many socialists and communists were especially critical of Gandhi and characterized him as an arch-reactionary. Though in economic matters Gandhi's views were sometimes backward-looking, in social matters, such as fighting untouchability, working for the elevation of the status of women and campaigning for the establishment of Hindu-Muslim unity, Gandhi was a progressive. Gandhi's social radicalism was particularly apparent in his attack on the outrage of untouchability which he, unlike the socialists and communists, considered as an independent problem.

The communists have always entertained a profound antipathy for Gandhi's basic ideological doctrines "not only because," claimed S. G. Sardesai, a prominent Indian communist, "of their medievalism and mysticism, but also because in practical politics they involved innumerable compromises with imperialist, feudal and Indian bourgeois interests."[53] Gandhi, in his turn, was fundamentally opposed to Marxism and particularly to its doctrine of class struggle.

Throughout the period of Gandhi's leadership of the national movement, the Indian communists contended that Gandhi, notwithstanding his sincerity, was the leader only of the national bourgeoisie, and, accordingly, they agitated for the development of the Indian working-class as an independent class which would act "as the leader, the hegemon of the national revolution." In this the communists were not successful, and to this lack of success they attribute the fact that the "freedom movement brought us a freedom which was bourgeois in character, and also based on various compromises with imperialist and Indian feudal interests."[54] But the CPI could not, in any event, gain leadership of the nationalist movement because it failed altogether to recognize the anti-imperialist role that a section of the Indian bourgeoisie was playing. As S. G. Sardesai put it: "Our failure fully to grasp Gandhi's role lay in our broader failure fully to grasp the role of the Indian national bourgeoisie itself in the freedom movement."[55]

Lenin, in his famous Preliminary Draft Theses on the National and the Colonial Questions presented to the Second Congress of the Comintern in 1920, had asked the communists to work not in opposition to but in cooperation with the national bourgeoisie in Asia. In his article, *Backward Europe and Advanced Asia* (May 1913), Lenin had referred to the progressive role that the bourgeoisie in Asia was playing as distinguished from the European bourgeoisie which had "gone over to reaction."[56] It is because of this analysis of the progressive role of the Asian bourgeoisie, that Lenin stated: "It is particularly important to bear in mind: first, that all communist parties must assist the bourgeois-democratic liberation movement in these countries."[57]

The Communist parties were not to lose their identity in these national liberation movements. In supporting these movements they were to bear in mind their future task of waging in due course a struggle against the national bourgeoisie. In the Preliminary Draft Theses Lenin said that "the Communist International must enter into a temporary alliance with bourgeois-democracy in colonial and backward countries but must not merge with it, and must under all circumstances preserve the independence of the proletarian movement even if it is in its most rudimentary form."[58]

According to Marxist analysis the bourgeoisie, which plays a progressive role in the fight for national independence, attempts at the same time to restrain and crush the revolutionary ardour of the people so that they may not be able to transform the national bourgeois state into a socialist state. The national bourgeoisie stands for national independence, but it also launches counter-revolutionary movements against the aspirations of the people for socialism. Because of its dual role Lenin did not regard every compromise and every temporary alliance with the national bourgeoisie as a deviation from revolutionary principles. Since Lenin "saw that M. N. Roy, the most prominent Indian communist at the Second Congress, was deviating," states an official publication of the CPI, "towards a sectarian approach to the mass movement led by Gandhi, by shouting himself hoarse about Gandhi's antiquated social ideology, Lenin admonished him to think more about how to carry forward the masses under Gandhian leadership than about Gandhi's social philosophy."[59]

Lenin recognized the historically progressive role of the national bourgeois liberation movements when he paid tribute to Tilak and Sun-Yat-sen, the nationalist leaders of India and

China respectively. Even Tolstoy, whose ideas Lenin regarded as harmful, was characterized by him as the mirror of the Russian revolution. It might seem strange to regard Tolstoy as the mirror of a revolution which Tolstoy did not fully comprehend and from which he stood apart, but Lenin pointed out that Tolstoy was to be appraised not merely from "the stand-point of the present-day working class movement and present-day socialism (such an appraisal, is, of course, needed but it is not enough), but from the stand-point of protest against advancing capitalism ... a protest which had to arise from the patriarchal Russian countryside." Though the ideological content of Tolstoy's views were considered revivalistic and reactionary by Lenin, he yet considered that Tolstoy played a historical part in the revolution in portraying the sufferings and protest of the peasantry against the exploitation involved in an advancing capitalistic system.

Gandhi was considerably influenced by Tolstoy. Gandhi corresponded with Tolstoy and considered him as one of his *gurus*. Both stood for the peasant and against the advancing industrial and capitalistic civilization. Both took their stand on religion and a pre-industrial civilization. Both were acutely conscious of the sufferings of the poor peasants. But while Tolstoy was pre-eminently a thinker, Gandhi was essentially a man of action. Tolstoy felt at home with ideas, and Gandhi among the masses. Tolstoy was an intellectual and individualist, but Gandhi was a leader of men and maker of history. But though Gandhi could move the masses, according to the early communists of India, the quasi-religious, semi-mystical, and medieval ideas that inspired Gandhi merely represented the contradictions of the capitalist system in its contact and conflict with the pre-industrial feudal Indian economy and, accordingly, Gandhi did not play any progressive role.

The early Indian communists criticized the ideological revivalism of Gandhi's philosophy but failed to analyse why he could move the masses and create history. "If Lenin considered it correct to explain Tolstoy's contradictions 'not as the ideological sophistry of a reactionary, unctuous landlord, but as the reflection of the shortcomings and weakness of our revolution'; how much more was it necessary for us," asked the later Indian communists, "to make a similar effort to understand Gandhi and his contradictions since we had to deal with a person who did not stand apart from the struggle but was always in the very thick of it?"[60]

Lenin recognized the historical role played by Tolstoy in Russia, Tilak and Gandhi in India, and Sun-Yat-sen in China. Sun-Yat-sen's ideology was vastly different from that of the Marxists. Sun-Yat-sen believed, like the Russian Narodniks, that socialism could be achieved on the basis of radical agrarian reforms and without going through a capitalistic phase. Lenin regarded this belief as both impractical and reactionary, in fact, as the belief "of a petty-bourgeois 'socialist' reactionary. For the idea that capitalism can be 'prevented' in China and that 'social revolution' there will be made easier by the country's backwardness, and so on, is altogether reactionary." But notwithstanding the assessment that Sun-Yat-sen's ideology was reactionary, Lenin did not fail to recognize the historical role that he was playing as a fighter for freedom. It is on the basis of this distinction between the ideological content of a philosophy and the historical role that the propagator of such a philosophy might play that Lenin differed from M. N. Roy in his assessment of Gandhi.[61]

Roy consistently and persistently criticized Gandhi's social and economic ideology. In fact, after the withdrawal of the non-cooperation movement by Gandhi in 1922 because of the Chauri-Chaura incidents, Roy denounced Gandhi as "the acutest and most desperate manifestation of the forces of reaction."[62] The withdrawal of the non-cooperation movement after the Chauri-Chaura incidents had also distressed many nationalist leaders, including Jawaharlal Nehru, but they continued to follow Gandhi, the leader of the Indian nationalist movement. The communist assessment of Gandhi, however, as representing the forces of reaction separated the communists at once from Gandhi and from the national liberation movement waged under his leadership.

The socialists in India, and particularly those who belonged to the Congress Socialist Party, fundamentally disagreed with the Indian communists on the attitude that should be adopted towards Gandhi and the Indian nationalist movement. They considered that Gandhi's leadership was essential for the Indian nationalist movement and it was "madness" to attack Gandhian leadership or to seek to discredit or weaken it.[63] It is for this reason that most socialists participated in the civil disobedience movements launched by Gandhi while the communists did not.

In their incapacity to extricate the political from the economic freedom movement many communists failed to appreciate Gandhi's role in India's political liberation. They denounced Gandhi for believing that the cooperation of all classes should be sought in the nationalist struggle against an alien rule. On the other hand, they wanted to rely only on the industrial workers, the peasants, and the lower middle class for waging a war of national liberation against British rule.[64] But Nehru, who also declared himself to be a socialist and was considerably attracted to Marxism, did not believe in the theory of proletarian leadership of the anti-imperialist struggle. It was revolutionary romanticism to talk of proletarian leadership while the proletariat was still to form itself into a social class. The upper middle class and the professional classes might oppose a socialist revolution, but many of them willingly joined hands in the struggle against foreign rule and in the movement for the establishment of a free India. A recent Communist Party publication states that the party made "costly mistakes" in keeping away from the civil disobedience movements launched by Gandhi.[65]

In the West socialism was developed as a theory to fight capitalism and not imperialism. Relying only on the Western experience some socialists and most communists failed to appreciate adequately the tactics essential for a national fight against an alien imperial rule. But as imperialism and foreign rule have been eliminated, the difficulties which beset the socialist and communist movement in India in the early years on this account no longer exist.

IV. SOCIALISM AND INDIAN TRADITION

Individualism has been a prominent motif of Indian culture. The very term socialism has therefore been suspect. But the old individualism of India aimed at the perfection of the individual and not at any self-seeking individualism, and, accordingly, argued the socialists, the ideals of individualism and of socialism do not differ in essence. They echoed the saying of Trotsky: "Only in a socialist society can the average of humanity rise to the level of a Plato or a Marx." Jayaprakash Narayan, the socialist leader, said: "As for Indian traditions, as far as I know them, they are not averse to the sharing of life and its privileges. It is said that individualism has always been the dominant feature of Indian civilization and, therefore, the latter is opposed to socialism. To put the problem in this manner is not to understand either of the ideals and to get lost in words. . . .Individualism has been the prominent motif in our culture only in the sense that perfection of the individual has been its ideal; never in the sense of narrow, self-seeking individualism, which is the motif in capitalist society. And if individual perfection is the goal, the socialist has not the least difficulty in showing that such perfection can come about only by aiming at the utmost common good."[66]

Some argued that Indian thought had in the past emphasized the group, such as the joint family and the caste and not the individual, and inasmuch as socialism also placed emphasis on the group and the community, socialism should be regarded as the natural evolution of Indian thought.

Again, some ardent socialists have even sought to find the up-to-date ideas of the modern economic world in ancient India of the fourth century B.C. They say that traces of state socialism are to be found in the *Arthasastra* in which a positive role is envisaged for the state. But the economic condition of ancient or medieval India bears a fairly close resemblance to that which existed in almost every European country in ancient or medieval times. Instances were not unknown in those countries of state interference and state participation in industries. But this state interference came into existence not with the object of radically altering any economic system or of establishing socialism but rather to make the state militarily or politically strong or self-sufficient.

Communism is associated with the name of Marx, a German Jew. Some have tarred communism with the brush of foreignism. For them any "ism" or ideology must grow out of India's soil, it must be rooted in India's past. Dr Bhagawan Das, the noted theosophist, suggested an Indian solution to the modern economic problem which has inspired communism and modern socialism and he spoke in favour of some kind of ancient Indian socialism as distinguished from modern scientific socialism.[67]

Bhagawan Das finds in the ancient Indian scheme of social organization the just desiderated compromise between indivi-

dualism and socialism, egotism and altruism, only private enterprise and only state-management, too little government and too
much government. This compromise is effected by the definition
and partition of the rights and duties of each individual in the
successive stages of life and as an adult member of society. This
is described as the permanent plan of the ancient Hindu law-
maker Manu and not a five-year plan or any other temporary
plan of modern times. Under this ancient Hindu scheme society
is to be divided into four functionally correlated professions.
To most people, however, it is not obvious how any solution
propounded by Manu in ancient times, or how the division of
society into four or any number of professions, can solve the
problem of present-day inequality and lack of opportunity. The
basic economic problems of the modern age are new and quite
naturally neither Manu nor any other ancient *rishi* of India did or
could devise any solution for them. In the past the means of
production were simple and agriculture and small cottage industries were carried on in the villages. There were neither the big
machines nor the problems of large-scale industrialization and
urbanization of the present-day world. The problems of the
modern industrial age were not and could not be foreseen or
anticipated by ancient Indian thinkers and for these modern
problems modern solutions have to be found.

No society is divided artificially according to a *priori* theories
of social thinkers. Social division is an organic process of society.
Manu or the intellectual efforts or social forces whose consumma-
tion he personified perhaps represented an attempt at codification
of natural social divisions. Bhagawan Das rightly found fault
with the present divisions of society, but the present divisions
were not super-imposed from above, they had grown up
naturally from their respective social soil. Bhagawan Das did not
show how he would impose his solution from the branches
downwards and not from the roots upwards. His scheme would
redistribute wealth, power, privileges, duties, and occupations,
but this could not be achieved without a revolution in the constitution of society. To effect this revolution Bhagawan Das
relied upon a class of *Brahmins*, the missionaries of *Brahma*. This
would be the permanent class of persons from whom good and
wise legislation would emanate. This class would provide trust-
worthy rulers. This is reminiscent of Plato's conception of

philosopher-kings. According to Bhagawan Das if the system of *Ashrams* was revived properly and people began to retire from the life of the household and competitive bread-winning soon after reaching their fiftieth year, then there would be a sufficient number of persons in the third stage of life, *vanasth*, who would be sages worthy of all trust and be fitted to make good laws and to guide the executive by their moral force. Under this scheme the diseases of the world can be exorcised and genuine equality achieved if men devoted to the worship of learning add to their achievement the virtue of resolute public spirit to make them fit for becoming the social missionaries of *Brahma*. But there is hardly any sign of the missionaries of *Brahma*, such as Bhagawan Das envisaged, emerging in the modern world.

While Dr Bhagawan Das sought in the ancient Indian social system the basis of true socialism, there were others who sought to reconcile the egalitarian ideas of the ancient Indian *rishis* of India with the thought of Bolshevik Russia. The ancient *rishis* were said to be the truest communists, for they did not consider private property as the exclusive possession of any single individual and desired that the same should be held in trust for the benefit of all. This line of thinking was, to some extent, developed by Bepin Pal, the extremist leader. "Socialism," he wrote, "in the highest and truest sense of the term, and not merely what it is understood to mean by the followers of Marx . . . are the rudimentary concepts of our social and political philosophy."[68] And it is in this context that Pal used the term "Hindu Socialism."[69] This attempt at a synthesis of ancient Indian ideas with modern socialism and of the old with the new is a manifestation of the curious Janus-like outlook of a certain aspect of modern Indian thought.

In India attempts were made to establish not only that there was no conflict between Hinduism and Socialism but also that there was no basic contradiction between the spirit of Islam and the spirit of socialism. In fact, it has been claimed that Islam is socialism, but few have explained what is meant by socialism when the word is used in this context. When it was said that Islam was socialism, what the conservatives really meant was that Islam being already socialistic was wholly perfect and did not need any further reform; whereas the progressives meant that if Islam was really followed then it would usher in a better and egalitarian social order and that it was the duty of every Muslim to seek to construct such a better social order based on Islamic principles of equality.

During the very first period of Islam (*Khilafat* and *Rashidah*), that is the period of about forty years from the time that the Prophet set up his rule in Madinah until the establishment of the Damascus empire, Islamic polity was pure and simple. The simple life of Muhammad, the crude democracy and the absence of social gradation or stratification has often been referred to by Indian Muslims. It has been said that the Prophet did not address his followers as his disciples, but called them "Ashab" which, in a sense, means comrades. References have been made to the egalitarians from the desert who at the splendid and luxurious court of Syria, immediately after the establishment of the empire, denounced in unmistakable terms the pomp of the royal court and the luxury of the rich. The Indian Muslims looked with pride and satisfaction to the period of Islamic history during the rule of Muhammad and his first four successors when what was preached was justice for all and there was no vulgar display of riches. This nostalgic reference to the early period of Islamic history and the painting of a roseate picture of the Islamic past had given rise to the belief among a section of the Muslims that it was not necessary to be socialist, for Islam included all that was good in socialism and that the holy Prophet was the greatest socialist ever born.

On the other hand, it has also been asserted with equal force and vehemence that socialism is un-Islamic because it denies the existence of God and repudiates the religious basis of morality. Islam, unlike communism, recognizes private property though it conceives it as a trust from God and not as something which remains absolutely at the disposal of the owner. Islam does not recognize class-struggle in which the communists believe. It has been said that genuine class-collaboration can be secured through Islam and that Islam can give a social code in which the claims of labour and of capital are reconciled. Islam holds that the rich are morally responsible for the way they spend their money, and in this respect there were similarities between the Islamic view of property and Gandhi's theory of trusteeship.

In modern India, Iqbal, the great Muslim poet, first denounced communism because of its antipathy to religion, He said "the encouragement in India of religious adventure on the ground of modern liberalism tends to make people more and more indifferent to religion. ... The Indian mind will then seek some other substitute for religion which is likely to be nothing else than the form of atheistic materialism which has appeared in Russia." Later, however, Iqbal changed his views and wrote many poems in praise of Lenin and communism and said that Islam and socialism had the same objective.

Among modern Indian leaders Gandhi referred to the passion for justice that was the basis of communist ideology, but he denounced and deprecated its reliance on violence and its disbelief in religion and, accordingly, he considered communism as being unsuited to Indian tradition. Nehru, who declared himself to be a socialist, was greatly attracted to communism though he had reservations about the communist approach to violence and parliamentary democracy. Nehru, who was not, however, religious in the traditional sense, offered no criticism of communism for its neglect of or antipathy to traditional religion. Subhas Bose explained that the opposition of communism to religion had mainly a historical basis, that is to say, the opposition was primarily based on the fact that the Orthodox Church of Russia was the supporter of the Tsarist regime, which the Bolsheviks opposed and eventually destroyed. Though both Nehru and Bose spoke in favour of socialism, they (particularly Bose) said that an Indian form of socialism would have to be devised which would be in harmony with Indian history and tradition. Subhas Bose used to say that socialism in India did not derive its birth from the books of Karl Marx but from Swami Vivekananda's gospel for the uplift of the poor or *Daridra Narayan*.[70]

Socialists, and particularly the communists, criticized not only the economic inequalities prevalent in Indian society but also various features of Indian society and culture. The spread of communism or Marxism was, therefore, interpreted by some as a relapse into the days of Derozio when everything European seemed good in Indian eyes and everything Indian appeared unprogressive. Many Indian religious and spiritual leaders, such as Vivekananda and Gandhi, had denounced the wholesale denigration of Indian culture, but both Vivekananda and Gandhi had also said that to improve India spiritually the first task of an Indian would be to improve the lot of the poor. Vivekananda had envisaged that power would gradually go to the poor. He said: "The world is in the third epoch under the domination of the *Vaishya* (the merchant, the third estate). The fourth epoch will be under that of *Sudra* (the proletariat)." Vivekananda believed that in the conditions existing in India what had to be preached was the gospel of *Daridra Narayan* (God as the poor). But the communists claimed that the worship of *Daridra Narayan* was fully realized in Russia where Vivekananda's *Daridra Narayan* had risen to the seat of power. India had, therefore, nothing to fear from communism.

The early communists of India had indiscriminately criticized Indian tradition. This attitude of indiscriminate criticism of the past was similar to the attitude that the Indian intelligentsia had developed towards the end of the nineteenth century under the impact of English utilitarianism when they came to despise India and everything Indian. Likewise, in the thirties of this century some communists under the impact of Marxism saw error or reaction everywhere and became vigorous critics of almost all aspects of Indian society, economy, and polity. A recent publication of the CPI states that it "has also to be admitted that the Communist Party of India, in that period, with all its valuable contribution to the development of the contemporary communist movement did not really make such an effort," that is to say, an effort of considering that "Marxism . . . is both a break and a continuity with the past" which required that instead of repudiating the past altogether, the Marxist should carry forward what was valuable in the past and integrate it with the new.[71]

Nehru often admonished the Indian communists with the remark: "For you, history begins with 1917." "That," states the said Communist Party publication, "of course, was uncharitable and untrue. But, it is equally true that numberless Indians, very favourably disposed towards communism and appreciative of many of our activities, entertained the same feeling . . . it has to be admitted that this was a barrier in the more rapid advance of the communist movement and party in India. This would be bad enough for any communist party, it was worse for the party of a country with a vast and ancient heritage, a heritage which was prized and held in very high esteem by progressive and forward-looking opinion in the country."[72]

At the Extraordinary Congress of the Communist Party of

India held in April 1958 emphasis was laid on the fact that the Indian communist movement must give due regard to Indian history and experience. The statement issued by this Congress declared that though the party would continue to be based on the philosophy of Marxism and Leninism, it should make conscious efforts to integrate the Indian communist movement with Indian history and Indian experience so that Marxism could be applied creatively to the realities of the Indian situation.

As early as 1951 the Communist Party of India had stated that the Indian communists should not blindly follow either the Russian or Chinese method of revolution but should evolve its own methods while learning from the experiences of the Russian as also the Chinese revolution.[73] Later, when the Indian Communist Party split into two the official CPI was ideologically closer to the Russian communists and the CPI(M), which seceded from it, was ideologically closer to the Chinese communists. But since 1967 the CPI(M) has criticized the methods not only of the Russian party but also of the Chinese communists, and it asserted that it would seek to apply Marxism-Leninism to India after taking Indian realities and conditions into account and that it would not be guided ideologically either by the Russian or the Chinese communists.

In 1925 when an attempt was made to form a communist party in India. Moulana Hazrat Mohani, the Chairman of the Reception Committee, had declared that the new party would be a purely Indian organization and would not be connected with the Communist International. Singaravelu, a leading member of the party, said that Indian communism was not Russian Bolshevism and that Indians must evolve their own form of communism.[74] M. N. Roy, then a leading member of the Comintern, had vehemently denounced these utterances saying that nothing could be more non-communistic than to say that an Indian communist movement could grow up independently of the international proletarian movement.[75] The Communist International guided the Indian communist movement in its early stages. But the Communist International was dissolved in 1943. Later, the world communist movement was split first by Tito in Yugoslavia and then by Mao Tse-tung in China. The first split in the Indian communist movement took place in 1964 when the CPI(M) seceded from the CPI, and the second split took place in 1967 when an extremist section seceded from the CPI(M) and later formed a new party, namely, the CPI(ML). When the first split in the Indian communist movement took place in 1964 the CPI(M) was ideologically closer to the Chinese communists, but when the second split took place in 1967 and a new party, the CPI(ML), was formed, it is this new party and not the CPI(M) that was ideologically closer to the Chinese communists.

NOTES AND REFERENCES

1. Sophia Collet, *Life and Letters of Raja Rammohan Roy*, 1913, p. 200. Collet wrote: "As the Scot finally lost his temper the Hindu was considered to have had the best of the argument."
2. R. P. Masani, *Dadabhai Naoroji*, p. 398.
3. Ibid., p. 420.
4. Dadabhai Naoroji, *Poverty and Un-British Rule in India*, p. 203.
5. Ibid., p. 38.
6. According to Digby "probably between Plassey and Waterloo £1,000 millions were transferred from Indian hoards to English banks." According to Professor Furber the drain did not reach vast proportions. The drain towards the West "should not be reckoned as exceeding £1.9 millions annually during the period 1783-93" (Furber, *John Company At Work*, Cambridge 1948, p. 305).
7. *Essays, Speeches, Addresses and Writings of the Hon'ble Dadabhai Naoroji*, 1887, pp. 135-36.
8. Asoka Mehta, *Democratic Socialism*, Bharatiya Vidya Bhavan, 1959, p. 103.
9. Ibid., pp. 103-4.
10. Romesh Dutt, *The Economic History of India Under Early British Rule* (1759-1837), 1963, p. xxxi.
11. Ibid., xxv-xxvi.
12. K. T. Telang, *Select Writings and Speeches*, ed. V. V. Thakur, pp. 153-56.
13. J. S. Mill, *Principles of Political Economy* (People's Edition, London, 1886), pp. 570-71.
14. K. T. Telang, *Select Writings and Speeches*, pp. 147-49.
15. M. G. Ranade, *Essays on Indian Economics*, pp. 19-20. See also Gide and Rist, *A History of Economic Doctrines*, London, 1948, p. 393.
16. M. G. Ranade, *Essays on Indian Economics*, pp. 33-34.
17. Lenin, *The National Liberation Movement in East*, pp. 14-15.
18. Lajpat Rai, *The Political Future of India*, p. 202.
19. Lajpat Rai, *Ideals of Non-cooperation*, p. 32.
20. *The People*, 23 September 1928.

21. *The People*, 20 March 1927.
22. Lajpat Rai, *India's Will to Freedom*, Madras, 1921, pp. 23-24, 29-30.
23. Ibid., p. 36.
24. Ibid., p. 33; Lajpat Rai, *The Political Future of India*, p. 203.
25. B. C. Pal, *Nationality and Empire*, Calcutta, 1914, pp. 196-98.
26. B. C. Pal, *The World Situation and Ourselves*, Calcutta, 1919, pp. 40-41.
27. Ibid., pp. 61-63.
28. Ibid., p. 64; Lajpat Rai, *The Political Future of India*, p. 206.
29. B. C. Pal, *The World Situation and Ourselves*, pp. 42-43.
30. Lajpat Rai, *The Political Future of India*, p. 204.
31. Lajpat Rai, *India's Will To Freedom*, pp. 36-37.
32. *Important Speeches of Jawaharlal Nehru*, pp. 4-14.
33. Rabindranath Tagore, *Nationalism*, pp. 102-6.
34. Rabindranath Tagore, *Letters from Russia*, Calcutta, 1960, pp. 97, 106.
35. Ibid., p. 108.
36. Ibid., p. 121.
37. Ibid., p. 122.
38. Ibid., p. 114.
39. Ibid.
40. Ibid., p. 111.
41. Ibid., p. 117.
42. Jawaharlal Nehru, *The Discovery of India*, 2nd ed., 1947, London, p. 472.
43. *The People*, 20 March 1927.
44. Jawaharlal Nehru, *The Discovery of India*, p. 488.
45. Subhas Bose, *The Indian Struggle*, p. 311.
46. M. N. Roy, *India in Transition*, 1922, p. 130.
47. M. N. Roy, *One Year of Non-Cooperation*, 1923, pp. 56-60.
48. R. P. Dutt, *Modern India*, 1926, pp. 17-18.
49. Jawaharlal Nehru, *The Unity of India*, 1944, pp. 121-22.
50. *Indian Annual Register*, 1923, Vol. I, pp. 957-58.
51. *Selected Speeches of Subhas Chandra Bose*, 1962, p. 33.
52. M. A. Jinnah, *Speeches and Writings*, p. 40.
53. S. G. Sardesai, "Gandhi and the CPI," in *The Mahatma, A Marxist Symposium*, 1969, p. 8.
54. Ibid., p. 9.
55. Ibid., p. 10.
56. Lenin, *Selected Works*, Foreign Languages Publishing House, Moscow, 1947, Vol. I, pp. 550-51.
57. The full text of the Theses is contained in Lenin, *Selected Works*, Vol. II, pp. 654-58.
58. Ibid.
59. S. G. Sardesai, op. cit., p. 13.
60. Ibid., p. 15.
61. *M. N. Roy's Memoirs*, 1964, p. 379.
62. M. N. Roy, *India in Transition*, p. 205.
63. Narendra Dev's Presidential Address at Patna Conference, 17 May

3

1934, *The Indian Annual Register*, 1934, Vol. I, p. 341.

64. M. N. Roy, *The Future of Indian Politics*, pp. 17, 85; M. N. Roy, *One Year of Non-Cooperation*, 1923, pp. 56-60.

65. S. G. Sardesai, *India And the Russian Revolution* (Communist Party Publication), 1967, pp. 49-50.

66. Jayaprakash Narayan, *Why Socialism?*, 1936.

67. Bhagawan Das, *Ancient Versus Modern Scientific Socialism*, Madras, 1934.

68. B. C. Pal, *Nationality and Empire*, pp. 85-86.

69. Ibid., p. 28.

70. *Selected Speeches of Subhas Chandra Bose*, 1962, p. 32.

71. S. G. Sardesai, *India And The Russian Revolution*, Communist Party Publication, 1967, p. 60.

72. Ibid., pp. 60-61.

73. *Statement of Policy Adopted by the All India Conference of the Communist Party of India, October, 1951*, p. 4.

74. *Indian Annual Register*, 1925, II, p. 367.

75. Overstreet & Windmiller, *Communism in India*, 1960, p. 79.

CHAPTER TWO

The Economic Background

I. RISE OF MODERN INDUSTRIES

Before the British introduced modern means of communication and transport and modern industries in India, self-sufficient village communities, based on agriculture, carried on with the primitive plough and bullock-power, and handicrafts, carried on by means of simple instruments, formed the basic features of the Indian economy. These self-sufficient village communities were like little republics, having almost everything that they wanted. There was hardly any interference in the internal life of these village republics by any central sovereign power or the overlord of the village. These village republics had a vitality of their own and, notwithstanding constant changes at the centre, they preserved their character almost intact till the advent of the British in India.

The village community was the virtual owner of the land in the villages. Each peasant family cultivated a particular holding and had a customary right to cultivate such holding from generation to generation. The peasant families were subject to various collective restrictions and were entitled to the benefits of divers collectively managed "municipal" services, such as watch and ward, the right to use the common grazing grounds and woodlands of the villages, and the right to village irrigation facilities and water supply. Further, the villagers collectively had to meet the revenue or rent demands of the overlord of the village. For paying such revenue and for providing the "municipal" services, the peasant families in the villages had to cooperate. All these developed a spirit of cooperation rather than competition and emphasized the duty that the villager owed to the community rather than the right that he possessed as an individual.

In pre-British times the king or the emperor did not claim

ownership of the land, which virtually belonged to the village community. The king or the emperor was satisfied with a share of the produce of the village or with his tribute or tax. The village community regulated the affairs of the village. The king or the emperor or the overlord of the village claimed no right within the village but only over it. The overlord of the village claimed revenue or tax or tribute, but did not seek to interfere with the internal working of the village community or with its methods of production.

The village produced not for the market but for the village community itself. A share of the produce went to the overlord of the village or to the Hindu king or the Delhi emperor as tribute or revenue or rent or tax, but otherwise the produce of the village was consumed in the village.

The village society was autarchic. Modern means of transport and communication had not opened up the village to any market within the country or outside. Within the village there was hardly any trade or commerce in exchange for money. The artisan was remunerated by the village community for the services he rendered to the peasants of the village. The artisan would get some portion of the grain from the village community at harvest time as his remuneration. The artisan was, therefore, not a private producer but virtually a public servant engaged by the village community.

Further, there was no water-tight distinction between the peasant and the artisan or between agriculture and industry. The peasant might also do some domestic spinning, whereas the artisan may also cultivate the small plot of land that the village community gave him. Division of labour was in a rudimentary stage.

The village was self-sufficient. For producing for the village no large-scale farming was necessary and simple agricultural equipments and hand-manipulated tools were all that were needed. The simple implements that were used for agriculture and industry remained the same in the villages for centuries. The plough and the bullock-cart were the symbols of agriculture as the spinning wheel was of industry. The village communities were based on possession of the land in common, on the blending of agriculture and handicrafts, and on production for use rather than for exchange.

The social institutions of ancient India were not individualistic or competitive but were collectivistic and cooperative. The unit of social life was not the individual but the village. The relationship between individuals was based not on contract but on caste and status. The individual existed as part of his family, caste, and village and not in his own right or by himself. The individual hardly existed except as part of a group, that is, as part of his family or caste or village. The state did not interfere with the family or the caste. The family and caste were governed by customary and religious laws and practices and not by the state or by secular law.

India has always been a land of villages. There were only a few towns. Some towns had political significance being the seat of the government; some others were trading centres; and the remaining were places of religious pilgrimage, such as Benares or Puri. But it is in the villages that India lived and the invincibility and toughness of the self-sufficient and autarchic Indian villages prevented the development in India of a spontaneous industrial order. It is the advanced bourgeoisie of England which brought India into contact with the modern industrial system and also destroyed the self-sufficiency of the Indian village. The British conquest of India, which introduced modern means of transport and communication and modern industries into India, thus helped to bring about a revolution in Indian economy and society.

During pre-British times India attained political unity for short intervals. Political unification of India was brought about by Samudra Gupta during the Hindu period and by Akbar during the Mughal period, but such political unification of the country did not affect the self-sufficiency and autarchy of the Indian villages. Such self-sufficiency of the villages and the old feudal economy of India was, however, destroyed with the establishment of British rule in India.

The British brought about an agrarian revolution in India by introducing individual ownership of land. This was done by introducing landlordism in some parts of the country and peasant proprietorship in others. Lord Cornwallis by introducing Permanent Settlement in Bengal, Bihar, and Orissa in 1793 converted the old revenue collectors, who had no proprietary right over the land, into landlords. In certain other parts of the country, at the instance of Sir Thomas Munro, the ryotwari system of peasant proprietorship was introduced. But both landlordism and peasant proprietorship destroyed village ownership of land and thereby laid the foundations of the individualistic and capitalistic development of agriculture. As a result of the new system of land tenure introduced by the British, the old village commune was destroyed and there emerged the modern peasant proprietor and zamindar.

Before the advent of the British in India a native merchant or middle class was coming into existence, but the transformation of Indian economy from feudalism to modern industrialism was hastened as a result of the imposition of British rule. In the early years of the eighteenth century, at a time when the Mughal Empire was disintegrating, there was emerging a new middle class in India.[1] Urban trading centres were coming into existence in which the emerging middle class was engaged in the exchange and distribution of commodities. These urban trading centres had attracted handicraftsmen, who produced not for local use but for exchange and export. But before this middle class could develop, consolidate its position and obtain ascendancy over the feudal classes, the British came and politically and administratively unified the country and thereby laid the foundations of a modern industrial economic order in India.

Prior to the coming of the British, India had been overrun by conquerors coming from divers parts of the world. Arabs, Turks, Tartars, and Mughals came in turn, conquered India but, eventually, they themselves were conquered by the superior civilization of the country they conquered. These conquerors did not affect the economic structure of Indian society.

The British, however, represented a completely different economic order. The British industrial class had in their own country overcome the feudal class as well as feudal disunity and had established a modern industrial nation-state. It is this unified and industrial Britain which conquered India. The British impact therefore destroyed ancient Indian society and the self-sufficiency of the Indian village.

The establishment of railways in India by the British during the middle of the nineteenth century at once commercialized agriculture and helped in the development of modern industries. Lord Dalhousie in his famous Minute on Railways referred thus to the enormous advantages of the introduction of railways:

"England is calling aloud for the cotton which India does already produce in some degree, and would produce sufficient in quality, and plentiful in quantity, if only there were provided the fitting means of conveyance for it from distant plains to the several ports adopted for its shipment. Every increase of facilities for trade has been attended, as we have seen, with an increased demand for articles of European produce in the most distant markets of India. . . . New markets are opening to us on this side of the globe under circumstances which defy the foresight of the wisest to estimate their probable value or calculate their future extent."

The railway system became the forerunner of modern industries in India. By the middle of the nineteenth century the British introduced plantation industries, such as, those in indigo, tea, and coffee. Gradually cotton and jute industries developed but up to the beginning of World War I engineering industries, except mostly as repair shops for railways, had not developed and only the barest beginning in iron and steel industries had been made.

The policy of *laissez-faire* that Britain had pursued, both on doctrinaire grounds as also from the point of view of its own economic interest, had stood in the way of the development of modern industries in India. From the assumption of direct rule by the Crown in 1858 till the end of the nineteenth century the government of India persisted in pursuing the doctrinaire policy of *laissez-faire* in the industrial field. "It was thought inevitable," writes Vera Anstey, "that India should remain predominantly agricultural, whilst the government wished to avoid both the active encouragement of industries that (like the cotton mill industry) competed with powerful British interests, and increased State expenditure."[2]

In the first decade of the twentieth century the Madras government took some little step for the development of industries. This participation of the Madras government in the industrial development of the province was regarded by the local European commercial community as "a serious menace to private enterprise and an unwarrantable intervention on the part of the state in matters beyond the sphere of Government."[3] Morley substantially agreed with this point of view, and, in a dispatch of 29 July 1910, while conceding that state funds could be spent in order to familiarize Indians with the scientific methods of production which were

prevalent in the advanced European countries, he strongly deprecated, in accordance with his doctrinaire *laissez-faire* creed, any
active participation of the government in the development of
industries.[4] It is interesting to note that when Morley asked
Hardinge if he would like to succeed Minto as Viceroy of India,
the only question he put to Hardinge was whether he was a
free-trader. Hardinge replied in the affirmative.[5]

The industrial weakness of India, disclosed during World War
I, made it apparent that the barren policy of *laissez-faire* would
have to be given up. In 1915 Lord Hardinge, the Viceroy,
declared "that a definite and self-conscious policy of improving
the industrial capabilities of India will have to be pursued after
the war, unless she is to become the dumping ground for the
manufacture of foreign nations who will be competing the more
keenly for markets. . . . " Accordingly, the Industrial Commission
that was set up recommended that the government would have
to take a more active interest in the development of industries in
India. This was welcomed by Indian publicists, who had for a
long time been demanding not only state aid but also state protection for indigenous industries. Indian publicists used to draw
attention to the fact that state aid and protection had facilitated
the industrialization of Germany and the United States of
America,[6] that the British colonies, such as Australia and Canada,
had raised protective duties even against the goods of their
mother country, and that in Britain also faith in free trade had
declined for Chamberlain had advocated a policy of imperial
preference and Balfour had supported a policy of retaliation.[7]
Further, the success of Japan in adopting Western industrial
methods, with the help of state aid and protection, did much to
sustain and strengthen the nationalist belief in the desirability
of industrialization and in the necessity of state aid and protection.[8]

The Montagu-Chelmsford Report of 1918 also recommended
that "a forward policy in industrial development is urgently
called for to satisfy the aspirations of her people. . . . Imperial
interests also demand that the natural resources of India should
henceforth be better utilized."[9] Further, the Report drew attention to the fact that the theoretical free trader hardly existed in
India.[10]

The reforms introduced as a result of the Montagu-Chelmsford

Report made industry a provincial and "transferred" subject thereby placing it in the hands of provincial governments which were partly controlled by elected representatives. But the financial resources of the provinces were too meagre to permit them to embark on a vigorous policy of granting state aid for the development of modern industries.

In 1923 the government of India adopted the recommendations of the Indian Fiscal Commission that a policy of "discriminating protection" should be introduced into India,[11] and it set up a Tariff Board. Pursuant to the recommendations of the Fiscal Commission a number of industries including iron and steel, cotton, sugar, paper, and pulp were granted protection. The adoption of a policy of protection for these industries helped them and in 1941 protection could be withdrawn from the steel industry, in 1947 from the cotton mill industry, and in 1950 from the sugar industry.

The policy of discriminating protection was, however, haphazard in operation, and the protection granted to Indian industries during British rule was perfunctory in manner and grudging in nature inasmuch as "the British Government's interests in the industrialization of the country were not whole-hearted."[12] Moreover, from 1927 onwards the Indian tariff system was governed by the principle of Imperial Preference. This gave preference to British products "over both non-Empire and Indian production in the Indian market."[13]

As a result of the pursuit of the policy of discriminatory protection some impetus was given to the development of Indian industries. But the industrial development of India prior to the outbreak of World War II was such that though India was freeing herself from dependence on foreign countries so far as consumer goods were concerned, she was almost wholly dependent on foreign countries for securing capital goods. As a result of protection sugar, cotton, iron and steel industries had developed, but prior to the outbreak of World War II, India was still dependent on foreign countries for the supply of machinery and other capital goods, without which the development of modern industries was impossible.

Before World War II the large-scale industries that were set up in India were primarily in cotton and jute. These cotton and jute industries employed more than 40 per cent of workers

employed in large industrial establishments in India as would
appear from the following figures:

LARGE INDUSTRIAL ESTABLISHMENTS IN BRITISH INDIA
(average number of employees, 20 or more persons)
(1935)

Kinds of establishments	Number	Persons employed	Percentage
Textiles, primarily cotton and jute	753	827,441	44.95
Food, drink and tobacco	2,957	257,584	13.99
Engineering, primarily railway workshops	888	220,587	11.98
Gins and presses	2,729	216,233	11.74
Tile, brick, glass factories and saw mills	532	87,066	4.72
Chemicals	514	64,539	3.50
Minerals and metals, primarily iron and steel mills	144	58,159	3.05
Paper and printing	454	48,622	2.64
Tanneries and shoe & leather manufacture	68	10,276	0.55
Miscellaneous	222	52,285	2.84
Total	9,261	1,840,792	100.00

World War II, like the first great war, gave a fillip to industrialization but even then the development was more in consumer
goods than in capital goods industries. "Cotton, sugar, paper,
cement and even leather have all expanded, while the basic industries for the production of machine tools, automobiles, railway
engines, ships and aeroplanes have been left out."[14]

While the industrial inadequacy of India during the first great
war compelled the British Indian government to consider the
question of adopting a policy of discriminating protection for
developing Indian industries, the need for such protection, as also
the urgent need for the rapid industrialization of the country,
was again emphasized during World War II. In June 1940 the
government of India issued a Notification stating that it was
prepared to consider the question of giving protection to certain
industries which were considered essential during the war, such
as steel, pipes and tube industries so that they may survive even
after the war.

By 1947 India became independent and the political difficulties that existed in the adoption of a full-fledged scheme of protection for Indian industries, by reason of conflict with the interests of the British manufacturers, disappeared. Political independence enabled Indians to give concrete expression to their ideas of economic nationalism. After independence the Fiscal Commission that was constituted by the government resolution dated 28 April 1949 recommended that instead of the old ad hoc Tariff Board a permanent body should be set up to advise on the adoption of a policy of protection and that such policy should form part of the overall plan for the economic development of the country. Accordingly, the Tariff Board was replaced by the Tariff Commission in 1952 and the latter granted protection to various new industries. The Tariff Commission, being a permanent body, unlike the former ad hoc Tariff Board, could also integrate the policy of protection with the policy of planning, which the country pursued after independence.

Though the policy of planning which India pursued after the attainment of independence had a much larger objective, one of the aims of such planning was the development of Indian industries and the increase in the food supply of the country which was also the aim of protectionist economics. The long-range perspective of planning was to double the per capita income in 25 years. The first plan launched in 1951 aimed at strengthening the economy at the base and laid emphasis on agricultural development and multi-purpose river valley projects, whereas the second plan (1956-1961) laid emphasis on the development of basic and heavy industries and formulated for the state or public sector a key role in the economic development of the country. The third plan (1961-66) aimed at achieving self-sufficiency in food-grains by increasing agricultural production. It also provided for the expansion of basic industries like steel, chemicals, fuel and power and the establishment of machine-building capacity in India with the object that the requirements of further industrialization could be met within a period of ten years or so mainly from the country's own resources.[15]

Population in India has increased continuously and a considerable portion of the increase in production is offset by the increase in population. Population increase during the four decades between 1891 to 1921 was inconsiderable, but thereafter

population has continued to increase at an increasing rate as will
appear from the following figures:

POPULATION GROWTH IN INDIA SINCE 1891

Census year	Population in millions	Per cent increase or decrease as compared with the previous decades
1891	235.9	
1901	235.5	— 0.2
1911	249.0	+ 5.7
1921	248.1	— 0.4
1931	275.5	+ 11.0
1941	312.8	+ 13.5
1951	356.9	+ 14.1
1961	439.0	+ 21.6

The bulk of the Indian population still lives in villages. In 1951
and 1961 the rural population in India was 361.09 and 439.23
millions respectively whereas the urban population was only
62.44 and 78.93 millions respectively. The bulk of the Indian
people is engaged as cultivators or as agricultural labourers and a
small percentage thereof are employed in industries as would
appear from the following table:

INDIAN POPULATION HIGHLIGHTS
(1961 compared with 1951)

Population in millions engaged in various occupations	1951	1961
1. Cultivator	69.74	99.62
2. Agricultural Labourer	27.50	31.52
3. Mining, Quarrying, etc	3.83	5.22
4. Household Industry	— *	12.03
5. Manufacturing (other than 4)	12.77	7.98
6. Construction	1.30	2.06
7. Trade and Commerce	7.30	7.65
8. Transport, Storage and Communication	2.13	3.02
9. Other Services	14.85	19.57

* Included under 3 and 5.

Industrial population in India has, however, continuously increased as would appear from the following figures:

INDEX NUMBERS OF INDUSTRIAL PRODUCTION
(Base: 1956-100)

	1951	1955	1960	1961	1962	1965	1966
General Index	73.0	92.3	130.2	139.4	150.0	186.9	191.5
Mining and quarrying	87.0	97.1	137.2	147.3	161.3	184.3	190.4
Food manufacturing	79.6	93.3	117.4	129.3	127.4	144.4	147.8
Cigarettes	81.6	86.8	140.6	150.0	155.7	205.8	222.5
Cotton textiles	79.1	95.2	102.9	109.0	109.6	123.3	119.9
Woollen textiles	70.7	83.2	101.3	107.3	138.4	110.1	102.0

II. THE GROWTH OF LABOUR MOVEMENT IN INDIA

From the 1880s modern industries began to develop in India and with it an industrial bourgeoisie. The Indian industrial class wanted to establish cotton textile and other industries in India. Thus the Indian industrial class came into competition with the industrial interests of Manchester and Lancashire. To meet this competition the watchword of the Indian industrial class was protectionism and *swadeshism*.

The development of modern industries in India brought into existence not only an Indian industrial class but also an Indian working class. The growth of an Indian working class gave rise to labour movements in India. The workers were at first led by middle-class intellectuals. Gradually they began to use the weapons of strike and collective bargaining and, in the course of time, working-class movements in India developed a socialistic orientation.

The conquest of India by Britain and the administrative unification of India under British rule helped in the destruction of the old agricultural and industrial system of India. Increasingly India became a sort of agricultural farm of Britain which was to produce raw materials for export to Britain. To develop the raw materials of India, in the first part of the nineteenth century, Englishmen acquired lands and set up plantations in India. It is in these plantations, the earliest form of capitalist enterprise in India, that the labour movement first originated.

The labour movement in the plantations was spontaneous and not organized. It represented the unorganized protest of the coolies or immigrants against the working conditions that prevailed there. Such protest often burst into sporadic violence in the same manner as the protest of the frame-work-knitters in England later broke out in machine-breaking in the 1880s.

Since 1833, about the time when slavery was abolished in the West Indies, plantations were being set up in Assam in India. Some of those who started these plantations in Assam were originally slave drivers of the West Indies, and the plantation system that was initially set up in India was a "thinly veiled slavery." The condition of the coolies or labourers in the plantations was so intolerable that they sometimes indulged in sporadic acts of violence. The riots and assaults that are associated with the early plantation system in India are reminiscent of the Luddite movement of England.

The condition of these coolies in the plantations drew the attention of the Bengali intelligentsia or the *bhadralok* class. Dwarkanath Gangapadhaya, a Brahmo social reformer, lived among the coolies in disguise and came to know at first-hand the conditions in which they lived. On his return to Calcutta he recounted his experiences and the miserable plight of the coolies in *Sanjibanee* and *The Bengalee*, which was edited by Surendranath Banerjea. The question of the coolies or of "slave labour" in Assam was taken up by the first session of the Bengal Provincial Conference held in 1888. This Conference urged the abolition of "slave labour" in Assam and called upon the Indian National Congress to take up the cause of the coolies.

The attention of the Bengali social reformers and the literary class was next directed to the unsatisfactory conditions in which the labourers worked in the jute mill industries in Bengal, which had been set up in the second half of the nineteenth century. Bankim Chandra Chatterjee, the Bengali novelist whose *Anandamath* was later to become the Bible of the terrorists or revolutionaries, protested against the economic inequalities from which the workers suffered in a series of articles on *Samya* or equality. Similar protests were voiced by Pandit Shivnath Shastri, one of the founders of the Sadharan Brahmo Samaj, in the journal

Samadarshee and by Dwarakanath Gangapadhaya and Krishna Kumar Mitra in the *Sanjibanee*. The activities of the Bengali social reformers and literary class were not confined merely to such writings and protests. In 1874 one Sasipada Banerjee started a journal *Bharat Sramjibee* [The Indian Worker] which ventilated the grievances of the workers. This can be said to be the first Indian journal dedicated to the cause of the Indian working class. Sasipada Banerjee also founded the Baranagore Institute at Baranagore, in whose neighbourhood many jute mills were situated, for promoting the education and welfare of the jute mill workers.

Whereas the first spontaneous and unorganized labour movement started in the plantations, the first organized labour movement in India—though not, as yet, through the instrumentality of properly constituted trade unions—developed among the workers in the railways and the printing presses and then in the textile industry. Though some trade unions were formed among the workers in the railways and the printing presses, the real and effective beginning of the trade union movement in India took place in the textile industries in Bombay, Ahmedabad, Calcutta, and Madras. This was natural because of the large concentration of workers in the textile industry and the higher political consciousness prevailing in or in the neighbourhood of the towns and cities where the factories had been set up.

In these towns and cities the politically-conscious middle class and the intellectuals inspired and guided the labour movement. In the early days the workers were generally illiterate and were hardly conscious of their rights. It is the outside leaders, the intellectuals and the middle class, who roused the workers and organized them. It is these outside leaders who verbalized the mute aspirations of the workers and supplied theories and slogans for their movements.

The workers who came for employment to the industries that were being set up in India in those early days were weak and helpless. They came from socially and economically disabled groups. They were the pauperized peasants and ruined artisans. They migrated to cities in search of employment and were pushed, not pulled, to the cities. In those early days famines, to a great extent, were responsible for the exodus of the rural population to the cities. In the two decades between 1872-81 and

1891-1901, when there were widespread famines, there was a considerable movement of the rural population to the towns in search of employment.[16] The early workers that were driven to the factories in the towns were, at heart, villagers and, therefore, migratory in character.

By the beginning of the twentieth century, there came a change in the mentality of the Indian workers. By this time many workers in the cities of Calcutta and Bombay and in the steel-town of Jamshedpur had been able to sever their connection with the villages and to find their footing in the factories. They were, therefore, no longer migratory in character and were more organized and conscious of their rights. It is they who formed the nucleus of a city proletariat which, in course of time, became a mighty force.

After the introduction of modern means of transport and communication, the factory system began to develop in India. The foundations of the modern cotton textile industry and jute industry were laid in the 1850s. Apart from the large-scale cotton and jute textile industries, seasonal industries, such as cotton and jute pressing and rice-milling, were also being set up. In the 1880s there were 89 cotton textile mills employing 43,000 workers and 20 jute mills employing 20,000 workers. These jute and cotton textile mills began to draw a growing labour force from the villages. The workers that came to these factories were drawn from the landless proletariat class, who had found it impossible to make a living in the villages and who had been pushed to the towns by the increasing pauperization and impoverishment of the village population caused by the destruction of the old village communities, the fractionalization of land, rack-renting, increase of population and divers other factors.

The landless proletariat class or the displaced labour force of the villages at first found employment in the construction of roads, railways, and public buildings which were constructed by the British Indian government in the middle of the nineteenth century; later, some of them were sent under a system of indenture to South Africa, the Pacific Coast, and other places; and, finally, when in the fifties and sixties of the last century the plantations and then the mines and factories were established, this labour force found employment there.

This displaced labour force from the villages came to a completely different environment in the cities and factories. The process of adaptation and assimilation to this new environment was at once slow and painful. "Silent and patient, reluctant and bewildered they come, by boat, by road and by train. They come from the village, whose long history is written in custom and in mutual cooperation, to the city whose brief history is written in change and in cut-throat competition. These immigrants are the meeting place of two civilizations. . . . The civilization of the West with its industrial system, its individualism and its rapid changes is throwing wave after wave against the sand bar and the quiet waters of the Eastern civilization based on agriculture, on community life, on established custom. For the immigrants to the city the change comes as a vast upheaval in which they are uprooted from their past and shaken from the stable basis of their lives."[17]

The workers that came to the factories in the 1850s and 1860s were too weak to protect themselves against the employers, nor did the government, wedded to a policy of *laissez-faire*, initially take any steps to protect the interests of the workers. In fact, the attitude of the government was that the social system should be protected from the workmen, rather than that the workmen should be protected from the social system in which they had to work under unhygienic and unsatisfactory conditions. Accordingly, the worst features of the early industrial system of Britain were reproduced in India.

In fact, in some respects the conditions of the workers in India, in the early days, were worse than in the early factories of England. Women and children were employed indiscriminately in the factories. Some of the children employed were hardly eight years old. Further, the workers had to work from sunrise to sunset with only half-an-hour's rest and there was no weekly holiday. In 1874 attention to these evils were drawn by Major Moore, the Chief Inspector of the Bombay Cotton Department.

Before Major Moore drew attention to these evils, India had not produced its own Shaftsbury or Robert Owen to raise his voice against these evils. In the 1870s there was considerable social and religious ferment in India, but the Indian élite which was engaged in social and religious reform did not, except in the case of plantation labour of Assam and in the case of jute mill workers of Bengal, draw attention to the evils that the introduc-

4

tion of the factory system in India was generating. In fact, even after political associations began to be formed, these associations were, in the beginning, confined to the upper classes and they did not concern themselves with working conditions in the factories.

The publication of Major Moore's report in 1874 gave rise to some agitation in England. This led to the appointment of the first Factory Commission in 1875. As in England, employers in India opposed the introduction of any Factory Act on the basis of the twin principles of "Hands off industry" and "So good for the children." In fact, in 1875 the Mill Owners' Association of Bombay was formed to organize opinion against "vexatious and useless restrictions" in the condition of work of labourers.[18]

When the industrial and mercantile interests in India were agitating against the introduction of any factory legislation, a well-known Indian social worker in Britain, Sorabjee Shaprujee Bengalee, sent in April 1878 a draft bill on factory legislation to the Governor of Bombay. The Bombay Legislative Council was not prepared to support even a limited factory legislation as proposed by S. S. Bengalee but the Poona Sarvajanik Sabha evinced a keen interest in the matter. S. S. Bengalee then brought to bear the force of humanitarian opinion in Britain to exert pressure on the British Indian government. It is interesting to note in this connection that the cause of factory legislation in India was also helped by Lancashire millowners and their supporters who looked with jealousy at the development of a cotton textile industry in India.[19]

The draft bill of Bengalee left some imprint on the first Indian Factories Act of 1881. The scope of this Act was, however, limited. It only provided for the regulation of employment of children below 12 years of age and it was meant to apply only to factories using mechanical power and employing 100 or more persons. Yet this Act was a landmark, for it recognized for the first time the rights of the working class in a statute passed by the government.

The Indian Factories Act of 1891 was passed on the basis of the recommendations of the Indian Factory Commission of 1890, of which S. S. Bengalee was a member. The 1891 Act applied to all factories employing 50 or more workers, stipulated for a weekly holiday and an half-hour recess for the workers, fixed 9 years as the minimum age for children to be employed in factories, limited the hours of work of children to seven instead of nine per day and prohibited night work for women.

Neither the Indian Factories Act of 1881 nor the Indian Factories Act of 1891 came into existence as a result of any agitation or movement of the Indian working class or even of the Indian political leaders. These legislations were enacted as a result of the agitation of British philanthropists and Indian social reformers, and the Lancashire interest and its jealousy of the cotton mill industry that was being developed in India, had also some part to play.

The cause of the Indian working class was persistently espoused in the 1880s by S. S. Bengalee, and during this period one of the first labour leaders of India was N. M. Lokhandy. At a meeting of the Bombay millworkers convened in 1884 by Lokhandy a memorial was drawn up urging the limitation of hours of work of the workers, fixation of a weekly rest day, and a noon-time recess and the provision of compensation for injuries to workmen. This memorial was drawn up for presentation to the Bombay Factories Commission of 1884.

Lokhandy, who began his life as a factory worker, later started a journal *Dinabandhu* [Friend of the poor]. In 1884 Lokhandy also described himself as the "President of the Millhands' Association." This claim, however, was somewhat exaggerated for it does not appear that at that time the Bombay Millhands' Association existed as an organized body at all, certainly it had "no roll of membership, no funds and no rules."[20]

Before Lokhandy sought to speak for the Bombay workers in 1884, it appears that in 1879 one Rughabe Succaram and 578 other operatives had presented a memorial to the Bombay Legislative Council drawing attention to the deplorable conditions in which they had to work. This is perhaps the first time that a memorial was presented by the workers themselves in India, but it does not seem that by that time they had organized themselves through trade unions.

Organized trade unionism was a late development in India. But this does not mean that there was no solidarity or unity among the workers before trade unions were formed. "Despite almost universal testimony before Commissions between 1880 and 1908 to the effect that there were no actual unions, many stated that the labourers in an individual mill were often able to act in unison and that, as a group, they were very independent. The Inspector of Boilers spoke in 1892 of 'an unnamed and unwritten bond of union among the workers peculiar to the people'; and the Collector of Bombay wrote that although this was 'little more than in the air' it was 'powerful'. 'I believe' he wrote to the Government 'it has had much to do with the prolonged maintenance of what seems to be a monopoly or almost a monopoly wage'. Sir S. Sassoon David said in 1908 that if labour 'had no proper organization, they had an understanding among themselves'. Mr Barucha, lately Director of Industries in Bombay Presidency stated that 'the hands were all-powerful against the owners, and could combine, though they had not got a trade union'. If there is some degree of exaggeration in these statements, the word of the British deputy commissioner at Wardha certainly overshot the mark when he said that 'the workers were masters of the situation; and the millowners were really more in need of protection than the workers'."[21]

It is not known when for the first time the workers, through their concentrated action, utilized the weapon of strike, which later was to become such a mighty weapon in their hands. In the 1870s there were instances of workers pressing their demands by refusing to work. Perhaps the first instance of a strike in India was the weaver's strike in 1877 in the Empress Mills at Nagpur.[22] Thereafter strikes began to spread. Between 1882 and 1890 in the factories of Bombay and Madras alone there were 25 important strikes and many more minor strikes. After 1892 strikes began to take a more organized form, even in the absence of trade unions.

As already stated, the almost universal testimony before Commissions between 1880 and 1908 was that there were no actual unions among the Indian workers. The weakness and lack of organization of Indian workers would be apparent from the fact that, after a visit to India, Keir Hardie, the British labour leader, wrote a book *India: Impressions and Suggestions*, published in 1910, in which there was no reference to any working class movement. Similarly, another labour leader of Britain, Ramsay MacDonald, in his book *The Awakening of India*, published in 1910, referred merely to the possibility of the formation of trade combinations by the Indian workers in the future, which "combinations will probably be of a kind midway between the castes of India and the trade unions of Great Britain."[23]

In the early days the middle-class intellectuals and politicians gave leadership to the workers. During times of intense political activity, such as after the anti-partition agitation in Bengal or after Tilak's arrest and imprisonment in 1908, there were considerable labour unrest. After the anti-partition agitation, the political leaders of Bengal helped the workers in the printing and transport industries to win some of their strikes. One of the most impressive of the early strikes in India was the six-day political mass strike of the Bombay mill-workers in 1908 in protest against Tilak's sentence and imprisonment. This political strike of the Bombay mill-workers was hailed by Lenin who said: "In India, too, the proletariat has already developed to conscious political mass struggle and, that being the case, the Russian-style British régime in India is doomed."[24]

The growing strength of the Bombay mill-workers was recognized by the employers. This is evident from the speech of J. B. Petit, the Deputy Chairman of the Mill-Owners' Association, Bombay on 14 April 1914: "I would invite your attention to what we have now learnt to recognize as the Labour Movement in this country. It is a movement, the significance and force of which it is not possible to ignore. Indian labourers are now beginning to combine among themselves for the attainment of their common good and the removal of their common grievances; and I should not wonder if before long, they are in a position to dictate terms to capitalists as they are doing in Europe. Labour in this city has now commenced to realize the force of numbers and the power of combination."[25] Though the strength of the Bombay mill-workers in 1914 was somewhat exaggerated by Petit, his speech was an indication of the awareness on the part of the employers that the workers were a force to reckon with and that their strength had increased and was increasing.

Prior to World War I workers' organizations were weak and they "scarcely extended beyond better paid railway employees and some classes of Government servants."[26] Further, during this period leadership for the labour movement was provided mainly by the politically conscious middle class and the social workers so that labour movement was, to a great extent, for the workers rather than by the workers.

After World War I there emerged a proper labour movement

in India. The ferment of the war made the workers in the cities conscious of their rights. They increasingly realized the advantages of the formation of trade unions and the force of collective bargaining. And above all, they realized that strike was a mighty weapon for advancing their rights and for wresting from the employers higher wages and better conditions of work.

Various causes contributed to strengthen the labour movement in India during and after the first great war. The expansion of industry during the war increased the demand for labour. The rising prices and higher cost of living increased the unrest and discontent of the workers. The mounting tide of the national movement and the emergence of trade union leaders inspired by the success of the Russian Revolution of October 1917 also helped in the growth and organization of the labour movement in India.

In 1918 the Madras Labour Union was formed. It became a precursor of the labour movement and the forerunner of trade unionism in India. Within a period of three years a good number of unions were formed in Bombay, Ahmedabad, Calcutta, and elsewhere in the country. And between 1918 and 1921 there was a plethora of strikes in divers factories and industries throughout India. The textile workers of Ahmedabad, under Gandhiji's leadership, went on strike for three weeks to enforce their demand for a wage increase. After three weeks the workers began to falter. At that stage Gandhi went on a fast to support the demand of the workers and the employers had to agree to refer the dispute to a Board of Arbitration.

The Madras Labour Union was founded by B. P. Wadia, a Home Rule leader and pioneer of the trade union movement in India, and the Ahmedabad Textile Labour Union by Gandhi. In fact, even after the first great war many of the leaders of the labour movement in India came from the political field. Again, what first attracted B. P. Wadia to the cause of the workers was not so much the economic condition of the workers as the harsh and arrogant treatment that the European officers of the mills of Binny Company meted out to the workers.[27] B. P. Wadia, in supporting the Allied cause during the first great war said that "it was a war between Powers of Darkness and Powers of Light" but added: "The case of English people in India is rather peculiar. They are on the side of the good and yet the ways they adopt in this country seem very much like the ways of Germans, who are haughty, arrogant and careless of freedom and justice." This statement was regarded as defamatory by Binny Company and some of its European officers and Wadia was threatened with defamation proceedings.[28]

In 1920 the All India Trade Union Congress (AITUC), the first all-India organization of labour, was formed with Lajpat Rai as president. Without an all-India labour organization, Indian labour could not secure representation to the International Labour Conference (ILO) at Geneva. The desire to secure such representation hastened the formation of the AITUC. In fact, some of the trade union leaders of the time did not consider that there had then developed such an organization of the Indian working class as warranted the formation of an all-India labour organization. V. V. Giri, one of the early labour leaders and later in 1969 the President of India, said: "Lajpat Rai, as the president of the first session of the AITUC considered, perhaps with justification then, that the time was not ripe in the year 1920 to give an all-India name to this organization."[29]

From its very inception the AITUC had close links with the Indian National Congress. Lajpat Rai, who presided over the Special Calcutta session of the Congress in September 1920 where the resolution on non-cooperation was adopted, also presided over the inaugural session of the AITUC at Bombay in October 1920. In 1921 the Congress welcomed the formation of the AITUC.

In 1921 B. P. Wadia, one of the leaders of the AITUC, said: "It is very necessary to recognize the Labour Movement as an integral part of the National Movement. The latter will not succeed in the right direction of democracy if Indian working classes are not enabled to organize their own forces and come into their own. Unless this is done for all classes of labourers—peasants, plantation coolies, factory 'hands' and miners—even the Montagu Reforms will only succeed in transferring the powers of bureaucracy from foreign to native hands; that is not democracy."[30] The problem that the termination of British rule in India might merely mean the substitution of an Indian for a foreign bureaucratic rule unless the freedom movement had as its aim the establishment of a social democracy, which was raised again and again in later years, was raised clearly by B. P. Wadia as early as 1921.

The link between the Congress and the AITUC was maintained in subsequent years and many Congress leaders, such as C. R. Das, Motilal Nehru, Jawaharlal Nehru, and Subhas Bose presided over the AITUC at one time or the other. In the early years, however, the AITUC had no mass base. It was a top organization and was greatly concerned to secure representation at the ILO conference at Geneva. The existence of an all-India organization like the AITUC, however helped in the development of other labour federations in India. For example, in 1921 the All India Railwaymen's Federation was formed.

There were some in the AITUC who felt that the AITUC could become the nucleus for the development of a labour party in India. Lapat Rai was one of them, and this idea was propagated forcefully by F. J. Ginwala, general secretary of the AITUC, who in his report to the fifth session of the AITUC, said that the time was ripe for the formation of such a party.[31] But there were others, such as C. R. Das, who thought that the interests of the labour movement and the national movement in India were not conflicting. He felt that inasmuch as industrial and agricultural labour constituted the great majority of the people, a national movement could and should represent the interests of the majority, so that there could be no need or occasion for the formation of a separate labour party. In his presidential address at the third session of the AITUC in 1923 he said: "The question was asked, what is the necessity of the labour movement. My answer.... is that Labour represents 98% of the population of India. Labour includes peasants in India. Does anybody mean to say that the vast population of the country require no organization? ... To my mind bureaucracy is a bureaucracy, whether it is a white bureaucracy or a brown bureaucracy. That is why I have always claimed Swaraj for the masses.... Swaraj must be for the entire population and not for any particular class." There was yet another or a third group of leaders within the AITUC who desired neither that the AITUC should become the nucleus for the formation of a separate labour party nor that it should align itself with any political party. These leaders, such as N. M. Joshi, V. V. Giri, and Dewan Chaman Lal, desired that the AITUC should not concern itself with politics but primarily with the economic interests of the workers, and in advancing their cause it should not reject the help that it may get from any political party.

In its early days the AITUC was considerably influenced by political leaders, particularly by Congress leaders. The political leaders supported the cause of the workers partly from humanitarian motives and partly from the political objective of strengthening the freedom struggle against the British by securing the support of the workers. Some Congress leaders were also acutely conscious of the fact that if the Congress did not take up the cause of labour, the socialists and communists would. In his presidential address at the 1922 Congress C. R. Das said: "My advice is that the Congress should lose no time in appointing a committee, a strong 'workable committee' to organize Labour and the Peasantry in India. We have delayed the matter already too long. If the Congress fails to do its duty, you may expect to find organizations set up in the country by Labourers and Peasants detached from you, dissociated from the cause of Swaraj, which will inevitably bring within the arena of peaceful revolution class struggle."[32]

While in the early stages of the labour movement in India, it secured considerable support from political leaders, the Indian workers also did not remain aloof from political movements, such as the Swadeshi movement, the Khilafat movement, the Home Rule Movement, the non-cooperation and civil disobedience movements. The Indian labour movement, however, did not produce any distinctive political, social, or economic philosophy, such as Fabianism of England, Revisionism of Germany, Syndicalism of France, or class-collaborationism of America.

Due to the influence of outsiders the Indian labour movement was involved in international activities from an early stage. As early as 1919 B. P. Wadia, the labour leader, visited England and America and pleaded the cause of Indian workers at the British Labour Party Conference, Trade Union Congress, and other organizations. The early involvement of Indian labour in international activities also led to the first split in the AITUC between those who supported the International Federation of Trade Unions, having its headquarters at Amsterdan, and others who aligned themselves with the International Labour Union, having its headquarters at Moscow. In 1921 the Red International Labour Union from Moscow sent its greetings to the second session of the AITUC and called upon it to join the new world movement of international solidarity. The AITUC reciprocated the greetings sent by the Red International and asked the workers of India to stand by the side of the Russian workers.

Since about 1923 the early communists of India began to be active in the labour movement in Bombay and Calcutta. The policy that the Indian communists should pursue was stated by the fifth Congress of the Communist International in 1924: "The Indian Communist Party must bring the trade union movement under its influence. It must reorganize it on a class basis and purge it of all alien elements."

The emphasis on the class character of the labour movement gave rise to some conflicts within the AITUC. The communists wanted that the Indian workers should recognize the role that they should play against their class enemies, the national bourgeoisie. C. R. Das, the Congress leader and president of the 1923 session of the AITUC, however, warned the labour leaders of India against any such emphasis on class conflicts. He asserted that the concept of class conflict, which might be valid in European countries, was inappropriate to a subject country like India having different traditions and that in India there did not, in fact, exist any conflict between the classes and masses.[33]

During the 1920s there was intense political movement in India and the 1920-22 non-cooperation movement had its repercussions in the labour field. In the year 1924 there were many strikes in India and particularly among the textile workers first in Bombay and then in Kanpur. Most of these strikes were organized by the communists. In 1924 the government started the Kanpur Conspiracy Case, popularly known as Bolshevik Conspiracy Trial, against four leaders—Dange, Shaukat Usmani, Muzzafar Ahmed, and Das Gupta who were charged with having conspired to wage war against the King.

Among the prominent communists and labour leaders of Bombay in the 1920s were S. A. Dange, later the Chairman of the CPI, R. S. Nimbkar, K. N. Jogelkar, and S. V. Ghate. At the Kanpur session of the AITUC in 1927 the communists obtained a measure of control over the AITUC and S. V. Ghate was elected as one of its secretaries. The communists wanted that the AITUC should dissociate itself from all cooperation with the British Labour Party and the International Labour Organization and should pursue a more leftist policy. In 1927 Shapurji Saklatwala, the British communist MP, had come to India to help the organization of the left forces in the country. He also attended the 1927 session of the AITUC. Saklatwala corresponded with Gandhi and explained the nature of his "attacks" on Gandhi—why he considered that the labour union that Gandhi founded at Ahmedabad, Ahmedabad Majur Mahajan, was not based on real trade union principles, why Gandhi's theories about "the due share of labour" was reactionary, and why Ahmedabad Majur Mahajan should affiliate itself with the AITUC and join the broad stream of the Indian trade union movement. Gandhi replied that his policy was not anti-capitalistic, that his idea was "to take from capital labour's due share and no more, and this not by paralysing capital, but by reform among labourers from within and by their own self-consciousness." Gandhi added: "Labour, in my opinion, must not become a pawn in the hands of the politician on the political chessboard. It must, by its sheer strength dominate the chessboard."

The first day of May 1927 was for the first time celebrated in India as a Labour Day in Bombay. Since then the first of May of each year has been celebrated as May Day or Labour Day in various parts of India.

In Bombay the influence of the communists in the trade unions were considerable. The leadership of the trade union movement in Bombay was divided between the moderates and the communists. Shiva Rao, the Chairman of the Executive of the AITUC and a moderate, said in 1928: "The time has come when the trade union movement in India should weed out of its organization mischief-makers. A warning is all the more necessary because there are certain individuals who go about preaching the gospel of strike."[34] The communists, on the other hand, believed that it is only through strikes that the workers could develop class consciousness and secure their demands from the employers.

In 1928 there were 203 strikes in the country out of which 111 took place in Bombay. In 1929 the number of strikes was less, but a call for a general strike of the textile workers of Bombay was given in April 1929 by Girni Kamgar Union, which was controlled by the communists. Labour unrest spread from the textile workers of Bombay to the jute workers of Bengal and the railway employees of the GIP Railway. In 1929 the government sought to counteract labour unrest first with the Public

Safety Ordinance and then with the Trade Disputes Act of 1929, which prohibited lightning strikes.

In March 1929 the government also launched the Meerut Conspiracy Case in which at first 31 leading trade union leaders were charged with having conspired to deprive the King Emperor of his sovereignty of India. The trial lasted for more than four years. Among those charged at the trial were S. A. Dange, Muzzafar Ahmed, and others who later became leading communists of India. This trial received great publicity and Harold Laski has even compared it to the Sacco-Vanzetti trial of America, the Dreyfus trial of France, and the Reichstag Fire Trial of Germany. Jawaharlal Nehru, the then president of the AITUC, appealed to the British Trade Union Congress for support, claiming that the trial had been launched for political reasons and for suppressing trade union activities in India. The British Trade Union Congress, however, through Sir Walter Citrine, its secretary, asserted that the accused were charged with political offences, that the trial did not affect the Indian trade union movement and should be expedited.

In January 1933 judgment was delivered in the Meerut Conspiracy Case. It provided for transportation for life for Muzzafar Ahmed; twelve years' transportation for Dange, Ghate, Jogelkar, Nimbkar, and Spratt; ten years' transportation for Bradley, Mirajkar, and Usmani; and lighter sentences for others. But instead of curbing trade unionism or even communism, the trial helped to give communism some sort of respectability among a section of the youth and the intellectuals of India.

In 1929 there took place a split in the AITUC between the moderate group led by N. M. Joshi, V. V. Giri, Shiva Rao, and Dewan Chaman Lal, and the extremist group led by the communists who were supported by the left nationalists. After 1929 the moderates came out of the AITUC and formed the Indian Trade Union Federation. Though in 1929 the communists, with the help of the left nationalists, gained control of the AITUC, it was still working in alliance with, and not in opposition to, the nationalist political movement in India. But in 1931 the communists led by B. T. Ranadive and S. V. Deshpande clashed with the left nationalists, then led by Subhas Chandra Bose, within the AITUC on the question as to what should be the relationship of the AITUC towards the nationalist movement in India. At the 1931

session of the AITUC a message from Saklatwala, the British communist MP, was read out in which he attacked the "treacherous
role of Gandhi and his satellites masquerading as revolutionary
leaders." The approach of the communists and the left nationalists
towards Gandhi and the nationalist movement were widely
divergent and a split was unavoidable. The communist group
left the AITUC and formed a separate All India Red Trade Union
Congress.

The Communist Party of India (CPI) which controlled the
All India Red Trade Union Congress was banned in 1934. In
1935 the Red Trade Union Congress merged with the AITUC.
By this time a new political group had organized itself within
the Indian National Congress under the name of the Congress
Socialist Party and this group joined the AITUC. After the CPI was
banned, the communists functioned from within the Congress
Socialist Party (CSP) and they could thereby exert some influence
both within the Congress and the AITUC.

Though the communists for some time functioned from within
the CSP and the AITUC, they considered both as reformist organizations lacking a leftist and revolutionary orientation. Writing in
India Today in 1940 R. P. Dutt, the British communist leader who
had considerable influence over the Indian communists, commented: "The special character of the Congress Socialist Party
was that membership was made conditional on membership of the
National Congress; the party thus constituted a wing within the
National Congress; it operated mainly as an apparatus within the
Congress and discouraged mass membership. The objective effect
of this programmatic and constitutional basis (whatever the
intentions of the progressive elements among its founders) inevitably represented an attempt to subordinate the independence of
the working-class movement to the control and discipline of the
existing dominant leadership of the National Congress, which
meant, in practice, of the bourgeoisie. This contradiction showed
itself further in the conflict between the left wing of the party,
which sought cooperation with the Communist Party and the
working class forces, and the dominant reactionary right wing,
which was hostile to the Communist Party and to all independent
working class activity."[35] The communists proclaimed that they
wanted to build up an independent working class movement
"freed from the alien channel of bourgeois influence (whether

imperialist influence, or bourgeois national influence, both of which have sought to deflect it from its aims), but at the same time participating in the broad front of the national struggle for independence. . . ."[36]

The next stage in the development of the labour movement in India was reached when the Government of India Act, 1935, was introduced. Prior to the 1935 Act, labour had for the first time under the Montagu-Chelmsford Reform Scheme of 1919 secured some, though very inadequate representation, in the legislatures. Under the 1935 Act the representation of labour in the legislatures was improved. They were allotted 38 seats in the provincial assemblies and 10 in the Federal Assembly. After winning the elections held under the 1935 Act, the Congress in 1937-38 formed elected governments in seven out of nine provinces. In terms of the famous Karachi resolution of the Congress passed in 1931 on Fundamental Rights, the Congress in its election manifesto of 1936 had enunciated its policy as securing to industrial workers a decent standard of living and hours of work and conditions of labour, the establishment of suitable machinery for settlement of disputes between the employers and workmen, and the making of adequate provision for the protection of the workers against the economic consequences of old age, sickness, and unemployment.

The Congress ministries took some steps to ameliorate the conditions of the workers, but these could not meet the revolution in expectations which the installation of elected ministries had given rise to. The Parliamentary Secretary of Labour in the Congress Ministry of Bombay appraised the situation thus: "The textile labour in the Province generally and in the Bombay City particularly had legitimate grounds for dissatisfaction. The earnings of the workers bore no sensible relation to the human requirements of the simplest possible life in a large urban area. Wage-cuts in the textile industry had aggravated the difficulties of a worker's life. The extent of unemployment and underemployment was fairly wide, but no attempts had been made to measure them or deal with them. It was apparent that the incoming of a popular Government would awaken aspirations, create expectations and give a fillip to labour legislation for better things."[37]

During the period the Congress ministries were in power the workers got a certain measure of sympathy from Congress ministers and this helped in the rapid growth of trade unions as would appear from the following figures:

Year	Number of registered unions	Membership of unions submitting returns
1936-37	271	2,61,047
1937-38	420	3,90,112
1938-39	562	3,99,159

The Congress ministries resigned from office in protest against the unilateral declaration made by the British Indian government, at the outbreak of World War II, that India was also at war with Germany. During this war another split took place in the AITUC. The supporters of the policy of M. N. Roy (Royists) declared that the war against Germany was an international civil war against Fascism, the enemy of liberty and all working class movements; and that, accordingly, the Indian working class should support the British war effort unconditionally. By taking this stand the Royists isolated themselves from the broad stream of the Indian nationalist movement, which opposed participation in the war-effort unless the freedom of India was guaranteed or assured. On the question of support to the war-effort the Royists seceded from the AITUC in 1940 and formed the Indian Federation of Labour. The government naturally welcomed this new organization, granted it Rs 13,000 per month for war propaganda, and in 1944 nominated one of its representatives for attending the International Labour Conference held at Philadelphia.

After Russia entered the war in 1942, the communists in India declared that the war had become a people's war. On this basis the communists supported the British war-effort and called upon the workers to do so. In 1942 the Congress, under Gandhi's leadership, started the Quit India Movement for the ending of British rule in India. As a result of this movement most of the nationalist and socialist leaders were either in prison or went underground. During the period of the war the communists dominated the AITUC.

During the war labour unrest was kept under check by various wartime measures, such as the Defence of India Rules, National

Service (Technical Personnel) Ordinance, and the Essential
Services (Maintenance) Ordinance. But the period of World
War II also witnessed a steady rise in the growth of trade unions
in India.

During the war industrial activities considerably increased
and the employers made large profits. The employers, therefore,
readily cooperated with the industrial adjudication machinery and
implemented industrial awards in order to secure the cooperation
of the workers for increasing production. But after the war
profits declined and there was less readiness to settle the claims
of labour through conciliation or to implement industrial awards
and, accordingly, there was more labour unrest.

The end of the war witnessed a steady increase in strikes
reminiscent of the wave of strikes of the late twenties. During
and after the war prices had gone up. This had increased the
cost of living of the workers and stimulated demands for wage
rise. Further, the period after the war witnessed a revival of
political activities and a great increase in the hopes and aspirations
of the people generally, including the working class, and all these
gave rise to more labour disputes and strikes.

After the war two important labour legislations were passed,
namely, the Indian Trades Union (Amendment) Act, 1947 and the
Industrial Disputes Act, 1947. The first Act provided for com-
pulsory recognition of trade unions but the necessary notification
for bringing the same into effect was not issued. The Industrial
Disputes Act, 1947, on the other hand, marked a milestone in
the development of labour legislation in India. It set up Works
Committees and Industrial Tribunals, which could make binding
awards in respect of industrial disputes referred to them. The
awards of Industrial Tribunals have in numerous cases provided
real relief to the workers.

By the end of the war the communists had come to dominate
the AITUC. Congress leaders after coming out of prison at the end
of war began to think of forming a separate all-India trade union
organization. The reason for starting such a separate all-India
labour organization was stated by Gulzari Lal Nanda in a communication addressed to Congress-minded trade unionists thus:
"Congressmen in general, and particularly those working in the
field of labour, have found it very difficult to cooperate any
longer with the Trade Union Congress which has repeatedly

been adopting a course completely disregarding, or even in opposition to, the declared policy and advice of the Indian National Congress." On 13 August 1946 the Congress Working Committee advised Congressmen engaged in the labour field to follow the lead given by Hind Mazdoor Sevak Sangh (HMSS). The HMSS had been founded in 1937 by those associated with the Ahmedabad Textile Labour Association, which had been founded by Gandhi. The circumstances relating to the founding of HMSS were stated thus by Professor N. G. Ranga: "It was not until 1938 that Gandhian Trade Union leaders realized the need for a national organization to develop Trade Unionism on the lines popularized by Mahatma Gandhi and they formed the HMSS with a view to training workers. . . . It was only then that a large number of Congressmen began to understand the full significance of the sudden outbreak of communist-inspired strikes in 1937-38 when the Congress Ministries were functioning. . . . Therefore, it was during this period of disillusionment, that Congress came to feel the necessity of the HMSS and began to rally round its banner."

Pursuant to the recommendation of the Congress Working Committee that Congressmen working in the labour front should follow the lead given by HMSS, the Indian National Trade Union Congress (INTUC) was formed at a conference presided over by Sardar Vallabhbhai Patel. This conference was attended by Congress leaders, such as Jawaharlal Nehru, J. B. Kripalani, Jagjivan Ram, Ravi Shankar Shukla, Hare Krishna Mahatab, Kamala Devi Chattopadhyaya, Aruna Asaf Ali, and Asoka Mehta.

In 1947 India attained freedom. This was also a year of strikes. The number of industrial disputes in 1947 was 1,811, involving loss of 16,562,666 working days as compared to 1,629 industrial disputes involving loss of 12,717,762 working days in 1946, and 820 industrial disputes involving loss of 12,717,762 working days in 1945.[38] The increase in strikes made the government uneasy and Prime Minister Nehru referred to the "the slow drying up of the productive capacity of the nation."

To promote better relations between employers and employees and to bring about an industrial truce an Industries Conference consisting of representatives of employers, workers, and the government was held at New Delhi in December 1947. The Conference revealed basic differences in the viewpoints of labour and

5

management, but eventually an Industrial Truce Resolution was arrived at unanimously. The Conference recommended that fullest use should be made of statutory and other machinery for peacefully solving industrial disputes, that a machinery for fixing fair wages and conditions of labour should be set up, and in each industrial undertaking Works Committees should be constituted. The Conference also requested labour and the management to maintain industrial peace and avert lock-outs and strikes for three years.

After this Industrial Truce Resolution was passed the government of India incorporated the same in its Industrial Policy Resolution of 6 April 1948. In pursuance of the Industrial Truce Resolution the government also appointed two committees, namely, the Profit-Sharing Committee and Fair Wages Commitee in 1948.

The recommendations of the Profit-Sharing Committee were not unanimous and the labour representatives in the Committee, namely, Asoka Mehta, Khandubhai Desai, and V. B. Karnik dissented from the recommendations of the Committee. The question of profit-sharing, one of the major causes of industrial strikes, therefore remained to be resolved by collective bargaining or through awards of industrial tribunals.

The Report of the Committee on Fair Wages was published in 1948. The Committee recommended that the lower limit of fair wage shall be the minimum wage and the upper limit would be fixed according to the industry's capacity to pay, and that in between these two limits the actual wages would be fixed on the basis of the productivity of labour, the level of income, the place of the industry concerned in the economy of the country, and other factors. To implement the recommendations of this Committee the government introduced a bill, but this bill eventually lapsed. The recommendations of the Committee, however, remained as guiding principles which were subsequently followed by many Industrial Tribunals.

After 1947 the number of industrial disputes diminished somewhat. Whereas in 1947 the number of strikes and stoppages of work were 1,811, in 1948 they were 1,259, in 1949 they were 920, and in 1950 they were 814.[39] Some of the factors which reduced industrial tension and lessened the number of strikes were the introduction of certain enactments and ameliorative measures by the government since 1946. They were mainly the Industrial Employment (Standing Orders) Act, 1946, the Mica Mines Labour Welfare Act, 1946, the Industrial Disputes Act, 1947, the Mines Labour Welfare Fund Act, 1947, the Indian Factories Act, 1948, the Coal Mines Provident Fund and Bonus Schemes Act, 1948, the Employees' State Insurance Act, 1948, and the Dock Workers (Regulation of Employment) Act, 1948.

After 1947, when the non-communists left the AITUC, the communists were in complete control. The attitude of the communists to the Indian government was very different from that of other labour leaders. In February 1948 the Communist Party of India at its second Congress held at Calcutta adopted the tough Zhdanov line and stated that "though the bourgeois leadership parades the story that independence has been won, the fact is that the freedom struggle has been betrayed and the national leadership has struck a treacherous deal behind the back of starving people, betraying every slogan of the democratic revolution."

Believing that the central government was utterly reactionary, in 1948 the communists organized a number of strikes in the collieries, plantations, cotton textile mills and in the Indian railways and tramways. Some of the strikes in Bombay and Calcutta were followed by violence. The government at the centre and in the various states adopted repressive measures against the communists. In March 1948 the West Bengal government banned the CPI, arrested a number of communist leaders and sealed the office of the Bengal branch of the AITUC. The workers in the tea-plantations staged a mass demonstration against the action of the Bengal government. In April 1948 the Bombay government arrested a number of important communist leaders, including S. A. Dange, president of the AITUC, and S. S. Mirajkar, president of the Bombay branch of the AITUC. On 1 May 1948 some of the workers in the railways and the tea-gardens struck work in protest.

Leading communists were arrested in different parts of the country in 1948 under the Public Safety Acts. In protest, the communists campaigned for launching an all-India railway strike and for this a call was given by Jayaprakash Narayan, the socialist leader and the president of the All-India Railwaymen's Federation. The all-India railway strike was to take place from 9 March 1949 but was averted as a result of negotiations between Jayaprakash Narayan and Gopalaswami Ayyanger, the Minister of State and Transport. The communists, however, continued to organize strikes in different parts of the industrial sector. In the second half of 1949 the communists gave a series of strike calls, namely, an all-Bengal general strike, Calcutta Municipal Corporation workers' strike, and all-Bengal Jute workers' strike. Only a few of these strikes materialized, or were successful.

Throughout the period from 1948 to 1950 the communists campaigned for intensifying the strike offensive. Jayaprakash Narayan, the socialist leader and the then president of the All-India Railwaymen's Federation, had at first supported the communist campaign for calling an all-India railway strike, but later he arrived at a mutually acceptable settlement with the government. Jayaprakash Narayan apprehended that the militant and extremist policy advocated by the communists might wreck the All-India Railwaymen's Federation, and in February 1949 he said: "If you consider dispassionately all that the communists have been doing in the railways for the past months, you will agree with me that if there is any one who can be accused of betraying the workers it is they. If they are allowed to carry on as at present, the result will be complete disruption of our organization and the end of the Federation. I have come to the conclusion therefore that we have now reached a parting of the ways."[40]

The militant policy pursued by AITUC during 1948-50 was countered by severe repressive measures by the government. This struggle with the government weakened the AITUC; its membership fell from 700,000 in 1948 to 100,000 in 1951 and it could hold its annual session again only after five years in 1954. Later, the leaders of the AITUC regretted that during 1948-50 the leadership of the AITUC was "provoked" by government to pursue an "adventurist policy." An official publication of the AITUC stated: "No doubt, the dominant section of the leadership of the AITUC during this period fell a victim to this [government's] provocations and pursued adventurist tactics which also helped to weaken the AITUC. Struggles were needed to expose the policies of the Congress but they had to be conducted cautiously with the least damage to the striking power and organization of the working class. The fact that this caution was thrown overboard at times during 1948-50 showed its weakness."[41]

Since India attained independence the working class movement in India has developed very rapidly. This would be apparent from the figures showing the growth in the number of trade unions in the decade following the attainment of independence in 1947:

REGISTERED TRADE UNIONS AND THEIR MEMBERSHIP
(1947-48 to 1957-58)

Year	Number of registered trade unions	Unions submitting returns	Percentage of unions submitting returns to total number of registered unions	Total membership	Average membership per union
1947-48	2,766	1,620	58.6	16,62,929	1,026
1948-49	3,159	1,848	58.7	19,60,107	1,061
1949-50	3,522	1,919	54.5	18,21,132	949
1950-51	3,766	2,002	53.2	17,56,971	877
1951-52	4,623	2,556	55.3	19,96,311	781
1952-53	4,934	2,718	55.1	20,99,003	772
1953-54	6,029	3,295	54.7	21,12,695	641
1954-55	6,658	3,549	53.2	21,70,450	612
1955-56	8,095	4,006	49.5	22,74,732	568
1956-57	8,554	4,399	51.4	23,76,762	540
1957-58	9,644	5,319	55.1	29,07,443	547

The labour movement in India is still considerably influenced by the different political parties of the country. This is one of the main reasons as to why Indian labour is not led by a single federation of labour like the British Trade Union Congress which represents the British workers, or by a joint front like the AFL and CIO which represents the American workers. The Indian labour movement, like the French or Italian labour movements, has been split up into several organizations.

The first all-India labour organization was the AITUC. In 1929 the communists, with the support of the left nationalists, succeeded in capturing the AITUC and in ousting the moderates therefrom. But in 1931 the left nationalists proved stronger than the communists, and the communists seceded from the AITUC

to form the All-India Red Trade Union Congress. In 1934 the
CPI was banned and in 1935 the communists joined the Congress
Socialist Party and the AITUC. After the 1942 Quit India movement, when the nationalists and socialists were either in prison
or were underground, the communists obtained complete control of the AITUC.

After coming out of jail in 1945 the nationalists and socialists
were faced with the alternative of joining the AITUC, in which
the communists had entrenched themselves, or of forming a
separate all-India labour federation. In the event, the nationalists
decided to form the separate Indian National Trade Union Congress (INTUC) in 1947.

From the time of the formation of the Congress Socialist Party,
the Congress socialists had functioned within the Indian National
Congress. In 1948, after Gandhi's death, a resolution was passed
by the Congress outlawing political groupings inside the Congress. The Congress socialists therefore left the Congress and set
up a separate Socialist Party of India after the Nasik Convention
of March 1948. In December 1948 the socialists formed the Hind
Mazdoor Panchayat (HMP) as a separate all-India federation for
labour. Thus there were organized three main all-India labour
federations in India namely, the AITUC, controlled by the communists; the INTUC, aligned with the Congress; and the HMP,
later known as HMS, associated with the socialists.

The objective of the AITUC is to establish socialism in India.
Its aim, as stated in its constitution, is to establish a socialist state
in India, to socialize and nationalize the means of production,
distribution, and exchange as far as possible, and to ameliorate
the economic and social conditions of the working class.

The INTUC, unlike the AITUC, does not in its constitution include
any provision for the establishment of a socialist state or the
nationalization or socialization of the means of production, distribution, or exchange. The INTUC declares that it is opposed to all
kinds of exploitation, economic, political, or social. It also stands
for the progressive elimination of the profit-motive in the
economic organization of society and for greater participation
of the workers in the management of industries. The roots of
INTUC's philosophy can be traced to Gandhian socialism or
sarvodaya, just as the roots of AITUC's philosophy can be traced
to Marxian socialism.

The main objectives of the INTUC are to establish a society which would remove hindrances in the way of the all-round development of its individual members, which would progressively eliminate social, political, and economic exploitaton and inequality, which would restrict the profit-motive in the economic organization of society, which would curb anti-social concentration of power, which would place industry under national ownership and control in suitable form in order to realize the aforesaid objectives, which would organize society in such a manner as to ensure full employment, and which would secure increasing association of the workers in the administration and control of industry.

Whereas the INTUC seeks to end exploitation in the economic field and the AITUC seeks to establish a socialist state, the declared objective of the HMS is "to organize for and promote the establishment of a democratic, socialist society in India." Both the AITUC and the HMS declare in their constitutions that they stand for socialism, but while the former is controlled by the communists the latter is controlled by the socialists. According to the socialists their basic difference with the communists stems from their approach to democracy and the emphasis on the adoption of peaceful methods for bringing about large-scale socio-economic changes. It is for this reason that HMS declares that its aim is not merely to establish a socialist society but "a democratic, socialist society."

It is the adoption of the words "a democratic, socialist society" by HMS which again became a source of dispute among some trade unionists and was partly responsible for the formation of a fourth all-India labour federation, the United Trades Union Congress (UTUC). The UTUC was formed by Professor K. T. Shah and Mrinal Kanti Bose. Mrinal Kanti Bose, who had some hold over the working class of Bengal, did not wish to align himself either with the communist-dominated AITUC or the Congress-oriented INTUC, and when the HMS was about to be formed, he had hoped that he would be able to join it. He wanted the HMS to accept the establishment of a socialist state as its objective but objected to the expression "democratic, socialist society" on the ground that to qualify "socialist society" by the word "democratic" "would create an absolutely false notion that socialism is something which is a negation of democracy."[42] The UTUC aims

at the establishment of a socialist society or the formation of a
workers' and peasants' state in India and believes in the nationalization and socialization of the means of production, distribution, and exchange. The constitution of the UTUC, however,
contains provisions which would prevent any political party from
dominating the organization.

The AITUC, HMS, and UTUC declare in their constitutions that
they stand for a socialist state or society. They also believe in
class struggle. The INTUC, which lays emphasis on the principles
laid down by Gandhi in forming the Ahmedabad Textile Labour
Association, does not rely on class struggle and does not rule out
class collaboration though it stands for the ending of all exploitation, the eradication of profit-motive in the economic organization of society, and the greater participation of the workers in
the management of industries. While the AITUC stands for Marxian
socialism, the INTUC stands for Gandhian socialism or *sarvodaya*,
and the HMS stands for democratic socialism.

Though communists belonging to both the CPI and the
CPI(M) participated in the AITUC, the political conflict between
the two was reflected in the functioning of the AITUC. Both
struggled to attain mastery over that organization, and this struggle and conflict eventually led to a split in the AITUC. The trade
union wings of the CPI(M) and of certain small parties allied to
it, such as the Marxist Forward Bloc and the Revolutionary
Communist Party of India, came out of the AITUC, and in May
1970 they formed a new all-India trade union organization called
the Centre of Indian Trade Unions (CITU).

In *Peoples' Democracy*, the organ of the CPI(M), B. T. Ranadive asserted that the split was "a historic necessity to unify the
working class,"[43] but the CPI described the split as "criminal" and
characterized it as "the biggest blow to the working class movement."[44] The CPI(M), however, continue to accuse the CPI-domi-
nated leadership of the AITUC as being guilty of the "vices of
economism and collaborationism"[45] and assert that CITU, the new
all-India trade union organization, would follow a militant
anti-collaborationist trade union policy for the attainment of
socialism.[46]

Though the leadership of the Indian working-class movement
is divided among different central organizations of labour, the
strength of the Indian labour movement has consistently increased

since the 1920s, when Indian labourers increasingly began to organize themselves into unions. A chart showing the number of strikes organized by the workers, mainly through their unions, since the 1920s would, in this connection, be instructive:

NUMBER OF STRIKES IN INDIA SINCE 1921

Year	Number of strikes and lock-outs	Number of work-people involved
1921	396	600,351
1923	213	301,044
1929	141	531,059
1937	379	647,801
1938	399	401,075
1939	406	409,189
1940	322	452,539
1942	694	772,653
1946	1,629	1,961,948
1947	1,811	1,840,784
1948	1,259	1,059,120
1949	920	685,457
1950	814	719,883
1951	1,071	691,321
1952	963	809,242
1953	772	466,607
1954	840	477,138
1955	1,166	527,767
1956	1,203	715,130
1957	1,630	889,371
1958	1,524	929,566
1959	1,531	693,616
1960	1,583	986,268
1961	1,357	511,860
1962	1,491	705,059
1963	1,471	563,121
1964	2,151	1,002,955
1965	1,835	991,158
1966	2,556	1,4120,056

III. LANDED ARISTOCRATS AND PEASANT MOVEMENTS

Working-class movements developed in India much later than political movements. The workers were illiterate and backward and were able to form their organizations or trade unions long after the educated middle class had formed their political associations or organizations. Furthermore, in the early stages it is the educated middle class which roused the consciousness of the workers, verbalized their mute aspirations, supplied slogans for them, and helped the workers to organize their trade unions. But though the workers organized themselves into groups and trade unions after the educated middle class had organized themselves, the workers, as a whole, were more active, organized, and militant as compared to the peasants of India.

Workers do not own the machines they operate nor do they own any land, unlike the peasants who might own the meagre plot of land which they till. Being propertyless, the workers are more militant than the peasants. Further, as the workers are concentrated in factories it is easier for them to organize themselves and to form trade unions than it is for the peasants who are widely scattered in the fields and farms. The workers have to cooperate with many others of their kind in working the machines in the factories. This develops in the workers a capacity to cooperate with others, to work in an organized way, and to act collectively for the purpose of forming a trade union or launching a strike. Unions of workers were, therefore, formed in India much earlier than unions of peasants. Again, the workers who operate modern power-driven machines are, unlike the peasants, not dependent on the forces of nature. This makes the workers more self-confident, active, and militant as compared with the peasants and it is no wonder that the various all-India federations of workmen seek to effect radical socio-economic changes in India and some of them have the establishment of a socialist state or society as their main objective.

The system of private property in land that the British introduced under the Permanent Settlement in Bengal brought into existence zamindars or big landlords who owned the land and tenants who tilled them. The zamindari system was aristocratic and was, to some extent, inspired by English landlordism, as the Ryotwari system that the British introduced in Madras and certain other parts of the country, was inspired by the French peasant-proprietorship system.

The zamindars created under the Permanent Settlement by Lord Cornwallis were aristocratic in outlook. Lord Lytton stated that the landed aristocrats were a conservative force and could be relied upon to support British rule.

The interests of the big landlords of British India and of the princes of the princely states were generally the same. They stood for *status quo* and the continuance of British rule. The British first associated the princes and then the big zamindars in the running of the Indian administration. In 1862 the Maharaja of Patiala and the Raja of Benares were nominated to the Governor-General's Legislative Council.

The big landlords or zamindars formed their political association, the British Indian Association, as early as 1851. The big landlords were generally opposed to the political demands made by the educated middle class. The educated middle class opposed Lytton's repressive Press Act, but the landlords did not. Bepin Pal, one of the early leaders of the educated middle class, recorded: "To protest against the Press Act of Lytton, the Indian Association convened a public meeting of the inhabitants of Calcutta at the Town Hall. The British Indian Association, representing the Bengal Zamindars, refused to join the meeting. But the educated middle class, not only of Calcutta and Bengal but practically of all the other provinces, supported this protest of the Indian Association."[47]

Most landed aristocrats and princes in India wanted to preserve the existing socio-economic order and to stem the tide of the growing nationalist and democratic movement in India. The Raja of Bhinga, a representative of the landed aristocrats, gave expression to his views in a work entitled *Democracy Not Suited to India* published in the year 1888.[48] The Raja believed that it was undesirable "to give men of inferior origin and caste, power over men immensely their superior in birth and social position," and he emphatically maintained that the territorial aristocrats wanted to preserve the social distinctions that existed between man and man in India from time immemorial.[49] The territorial aristocrats had no love for democracy; they were conservative and orthodox and clung to the old established usages. But the light of orthodoxy had become dim in the minds of the English educated middle-class and Congress agitators who, the Raja lamented, were "seeking to introduce into India the strange and complicated institutions of the far West." The Raja claimed that the landed aristocrats represented the real interests of the people and advised the British rulers to govern India through the landed aristocrats.[50]

Similarly, another landed aristocrat, Raja Siva Prasad, declared in the 1888 Congress that the government should prohibit the extensive distribution of pamphlets and leaflets which contained criticisms of the British administration in India. Language such as "to what condition the nation has been reduced . . . how distressed she feels . . . is she alive or dead" he considered objectionable. This conservative Raja said that "to declare the value of the principles of democracy and that England owes its greatness to it; to hold up to admiration the Republican form of government in France; to show that in the colonies even the negroes enjoy the same rights as the British-born subjects, implying thereby that the conditions of the negroes is better than that of the people of India" was to use language that was inflammatory.[51]

A little known person by the name of R. C. Saunders, a Calcutta solicitor, suggested in 1890 that by forming an Indian House of Lords it would be possible to rule India through the territorial aristocrats. He computed that the Indian peerage would be composed of 1,280 aristocrats. There would be 230 ruling chiefs of native states, 100 survivors of extinct dynasties and other eminent men, and 950 zamindars of British India.[52] The Indian peerage was to have the right of trial by its own class and to have a voice in legislation.[53] It was not clearly specified as to how real the power of the Indian peerage was to be in this scheme of things, but probably the Indian House of Lords was designed to be merely a consultative body and it was not intended that it would be invested with any effective power over legislation.

Saunders suggested that some of the ambitious and relatively wealthy educated middle-class Indians could be elevated to the Indian peerage in the manner that some middle class persons in Britain had been incorporated in the British nobility. The purpose that Saunders had in mind when he suggested the creation of an Indian House of Lords was that it would provide a "proper counterpoise" to the Congress movement that was dominated by the English-educated middle class.[54] Saunders wanted to check the growing influence of the English-educated class which was seeking to familiarize its countrymen with Western political institutions and ideas and which was more enlightened than the territorial artistocrats of India. As the Raja of Bhinga himself admitted, the majority of the ancient nobility of India had not received the benefits of English education and they found it difficult to keep pace with the tide of progress.[55]

Even Syed Ahmed Khan, the great Muslim leader, opposed the Congress movement not merely because it formulated reform proposals on the assumption that Indians were a nation,[56] but also because it sought to import democratic institutions in India which, he maintained, were totally unsuited to Indian conditions. Syed Ahmed asserted that the Viceroy would be specially justified in appointing persons of good family as members of the Governor-General's Legislative Council. "None but a man of good breeding," he declared, "can the Viceroy take as his colleague, treat as his brother, and invite to entertainments at which he may have to dine with Dukes and Earls."[57] The suggestion that those who enjoyed the accidental advantages of rank and birth should be given special preference in the matter of appointment to the Governor-General's Legislative Council was strongly criticized in the nationalist press.[58] "India," wrote the *Indian Spectator*, "does not want government managed by the native aristocracy. It requires the fittest men it can find."[59] The *Tribune* drew attention to the fact that even the landed gentry of Bengal had once suggested as its nominee in the Governor-General's Legislative Council the name of that fine representative of the English-educated class, Kristo Das Pal, even though Pal was born in the "low" *teli* or oilman caste.[60]

The question of providing a counterpoise to the growing nationalist movement represented by the English-educated middle class, which dominated the Congress, assumed greater importance at the time of the Morley-Minto reforms. This was the question which was uppermost in Minto's mind. On 27 June 1906 Minto wrote that Congressmen, who could easily imitate Western political methods, had secured for their political utterances much greater importance in Britain than they ever could aspire to obtain in India.[61] He believed that the most important factor with which the government had to deal was "not impossible Congress ambitions."[62] He desired to satisfy the aspirations of big landowners and others who wanted Indians to have a greater share in the highest councils of the government but who were not enthusiastic about the Congress demand for the increase of representative government in India. On 28 May 1906 Minto wrote to Morley: "I have been thinking a good deal lately of possible counterpoise to Congress aims. I think we find a solution in the Council of princes, or in an elaboration of that idea; a Privy Council not only of Native Rulers, but of a few other big men.... We should get (from them) different ideas from those of Congress."[63]

In order to provide a counterpoise to the Congress influence Minto desired to have a large representation of the landed interests in the Councils and in a letter written to Morley on 1 July 1906 Minto said: "But I am inclined to apprehend that we might perhaps find our university members too much connected with Congress aspirations, and I think that their influence should be balanced by representatives on the Council nominated, for instance, by the Taluqdar Association and other such associations representing the landed interest."[64] It is significant that this portion of the letter was omitted by Lady Minto from the official version of the letter which was published by her.[65]

To counteract the influence of the Congress and the educated class the government of India suggested the formation of an Imperial Advisory Council to be composed of ruling chiefs and territorial magnates, and of provincial advisory councils to be composed of substantial landholders, representatives of the smaller landholders, of industry, commerce, capital, and also of the professional classes.[66] These advisory councils would have borne not the slightest resemblance to the English Parliament. They were to be purely consultative bodies. The advisers could be consulted individually as well as collectively, and consultations as a general rule were to be private and confidential.[67]

The Ruling Chiefs even objected to a mixed Imperial Advisory Council on the ground that they would have to sit with the subjects of the British government who were "necessarily of an inferior status."[68] Ultimately the idea of creating an Advisory Council was dropped.[69] The dropping of the idea pleased Congressmen for they knew that such Councils would have merely provided a counterpoise to the influence of the educated middle class.[70]

In the reform proposals suggested by the government of India it was stated that the operation of the quasi-elective system since 1893 had resulted in an excessive representation of the professional middle classes,[71] and that "the requisite counterpoise to their excessive influence" could be found by the creation of an "additional electorate recruited from landed and monied classes."[72] But the very fact that few landlords, but many members of the professional classes, had been elected to the councils showed that the professional classes had a greater representative character than the landed classes.

The extent of representation granted to the landlords by the Morley-Minto reforms was considered by Congressmen to be excessive,[73] and many of them also criticized the provision for the separate representation of the landlords.[74] Pandit B. N. Dhar referred to the landlords as an extremely conservative force.[75] "You want in the Councils," he said, "men who are educated . . . who have the intelligence to appreciate the ideals of British civilization and British government, and who alone are suited by their training to help the government in moulding our institutions according to the needs of the new times. The landed magnates are at least a conservative force not in the sense in which that phrase is applicable to the landlord class in England, which is educated, intelligent, and conversant with public affairs —but a body of men who are backward in knowledge and wedded to retrospective habits of thought, and whose golden age lies behind the mists of the past."[76]

Before the Montagu-Chelmsford Reforms Scheme of 1919 was introduced the landed aristocrats again adopted the same conservative approach as they had done at the time of the Morley-Minto Reforms of 1909. Referring to the British Indian Association, the organization of the landlords, Montagu wrote in his *Indian Diary*: "The British Indian Association [is] more or less a conservative body headed by the Maharaja of Burdwan, the best type of conservative Indian. . . . He has a fierce love of the British connection—not a passive acquiescence, but a firm belief in it. . . . He is a large and very rich zamindar, and wishes to be made an independent Chief."[77]

The zamindars opposed political reforms in India but the tenants, who tilled the land under the zamindars, increasingly came to participate in diverse kinds of movements for securing greater political and economic rights. In the beginning these movements of the tenants or kisans were spontaneous and unorganized, and took place when conditions became so miserable that the peasants became reckless.

There were famines in India in 1870, 1896, and 1897. During these famines peasants or kisans suffered miserably. Such miserable conditions, on occasions, generated a spirit of recklessness and gave rise to peasant movements or struggles against the zamindars and the government. In 1870, for example, the tenants of Bengal were so hard hit by famines that many of them refused to pay rent or obey the orders of the courts directing their eviction. Near anarchical conditions came to prevail in some parts of Bengal. The government appointed an inquiry committee and subsequently enacted the Bengal Tenancy Act of 1885 giving some relief to the tenants.

Again in 1875 the Maratha peasants, who were in very straitened circumstances, raided the houses of the moneylenders to whom they were indebted, and even killed some of them. Realizing the gravity of the situation the government passed the Deccan Agriculturists' Relief Act of 1879 to give the peasants of the Deccan some protection against the moneylenders. Similarly, the Punjab peasants, fearing loss of their lands to the moneylenders, rose against them in the last decade of the nineteenth century and the government had to pass the Punjab Alienation Act in 1902-3.

During Lord Curzon's regime a resolution of the government on land revenue policy was adopted with the object of protecting the tenants from the zamindars. In the early days the English educated middle class, which dominated the Congress, spoke more for the industrialization of the country and for state aid and protection to help such industrialization and the industrialists, than for the amelioration of the condition of peasants. It is no wonder that Curzon challenged Romesh Chandra Dutt, who had led an agitation against temporary settlements, with the remark that the government had done more for protecting the peasants from the rapacity of the zamindars.

Gandhi was one of the first political leaders of India to organize peasant resistance. In 1917-18 Gandhi organized the peasants of Champaran in Bihar against the indigo planters who were mostly Europeans. The Champaran agitation forced the government to appoint an inquiry committee, of which Gandhi was also a member, and on the basis of the report of the committee a legislation was passed which gave some relief to the peasants. Later, Gandhi led a satyagraha movement of the peasants in

Kaira who were protesting against the collection of land revenue which they could not pay due to failure of crops.

Though Gandhi was the pioneer among the Indian political leaders in organizing kisan movements, he did not denounce the zamindari system as such. For this he has been criticized by N. G. Ranga, a peasant leader who later joined the Swatantra Party. Ranga wrote: "Just as the earlier Congress agitation led by Romesh Chandra Dutt against temporary settlements did not embrace the exploitation of our peasants by Zamindars, so also this agitation led by the Mahatma in Champaran did not lead up to any fight against the main causes for the terrible poverty and sufferings of Champaran peasants, namely, the excessive rents and exorbitant incidence of debts. . . . It does strike us as rather significant that both he [Gandhi] and Rajen Prasad should have remained scrupulously silent upon the ravages of the zamindary system."

The call for the non-payment of land tax given by the Congress during the non-cooperation movement of 1919 naturally appealed to the peasants. Later, in 1921, there were certain peasant struggles in the Guntur District, Karnatak, and the Oudh Rent Act of 1921 was passed to give a measure of relief to the peasants.

Another significant peasant rising was the Moplah Rebellion of 1922, which was both an economic and communal movement. This was a movement by Muslim agriculturists against the Brahmin landlords of Malabar. This movement which was a protest of the exploited agriculturist took a religious turn and led to loss of life and property.

After the non-cooperation movement of 1919, peasant organizations began to be formed in the country. Ryots' associations were formed in Andhra in 1923 and kisan sabhas were organized in Punjab, Bengal, and Uttar Pradesh during 1926-27.

In 1928-29 Sardar Vallabhbhai Patel, who later came to be known as the strong man of the Congress and the leader of the rightist wing of the party, organized and led a successful peasant movement in the Bardoli district in Gujarat.

In 1930 Gandhi submitted his Eleven Points demand to the British government. In this he did not include the demands of the peasants against the landlords. Gandhi did not desire to split the Indian nationalist movement by raising such a demand, and

6

for this he was criticized by some left nationalists and socialists. N. G. Ranga said: "Mahatmaji should certainly have asked for a considerable reduction of rents charged by zamindars, redemption of our agricultural indebtedness ... a minimum wage for our labour, nationalization of our key industries.... But he would not do it consistently with his class collaboration convictions and his anxiety not to divide our people into two political groups basing their difference on economic interests."

The world economic depression of 1929 adversely affected the Indian peasants and there were peasant movements in Uttar Pradesh, Andhra, Gujarat, and certain other parts of the country. The Congress supported some of these movements, but not all.

After the end of the non-cooperation movement of the 1930s the need was felt for forming separate organizations of kisans. The need for forming such associations was stressed by the Congress socialists and the left nationalists, such as Jawaharlal Nehru and Subhas Bose, as also by the communists.

Between 1935 and 1938 diverse associations of ryots and agriculturists were formed in Madras. A Provincial Kisan Sabha was formed in Uttar Pradesh in 1935. In Bihar as early as 1927 a Bihar Kisan Sabha had been formed, but since 1934 it developed into an extensive organization due mainly to the drive and organizing ability of Swami Sahajanand Saraswati. The Bihar Kisan Sabha became the strongest unit of the All-India Kisan Sabha that was subsequently formed in 1935 in Lucknow.

The formation of the All-India Kisan Sabha was a landmark in the development of the kisan movement in India for the Sabha gave the movement for the first time an all-India character. Jawaharlal Nehru strongly supported it. Later, the All-India Kisan Sabha asked for collective affiliation to the Indian National Congress but this was not granted.

In the election manifesto that it issued to fight the 1937 elections held in terms of the Government of India Act, 1935, the Congress had enunciated a socio-economic programme *inter alia* for the radical improvement of the condition of the kisans. After the elections the Congress formed governments in seven out of nine states. The Congress governments introduced certain agrarian reforms, but the kisan leaders considered them inadequate. The Kisan Sabhas from time to time organized meetings and kisan marches to induce the Congress to implement a more radical agrarian reform policy. These extra-parliamentary activities of Kisan Sabhas were encouraged by the left wing within the Congress but were disapproved of by the right wing.

After independence was attained there were peasant movements in Telengana in Hyderabad which led to violence. At a time when the question of the accession of Hyderabad to India was not yet settled, two districts of Hyderabad on the border of Madras came under the control of communist guerrillas who aimed at establishing a Telegu-speaking state composed of a part of the territory of the Nizam of Hyderabad and a part of Madras. The peasants of Telengana, led by communists, sought to set up a parallel government in Telengana. The government of India countered the Telengana movement with severe repressive measures.

While the government of India met violence with violence in Telengana, Vinoba Bhave, the spiritual successor of Gandhi, sought to wean over the dissatisfied peasants of Telengana to the path of peace on the basis of his *bhoodan yajna* (land-gift sacrifice) movement. Vinoba trekked the villages of India calling for *bhoodan* or gift of land which was to be distributed to the landless. As the *bhoodan* movement gained in momentum, Vinoba called for *gramdan* or the gift of villages which were to be utilized for cooperative community service. The final aim of Vinoba was the same as that of Gandhi: the attainment of sarvodaya, that is, a society based on love and compassion. Such a society was to be casteless and classless, a society in which the state would wither away. The aim was not to socialize the means of production and to make the state at once powerful and beneficent, but to reduce the powers of the state and to disperse and decentralize power among the thousands of villages of India. Vinoba aimed at an agrarian revolution to be achieved not through violence or through the coercive power of the state but through persuasion and by change in the character of men. The economic reform of society was to come through the ethical transformation of man, and the aim of politics was the ending of all politics by the establishment of a casteless, classless society in which the state had withered away.

Vinoba came into prominence when he opposed the communist led armed struggle of the Telengana peasantry with his alternative of *bhoodan* movement. This *bhoodan* movement was presented as an alternative both to the communist method of revolutionary seizure of land as also to the land reform programme of the Congress to be effected through the instrumentality of the coercive power of the state. Vinoba invoked *lokshakti* or the power of the people and not *rajashakti* or the power of the state. In this Vinoba was again following the last wish of Gandhi that the Congress should dissolve and be replaced by a *Lok Sevak Sangh* which would serve the people and not run the government.

Vinoba started his campaign with the slogan that every man should part with one-sixth of his land for the landless. This *bhoodan* movement later developed into the *gramdan* movement. The aim was to abolish private property in land and to revive the ancient Indian village community with common cultivation of the land, owned by the village, and distribution of the produce of the land equitably to all, as also the organization of village handicrafts on a cooperative basis.

Jayaprakash Narayan, the erstwhile leader of the Congress socialists, joined the *bhoodan* movement in the belief that large-scale socio-economic changes could only be brought about in a non-violent peaceful manner and not by revolutionary violence or through the coercive power of the state.

The communists have, however, characterized the *bhoodan* and *gramdan* movement as a "colossal failure." They assert: "The land donated has often enough turned out to be unfit for cultivation or encumbered with litigation" and that "the achievements of the *sarvodaya* movement are worse than negative."[78]

The extremists within the CPI(M), who later seceded from it and came to be known as the Naxalites, preached that the only path that a peasant movement could or should take was one of guerrilla warfare and revolutionary violence. After independence this path was first adopted in Telengana. Later, this path was again adopted in Naxalbari and in the neighbouring districts of Darjeeling in 1967 when the communist extremists led the land-poor peasants to mount attacks on landlords, plantation owners, and governmental authorities in order to seize land and arms and to set up a parallel government as a centre of revolutionary resistance.

The CPI(M) disowned these extremists or Naxalites. The CPI,

while condemning the Naxalite method of agrarian revolution, commented that the Naxalites were really putting into practice the theories which the cpi(m) had preached.

Both the cpi and cpi(m) continue to attack the methods chosen by the Naxalites for bringing about an agrarian revolution. In October 1969 while presenting his report at the twentieth session of the All-India Kisan Sabha, Hare Krishna Konar, the general secretary of the All-India Kisan Sabha [cpi(m)] (the other All-India Kisan Sabha is dominated by the cpi), referred to the adventurist policies of the Naxalites and stated that even though this adventurist trend did not pose a serious threat in West Bengal "it created considerable disruption in Andhra, up, Jammu and Kashmir." In Andhra, he said, the Naxalites "directed the peasant struggle that had great possibilities into adventurist suicidal channels. The Girijans in Srikakulam are the worst exploited. A powerful struggle backed by wide democratic support could have been created. But the adventurists have successfully isolated the movement from that democratic support and have made it a premature victim of brutal police terror."[79]

Kisan movements are weak in most states, except in West Bengal and Kerala. In these two states kisan movements got support from United Front governments. Konar claimed that in West Bengal millions of peasants unleashed all over the State an unprecedented struggle with the backing of the United Front government for recovering benami land, for possession and distribution of surplus land, and for checking hoarding and black-marketing.[80]

The peasants in India do not have one *apex* centralized organization or federation. The cpi and the cpi(m) control two separate All-India Kisan Sabhas. In October 1969 Z. A. Ahmed, the president of the All-India Kisan Sabha (cpi), pleaded for the setting up of a coordination committee to unite the kisan movements of the cpi and the cpi(m) on a countywide basis. Such a coordination committee was not set up and each of these two communist parties continue to charge the other of indulging in disruptive activities in the kisan front.[81]

For improving the lot of the peasants or kisans different roads have been suggested. The Naxalites seek to organize the kisans into guerrilla bands who would first get control of the countryside and then encircle the cities for a revolutionary seizure of power. The communists seek to build up peasant resistance against the big landlords, moneylenders, and governmental authorities. The Congress government, which has ruled India for more than two decades, seeks to improve the lot of the peasants by agrarian reforms and community development projects. Vinoba and his followers seek to revive the old village panchayats of India through their *bhoodan* and *gramdan* movements in order to regenerate rural India.

In the 1880s Lord Ripon had suggested the setting up of village councils which would be built upon the foundation of the ancient Indian panchayats of India. In the 1920s various attempts were made to revive the ancient Indian village panchayats, but the village panchayats had limited resources and functions. In place of the panchayat experiment another method of rural uplift or rural reconstruction was suggested and was pursued by some enthusiastic British officials, such as Sir Malcolm Darling and F. L. Brayne. Darling laid emphasis on the development of village cooperatives as agencies for agricultural credit, for adoption of better farming techniques and improved marketing facilities. Brayne emphasized the importance of having village guides who would stimulate village initiative and act as intermediaries between the simple villagers and the governmental authorities.

When Gandhi appeared on the Indian scene he emphasized the village and its importance. Gandhi started a resistance movement of the kisans of Champaran in 1917. Gandhi sought to revive the old self-sufficient village community and to liberate India at once from Western industrialism and "Western materialism" and to set up a Panchayat Raj in place of the British Raj. But Gandhi's conception of Indian polity was not accepted by the framers of the Indian Constitution, though Article 40 of the Constitution spoke of village panchayats as "units of self-government."

Partly due to Gandhi's inspiration, the government of India launched the community development project in October 1952. The community development project was intended to develop a sense of community spirit among the villagers and to hasten the agricultural development of the country. But the Balwantrai Mehta Committee Report, which appeared in November 1957, observed that there had not been the requisite people's participation in the community development projects and that there was still an excessive dependence on governmental initiative. The Report made radical proposals for devolution and popular control so as to establish Panchayati Raj or government of the villages and not Panchayat Raj or village self-government. The Report recommended that the responsibility for economic and social activity should rest with the panchayat samiti, a local representative council at the level of the block, that within the block the villages would be grouped into circles, that the gram panchayat would be elected by the people, and it is the members of these gram panchayats who would choose from among themselves representatives for the panchayat samiti. The presidents of all panchayat samitis in a district together with the local MPs and MLAs and the heads of various departments were to constitute the Zila Parishad or district council, which was to replace the existing units of local self-government as a coordinating body but without assuming the latter's executive powers. The recommendations of the Committee, which had suggested the replacement of the old autocratic system and the self-sufficient village by a system of panchayati raj where the village would not remain an isolated unit but would become part of the block and the district and where decisions would be taken more at the block level than at the district level, were accepted by most of the states.

The idea of people's participation at the village level which found expression in the Balwantrai Mehta Report was further developed by Jayaprakash Narayan in his "A Plea for Reconstruction of Indian Polity" which he had prepared for private circulation in 1959. Jayaprakash, in the tradition of Gandhi and Vinoba, aims at replacing centralism by a communitarian and participating democracy. His objective is to establish a pyramid of politics to be based on village communities. Under this scheme the higher organs of state power would be derived electorally from these village communities at the base and would have only residual coordinating functions. But this scheme of Jayaprakash has not received general acceptance.

Vinoba and Jayaprakash have sought to bring about a radical transformation of village life and of the condition of the peasants through the *bhoodan* and *sarvodaya* movement and since independence various state governments have sought to improve the condition of the peasants through land reforms. But the condition of the peasants—many of them landless—is still deplorable. In August 1970 many of the left parties of India, including the CPI, the SSP and the PSP, started a land grab movement with the object of forcibly occupying lands belonging to the big land-lords and for distribution of the same to the landless tillers of the soil. Of about 130 million Indians who work on the land about 30 million are landless. The land grab movement naturally led to clashes with the police and the leftist leaders who participated in the land grab movement, such as Dange, Bhupesh Gupta, Raj Narain, Madhu Limaye and others, were arrested. But this land grab movement, sponsored by a coalition of leftist parties, did not generally lead to violent clashes and the killing or extermina-tion of "class enemies," such as big landlords on a scale which had taken place during the Naxalbari movement in West Bengal in 1967 and later during the Girijan tribal revolt in Srikakulam district in Andhra Pradesh. The peasant uprising in Naxalbari and the tribal revolt in Srikakulam were led by the Naxalites and the Indian Maoists, characterized as "the front paw of the Indian revolution" by Radio Peking. Though the land grab movement launched in August 1970 by a coalition of leftist parties in India, who are much less militant or extremist than the Naxalites, have not resulted in the large-scale extermination of "class enemies" or big landlords as had taken place in Naxalbari and Srikakulam, it is clear that discontent among the peasants in India is develop-ing fast and unless a radical agrarian policy is rapidly implemented the Indian countryside faces an explosive situation.

NOTES AND REFERENCES

1. Joan Beauchamp, *British Imperialism in India*, 1935, p. 16.
2. Vera Anstey, *The Economic Development of India*, London, 1929, p. 210.
3. *Report of the Indian Industrial Commission*, para 107.
4. Lord Crewe, who succeeded Lord Morley as Secretary of State for India, however, said that the Madras Government had put a too limited construction on Morley's dispatch (ibid., para 108).
5. *The Reminiscences of Lord Hardinge of Penshurst*, pp. 3-4.
6. See speech of V. G. Kale in the *Report of the Twenty-Ninth Indian National Congress*, p. 94.
7. See speeches of A. C. Mazumdar and V. V. J. Pantulu in the *Report*

of the Twenty-Seventh Indian National Congress, pp. 81-82; and the views of R. C. Dutt in *The Swadeshi Movement : A Symposium* (published by G. A. Natesan, Madras), 2nd ed., p. 92.

8. See the speeches of G. Subramanian Iyer and of N. K. Ramaswami Aiyar in the *Report of the Seventeenth Indian National Congress,* pp. 122-25, 132; and a speech of Dadabhai in the *Proceedings of the Council of the Governor-General of India, April 1910 to March 1911,* p. 649.

9. *Montagu-Chelmsford Report,* p. 267.

10. Ibid., para 342.

11. *Report of the Indian Fiscal Commission* (1921-22), para 55.

12. S. B. Jathar and K. G. Jathar, *Indian Economics,* London, 1947, p. 189.

13. Wadia and Merchant, *Our Economic Problem,* 1943, p. 285.

14. L. C. Jain, *Indian Economy during the War,* 1949, p. 48.

15. *Towards A Self-Reliant Economy : India's Third Plan, 1961-66,* Publications Division, Government of India, pp. 62-63.

16. D. R. Gadgil, *The Industrial Evolution of India in Recent Times,* 1944, p. 148.

17. Margaret Mead, *The Indian Peasant Uprooted,* 1931, pp. 2-3.

18. G. K. Sharma, *Labour Movement in India,* 1963, p. 49, footnote 4.

19. Dr R. K. Das, *The Indian Labour Movement,* 1923, p. 7.

20. *Report of the Working of the Factory Act in Bombay for 1892,* p. 15.

21. D. H. Buchanan, *The Development of Capitalistic Enterprise in India,* 1934, p. 425.

22. Ibid., p. 416.

23. Ramsay MacDonald, *The Awakening of India,* 1910, p. 179,

24. Lenin, *The National Liberation Movement in the East,* pp. 14-15.

25. S. D. Saklatwala, *History of the Mill-Owners' Association,* 1875-1930.

26. *Report of the Royal Commission on Labour in India,* 1931, p. 317.

27. B. Shiva Rao, *Industrial Worker in India,* 1939, p. 14.

28. B. P. Wadia, *Labour in Madras,* 1921, pp. 34-38.

29. *Report of the Sixth Session of the All India Trade Union Congress,* 1926, p. 8.

30. B. P. Wadia, *Labour in Madras,* 1921, pp. xvi-xvii.

31. V. B. Karnik, *Indian Trade Unions : A Survey,* 1960, p. 50.

32. *Indian Annual Register,* 1923, Vol. I, pp. 843-44.

33. *Indian Annual Register,* 1925, Vol. I.

34. R. P. Dutt, *India Today,* London, 1940, p. 376.

35. Ibid., p. 383.

36. Ibid., p. 386.

37. G. K. Sharma, *Labour Movement in India,* 1963, pp. 99-100.

38. *The Indian Labour Year Book,* 1950-51, p. 175.

39. Ibid.

40. *Address of Jayaprakash Narayan at the All India Railwaymen's Federation on 16 February 1949.*

41. K. B. Panikkar, *An Outline of the History of the AITUC,* 1959, p. 15.

42. Mrinal Kanti Bose, *Parties and Paradoxes : Plan of a Labour Party,*

United Trade Union Congress, 1953, p. 2.

43. *People's Democracy*, 24 May 1970.

44. *New Age*, Central Organ of the Communist Party of India, 31 May 1970.

45. See speeches at the rally organized by CITU at Calcutta and reported in the *Statesman*, 1 June 1970.

46. "For a Fighting Trade Union Centre," in *People's Democracy*, 31 May 1970.

47. B. C. Pal, *Memories of My Life and Times*, p. 288.

48. On 26 September 1888, *The Pioneer Mail*, which voiced the opinions of an important section of Anglo-Indian officials, very favourably reviewed this book.

49. The Raja of Bhinga, *Democracy Not Suited to India*, p. 26.

50. Ibid., p. 102.

51. *Report of the Fourth Indian National Congress*, pp. 24-25.

52. R. C. Saunders, *A Glance at India's Aristocracy : Or should there be a House of Lords for India?* pp. 4-10.

53. Ibid., p. 6.

54. For Saunders' views see *The Journal of the East India Association*, 1889, pp. 75-77.

55. See the Raja's article "The Decay of the Landed Aristocracy in India," *The Nineteenth Century*, May 1892, p. 835.

56. Syed Ahmed Khan, *The Present State of Indian Politics*, p. 59.

57. Ibid., p. 4.

58. *The Indian Mirror*, 17 January 1888; *The Hindoo Patriot*, 23 January 1888.

59. *The Indian Spectator*, 22 January 1888; *The Indian Spectator* was edited by Behramji Malabari, who was an ardent social reformer.

60. *The Tribune*, 25 January 1888.

61. Lady Minto, *India : Minto and Morley*, p. 31.

62. Letter to Morley dated 27 February 1907 (ibid., p. 104).

63. Ibid., p. 29.

64. *Evolution of India and Pakistan, 1858-1947, Select Documents*, ed. C. H. Philips, p. 76.

65. Lady Minto, *India : Minto and Morley*, pp. 97-99.

66. *Circular from the Government of India, to Local Governments and Administrations dated 24 August 1907* (Cd. 3710), paras 5-6.

67. Ibid., paras 4-5.

68. *Proposals of the Government of India dated 1 October 1908*, paras 4-6.

69. *Dispatch of the Secretary of State dated 27 November 1908*, para 4.

70. *Congress Presidential Addresses, First Series*, p. 808.

71. *Proposals of the Government of India, 1 October 1908*, para 20.

72. *Circular of the Government of India, 24 August 1907*, para 7.

73. *Report of the Twenty-Sixth Indian National Congress*, p. 24.

74. See a speech of Pandit Malaviya of 24 January 1911 (*The Proceedings of the Council of the Governor-General of India, April 1910 to March 1911*, p. 136). Gokhale, however, was not opposed to the separate

representation of landlords (ibid., p. 146).

75. B. N. Dhar, "The Reform Scheme and the Councils Regulation," *The Indian World*, April-May 1911, p. 266.
76. *Report of the Twenty-Sixth Indian National Congress*, p. 24.
77. E. S. Montagu, *An Indian Diary*, 1930, pp. 79-80.
78. Mohit Sen, "Gandhism after Freedom," in *The Mahatma: A Marxist Symposium*, 1969, p. 65.
79. *The Statesman*, 31 October, 1969.
80. Ibid.
81. For the views of cpi(m) see "Dange Out To Split aituc" in *People's Democracy*, 28 December 1969. For the views of the cpi see "cpm Leaders Walk Out" in *New Age*, 28 December 1969, p. 6.

CHAPTER THREE

Gandhi on Socialism and Communism

I. GANDHIAN SOCIALISM

Once when some socialist students visited him, Gandhi expressed his views on socialism thus: "Now tell me how many of you have servants in your homes? [They said they each had a servant at home.] And you call yourselves socialists while you make others slave for you! It is a queer kind of socialism which, I must say, I cannot understand. If you will listen to me, I will say, do not involve yourselves in any ism. Study every ism. Ponder and assimilate what you have read and try to practise yourself what appeals to you out of it. But for heaven's sake, do not set out to establish any ism. The first step in the practice of socialism is to learn to use your hands and feet. It is the only sure way to eradicate violence and exploitation from society. We have no right to talk of socialism so long as there is hunger and unemployment and the distinction between high and low amongst us and around us."[1]

For Gandhi, socialism was a mode of personal conduct and a form of social service, and was neither a gospel for the expropriation of the rich nor a programme for the socialization of the means of production. Under Gandhi's socialism there would have been the poor and the rich but they would have been on the same level. He said: "Socialism is a beautiful word and so far as I am aware in socialism all the members of society are equal —none low, none high. In the individual's body the head is not high because it is [at] the top... nor are the soles of the feet low because they touch the earth. Even as members of the individual's body are equal so are the members of society." Hence under Gandhian socialism there was room for both the rich and the poor. "The prince and the peasant will not be equalled," said Gandhi, "by cutting off the prince's head nor can the process of cutting off equalize the employer and the employed."[2]

Addressing the Delhi Provincial Political Conference on 2 July, 1947 Gandhi pointed to the socialist leader Jayaprakash Narayan and said: "He holds the reins of the Socialist Party. But I, too, am a socialist." "Nearly fifty years ago," Gandhi went on, "when I was practising law in South Africa, many people used to call themselves socialists. But they were less of socialists than I was. I used to work among the labourers. I have made this part of my life's work. This is true socialism. I have always considered myself a true servant of the peasants and of the workers. There is a difference in my and Jayaprakash Narayan's method of approach towards socialism. I am of the opinion that even a king can be a socialist by becoming a servant of the people."[3]

For Gandhi socialism was service of the people. And inasmuch as for Gandhi the highest virtues were belief in God and the pursuit of truth and nonviolence he asserted that the essence of socialism should consist in belief in God, truth, and non-violence. "Truth and nonviolence," he said, "must incarnate in socialism. In order that they can, the votary must have a living faith in God. . . . Nevertheless, it is possible to say that it has perhaps never occurred to a believing socialist that there is any connection between his socialism and belief in God. It is equally safe to say that godly men as a rule never commended socialism to the masses."[4]

If Gandhi was a socialist then he was a humanitarian socialist and not a "scientific" socialist in the Marxian sense. Gandhi was not a socialist who believed in the nationalization of the means of production, exchange, and distribution, or in the establishment of a centralized, socialized state. Gandhi believed in decentralization and in the dispersal of power. He wanted to establish an autonomous self-governing society, based on the village. Gandhi loved the villages and idealized them. His symbol was the spinning wheel and not the machine.

Gandhi sought to bring about large-scale social changes not through the coercive power of the state but through a change of heart of the individual. Gandhi wanted to strengthen the power of the individual and believed that it could grow only in a decentralized, village-based society.

Socialists generally believed in industrialization and in a centralized state. Industrialization could raise the standard of living of the people and a socialistic state could ensure equitable distribution. But Gandhi believed neither in industrialization nor in centralization. In fact, the mere raising of the standard of living, through industrialization or otherwise, did not appear to Gandhi to be a particularly worthwhile ideal. For Gandhi believed in a simple life and in the limitation of wants. If wants were restricted then the people could at once be free and happy. They could be liberated not only from the tyranny of wants but also from the power of the big machine and the grip of the bureaucratic and centralized state.

Gandhi's aim was not to establish a centralized, socialized state which would ensure work, wages, and equality to all, but to establish a village-based society where the people would rule themselves in autonomous villages. In such a village-based society not only centralization will be avoided but the system of values would be different. In such a society the people would aspire for a simple life and would find satisfaction in doing physical and manual work.

For Gandhi an ideal system of production was one which not merely spurned industrialization and the big machines but which also emphasized the importance of physical or manual work. Gandhi imbibed from Ruskin the idea that a lawyer's work had the same value as a barber's.[5] "May not men earn their bread by intellectual labour? No, the needs of the body must be supplied by the body. Render unto Caesar that which is Caesar's perhaps applies here as well," wrote Gandhi in the *Harijan* in June 1933.[6] For Gandhi the life of the tiller and the handicraftsman was the life worth living. Accordingly, Gandhi desired all men to turn themselves voluntarily into manual labourers.

Equality could be achieved if all men worked simply and did physical labour. If everyone voluntarily became manual workers then the distinction between man and man would disappear and a truly egalitarian society would be established. This, according to Gandhi, should be the aim of socialism—that is, to break down the aristocracy of brain as also the aristocracy of wealth. Like Tolstoy, Gandhi wanted to break down the aristocracy of brain. Gandhi believed that the brain workers would not be able to appreciate the lot of manual workers unless physical labour was made the supreme source of wealth. "In my system," said Gandhi, "it is labour which is current coin, not metal. Any person who uses his labour has that coin, his wealth." Gandhi said that the "law of bread labour" was the first moral law of life. According to this law every man should earn his bread by the sweat of his brow in some labour connected with agriculture or its allied industries. For it was physical labour alone which could help to keep the mind under control and enable an individual to maintain his poise. The ideal society for Gandhi was not a society where a centralized, socialized state ensured adequate wages or a satisfactory standard of life for all, but a society where each individual found fulfilment in doing physical or manual work in autonomous village societies.

Gandhi's socialism was humanitarian. He gave his own definition to the word socialism. Socialism, for Gandhi, was love for and identification with the poor, and socialistic endeavour consisted in service for the poor. Gandhi represents in India the anarchistic-communitarian socialism whose exponents in nineteenth-century Europe were Proudhon, Ruskin, and Tolstoy.

Gandhi's socialism was more a code of personal conduct or service for the poor and renunciation of riches than an economic ideology. Gandhi's socialism was founded on ideas of non-possession, trusteeship, nonviolence, and human equality, and was not an ideology of industrialization of the economy or the socialization of the means of production. Consequently, it had only a limited appeal to the urban intelligentsia.

For realizing the ideal society Gandhi relied not on the increase of state power but on the increase of goodness in individual human beings. He said: "I look upon an increase of the power of the State with the greatest fear because, although while apparently doing good by minimizing exploitation, it does the greatest harm to mankind by destroying individuality which lies at the root of all progress."[7]

II. THE THEORY OF TRUSTEESHIP

Gandhi believed in *Ram Rajya*. *Ram Rajya* of Gandhi's dreams enshrined and protected the rights of princes and paupers alike. The pauper exists in Gandhi's *Ram Rajya* or ideal state but the pauper would be absent in any socialistic or communistic state. But though princes exist in Gandhi's ideal state such princes would have no exclusive right over their properties. They must hold the property in trust for the people. Gandhi had come upon the idea of trust from the English law of trust which he had imbibed while studying for the bar in England. Gandhi's whole economic ideology was based on this idea of trusteeship.

According to communist ideology the capitalist cannot be trusted with the property of the worker. The capitalist has appropriated the surplus labour of the worker and has thereby expropriated the worker's property. Such acquisition of property by the capitalist is nothing but theft, and it is in the expropriation of the expropriator that communistic justice consists.

Gandhi would have allowed talented people to earn more than others, if their talents were likely to be stifled unless they were allowed to earn more. But the bulk of the greater earnings of such talented persons must be used for the good of the state "just as the income of all earning sons of the father goes to the common family fund."[8] In February 1942 Gandhi wrote in the *Harijan*: "The most effective *mantram* is enjoy thy wealth by renouncing. Earn your crores by all means. But understand that your wealth is not yours ... take what you require for legitimate needs, and use the remainder for society."[9] The emphasis in this conception is not on what one earns, but how one spends.

But though Gandhi believed in the doctrine of trusteeship he was discerning enough to realize that in this age the poor would, in any event, come into their own and achieve their rights. Gandhi hoped that the just rights of the poor would be secured through nonviolent means, though, on occasions, he apprehended that violence may come to be used for that purpose. "I see," said Gandhi, "the coming of the rule of the poor, whether that rule be through force of arms or of nonviolence."

Many socialists and communists derided the Gandhian idea of trusteeship. They said that it was futile to expect that the rich would voluntarily give up their wealth and asserted that equality could be achieved only through the coercive power of the state. But Gandhi wanted not so much to change institutions as to change men. Gandhi had little faith in the perfectibility

of institutions but unbounded faith in the perfectibility of individuals. "Socialism and communism of the West is based," wrote
Gandhi, "on certain conceptions which are fundamentally different from ours. One such conception is the belief in the
essential selfishness of human nature." Gandhi did not believe
that the capitalists were essentially selfish. "In the application of
the method of nonviolence one must believe in the possibility
of every person, however depraved, being reformed under
humane and skilled treatment."

Gandhi said that the landlords and capitalists must regard
themselves, even as the Japanese nobles did, as trustees holding
their wealth for the good of their wards, the peasants and workers. He asked the trustees to take no more than a reasonable
amount of commission for their labour. Gandhi was acutely
conscious of the fact that in India there was a great dispropor-
tion between the pomp and extravagance of the moneyed class
and the grinding poverty of the ryots. In these circumstances a
model Zamindar, said Gandhi, had no other alternative but to
"reduce himself to poverty in order that the ryot may have the
necessaries of life."[10] "I am convinced," he wrote, "that the
capitalist, if he follows the samurai of Japan, has nothing really
to lose and everything to gain. . . . If the capitalist class will read
the sign of the times, revise their notions of God-given right to
all they possess, in an incredibly short space of time the seven
hundred thousand dung-heaps which today pass muster as villages, can be turned into abodes of peace, health, and comfort."
Gandhi felt that there was no alternative for the wealthy but to
voluntarily surrender their riches. Otherwise the famishing millions may rise up in revolt which even the armed force of a
powerful government would not be able to avert.

The Gandhian belief that the holders of economic power
would surrender power voluntarily have been criticized by many
communists and socialists. M. N. Roy characterized this theory
as an attempt to lull the have-nots into contentment with their
existing conditions.[11] But Gandhi believed that it was possible to
change the economic system peacefully and through persuasion.
In fact, he believed that any attempt to change the economic
system violently would not lead to any fruitful result. In September 1934 Gandhi wrote in the *Harijan*: "It is because the
rulers, if they are bad, are so, not necessarily or wholly by

birth, but largely because of their environment, that I have hopes of their altering their course.... But the environment are ... the people who make the rulers what they are in the aggregate ... any violence done to the rulers would be violence done to ourselves. It would be suicide. Moreover, violence may destroy one or more bad rulers, but like Ravana's head, others will pop up in their places, for the root lies elsewhere. It lies in us. If we reform ourselves, the rulers will automatically do so."[12]

Gandhi asked his countrymen to seek to change men and rulers and not to destroy them. In March 1927 he wrote in *Young India*: "Those who seek to destroy men rather than manners ... become worse than those whom they destroy under the mistaken belief that manners will die with men."[13] Gandhi felt that violent action would not benefit society. Through violence society will be poorer for it will lose the gifts of a man who knows how to accumulate wealth. If violence is dangerous, what was the solution? "In trying to find out the solution of this riddle," said Gandhi, "I have lighted on nonviolent non-cooperation and civil disobedience as the right and infallible means."[14] The rich could not accumulate wealth without the cooperation of the poor in society and, therefore, if the poor did not cooperate, the rich were bound to mend their ways. And if the rich did not act fairly the poor could start a nonviolent non-cooperation movement.

Gandhi said that a rich man should not possess a rupee more than his neighbour. Writing in the *Harijan* in August 1940, he said that only after one has given up wealth will it be possible for him to preach this ideal among his associates and neighbours. To live up to his ideal Gandhi gave up all he had and took a vow of poverty. In March 1942 Gandhi said that "it is better not to desire wealth than to acquire it and become a trustee. I gave up my own long ago which should be proof enough of what I would like others to do. But what am I to advise those who are already wealthy or who would not shed the desire for wealth? I can only say to them that they should use their wealth for service."[15] Gandhi added: "Personally I do not believe in inherited riches." But seeing that rich children recite verses in praise of poverty but had no compunction about helping themselves to paternal wealth, Gandhi declared in 1938 that a "trustee has no heir but the public."[16] The final aim of the Gandhian theory of trusteeship was the amelioration of the condition of the poor. Under the Gandhian scheme freedom was to be attained for the sake of the dumb millions and every class that was hostile to the interests of the masses would have to give up its privileges.[17]

Gandhi believed in economic equality but he felt that the ideal of economic equality could not be immediately realized. "My ideal," he wrote in March 1927, "is equal distribution, but so far as I can see, it is not to be realized. I, therefore, work for equitable distribution."[18] In April 1940 Gandhi explained that "the real implication of equal distribution is that each man shall have the wherewithal to supply all his natural wants and no more."[19]

Gandhi's faith in the doctrine of trusteeship arose from his disbelief in the state and from his horror of the concentration and centralization of power. He said: "What I would personally prefer would be not a centralization of power in the hands of the state, but an extension of the sense of trusteeship, as in my opinion the violence of private ownership is less injurious than the violence of the state. . . . If the state suppressed capitalism by violence it would be caught in the coils of violence itself and fail to develop nonviolence . . . the individual has a soul, but as the state is a soulless machine, it can never be weaned from the violence to which it owes its very existence. Hence I prefer the doctrine of trusteeship."[20] It is this Gandhian distrust of the state that was later relied upon by those Indian parties, such as the Swatantra Party, who warned against the acquisition of large economic powers by the State.[21]

Gandhi said that the French had a noble motto of liberty, equality, fraternity but they failed to realize these ideals in actual practice. "What the French never realized," said Gandhi, "it is open to us to do. It is for the princes to take the lead and not for the have-nots who have nothing to share except their pauperism."[22] Gandhi wanted the princes and the rich people to shed their wealth and to become trustees. In some of his later writings, however, Gandhi expressed disillusionment with the princes and said that because he despaired of response from the princes he had thought of moving the masses. But yet Gandhi did not advocate state ownership of the means of production.

Gandhi was essentially a philosophical anarchist who believed in restricting the functions of the state to the narrowest possible limits. He relied on individual liberty and initiative. Socialists and communists, on the other hand, had no such faith in human nature and they asserted that large-scale social changes could be effected only by the compulsion of the state and not through voluntary endeavour.

Gandhi was against exploitation of all kinds and believed that if the exploiter shed selfishness and the exploited shed fear then exploitation would end. Gandhi had trust in the potential goodness of human beings. He believed that if a *satyagrahi* suffered and did not retaliate the heart of the exploiter would be touched and he would change. Love and suffering could effect this change. Real changes, Gandhi asserted, could not come through the enforcement of any particular form of social order by the exercise of the coercive power of the state, but such changes could be effected only by means of nonviolence and persuasion.

Many did not share Gandhi's belief in nonviolence or in the theory of trusteeship or in the possibility of the attainment of an ideal society by appealing merely to the innate goodness of men and without the use of the compulsive force of state power. Socialists and Marxists pointed out that mere appeals to the innate goodness of capitalists and landlords would not yield any fruitful result, for they would not shed their riches or power as a result only of moral persuasion. They derided the idea that the Indian capitalist or landlord was more spiritual or less rapacious than his counterpart in the West. Nehru said that Indian capitalists were no better than the Western capitalists and quoted an English socialist's remark that "Indian usurers and landlords are the most rapacious parasites to be found in any contemporary social system."

But some have hailed Gandhi's theory of trusteeship as preeminently Indian and as suited to the nonviolent spirit of the country. The theory of trusteeship cut across the theory of class war. The very words "class war" breathed conflict and violence. Tagore, who sought harmony rather than contradiction and conflict in the processes of history, found the doctrine of dialectical materialism and of class war unacceptable. Nehru, however, believed that class conflict was inherent in the modern capitalistic society. But association with Gandhi exposed him to the criticism by staunch socialists that Nehru would avoid class war if he could, that he wanted Russia's fruit without Russia's blood and that he was out to evolve an Indian version of communism which was a cross between Gandhism and Marxism. Gandhi's emphasis on nonviolence also influenced some Indian socialists and inclined them towards socialism of a Fabian and evolutionary type in place of Marxism of a revolutionary variety.

It has often been said that the Indian version of communism will have a rich deposit of Gandhism even while being dialectically developed against it. The followers of Gandhi, such as Vinoba Bhave, have, however, declared that communism will have its real trial of strength with Gandhism. Vinoba Bhave said: "Ideologically the latter [capitalism] has lost all vitality and though it might appear doughty on the strength of its military force I do not regard it as really existent as a rival against communism. On the other hand, though the Gandhian ideology stands nowhere in an organized form, yet inasmuch as it is impregnated with the virility of right thinking, I believe that ultimately it will be Gandhism with which communism will have its trial of strength."[23]

Socialists and communists, however, have repeatedly stated that theories of trusteeship, of class collaboration and the discovery of substitutes for class struggles are not original discoveries of Indian thought. The language might be Indian but the essential theory is international. In communist literature such theories are known as "reformism." Before the modern industrial era, when there was not enough to go round, moralists exhorted the rich to be kind to the poor and to behave like trustees. A century and a half before Gandhi propounded his theory of trusteeship, William Godwin in his *Political Justice* wrote that the most energetic teachers of religion "taught the rich that they hold their wealth as a trust . . . that they are merely administrators and by no means proprietors-in-chief."

III. GANDHI AND MODERN INDUSTRIALISM

Socialists accepted modern industrialism. They welcomed the machine and large-scale production. True, they referred to the inequalities and certain other evils of modern industrialism. But to remove these evils they wanted not to eliminate industrialism but to destroy capitalism. Modern industrialism, as such, was not harmful. What the socialists regarded as harmful was private ownership of the means of production, exchange, and distribution. According to this analysis the solution lay in the establishment of public or state ownership of the means of production, exchange, and distribution.

Gandhi, on the other hand, had as early as 1908, in the *Hind Swaraj*, denounced all the instruments and institutions of modern industrialism and Western civilization. The British had introduced in India railways, telegraphs, and telephones, established large cities, set up modern law courts and popularized European medical science. Gandhi wrote that the salvation of India consisted in unlearning most of the things that she had learnt from the British.

Gandhi criticized modern civilization not because it was a Western civilization but because he believed it to be a purely materialistic civilization. In December 1916 he said that Western nations worshipped the god of Mammon and measured their progress in pounds, shillings, and pence.[24] The modern industrial system, according to Gandhi, had merely stimulated the money-making propensities of mankind. But men of high ethical stature, such as Buddha, Jesus, Sankara, and Ramakrishna, never sought wealth or riches. Gandhi described Jesus as the greatest economist of his time, and approvingly quoted his saying that it was easier for a camel to go through the eye of a needle than for a rich man to enter into the kingdom of God.[25] In a lecture on 22 December 1918 Gandhi said that he had not read the works of Adam Smith, Mill, Marshall, and other eminent economists, but he argued that one could get sounder economic ideas from religious scriptures than from modern economic textbooks.[26]

Gandhi was not impressed by the economic progress made by modern Western countries. He did not believe that the Western peoples by inventing new machinery and by increasing national production had made any spiritual progress. In fact, for Gandhi the source of all economic misery was the love of material wealth and luxury. According to Gandhi, Rome suffered spiritually when it attained high material affluence and so did Egypt.[27] Great riches were incompatible with a highly developed moral life. Gandhi said that though people would not deny to the Rockefellers and the Carnegies possession of an ordinary measure of morality, they would gladly judge them indulgently for they would not even expect them to satisfy the highest standard of morality.

To gain true economic knowledge, one had to turn not to professional economists who dealt with the science of wealth but to the saints and religious teachers who spurned wealth. Gandhi considered the scriptures of the world as far safer and sounder treatises on the laws of economics than economic textbooks. Jesus, on this view, was one of the greatest economists for he "succeeded in economizing time and space; he transcended them." One of Jesus's disciples came to him running, knelt down and asked: "Good Master, what shall I do that I may inherit eternal life?" Jesus answered: "Why callest thou me good? There is none good but one, that is God. Thou knowest the commandments. Do not commit adultery, do not kill, do not steal, do not bear false witness, defraud not, honour thy father and mother." The disciple replied: "Master, all these have I observed from my youth." Then Jesus said unto him: "One thing thou lackest. Go thy way, sell whatever thou hast and give to the poor, and thou shalt have treasure in heaven...." The disciple went away grieved for he had great possessions. Then Jesus looked round and told unto his disciples: "Children, how hard is it for them that trust in riches to enter into the Kingdom of God. It is easier for a camel to go through the eye of a needle than for a rich man to enter into the Kingdom of God."

It is this example of Jesus that Gandhi quoted in December 1916 in a lecture he delivered to the students of Muir College Economic Society at Allahabad. Gandhi asked the students to read Jesus and not Adam Smith or Marshall to gain knowledge of true economics, which dealt not with wealth but welfare. Referring to the words of Jesus, Gandhi said: "There you have an eternal rule of life stated in the noblest words the English language is capable of producing. But the disciples nodded unbelief as we do even to this day." Gandhi believed that the saying that God and Mammon could not be served at one and the same time was an economic truth of the highest value. He asked his countrymen to discard the God of materialism. "I have heard many of our countrymen say that we will gain

American wealth but avoid its methods. I venture to suggest," remarked Gandhi, "that such an attempt, if it were made, is foredoomed to failure. . . . I would have our leaders to teach us to be morally supreme in the world."[28]

The modern industrial system led to the concentration of wealth and the growth of cities. Gandhi was against modern industrialism and urbanization and he requested educated Indians, who lived in modern cities, to return to the villages, because he believed that the villages of India, which were not polluted by railways or touched by modern civilization, preserved all that was best in the ancient Indian civilization which did not glorify wealth or power but set a limit to man's indulgences.[29] In the manner of Ruskin, Gandhi considered that the life of the tiller of the soil and the handicraftsman was the life which alone was worth living.[30]

In the *Hind Swaraj* (1908) Gandhi had written that machinery was like a snake-hole which might contain from one to hundreds of snakes and that machinery had enslaved nations by creating money which was "as much poison as sexual vice." Machinery, the chief symbol of modern civilization, represented to Gandhi "a great sin which had begun to desolate Europe."[31] By using Manchester cloth we could only waste our money, but by reproducing Manchester in India, we shall "keep our money at the price of our blood, because our very moral being will be sapped. . . . Better for us to send our money to Manchester than to multiply mills in India."

Gandhi's ideas as regards machines and industrialism did not always remain the same as they were in 1908, when he wrote the *Hind Swaraj*, but throughout his life Gandhi retained a horror of large-scale industrialization and of big machines and there was a decentralist and agrarian bias in all his writings. All through his life Gandhi asked the people to use the spinning wheel. Hand-spinning was to be a remedy for underemployment and poverty and through hand-spinning India was to attain self-sufficiency.

In the face of the trend for urbanization all over the world, Gandhi thought it nevertheless a practicable policy to shift back the population from the towns to the villages. Gandhi aimed at blotting out the Industrial Revolution. His Utopia was a federation of village societies each of which managed its own affairs. Through the *panchayats* each of the villages would maintain order, administer justice, and provide for the severely simple needs of each such village. To the vast majority of the villagers who populated agricultural India such views of Gandhi had an instinctive appeal, and Gandhi gained ascendancy over the minds of Indian masses partly through his advocacy of village industries and the spinning wheel.

The introduction of modern industrialism and Western institutions into India was mainly the result of political contact. Industrialism seemed an exotic growth and an instrument of political and economic exploitation. Cottage industry represented a defence not only against Western industrialism but also against Western domination. Even C. R. Das, the Swarajist leader, declared that industrialism never was and never could be a part of Indian nature. "Mills and factories—like some gigantic monster—will crush out," he said, "the little of life that still feebly pulsates in our veins ... and the rich capitalist operating at a distance will lick us dry of what little blood we still may have."

Western industrialism in its early stages was associated with slums, ugliness, and exploitation. To Gandhians industrialism appeared to mean the establishment of the prototypes of Manchester, Liverpool, and Birmingham in India. Socialists in India, however, argued that the West brought also the antidote to the evils of competitive industrial civilization in the principles of cooperation, social insurance, and socialism. But, was it not creating a disease and then setting out to cure it, asked the Gandhians.

Gandhi pleaded for the revival of self-sufficient village communities "in which every man and woman knows what he or she wants and, what is more, knows that no one should want anything that others cannot have with equal labour. ... In this structure composed of innumerable villages, there will be everwidening, never ascending circles. Life will not be a pyramid with the apex sustained by the bottom. But it will be an oceanic circle whose centre will be the individual. ... "

If cities proved to be inevitable for human welfare Gandhi would vote for them but only as a necessary evil. It is here that he differed most from the advocates of industrialization and free enterprise as also the champions of socialism. "You cannot build nonviolence on factory civilization," said Gandhi, "but it can be built on self-contained villages. Even if Hitler was so minded, he could not devastate seven hundred thousand nonviolent villages. He would himself become nonviolent in the process," wrote Gandhi in the *Harijan* of 4 November 1939.

Modern industrialism led to inequitable distribution and to the concentration of wealth in a few hands. We want, said Gandhi, not only the best method of production but also ideal distribution so that there would be no exploitation. "Indeed, the West has had," said Gandhi, "a surfeit of industrialism and exploitation, the fact is that this industrialized civilization is an evil. I have no quarrel with steamships and telegraphs. They may stay, if they can, without the support of industrialism and all it connotes. Our concern is therefore to destroy industrialism at any cost." After Gandhi had made a distinction between machinery of one kind and another and had admitted that some machinery might lighten human toil, the virulence of his attack on industrialism grew. "Industrialism is, I am afraid," said Gandhi, "going to be a curse for mankind. Industrialism depends entirely on your capacity to exploit, on foreign markets being open to you. . . . "

In spite of all the arguments against the evils of industrialism, it was undeniable that a modern industrial order increased production and could raise the standard of living of the people. But Gandhi had no desire to raise the standards of the masses beyond a certain very modest competence. In 1908 in the *Hind Swaraj* Gandhi wrote: "Millions will always remain poor."[32] Believing that millions of people would always remain poor Gandhi maintained that ancient Indian society, which did not despise poverty, was superior to modern Western society in which most men wanted to be rich.[33]

For Gandhi higher standards and leisure would merely lead to self-indulgence. It was bad enough that a handful of well-to-do were self-indulgent, it would be worse if their numbers are added to. European industrialism led to Fordism or the multiplication of wants in excess of needs. Wants were endless and could never be fully satisfied and, accordingly, in the Gandhian theory it would be wise to set a limit to man's indulgence.

What Gandhi wrote in the *Hind Swaraj* in denunciation of industrialism and urbanization gives a clue to the understanding of his entire philosophy. He wrote: "Our ancestors dissuaded us from luxuries and pleasures. We have managed with the same kind of plough as existed thousands of years ago. We have retained the same kind of cottage that we had in former times and our indigenous education remains the same as before. We have had no system of life-corroding competition. Each followed his own occupation or trade and charged a regulation wage. It was not that we did not know how to invent machinery, but our forefathers knew that if we set our hearts after such things, we would become slaves and lose our moral fibre. They, therefore, after due deliberation decided that we should only do what we could with our hands and feet. They had seen that our real happiness and health consisted in a proper use of our hands and feet. They further reasoned that large cities were a snare and useless encumbrances and that people would not be happy in them, that there would be gangs of thieves and robbers, prostitution and vice flourishing in them and that poor men would be robbed by rich men. They were, therefore, satisfied with small villages. They saw that kings and their swords were inferior to the sword of ethics, and they, therefore, held the sovereigns of the earth to be inferior to the Rishis. . . . A nation with a constitution like this is fitter to teach others than to learn from others."[34]

It is because of this indiscriminate criticism of modern civilization in the *Hind Swaraj* that Gokhale, whom Gandhi claimed as his political *guru*, said that Gandhi would destroy the book after spending a year in India. But Gandhi did not. There were such basic differences between Gandhi and Gokhale that Gandhi was refused admittance to Gokhale's Servants of India Society. In 1921 Gandhi wrote: "The booklet is a severe condemnation of 'Modern Civilization'. It was written in 1908. My conviction is deeper than ever."[35] In the preface to the 1938 edition of *Hind Swaraj* Mahadev Desai, Gandhi's private secretary, wrote that Gandhi would alter nothing in the book except the language in some parts.

Most Indian nationalists and publicists, however, thought that India could preserve her individuality and yet incorporate what was best in the Western industrial civilization. The scientific achievement of the West, however perverted to material ends, was, as Tagore said, essentially a spiritual achievement, as spiritual as anything India had achieved in religion and philosophy and India could not, therefore, reject all that was in the West.

Of Asian nations Japan was the first country which whole-heartedly welcomed modern industrial civilization. Japan was an ideal and a beacon light for many Indian nationalists who claimed that Japan had "borrowed the military system of Germany, the naval system of England, the industrial system of America" but had yet retained her native religious faith. But as time went on it became apparent, however, that though Japan had retained her Shintoism she had also borrowed the imperialistic and aggressive policy of some of the modern nations of the West. The progress of Japan from nationalism to imperialism during the decade preceding World War II distressed Indian advocates of industrialism and modernism. To some it even appeared that militarism was associated inextricably with industrialism whereas socialists, on the one hand, argued that what was at fault was not industrialism but capitalistic imperialism. Internationalists, on the other hand, argued that what was at fault was chauvinistic nationalism.

The debate on industrialism went on. But industrialism is a world historic force and almost inevitable in the modern world, and neither tradition nor inertia could check the progress of industrialism in India. The realists who spurned the spinning wheel as the symbol of the modern age won the day. But Gandhi's cult of the spinning wheel emphasized the need of an economic thought with a bias in favour of cottage industries and decentralization. Gandhi placed cottage industries on the map of Indian industrialism. He could not, however, counter the mighty and irresistible force of modern industrialism. Notwithstanding Gandhi, the Congress had always been in favour of the modern industrial order. The Congress stood not for Gandhi's economics of *Khaddar* but for the economics of large-scale industrialization.

IV. GANDHIAN NONVIOLENCE AND COMMUNISM

Gandhi, the prophet of nonviolence, did not believe in communism or Bolshevism. But Gandhism is not "communism plus God or Marxism minus violence."[36] There were basic differences between Gandhi and Marx. Writing about Bolshevism in *Young India* in November 1928 Gandhi said that all he knew of Bolshevism was that it aimed at the abolition of private property; that is to say, it was only an application of the ethical ideal of non-possession in the realm of economics. If people adopted this ideal of their own accord or could be made to adopt the same by peaceful persuasion, then there would be nothing like it. "But," said Gandhi, "from what I know of Bolshevism, it not only does not preclude the use of force but freely sanctions it for the expropriation of private property and maintaining the collective ownership of the same. And if that is so, I have no hesitation in saying that the Bolshevik régime in its present form cannot last for long. For it is my firm conviction that nothing enduring can be built on violence."[37]

Gandhi recognized the passion for justice behind the Bolshevik movement but its resort to violence repelled him. Referring to the sacrifice of Lenin and countless other men Gandhi wrote that "the noble example of their renunciation will be emblazoned for ever, and quicken and purify the ideal as time passes." But Gandhi believed that economic justice could be attained only through nonviolence. Gandhi wanted not to destroy the capitalists, but only capitalism. In July 1940 Gandhi wrote in *Harijan*: "Exploitation of the poor can be extinguished not by effecting the destruction of a few millionaires, but by removing the ignorance of the poor and teaching them to non-cooperate with their exploiters. This will convert the exploiters also. I have even suggested that ultimately it will lead to both being equal partners."[38]

Gandhi had a passion for social justice and, therefore, the underlying idea of socialism appealed to him though he could not accept all its doctrines. No man could be actively non-violent and not rise against social injustices, said Gandhi; but he complained that Western socialists believed in the necessity of violence for enforcing socialistic doctrines. Gandhi's belief in nonviolence made him a crusader for social justice, but the belief of the socialists that violence may have to be resorted to in certain eventualities prevented Gandhi from becoming a socialist.

Gandhi's antipathy to violence and his aversion to the power of the State made him an anti-communist. Gandhi said that Bolshevism was the necessary result of modern materialistic civilization and he warned that if the "insensate worship of matter" continued then "in a few years' time we shall have

Bolshevism rampant in this land which was once so holy."[39] Though Gandhi admired the self-denial and spirit of sacrifice of his communist friends he said: "I have never concealed the sharp differences between their method and mine. They frankly believe in violence and all that is in its bosom."[40]

Gandhi believed that neither freedom nor democracy could be achieved through violence. In an article entitled "Nonviolence and Democracy and Freedom" published in the *Young India* in 1925 Gandhi said that "warfare may give us another rule for English rule, but not self-rule in terms of the masses."[41] Through violence only a dictatorship could be established. "I feel," wrote Gandhi in the *Young India*[42] in September 1925, "that fundamentally the disease is the same in Europe as in India, in spite of the fact that in the former country, the people enjoy self-government.... The people of Europe have no doubt political power but no *Swaraj*. Asian and African races are exploited by the ruling class or caste under the sacred name of democracy."

The nonviolent method preached by Gandhi found support even from unexpected quarters. Many leftists inspired by socialist thought contended that violence is common to both capitalistic and communistic society but that while in the capitalistic society violence was inherent, only in a socialistic society could, they claimed, the amount of violence that had to be employed be reduced to the minimum. But believing that a rapid and violent change might frighten the people into the arms of Fascism, many ardent progressivists turned moderates and mild revisionists and came to believe in the Gandhian method of nonviolent resistance as a good practical policy. Consequently, many Indians whose political and economic views were far more radical than those of Gandhi came to support the Gandhian method of nonviolent resistance.

Gandhi denounced the violence that seemed to him to be associated with communism. Purges and suppressions that took place in Russia repelled not only Gandhi but also the socialist Nehru and the internationalist Tagore. Tagore feared that what Russia sought to build up overnight by violence could not be relied upon, for upon violence a permanent or abiding society could not be founded. He said that those who had not the patience to wait for human nature to change and to be reformed believed in persecution. Violence was a sort of medical treatment. Tagore said that it may be that in this age of Bolshevism such a treatment was unavoidable but such treatment could not be a permanent solution.

Gandhi denounced violence as such and under all circumstances. Most Indian nationalists, however, did not condemn violence from any *a priori* absolute standpoint but on practical grounds and primarily because they felt that in the conditions then prevailing in India an armed rebellion against the British was impracticable. Most Indian nationalists did not agree that violence had to be abjured at all costs and in this connection they referred to Gandhi's own saying that in a choice between cowardice and violence he would have chosen violence. Socialists similarly argued that in a choice between capitalistic exploitation and socialistic violence, violence was to be chosen.

But Gandhi held fast to his unshakeable faith in nonviolence. "The socialist conception of the West," Gandhi wrote in the *Harijan* in 1940, "was born in an environment reeking with violence."[43] Gandhi felt that the coming into power of the proletariat through violence would not lead to any permanent or satisfactory solution. "What is gained by violence," said Gandhi, "must be lost before superior violence."[44]

Gandhi said that communism had demonstrated the possibility of organizing the masses but that such organization was based on a dictatorship whereas he favoured the decentralization of power. Gandhians believed that the socialization of the instruments of production would transfer only the *de jure* ownership of such instruments into the hands of the workers, but the real control and power would pass into the hands of the managers and bureaucrats, so that bureaucracy and dictatorship would reappear. For Gandhians the alternative was a society in which the instruments of production were so simplified that the common man could ply them and understand them. Only in such a society, they argued, could the state wither away and the Marxian dream be fulfilled.

Gandhi's conception of an ideal economy was one in which there was an utter simplification of the means of production and a complete decentralization of power to village units. But even though decentralization of power to the village units might possibly have solved the problem of economic power, though not necessarily of economic prosperity, the attempt to decen-

tralize power to the village units would have involved a radical
alteration in the distribution of economic power. The question
arises how such a radical alteration of economic power could
at all be achieved by consent or by peaceful methods. In fact,
an economic system which would simplify all the means of
production and do away with the large machines was not acceptable either to the advocates of modern industrialism and free
enterprise or to the champions of socialism.

Gandhi believed that real economic change could only come
from change in the character of men. Lenin, on the other hand,
believed that though in the end men would melt the sword for
making the plough, yet till the communist society was established there would be violence and that this was the inevitable
law of history. The moral passion behind the doctrines of
socialism and communism appealed to Gandhi but on the question of using violence as a means for attaining the ideal society
Gandhi held views diametrically opposite to those of the communists. "The underlying belief of communism is good and as
old as the hills," said Gandhi. But Gandhi would employ methods
different from the methods of communism for attaining his ends.

Gandhi apprehended that the communists believed in the
adoption of any means for attaining their ends. In 1946 Gandhi
said: "The communists seem to make trouble-shooting their
profession. I have friends among them. Some of them are like
sons to me. But it seems they do not make any distinction between fair and foul, truth and falsehood. They deny the charge.
But their reported acts seem to sustain it."[45]

Gandhi believed that God has given us no control over the
end and only a limited one over the means, and accordingly men
must ensure that the means were scrupulously pure and nonviolent. Gandhi wanted to change not so much circumstances
in which men lived as the character they had. For Gandhi, permanent changes could come only from within, by a change in
the character of men and through love. A revolution that was
to be effected through love could only be a slow process but for
Gandhi it was the only process that could yield abiding results.
Gandhi's essential contribution lay in emphasizing the individual
and in recognizing the power of the individual to transform
himself and also to transform society. In his emphasis on the

purity of the means, Gandhi's message was continued by his spiritual successor Vinoba Bhave.

Vinoba 1 have was born in 1895. From his early days Vinoba had felt a call for leading an ascetic and spiritual life. While in his late teens Vinoba left his studies and went to the holy city of Benares in search of a spiritual leader. Later, after reading in a newspaper one of Gandhi's speeches he was so drawn to Gandhi's ideas that he joined Gandhi's ashram at Sabarmati. In 1921, at the instance of Gandhi, Vinoba opened another ashram at Wardha and in the civil disobedience movement of 1940 Vinoba was chosen by Gandhi to be the first *satyagrahi* to court arrest. In prison Vinoba, already a master of Sanskrit, learned four Dravidian languages of South India. After Gandhi's death, Vinoba was regarded as Gandhi's spiritual successor. Vinoba came in direct contact with communist methods in Telengana where there was a peasant rising accompanied by violence. To the revolutionary call to seize land by force, Vinoba put forward his alternative of *bhoodan yagna* movement or voluntary sacrificial land-giving by the landlords.

Vinoba said that there was no difference between his goal and that of the communists and that the real difference was on the question of methods that were to be employed for reaching the common goal. Vinoba was no traditionalist and he claimed that like the communists he believed in change and revolution, but where he differed from the communists was in the belief that he held that to bring about a new order of society violence had to be eschewed altogether.

Vinoba referred to Marx as the *Maha Muni* (Great Sage) and thought that communist ideology was worthy of consideration though, according to Vinoba, real progress could come only through peaceful means and on the basis of the ideology of *sarvodaya* (welfare for all). Addressing the *sarvodaya* workers in Kerala in 1957 Vinoba said that a study of Marx had brought about a great change in the minds of innumerable people and that, accordingly, he considered it a dilemma of the communists that there was no room in their philosophy for a change of heart while their own lives bore testimony to the fact that there could be a change of heart. "And, therefore," said Vinoba, "I consider communism by itself is a very good and great thing. But what is the means to realize it? ... Those who say that *satya-yuga* is yet to come are communists. The traditionalists and the communists are both believers in *satya-yuga*. One group describes the one that had passed away and the other that of the one yet to come. But what do I say? The past is not in my hands nor the future. The present only is in my hands, and, therefore, we want to make the *satya-yuga* a reality of the present. . . . Some of the Jana Sangh Party used to meet me. They used to tell me: 'You talk about *ahimsa*, but it will never be practicable in this *kali-yuga*; it was only possible in the *satya-yuga* of the past.' These are traditionalists. They do not believe that nonviolence would go well with the present. They oppose us thus, while the communists oppose us by saying that we are only wandering in an utopia. They say: 'For the present we have to be prepared to make use of violence. But ultimately nonviolence will come to prevail, that is, for achieving nonviolence in the end we have to use a little violence today and we must be prepared for it. Therefore, you have to suspend your nonviolence for a little. . . .' I ask the communists also to tell me how to reach their paradise. They answer that I should now be prepared for some violence and killing. One says that paradise can be reached after death and the other tells me that the paradise will come after I kill another. Therefore both ways do not appear to be helpful to us. . . . We have to demonstrate the power of both love and peace. . . . It behoves us to take the responsibility to demonstrate that every issue in this world can be solved through peace."[46]

In saying that there was no difference between him and the communists as to the ultimate aims and that they differed only on the question as to whether violence could be used for attaining the common ends, Vinoba did not explain or develop his other differences with the communists. The aim of Vinoba was the creation of small, self-sufficient, and self-governing villages, as Gandhi had envisaged them, and in this respect there were serious differences between Vinoba and the communists. Vinoba's follower Jayaprakash has laid greater emphasis on these differences. He said that he rejected the communist ideology not merely because of his belief in the purity of means and disbelief in the justification of the use of violence to effect social revolution, but also because he was opposed to the socialization of the means of production by the state and to the establishment of a monolithic party rule and, further, because he wanted to establish a society based on complete political and economic decentralization.[47]

V. GANDHIAN DECENTRALISM, NEHRU AND SOCIALISM

One of the reasons why Gandhi did not approve of socialism or communism was that he believed in plain living and in the ideal of economic simplicity whereas the advocates of socialism were supporters of large-scale production. Gandhi was opposed to large-scale production and he believed that it would only lead to exploitation and urbanization. Gandhi said: "Machinery would concentrate production in particular areas so that you would have to go in a round-about way to regulate distribution whereas if there is production and distribution both in the respective areas where things are required, it is automatically regulated."

Gandhi stood for village industries and decentralized production. If the state monopolized all the means of production then that would lead to concentration of power and to the establishment of the dictatorship of a party or of the bureaucracy.[48] It is this aspect of Gandhi's thought that later impressed erstwhile advocates of the socialization of the means of production by the state, such as Jayaprakash Narayan, who eventually came to believe in decentralization of power. Again, it is Gandhi's distrust of centralization and concentration of power in the hands of the state that is referred to constantly by C. Rajagopalachari, the founder of the Swatantra Party in India.

"If our desire," wrote Gandhi, "is to establish *Swaraj* for the people, not to substitute one class rule by another, which may be even worse," then village industries would have to be encouraged.[49] Referring to the town-bred he said that "hitherto the villagers have died in their thousands so that we might live." It is again this emphasis on villages and village life that recurs later in the writings of Vinoba Bhave and in the later writings of Jayaprakash Narayan. After his conversion to *Sarvodaya*, Jayaprakash denounced the extremes of modern industrialism and centralization and said that democracy could be founded only on the basis of the village which was "a primary face-to-face community" and not a "human jungle where impersonal relationships govern the life of the individual."[50]

In a situation where production would not be primarily mechanical but would be decentralized and mostly in the villages, there would be no accumulation of wealth in the pockets of a few nor would there be poverty in the midst of plenty for the rest, and a simple form of communitarian democracy would prevail. In support of such economic decentralization Jayaprakash said: "At one time socialists used to believe that if the means of production, distribution, and exchange were nationalized economic democracy would automatically come into being. The experience, however, of totalitarian communism has proved that even the complete nationalization of all these means does not necessarily result in economic democracy; on the contrary, it might even end up in the most rigorous economic dictatorship, giving rise at the same time to new forms of economic exploitation and inequality. Therefore, democratic socialists have come to realize that if they were not to give up the aim of economic democracy, they must not be content with the traditional means of nationalization, but seek ways of decentralizing the economic institutions and processes of society."[51] The decentralized economy of Jayaprakash's conception was to have an agrarian bias and was to be of the "owner-worker or cooperative type"[52] as distinguished from a socialized economy where the state owned all or the major means of production.

The decentralist bias in Gandhian thought is also continued in the ideas of Chakravarti Rajagopalachari who is generally known as C. R. C. R. had been an intimate associate of Gandhi and had also been the first Indian Governor-General of the Dominion of India. C. R. and the Swatantra Party he founded are opposed to socialism and centralization. When the decision to form the Swatantra Party was taken in Madras in June 1959 the party's aims were stated thus: "We are of the opinion that social justice and welfare can be reached more certainly and properly in other ways than through techniques of so-called Socialism. . . . Social justice and welfare should not be brought about by violence or State compulsion . . . but must be brought into being by the spread of the doctrine of trusteeship as suggested by Gandhiji. . . . The educational activities of government, direct and indirect, should be such as to emphasize the moral obligations of those who possess wealth to hold it in trust for society, and a doctrine of life based on that moral obligation as distinguished from seeking to establish a socialist structure based on legislative sanctions involving expropriation and loss of incentive for the individual to work and increasing dependence on the State and its official in every walk of life."

The immediate cause for the formation of the Swatantra Party was the resolution that the Congress passed at its Nagpur Session in 1959 regarding cooperative farming which C. R. regarded as nothing but "the royal road to communism." Apart from C. R. the main promoters of the party were Professor Ranga, who had once been the general secretary of the Indian National Congress, M. R. Masani, who had been a founder-member of the Congress Socialist Party, and K. M. Munshi, a scholar and a former leader of the Congress Party. C. R. asserted that the Congress under Nehru's leadership had in effect accepted communistic principles and that Nehru had sought to lead the Congress along the socialistic or communist path. This, claimed C. R., was because Nehru was not restrained by Gandhi, who had been assassinated, or by the conservative or rightist Patel, who was no more, "After Gandhi is dead," declared C. R , "we have socialism. Socialism is now preached boldly because there is no Gandhi to answer it. I say the same things as Gandhi said. . . . If Gandhi had been alive or Vallabhbhai Patel had been alive I would not have had to do all this work." The Swatantra Party is a party with conservative leanings and is wholly opposed to socialism and Jayaprakash Narayan, the erstwhile socialist, has even characterized the party as a balancing factor between the forces of radicalism and conservatism in India.

The Gandhian belief in decentralism was linked with his belief in simple living and the establishment of a pre-industrial, agricultural and village-based society. But Gandhi's love for pre-industrial agricultural India left Nehru, whom Gandhi described as his successor, cold. Nehru scathingly criticized Gandhi's doctrine for the revival of ancient Indian village societies as formulated in the *Hind Swaraj*. Nehru wrote: "All this seems to me utterly wrong and harmful doctrine, and impossible of achievement. Behind it lies Gandhiji's love and praise of poverty and suffering and the ascetic life. For him progress and civiliza-

tion consist not in multiplication of wants ... but in the deli-
berate and voluntary restriction of wants. ... " "Gandhiji is
always thinking in terms of personal salvation and of sin while
most of us," wrote Nehru, "have society's welfare uppermost in
our minds. ... He [Gandhi] is not out to change society or the
social structure, he devotes himself to the eradication of sin
from individuals."

Nehru stood for increased production through industrialization. He stood for higher standards of living. Nehru wanted to
establish a modern economy in India, and the "spiritual" basis
of ancient Indian indigenous economy did not appeal to him.
Nehru complained that Gandhi's activities led one to think that
he wanted "to go back to the narrowest autarchy, not only a
self-sufficient nation but almost a self-sufficient village." Nehru,
on the other hand, aimed at the "establishment of a socialist
order, first within the national boundaries and eventually in the
world as a whole, with a controlled production and distribution
of wealth for the public good." Nehru considered that the
Khadi movement, hand-spinning and hand-weaving, for which
Gandhi stood, would only lead to an intensification of individualism in production and would thus be "a throw-back to the
pre-industrial age."[53] It was both futile and wrong to seek to
stop the advance of industrialism and mass-production. "For not
only is our material and cultural progress bound up with it, but
also our freedom itself," declared Nehru.

Nehru had no faith in Gandhi's ideal of village self-sufficiency
or of complete decentralization. "The village could no longer be
a self-contained economic unit," said Nehru.[54] Nehru, however,
did not reject the idea of decentralization altogether. He wrote
that the village "can very well be a governmental and electoral
unit, each such unit functioning as a self-governing community
within the larger political framework and looking after the essential needs of the village."[55]

Nehru rejected altogether Gandhi's theory of trusteeship.
Gandhi hoped that the zamindars, princes, and the propertied
class would use their wealth and power as trustees for the poor.
Nehru had no faith in trusteeship and, for him, zamindari was a
semi-feudal system which was "out of date" and an impediment
to production and general progress. "The sole trusteeship that

can be fair," said Nehru, "is the trusteeship of the nation and not of one individual or a group."[56]

Nehru sought to interest Gandhi in Marxism and socialistic theories but Gandhi was never attracted to the ideology of Marxism. Gandhi's philosophy was mainly derived from indigenous sources of Indian culture and the book of life, being Gandhi's Experiments with Truth, rather than from any person or from any printed book. But though Gandhi was no Marxist, his feeling for the underdog was no less than that of any ardent Marxist.

In spite of the great differences in ideology and temperament between Nehru and Gandhi, they were still very close and in 1942 Gandhi declared: "It will require much more than differences of opinion to estrange us. . . . We have had differences from the moment we became co-workers, and yet I have said for some years and say now that not Rajaji but Jawaharlal will be my successor. He says he does not understand my language, and that he speaks a language foreign to me. . . . I know this, that when I am gone he will speak my language."[57]

The fact that Nehru, the idol of Young India, acknowledged Gandhi as his Master made Gandhi more acceptable to the young who might otherwise have turned away from Gandhi's apparent revivalism and conservatism and might have failed to discern his revolutionary political role. But Gandhi was really the messiah of the villagers, as Nehru was the idol of the intelligentsia. Nehru was influenced by all the modern trends and movements which have inspired and troubled the intelligentsia of modern India. Nehru had been brought up in the Western liberal tradition but he considered mere liberalism as inadequate. Like many among modern India's intelligentsia, Nehru sought to combine liberalism with egalitarianism, democracy and individual liberty with socialism and planning. Nehru acknowledged himself to be socialist, and though attracted to Marxism was not intoxicated by it. He derived much comfort from Marxist economic and social philosophy but did not give his absolute allegiance to it. Nehru was a nationalist and yet he did not consider the freedom movement in India as something apart from world movements. Nehru prided himself in being an Indian and was yet at home with Western culture. He came from a wealthy family but yet he spoke for the poor peasants and workers. Nehru seemed to have absorbed all kinds of forces and trends which affected the intelligentsia of India. But the apparent contradictions and paradoxes in Nehru's ways and views were part of his appeal to the intelligentsia.[58]

Though very different from one another Nehru complemented Gandhi in the same manner as Vivekananda complemented his great master Ramakrishna, from whom Vivekananda differed radically in temperament and way of life. Nehru can be regarded as the Plato to Gandhi's role as Socrates.[59]

VI. THE COMMUNIST CRITIQUE OF GANDHI

Gandhi was a complex and sometimes an enigmatic personality. It was not altogether easy to analyse Gandhi and Gandhism. The communists also did not find it easy to classify Gandhi according to any rigid formula.

The first Indian communist who dealt with Gandhi and his political and economic ideas was M. N. Roy, but his approach to Gandhi did not always remain the same and changed with the passage of time. M. N. Roy, however, started as an uncompromising critic of Gandhi. In his first book *India in Transition*, published in 1922, Roy described Gandhism as "the acutest and most desperate manifestation of the forces of reaction."[60] Roy took pains to emphasize that the fact that Gandhi denounced materialism and modern Western civilization did not make him a progressive, because Gandhi was merely a defender of Indian feudalism and was even opposed to the evolution of modern capitalistic enterprise in India.

Next year M. N. Roy and his wife Ellen Roy published a book *One Year of Non-Cooperation* in which tributes were paid to the moral qualities of Gandhi but, none the less, Gandhi was characterized as a reactionary. Ellen Roy, writing under the pen name Santi Devi, prophesied that Gandhi would be remembered by posterity in the same manner as his saintly prototypes of the past, such as Thomas Aquinas, Savonarola and St Francis of Assisi,[61] but she was bitterly sarcastic about the Gandhian creed of nonviolence. She considered it futile to expect that three hundred million Indians would "cheerfully endure all kicks and insults, all hunger and nakedness, all poverty and wretchedness at the hands of their exploiters" in the fond hope that the exploiting class would respond "by throwing away their machine guns and flesh-pots, their treasure hoards and princely power." She wrote: "Nonviolence, resignation, perfect love and release from the pain of living—this is the substance of Indian philosophy handed down through the ages by a powerful caste of kings, priests, and philosophers who found it good to keep the people in subjection. . . . Gandhi is nothing but the heir of this long line of ghostly ancestors. . . ."[62] The Gandhian belief in class collaboration was similarly denounced by Ellen Roy. The hope that the capitalists and the proletariat could unite in a common struggle for freedom, whose economic content remained undefined, was as futile as the hope that oil could mix with water.

After M. N. Roy and Ellen Roy, the most important communist who critically examined Gandhian philosophy was R. Palme Dutt. Dutt's evaluation of Gandhi, as contained in his book *Modern India* (1926), was somewhat different from that of M. N. Roy. In Roy's view Gandhi represented feudalism and the big bourgeoisie but Dutt regarded that Gandhi was aligned with the "petty bourgeois intellectual elements." According to Dutt the big bourgeois interests were represented by the moderates and the liberals outside the Congress, but the Congress under Gandhi represented the petty bourgeois intellectual elements. Dutt denounced the "spiritually reactionary propaganda of Gandhism" but did not fail to note the positive role of Gandhi as a political leader of the national movement. "The achievement of Gandhi," wrote Dutt, "consisted in that he, almost alone of all the leaders, sensed and reached out to the masses. This was the first great achievement of Gandhi. He did —at one point—reach the masses. This positive achievement of Gandhi is bigger than all the idiosyncrasies and weakness which may be brought against him, and constitutes his real contribution to Indian Nationalism."[63]

R. P. Dutt, however, criticized Gandhi for having withdrawn the civil disobedience movement after the violent incidents that took place at Chauri Chaura in 1922. The withdrawal of the movement Dutt attributed to Gandhi's class prejudices and his disinclination to rouse the masses to a revolutionary pitch. "Gandhi failed as the leader of the national struggle," argued

Dutt, "because he could not cut himself loose from the upper-class interests and prejudices in which he had been brought up. ... The 'spirituality' of Gandhi is only the expression of this class interest. All parasitic and propertied classes have to weave around themselves a fog of confused language, superstition, tradition, religion, revivalism, etc. in order to hide from the masses the fact of their exploitation."[64]

The next important communist who dealt with Gandhi and Gandhism was Shapurji Saklatwala, who had been returned to the British Parliament from a working-class constituency. Saklatwala visited India in 1927 and entered into controversial correspondence with Gandhi. Saklatwala regarded Gandhi's economic ideas as reactionary and also denounced Gandhi's belief that labour and capital could collaborate. Saklatwala realized that Gandhi had a great hold upon the Indian masses, but he asserted that in the absence of a progressive economic ideology Gandhi could not lead the Indian people in the right direction. "Let me say in my usual blunt way," wrote Saklatwala to Gandhi, "that I am returning to my 'attack' upon you. Of course, you understand the meaning and nature of my 'attacks' upon you, namely, that recognizing in you a man of indomitable spirit, with a real propagandist's heart and qualities, I want you to deal with the various Indian movements in the way in which success is made for such movements in other parts of the world."

Gandhi replied: "So far as our ideals are concerned we stand apart. ... One word as to policy. ... It [my policy] is not anti-capitalistic. The idea is to take from capital labour's due share and no more, and this not by paralysing capital, but by reform among labourers from within and by their own self-consciousness; not, again through the cleverness and manoeuvring of non-labour leaders, but by educating labour to evolve its own leadership."

Since 1920 Gandhi had often spoken and written about communists and Bolshevism. He never failed to recognize the spirit of dedication of the communists in Russia, but he could not reconcile himself to the violence that appeared to him to be inevitable in any communist scheme of reconstruction of society. In December 1924 Gandhi wrote in *Young India*: "I am yet ignorant of what exactly Bolshevism is. I have not been able to study it. I do not know if it is for the good of Russia in the long run. But ... in so far as it is based on violence and denial of God, it repels me."[65] Again in November 1928 Gandhi wrote: "It is my firm conviction that nothing enduring can be built on violence. But, be that as it may, there is no questioning the fact that the bolshevik ideal has behind it the purest sacrifice of countless men and women who have given up their all for its sake, and an ideal that is sanctified by the sacrifices of such master spirits as Lenin cannot go in vain; the noble example of their renunciation will be emblazoned for ever and quicken and purify the ideal as time passes."[66]

While Gandhi criticized the communists for their lack of faith in the creed of nonviolence, the communists asserted that the Gandhian creed of nonviolence was being utilized by the vested interests to preserve the *status quo* and to dampen the revolutionary ardour of the Indian people. Gandhi's belief in nonviolence was linked with his theory of trusteeship, that is to say, that the wealthy should hold their wealth in trust for the people, and also with his theory that it was possible to bring about a change of heart in the wealthy so that they would act truly as the trustees of the people. All these theories of non-violence, trusteeship, change of heart and class collaboration were steadfastly and constantly criticized by the communists.

The Sixth Congress of Comintern held in 1928 scathingly attacked Gandhism and all nationalist and reformist ideologies. The Sixth Congress met after the communist debacle in China in 1926. The Chinese communists had previously cooperated with the Kuomintang and Chiang Kai-shek but in 1926 the Chinese communist movement was severely attacked by Chiang Kai-shek, and it is no wonder that the Sixth Congress considered the national bourgeoisie in colonial and dependent countries as treacherous and unreliable. The Sixth Congress gave a call to the communists to fight Gandhism and the Indian National Congress. It said: "The communists must unmask the national reformism of the Indian National Congress and oppose all the phrases of the Swarajists, Gandhists, etc. about passive resistance with the irreconcilable slogan of struggle for the emancipation of the country and the expulsion of the imperialists."

The Sixth Congress declared that the bourgeois national movements in India, Egypt, and other dependent and colonial countries were going over to counter-revolution. It said: "The national bourgeoisie has not the significance of a force in the struggle against imperialism. . . . Its chief feature is that it exerts a braking, retarding influence on the development of the revolutionary movement. . . . In India and Egypt we still observe, for the time being, the typical bourgeois-nationalist movement—an opportunist movement, subject to great vacillations, balancing between imperialism and revolution. . . . It is necessary to reject the formation of any kind of bloc between the Communist Party and the nationalist reformist opposition. . . . It is no less important to mercilessly expose before the toiling masses the national reformist character of the swarajist, wafdist and other nationalist parties, and in particular, of their leaders. It is necessary to expose their half-heartedness and vacillation in the national struggle . . . their previous capitulations and counter-revolutionary advances . . . their empty nationalist phraseology. . . . "

It is clear from the formulations made at the Sixth Congress that the communists were not expected to cooperate with the Indian National Congress or to work from within that organization. The tenets laid down at the Sixth Congress could lead the communists only to pursue a policy of denunciation of the Congress led by Gandhi and not to a policy aimed at radicalizing the Congress from within. In this respect the Sixth Congress marked a radical departure from the policies adumbrated at the Second Congress by Lenin who had asked the communists not to work in opposition to but in cooperation with the national bourgeoisie. S. G. Sardesai, a CPI leader,, wrote in retrospect: "It cannot be denied that the Sixth Congress theses nowhere ask Indian communists to work inside the Congress and its movement. . . . This was the crucial point on which the Sixth Congress line departed radically from the preceding international communist line in respect of the Indian freedom movement pursued since the Second Congress on the basis of Lenin's understanding and guidance."[67]

In 1929 an article on Gandhi appeared in the *Large Soviet Encyclopedia* in which there were references to the writings on Gandhi by M. N. Roy as also by R. P. Dutt. This article referred to Gandhi as representing the interests of the propertied classes, but Gandhi was characterized not as the spokesman of feudalism as M. N. Roy had done in *India in Transition* (1922), but as the spokesman of the petty bourgeoisie as R. P. Dutt had done in *Modern India* (1927).

In 1929 the British Indian government launched the Meerut Conspiracy Case in which many Indian communists were accused of having conspired to deprive the King Emperor of his sovereignty in India. Gandhi visited the accused in Meerut jail and asked them to support the Indian National Congress. One of the communists whom Gandhi visited in jail asked if Gandhi would suspend his civil disobedience movement again as he had done in 1922 when violence had erupted in Chauri Chaura. Gandhi pondered for a while and replied: "No."[68]

In 1930 when Gandhi launched his civil disobedience movement the Indian communists took no part in it. This alienated them from the Indian people. The decision of the communists not to take part in this civil disobedience movement launched by Gandhi was later regretted by them, and they claimed that if the communists had not been arrested in 1929 in connection with the Meerut Conspiracy Case they might have adopted "less sectarian tactics towards the Congress-led movement."[69] "It was a tragedy that in 1930," wrote S. G. Sardesai, "we contraposed ourselves against Gandhi, against the Indian National Congress, and practically against the mass civil disobedience movement launched by it though, of course, with the sincere desire to liberate the Indian masses from reformist, compromising, Gandhian influence and unleash a genuine revolutionary national-freedom movement under the leadership of the working class."[70]

In opposing Gandhi and the non-cooperation movement started by him in 1930 the Indian communists were pursuing the militant and extremist policy laid down by the Sixth Congress of the Comintern and was developing it even still further. The Draft Platform of Action of the Communist Party of India published towards the end of 1930 stated that the Indian "capitalist class has long ago betrayed the struggle for the independence of the country . . . its present 'opposition' represents merely manoeuvres with British imperialists, calculated to swindle the mass of the toilers, . . . the assistance granted to British imperialism by the capitalist class and its political organization, the National Congress, takes the shape at the present time of a consistent policy of compromise with British imperialism; it takes the form of the disorganization of the revolutionary struggle of the masses and the preservation of the system of imperialism . . . the policy of Gandhism, on which the programme of the Congress is founded, uses the cloak of vague phrases . . . the most harmful and dangerous obstacle to the victory of the Indian revolution is the agitation carried on by the 'left' elements of the National Congress, led by Jawaharlal Nehru, Bose and others . . . the exposure of the 'left' Congress leaders is the primary task of our party. . . . "

The same extremist policy was reflected in the resolution adopted by the Executive Committee of the Communist International in March–April 1931 which called upon the Indian working class to counter the "treacherous and counter-revolutionary alliance concluded between the national reformist bourgeoisie and British imperialism and to organize the revolutionary action of the oppressed classes against British imperialism and the National Congress." The resolution stated: "The anti-imperialist struggle of the masses is more and more breaking through the framework of counter-revolutionary Gandhism."

In 1931 Gandhi addressed a meeting of the workers in Bombay. At this meeting B. T. Ranadive, who had led a demonstration on behalf of the communists, also spoke. Speaking after Ranadive, Gandhi explained that his *Swaraj* would be for the workers and peasants but that this did not mean that he sought to overthrow capitalism. Gandhi said: "I made the working man's cause my own long before any of the young communists here were born. I spent the best part of my time in South Africa working for them. I used to live with them and shared their joys and sorrows. You must therefore understand why I claim to speak for labour. . . . If the Congress sends its representatives to the conference [the Second Round Table Conference, which Gandhi was due to attend] they will press for no Swaraj other than the Swaràj for workers and peasants." But Gandhi also made it clear that he was not hostile to the capitalists. He said: "I do not want to deceive you. I must warn you that I do not bear any ill-will to the capitalists."[71]

When Gandhi was in London in connection with the Second Round Table Conference he spoke to Indian students there, many of whom were ardent leftists. Gandhi was asked: "How exactly do you think are the Indian princes, landlords, mill-owners, money-lenders and other proprietors enriched?" and he replied: "At the present moment, by exploiting the masses." But this did not mean that Gandhi subscribed to the communist theory of class war for when he was asked: "If you will benefit the workers and peasants can you avoid class war?" he replied: "I can, most decidedly, if only the people will follow the non-violent methods. By the nonviolent method we seek not to destroy the capitalist, we seek to destroy capitalism. We invite the capitalist to regard himself as a trustee for those on whom he depends for the making, the retention, and the increase of his capital."[72] Gandhi said that in order to bring about a society in which the wealthy would hold their properties in trust, he would rely not merely on the method of persuasion but also on the method of non-cooperation which he regarded as a revolutionary method.

In June 1933 in an article published by Valia in *Communist International* a virulent attack was launched on Gandhi and Gandhism. Valia considered Gandhi as the representative of the bourgeoisie and the landlords and characterized his teachings as utterly anti-revolutionary. Valia wrote: "An estimate of Gandhism as petty bourgeois philosophy ... still finds support among some of the followers of the revolutionary movement and is extremely harmful, hindering the process of the development of revolutionary Marxism.... The starting point in determining the class essence of Gandhism is the statement of Comrade Stalin in his report at the XVI Congress of the CPSU: 'As for assistants [i.e. of imperialism] of the type of Gandhi, Tsarism had shoals of them in the form of liberal conciliators of every kind, from which, however nothing but confusion arose....' Gandhism is now again demonstrating its liberal anti-revolutionary nature. ... Thus Gandhism was, and is, the philosophy of the bourgeoisie and the landlords. It is not right to state that its drawback consisted and still consists in reactionary, utopian petty bourgeois principles, because it was and is the teachings of the cowardly anti-revolutionary bourgeoisie, linked up with the landlord system and in deadly fear of a national revolution. This is the essence of the matter."[73]

The Communist Party of India was declared illegal by the British Indian government in 1934. The Indian communists were at that time pursuing an extreme militant policy in conformity with the formulations accepted at the Sixth Congress of the

Comintern in 1928 and they cherished an uncompromising hostility to the national bourgeoisie and the Congress movement led by Gandhi.

The Seventh Congress of the Comintern held in 1935 reversed the extreme militant and noncompromising policy which had been adopted at the Sixth Congress of the Comintern in 1928. The Seventh Congress gave a call for forging an international popular front against Fascism and its aggressive and militant designs. It also gave a call for forming a broad national front against imperialism in all colonial and semi-colonial countries. The Dutt-Bradley thesis, which followed the Seventh Congress, also called upon the Indian communists to develop a popular front against imperialism.

The policy laid down by the Seventh Congress and the line suggested in the Dutt-Bradley thesis gave a new orientation to communist policy in India. Thenceforward the communists did not denounce Gandhi and the Congress altogether but they aimed at radicalizing the Congress by joining that organization and developing it into a more militant and anti-imperialist body. Gandhi could, therefore, no longer be regarded a mere symbol of reaction nor could it be said, as was said by R. P. Dutt in 1931, that "to all that is young and generous in India the name of Gandhi is an object of cursing and contempt, the name of Judas."[74]

After the acceptance of the Dutt-Bradley thesis the communists could not regard Gandhi as an unmitigated anti-revolutionary. Gandhi was now regarded as the leader of the Indian freedom movement who had a positive role to play in the struggle between the national bourgeoisie and the British imperialism but who would, at the same time, attempt to stem the tide of the socialistic advance of the Indian working class and the peasantry against the Indian bourgeoisie. Gandhi, in his turn, also made it clear that he did not stand for the abolition of private property or of the capitalists, but that he aimed at the establishment of a just relationship between the capitalists and the workers. When the Congress Socialist Party was formed in 1934 he said: "I am not for elimination but for just regulation of the relation between landlords and tenants."[75] Again, in September 1934, Gandhi declared: "If the Congress socialists gain ascendancy in the Congress, as they well may, I cannot remain in the Congress."

Gandhi's leadership was challenged in 1938 when Subhas Bose, with the support of the leftists including the Congress socialists and the communists, was elected as the Congress President defeating Pattabhi Sitaramayya, whose candidature Gandhi had blessed. Gandhi declared Sitaramayya's defeat as his own defeat. A situation arose when it appeared that the Congress might be split into the rightists led by Gandhi and the leftists led by Subhas Bose. Later, the Congress socialists withdrew their support from Subhas Bose and the communists also did likewise. Nehru, the leader of socialists inside the Congress, also did not wish to break with Gandhi altogether.

In 1940 a treatise on Gandhi was issued by Communist Party of India. According to this treatise Gandhi had played a progressive and militant role during the first non-cooperation movement in 1920, and again in the next non-cooperation movement between 1930-33, but had later surrendered to the bourgeoisie. In 1940 the Indian communists characterized Gandhi as a decadent force, and in 1942 when Gandhi led the Quit India movement the Indian communists opposed it.

In 1942 P. C. Joshi, the general secretary of the Communist Party of India, characterized Gandhism as a negative force. He wrote: "Gandhism is the path of negation. This creed which has dominated the national leadership in the past, fails now to answer their needs. It has become the ideology of blank negation which satisfies the ethical needs of Gandhi and his immediate followers, but fails to offer an explanation of changing reality. ... The outlook of negation, the policy of passivity, and the practice of subservience—this is Gandhism today."[76]

The relation between the Indian communists and the Congress led by Gandhi was strained to the breaking-point during World War II when Gandhi started the Quit India movement. At a time when Gandhi started this movement [1942] the communists were saying that the war was a people's war and nothing should be done to embarrass the Allies in their war-effort. During this period the communists also supported the Muslim League demand for self-determination or Pakistan. All these created almost an impassable barrier between the Congress led by Gandhi and the Indian communists.

9

In 1946 Dutt came to India and worked for effecting a reconciliation between the Congress and the communists on the basis, *inter alia*, that the communists would give up their support for the Muslim League demand for self-determination. Dutt was also responsible for a new communist evaluation of Gandhi. Dutt, who in 1942 had referred to Gandhi as "the pacifist evil genius of Indian politics,"[77] now gave a new and more sympathetic evaluation of Gandhi. In an article, published in the *Labour Monthly* in March 1948, Dutt asserted, as before, that Gandhi lacked a systematic and comprehensive social and economic philosophy, but he yet claimed that Gandhi's "greatness of spirit, his honesty, courage, and love of humanity shine through and transcend the many inconsistencies and contradictions.... His detractors can with ease pick out his weaknesses and inconsistencies in a manner which only reveals their own pettiness and inability to understand the greatness that was in him."[78]

In 1949 A. M. Dyakov, a leading Soviet Indologist, made an evaluation of Gandhi which was very different from the sympathetic evaluation that R. P. Dutt had made in 1948 in the *Labour Monthly*. Dyakov denounced Gandhism as a purely counter-revolutionary ideology. He wrote: "The attempts to utilize the authority of Gandhi for a defence of democracy in India are extremely harmful and dangerous. Gandhi never headed the armed struggle against imperialism and has never come out against traitors from among the Indians. On the contrary, he has always been the principal traitor of the mass national liberation movement. The struggle against Gandhism—the ideology of the counter-revolutionary bourgeoisie of India—is impossible without a struggle against the authority of Gandhi, against the Gandhi cult, without an exposure of all the activities of Gandhi who has constantly betrayed the popular movement and by this rendered tremendous services to the British enslavers of India."[79]

In a similar vein an article appeared in January 1950 in the *Communist*, the CPI theoretical journal, to the effect that Gandhi played "a hampering and reactionary role in the development of national liberation movement."[80] "The paramount task of the Indian proletariat at this stage," the article continued, "consists in the emancipation of the millions of peasant masses from the ideological and political influence of the bourgeoisie and particularly from the influence of Gandhian ideology."81

In succeeding years, though the communists continued to criticize the economic and social philosophy of Gandhism, they increasingly referred to the moral greatness of Gandhi as a man. Writing in the *New Age* in June 1955, E. M. S. Namboodiripad observed: "Gandhi had no personal axe to grind; he represented the bourgeois class as a whole and not an individual or group among the bourgeoisie; he, therefore, was able to look at every problem from the point of view of the long-range interest of his class as a whole rather than from the narrow, petty, personal, or group interests of sections of the bourgeoisie.... Herein lies the greatness of Gandhi as the typical ideological-political leader of the Indian bourgeoisie."82

In June 1955 Nehru visited Russia. On the occasion of this visit, the Soviet Union published 100,000 copies of a Russian translation of Nehru's *Discovery of India*. In reviewing this book Dyakov and Balabushevich, Soviet Indologists, stated that it was entirely proper to give Gandhi a great place in the national liberation movement as Nehru had done.

In November 1955 Khrushchev and Bulganin visited India. Both of them spoke admiringly of Gandhi and his contribution to the Indian national movement. On 24 November 1955 Bulganin said in Bombay: "You had an outstanding leader who did much for your country. I am speaking of Mahatma Gandhi, ... We pay due tribute to his memory and to the work of his successor, Jawaharlal Nehru.... We, Lenin's pupils, do not share Gandhi's philosophical views, but we consider him an outstanding leader...."

On 2 February 1956 Zhukov, a leading Soviet expert on Asia, wrote in the *New Times* that many Soviet oriental scholars, including himself, had in the past failed to make a correct appraisal of Gandhi's contribution to the Indian national movement. He wrote: "Unfortunately, Soviet historical literature has failed to give a clear and lucid appraisal of the part played by Gandhi. Moreover, certain Soviet studies contain an incorrect assessment of his activities. What is the explanation? It is, I believe, that until quite recently we did not possess sufficient knowledge of the facts of Indian history. As a result, the characterization of so complex a figure as Gandhi was bound to be one-sided. Our authors concentrated on criticizing certain aspects of the Gandhi philosophy, regarding his activities in complete divorcement from the concrete conditions and level of the anti-imperialist movement in India. And it must be admitted that most Soviet oriental scholars, myself among them, at one time shared these views, which found expression in the press. In this connection, I should like to emphasize once again the vast importance of Premier Nehru's books for a correct understanding of many specific features of the national-liberation movement in India, and notably the part played by Gandhi."[83] Later, Dyakov also similarly asserted that Gandhi had played a positive role in the development of the Indian liberation movement and in transforming the Congress into a mass party.

The criticism of the philosophical foundations of Gandhism had in the past prevented many communists from recognizing the positive role of Gandhi as the leader of the Indian national movement. That this had in the past led to "sectarian errors" was acknowledged by Otto Kuusinen at the Twentieth Party Congress of the Communist Party of the Soviet Union held in February 1956. Kuusinen said: "The great political importance of the fact that in their statements in India Comrades Khrushchev and Bulganin justly acknowledged the prominent role played in the history of the Indian people by Mahatma Gandhi should also be noted. . . . By so doing Comrades Khrushchev and Bulganin actually took the initiative in correcting those sectarian errors which have found reflection in recent years in some of the statements made by Soviet Orientalists in the publications of the Communist International. Solely on the basis of criticism of Gandhi's philosophical views, which, as is known, are at great variance with the views of Marxism–Leninism, some of our publicists were at that time so one-sided that they totally denied that Gandhi played a positive role in history."[84]

In June 1955 Nehru had visited the Soviet Union and thereafter in November 1955 Khrushchev and Bulganin visited India. In 1955 the relationship between India and the Soviet Union was improving and it was natural that the Soviet leaders and Indologists would make a more sympathetic assessment of Gandhi, whom Indians held in very high regard. The Indian communists, who in the past had denounced Gandhi in unmistakable terms, had also to reckon with the fact that Gandhi's name was sacred in many parts of India, particularly in the villages.

The change in the attitude of Indian communists to Gandhi is reflected in the studies on Gandhi made by two leading communists of India, namely, by Hiren Mukherjee, the communist scholar and parliamentarian, and E. M. S. Namboodiripad, the communist leader from Kerala. These works evince considerable respect for Gandhi and seek to portray him in a historic role in the national liberation movement of India.

In his book *Gandhi : A Study*, first published in 1958, Hiren Mukherjee regretted Gandhi's lack of a clearly formulated social philosophy and economic ideology but paid tributes to his unique personality and argued that in order to account for the splendour of Gandhi's spirit Marxist thought would have to pay more attention to the individual and his uniqueness. He wrote: "What Gandhi has left as his legacy is not a set body of doctrines, consistent and closely argued, and eminently applicable to social phenomena. His life as a whole, rather than any of his specific teachings, remains, as Gandhi himself had said, his message to succeeding generations—a life of identification with the people, of ceaseless service for the common good, of courage and unobtrusive sacrifice. It was a life that showed a great personality, truly great in the stupendous strength that his links with the people gave him. No label need be placed on his thought but the expansive one of humanism, and while we shall no doubt study his career and examine his errors and paradoxes and waywardnesses, we shall cherish the best and finest of his qualities— simplicity and the quest for truth, gentleness and good cheer, equanimity in sorrow and danger, love and fellowship and unremitting labour—qualities without which the life that is yet to be, in the East or in the West, will wither before it is born. Such splendour of spirit might even require Marxist thought to pay more attention than has been possible so far to give to the question of the individual, his existence as an entity and resistance to external pressures, his uniqueness. Gandhi might conceivably have added to his greatness high qualities of intellect and a comprehensive insight into social reality which intellectual discernment alone could help him to achieve. But in that case, he would not have been the Gandhi that we have known —a grand man, unique and integrated, who spanned a whole epoch with power and with grace, but limited of understanding and unable to show India, except in beautiful flashes of stress on right conduct, the way ahead in an uncommonly complicated world."[85]

Namboodiripad in his book *The Mahatma and The Ism* (1959) also paid glowing tributes to Gandhi the man. He wrote: "Gandhiji, too, was great because the ideals and moral values to which he clung to the end of his life conformed to the requirements and desires of the millions of the Indian people. His teachings were for the nation, as a whole, a call of revolt. Particularly were they a call of revolt to the mass of the rural poor, the lowliest of the lowly in the villages, the 'Daridranarayans' as he called them. His conception of love, truth, justice, etc. were, in the context of the time, an inspiration for the mass of the rural poor to free themselves from the social, economic, and political bonds, which have tied them to imperialism and feudalism. The mass of the rural poor, therefore, looked up to him as a new messiah, their saviour and protector."[86]

But about Gandhi as a politician, Namboodiripad claimed that he was only the leader of the bourgeoisie and represented the bourgeois-democratic approach, and speaking about himself he wrote that he had made the "leap" from Gandhism to communism. Namboodiripad traces his transition from Gandhism to communism thus: "With the appearance of a left or radical tendency within the Gandhian School (the tendency represented by Pandit Jawaharlal Nehru), I became an ardent follower of the Nehru School. Later on, when this left trend within the Gandhian School went still more to the left leading to the formation of the Congress Socialist Party [whose founder-general secretary and foremost leader, Sri Jayaprakash Narayan, has now become one of the foremost leaders of what may be called the 'Gandhians after Gandhi'], I joined it. It was out of this leftist trend within the Gandhian School that I took the 'leap' from Gandhism to Marxism–Leninism. May I add that it was because respected colleagues like Sri Jayaprakash did not take this 'leap' that many of them took a swing back from a near–Marxist stand to Gandhism."[87]

While recognizing the moral greatness of Gandhi, Indian communists did not fail to criticize Gandhian ideas on class collaboration, the unity of labour and capital and trusteeship.

Writing in the *New Age* on 29 January 1956, E. M. S. Namboodiripad observed: "This passion for the unity of the entire nation proved, in practice, to be a force which retarded the further development of the democratic movement. For, one of the most important articles of faith which the Mahatma developed as part of his programme of building national unity was that the oppressed and exploited classes (the workers and peasants) are the brothers and partners of the classes which are oppressing and exploiting them.... It was this Gandhian conception of national unity that prevented the full unleashing of the revolutionary energies of the common people—an unleashing which he denounced as 'violence'. We communists, therefore, cannot forget that it is our duty even today to carry on a systematic struggle against all manifestations of this essential class basis of his philosophy and programme of action. At the same time, we cannot forget that Gandhi's was a national and democratic leadership."[88]

Though Indian communists came to recognize and emphasize Gandhi's role as the leader of the national movement as also his moral greatness, they continued to criticize Gandhism for the lack of a clear-cut economic ideology and for its adherence to nonviolence as a creed. The communists regarded that this adherence to the gospel of absolute nonviolence would only help the vested interests in maintaining the *status quo*. As early as 1923 M. N. Roy had said: "If India will not have freedom conquered by violent means, she will have to go without it."[89] Similarly Philip Spratt, an accused in the Meerut Conspiracy Case, had asserted: "It seems that we who are communists need not apologize, we need not be careful to disguise the brutal blood-thirsty side of our proposals. We say these things are inevitable. Modern society is based upon fierce brutality, and if we want to get rid of it, we have to use fierce brutality.... We shall not also disguise the fact that in the course of attainment of our aims and the establishment of communism, we shall have to indulge in brutal dictatorial methods. We shall have to indulge in civil wars in most countries."[90] Again in 1930 in the "Draft Platform of Action of the Communist Party of India" revolutionary armed insurrection or violence was advocated. It stated: "The Communist Party declares that the road to victory is not the method of individual terror but the struggle and the revolutionary armed insurrection of the widest possible masses of the working class, the peasantry, the poor of the towns and the Indian soldiers, around the banner and under the leadership of the Communist Party of India."

The communists never accepted the Gandhian gospel of non-violence. After India attained independence and set up parliamentary democracy the communists participated in the elections saying that it was not inevitable that armed violence would have to be resorted to for establishing socialism, but that if the ruling classes resorted to violence the communists would have no alternative but to resist likewise. They regarded the question as to whether the communists believed in violence or nonviolence as a poser of Gandhian ideology and not as a proper question to ask. The statement of policy adopted by the party at its All India Conference in 1951 stated that "the main question is not whether there is to be armed struggle or not, the main question is not whether to be nonviolent or not. It is the reactionary ruling classes who resort to force and violence against the people and who pose for us the question whether our creed is violence or nonviolence. Such a poser is a poser of Gandhian ideology, which in practice, misleads the masses and is a poser of which we must steer clear. Marxism and history have once for all decided the question for the Party and the people of every country in the world long ago. All action of the masses in defence of their interests to achieve their liberation is sacrosanct. History sanctions all that the people decide to do to clear the lumber-load of decadence and reaction in their path to progress and freedom."[91]

The communists had reservations about the Gandhian policy of *satyagraha* because in Gandhian thought *satyagraha* was linked up with the creed of nonviolence. But the Gandhian tradition of *satyagraha* had developed such strong roots in India that on many occasions when the communists started resistance movements some kind of *satyagraha* movement developed. This tendency could not be wholeheartedly welcomed by the communists. In 1952 S. A. Dange said: "Importation of *satyagraha* forms in strike struggles should not be encouraged, though today in some cases, the worker and the middle-class employees under the influence of past traditions easily take to such suggestions. If in certain circumstances such forms can help to initiate mass mobilization, we should not hesitate to use them but with caution and care."[92] Similarly in 1954 Ajoy Ghosh wrote: "In Calcutta, different left parties launched a *satyagraha* for food, but we kept out of the whole struggle on the ground that *satyagraha* is a Gandhian form of struggle, and since we could not go in for general strike, we stayed away from it. This was a mistake and was corrected. Subsequently at some places the deviation developed of looking upon *satyagraha* as the main form of struggle. The Party Congress made it clear that *satyagraha* is a form of struggle which disrupts mass participation and brings only some pressure upon the enemy. In fact, it is a counterpart of terrorism relying on the same principle of heroes leading passive masses and reducing the people to the role of spectators. While in some backward areas *satyagrahas* may become necessary at the first stage it should not be allowed to become a substitute for mass action."[93]

In spite of the revaluation of Gandhi by communists and their recognition of the moral greatness of Gandhi and of his political role as the leader of the national liberation movement, the communists always regarded Gandhi's social and economic ideology as retrograde and antiquated. They regarded Gandhism as the ideological reflex of the ruined but rising rich peasant. The communists had nothing but scorn for Gandhi's dream of reviving the ancient Indian village community. "One has here," they asserted, "the coming to the surface of that 'peculiar melancholy of the Hindu' about which Marx wrote so poignantly. The prayer meeting, the self-sufficient ashrams, the *nai talim* with its craft-centred outlook, even the message of nonviolent non-cooperation expressed the peasant's anguish and aspiration—the heart of a heartless world, the spirit of a spiritless situation, the opium of the peasantry."[94]

The communists complained that Gandhi was opposed to the independent action of the peasants. Gandhi's fasts, his assumption of dictatorial powers during non-cooperation movements and the rigorous conditions he laid down for a *satyagrahi* showed, they asserted, that Gandhi believed in élitist action and not in any mass movement directed against feudalism or landlordism.[95] The communists also complained that Gandhi steadfastly and consistently opposed any policy as a result of which the leadership of the national movement could be taken over by the working class.

The communists did not participate in the non-cooperation movements against the British which Gandhi launched from time to time. But after independence and, in retrospect, the communists have recognized that Gandhi was the foremost anti-imperialist leader that India produced and that he, more than any other individual, was responsible for transforming the Congress into a mass party. In an article in *The Mahatma*: A *Marxist Symposium* published in 1969 it was stated: "There is no doubt that he [Gandhi] was the foremost anti-imperialist leader produced by our mass struggle for freedom. It was he who accomplished the mass turn of the peasantry to the national movement and who built the Congress into the anti-imperialist, organized front extending into every village and town. It was he who strove for Hindu–Muslim unity, for the realization of Indian unity based on the recognition of its diversity. It was he who brought *Daridranarayan*, the harijan, to the centre of the national conscience."[96]

The communists generally, however, found Gandhi's creed of nonviolence and his emphasis on the need of bringing about political and economic changes in a purely peaceful manner as wholly unacceptable. But since the 1957 Moscow conference of 12 Communist and Workers' Parties of socialist countries where it was declared that, in the changed world circumstances, war was not fatalistically inevitable and, further, that peaceful transition to socialism was possible, communists in India belonging to the CPI have shown less antipathy to theories, such as those of Gandhi, that large-scale socio-economic changes could be affected through peaceful means. But the doctrine of peaceful transition to socialism was denounced first by the Chinese communists and later by those Indian communists who belong to the CPI(M). The evaluation of Gandhi and of his philosophy of peaceful change by the CPI(M), who did not accept the doctrine of peaceful transition to socialism adumbrated at the Moscow Conference, is less sympathetic than that of the CPI. But among the present-day Indian communists the staunchest critics of Gandhi are the members of the CPI(ML), or the Naxalites, who broke away from the CPI(M) in 1967. The Naxalites do not believe either in peaceful change or in parliamentarianism. For them, revolutionary transformation of society can be effected only through violence, and the name of Gandhi is anathema.

Since April 1970 bands of Naxalite young men have indiscriminately set fire to Gandhi's portraits and to books by or on Gandhi. Gandhi, the apostle of nonviolence, gave his life at the hands of an assassin, and even after his death violence is used against his portraits and books in an attempt that the philosophy of nonviolence may be replaced by the doctrine that power grows only out of the barrel of a gun.

NOTES AND REFERENCES

1. Pyarelal, *Mahatma Gandhi : The Last Phase*, Vol. II, Chapter 6, p. 133.
2. Ibid.
3. D. G. Tendulkar, *Mahatma*, 1963, Vol. VIII, p. 37.
4. Ibid.
5. M. K. Gandhi, *An Autobiography*, Ahmedabad, 1945, p. 238.
6. *Harijan*, 29 June 1923.
7. D. G. Tendulkar, *Mahatma : The Life of Mohandas Karamchand Gandhi*, Vol. IV, p. 15.
8. *Young India*, 26 November 1921.
9. *Harijan*, 1 February 1942.
10. *Young India*, 5 December 1929.
11. *M. N. Roy's Memoirs*, 1964, p. 543.
12. *Harijan*, 21 September 1934.
13. *Young India*, 17 March 1927.
14. *Harijan*, 25 August 1940.
15. *Harijan*, 8 March 1942.
16. *Harijan*, 13 April 1938.
17. M. K. Gandhi, *An Autobiography*, p. 362.
18. *Young India*, 17 March 1927.
19. *Harijan*, 25 April 1940.
20. Nirmal Bose, *Studies in Gandhism*, p. 43.
21. See M. R. Masani, *Congress Misrule and the Swatantra Alternative*, Bombay, 1966.
22. *Harijan*, 2 August 1942.
23. See Vinoba Bhave's "Introduction" to the book by K. G. Mashruwala, *Gandhi and Marx*, p. 15.
24. *Mahatma Gandhi : His Life, Writings, and Speeches*, Madras, 1918, p. 227.
25. Ibid., pp. 223-24.
26. Ibid., pp. 219, 223.
27. D. G. Tendulkar, *Mahatma*, 1960, Vol. I, p. 194.
28. Ibid., pp. 195-96.
29. M. K. Gandhi, *Hind Swaraj*, Madras, 1921, pp. 48-50, 226, and

Mahatma Gandhi's Writings and Speeches, Madras, 1918, p. 95.

30. It was after reading Ruskin's *Unto This Last* that Gandhi was convinced that the life of the tiller of the soil and the handicraftsman was the life worth living. (*An Autobiography or the Story of My Experiments with Truth,* Ahmedabad, 1945, p. 238). Gandhi wrote that the reading of *Unto This Last* brought about an instantaneous and practical transformation of his life.

31. M. K. Gandhi, *Hind Swaraj,* Madras, 1921, p. 85.

32. Ibid., p. 49.

33. *Mahatma Gandhi : His Life, Writings and Speeches,* Madras, 1918, pp. 95, 222-23.

34. M. K. Gandhi, *Hind Swaraj,* Madras, 1921, pp. 48-49, 87-89.

35. See also D. G. Tendulkar, *Mahatma,* 1960, Vol. II, p. 109.

36. K. G. Mashruwala, *Gandhi and Marx,* p. 87.

37. *Young India,* 15 November 1928.

38. *Harijan,* 28 July 1940.

39. Louis Fisher, *Mahatma Gandhi : His Life and Message for the World,* p. 88.

40. Discussion with Louis Fisher in July 1946, recorded by Pyarelal, in K. G. Mashruwala, *Gandhi and Marx,* Ahmedabad, 1951, Appendix II, p. 109.

41. *Young India,* 21 May 1925.

42. *Young India,* 3 September 1925.

43. *Harijan,* 27 January 1940.

44. Ibid.

45. *Harijan,* 6 October 1946.

46. Vinoba Bhave, "Communism and Sarvodaya," in *Sarvodaya,* May 1957.

47. Jayaprakash Narayan, "Organic Democracy," in *Studies in Indian Democracy,* ed. S. P. Aiyar and R. Srinivasan, 1965, pp. 337-40.

48. *Young India,* 17 April 1924.

49. Ibid.

50. Jayaprakash Narayan, *Socialism, Sarvodaya and Democracy,* ed. Bimla Prasad, 1964.

51. Jayaprakash Narayan, "Organic Democracy," in *Studies in Indian Democracy,* ed. S. P. Aiyar and R. Srinivasan, 1965, p. 337.

52. Ibid., p. 339.

53. Jawaharlal Nehru, *Autobiography,* London, 1955, p. 73.

54. Jawaharlal Nehru, *The Discovery of India,* London, 1956, p. 536.

55. Ibid., p. 537.

56. *Congress Presidential Addresses,* Second Series, 1911-34, p. 896.

57. *The Indian Annual Register,* 1942, Vol. I, pp. 282-83.

58. Krishna Kripalani, *Gandhi, Tagore and Nehru,* p. 73.

59. Hugh Toye, *The Springing Tiger,* London, 1959, p. 48.

60. M. N. Roy, *India In Transition,* 1922, p. 205.

61. M. N. Roy and Ellen Roy, *One Year of Non-Cooperation,* 1923, p. 45.

62. Ibid., pp. 48-50.
63. R. P. Dutt, *Modern India*, 1927, p. 72.
64. Ibid., p. 80.
65. *Young India*, 11 December 1924.
66. *Young India*, 15 November 1928.
67. S. G. Sardesai, "Gandhi and the cpi" in *The Mahatma: A Marxist Symposium*, 1969, p. 30.
68. Ibid., p. 31.
69. Ibid., p. 32.
70. Ibid., p. 31.
71. *Young India*, 26 March 1931.
72. *Young India*, 26 November 1931.
73. Valia, "The Constitution, for the Enslavement of the Indian People and the Policy of the Indian Bourgeoisie," in *Communist International*, X, 15 June 1933, pp. 388-90.
74. R. Palme Dutt, "India," *Labour Monthly*, XIII, May 1931, p. 264.
75. M. K. Gandhi, *My Socialism*, p. 9.
76. P. C. Joshi, *The Indian Communist Party: Its Policy and Work in the War of Liberation*, p. 26.
77. R. P. Dutt, "India—What Must Be Done," in *Labour Monthly*, XXIV, September 1942, p. 264.
78. R. P. Dutt, "Gandhi—The Last Phase," in *Labour Monthly*, XXX, March 1948, p. 84.
79. A. M. Dyakov, *Crisis of the Colonial System*, Bombay, 1951, p. 32.
80. S. M. Vakar, "The Class Essence of Gandhism," in *Communist*, January 1950, p. 15.
81. Ibid., p. 7.
82. E. M. S. Namboodiripad, "August 15: Gandhism's Triumph or Defeat?" in *New Age*, June 1955, pp. 21-22.
83. E. Zhukov, "Gandhi's Role in History," in *New Times*, 2 February 1956, pp. 15-16.
84. Overstreet and Windmiller, *Communism in India*, Bombay, 1960, p. 520.
85. Hiren Mukherjee, *Gandhiji: A Study*, 2nd ed., 1960, pp. 219-20.
86. E. M. S. Namboodiripad, *The Mahatma and the Ism*, 2nd ed., September 1959, "Introduction," p. xi.
87. Ibid., p. vii.
88. E. M. S. Namboodiripad, "Mahatma Gandhi," in *New Age*, 29 January 1956, p. 2.
89. M. N. Roy, *The Aftermath of Non-Cooperation*, London, 1926, p. 118.
90. *Judgment Delivered by R. L. Yorke in the Meerut Communist Conspiracy Case*, Simla, 1932-33, p. 225.
91. *Statement of Policy Adopted by the All India Conference of the Communist Party of India*, October 1951, pp. 7-8.
92. S. A. Dange, *On the Indian Trade Union Movement*, Bombay, Communist Party of India, 1952, p. 56.

93. Ajoy Ghosh, *On the Work of Third Congress of the Communist Party of India*, 1954, pp. 16-17.
94. Mohit Sen, "Gandhism After Freedom," in *The Mahatma : A Marxist Symposium*, 1969, p. 56.
95. Ibid., p. 57.
96. Ibid.

CHAPTER FOUR

M. N. Roy and Communism

I. ROY AS A COMMUNIST REVOLUTIONARY

One of the first Indian communists was Manabendra Nath Roy (1887–1954). M. N. Roy passed through three phases. In the first phase, which lasted up to 1919, Roy was a national revolutionary engaged in smuggling arms and money for the terrorist or revolutionary movement in Bengal. In the second phase, Roy was a Marxist engaged in active communist movement first in Mexico and then in Russia, China, and India. In the last and final phase, Roy emerged as a Radical Humanist who had disowned Marxism in favour of some kind of liberal humanism.

Roy was a revolutionary even while a student. As a student he was attracted to the revolutionary Yugantar Group. In 1910 Roy was sentenced to imprisonment in connection with the Howrah Conspiracy Case, and was again arrested in 1915 in connection with his alleged complicity in a political dacoity in Calcutta.

In 1915 Roy slipped out of India to the Dutch Indies. He made contacts in Java with German agents for bringing arms for an insurrection in India. This plot having failed, Roy proceeded to the United States of America, and from there he went to Mexico in 1919 where he settled under the name of Manabendra Nath Roy, his previous name being Narendranath Bhattacharya.

In Mexico Roy was converted to Marxism. In Mexico too Roy came in close contact with Michael Borodin, the Russian communist. Later, Roy was invited to Russia to attend the Second Congress of Comintern. He had gone to Mexico as a nationalist, and left Mexico for Russia as a confirmed Marxist. "I left the land of my rebirth [Mexico]," wrote Roy in his *Memoirs*, "as an intellectually free man, though with a new

faith. I no longer believed in political freedom without the
content of economic liberation and social justice. I had also
realized that the intellectual freedom from the bondage of all
tradition and authority was the condition for any effective struggle for social emancipation."[1]

At the Second Congress of the Comintern in Russia in 1920
Roy, the erstwhile extremist and militant nationalist, advocated
that the communists in colonial and semi-colonial countries
should pursue a militant uncompromising policy. Whereas Lenin
considered that in the early stages of the national liberation
movement in colonial and semi-colonial countries, the communists should work in cooperation, and not in conflict, with
the national bourgeoisie who sought freedom, M. N. Roy was
distrustful of the role of the national bourgeoisie altogether.
Further, as to the role of Gandhi in the Indian national movement, Roy and Lenin had differences. Lenin considered that
Gandhi was playing a progressive role in the conditions prevailing in India, but Roy regarded Gandhi as a purely mediaevalist
reactionary. This approach of Roy, to some extent, coloured
the thinking of the Indian communists at the early stages, though
later the Indian communists vigorously denounced Roy for his
"left-sectarian" attitude.[2]

In India Roy had been an extremist and had denounced the
politics of the moderates who represented the Indian national
bourgeoisie. It was natural that Roy would not favour a policy
which would make the Indian moderates and liberals, who were
seeking concessions for the national bourgeoisie from the British
imperialists, as the persons with whom the communists should
collaborate for taking the Indian people forward.

Further, Roy had no contact with the Indian moderates and
liberals. If the Comintern thought that the Indian moderates and
liberals were playing a progressive role and should be supported,
then Virendranath Chattopadhyaya, the leader of the Indian
revolutionaries in Berlin, rather than Roy, would have been a
more appropriate choice for the Comintern as the person through
whom the Comintern could establish contacts with the Indian
nationalist movement. Temperamentally and by conviction Roy
wanted the Comintern to pursue an extremist uncompromising
policy and, again, it is only if such a policy was pursued that
Roy, and not Chattopadhyaya, could be the natural choice of

the Comintern for organizing and directing such a policy.

The Supplementary Thesis that Roy produced at the Second Congress was, at the instance of Lenin, adopted along with the more moderate thesis that Lenin himself had produced. But it does not appear that after the Second Congress Lenin or anyone else paid any heed to Roy's thesis. The Comintern, at that time, wanted the communists to work in cooperation and not in opposition to the national bourgeoisie who were seeking national freedom.

Roy was chosen by the Comintern to organize the communist movement in India. Roy got in touch with those Indian revolutionaries who had come to Tashkent and had enrolled themselves in the communist university of Toilers of the East which had been established in Moscow in April 1921. Roy also got in touch with S. A. Dange and other radicals in India.

Roy prepared a report on the conditions obtaining in India and, at Lenin's suggestion, converted the report into a book. The book was written in collaboration with Abani Mukherjee and published as *India in Transition* in 1922. In this book Roy criticized the Indian moderates who believed in the British sense of justice and characterized them as the instruments of the Indian bourgeoisie. So far as the extremists were concerned, Roy ridiculed them because of their induction of religion into politics and this Roy characterized as mediaevalism and revivalism. Roy claimed that the only solution for India lay in the adoption of Marxist philosophy and ideology. Roy referred to the strikes at Bombay in the 1890's, the strikes of railway workers in 1906, and the strikes in the Calcutta jute mills in 1907, and observed that in India the struggle for national freedom was going on side by side with a raging class struggle.

In *India in Transition* Roy also explained that the British imperialists had started making concessions to the Indian bourgeoisie. The Indian bourgeoisie, therefore, were seeking to collaborate with the British, but they recognized at the same time that they would not be able to extort political and economic concessions from the British, if by an unconditional collaboration with the British they lost the support of the Indian people altogether. Roy was greatly distrustful of the role of the national bourgeoisie led by Gandhi, and wrote: "The impending wane of Gandhism signifies the collapse of the reactionary forces and their total elimination from the political movement."[3]

In those days Berlin was the centre of Indian revolutionaries. It was natural, therefore, that Roy, who sought to organize the Indian revolutionaries and to lead them towards communism, would shift his headquarters to Berlin. This he did in 1922. In Berlin Roy started publication of an English periodical, *The Vanguard of Indian Independence*, which later came to be known as the *Advance Guard*, and thereafter as the *Vanguard*. With the assistance of Indian seamen Roy sent his periodical to India, and *Amrita Bazar Patrika* of Calcutta was one of the newspapers which was, to some extent, influenced by the *Vanguard*.

Towards the end of 1922 Roy published another book, *India's Problem and Its Solution*. In this book he referred to the proceedings of the Ahmedabad Congress of 1921 and criticized Congress policies as a betrayal by the bourgeois leadership of the revolutionary forces. So far as Gandhi was concerned, Roy again attacked his mediaevalism and conservatism. Roy recognized that the nonviolent movement, advocated by Gandhi in place of the constitutional agitation of the moderate Congressmen, had harnessed the spontaneous mass discontent in support of the Congress and had made Gandhi the leader of the country almost overnight. Roy complained, however, that the religious ideology preached by Gandhi appealed really to the mediaeval mentality of the masses and, thereby, effectively discouraged any revolutionary mass action. Writing in retrospect in his *Memoirs*, Roy observed: "The quintessence of the situation, as I analysed and understood it, was a potentially revolutionary movement restrained by a reactionary ideology."[4]

According to Roy the non-cooperation movement of 1922 was inspired by the ideology of the lower middle class and did not contain any revolutionary programme. He called for mass strikes and militant action by the masses in place of the Gandhian policy of non-cooperation. The masses were to be the conscious vanguard of the revolution pledged absolutely to the acceptance of the thesis of class struggle. Roy complained that Congress had failed to develop the workers and peasants because big capitalists financially supported the Congress. The landlords welcomed Gandhi's religious ideology and the doctrine of trusteeship, and, similarly, the capitalists welcomed Gandhi's theory that the workers "should not look upon their employers as exploiters, but trust them as their elder brothers."[5]

In August 1922 Roy requested the Communist Party of Great Britain to send two Europeans to Calcutta to organize the communist movement there. Roy, who was receiving substantial funds from Comintern, agreed to provide for the expenses of these communist emissaries to India. The Communist Party of Great Britain could supply only one emissary, Charles Ashleigh, a communist who had served a term of imprisonment in the United States. But the British authorities came to know of Ashleigh's mission and immediately on his arrival at Bombay on 19 September 1922, Ashleigh was taken into custody and later deported to Britain.

Throughout 1922, in the periodical published from Berlin, Roy continued to write about the path that the Indian revolutionaries should follow in order to establish communism. Roy wanted those who had been imbued with the communist ideology to form an opposition bloc inside the Indian National Congress. This bloc was to carry on an intensive propaganda to win allies for the communist movement. Its aim was to be the eventual capture of the Congress organization, which lacked a clear-cut, positive economic ideology.

In a letter written on 2 November 1922 to S. A. Dange, which was disclosed in the Cawnpore Conspiracy Case, Roy suggested the development of a large mass party comprising all revolutionary elements, but this party would not openly proclaim itself as a Communist Party, and would be guided by an illegal Communist Party composed of true communists. This large mass party would function as an opposition bloc inside the Indian National Congress. The opposition bloc would seek to radicalize the Congress organization, to eventually capture its leadership.

Among those within the Congress who, Roy believed, would be able to give a more radical orientation to Congress policies were C. R. Das, Sampurnanand, and Singaravelu Chettiar. C. R. Das in some of his speeches had declared himself in favour of Swaraj for the masses. On 1 November 1922 Das had said: "The Liberals fight shy of revolution. What is revolution but a part of that growth the totality of which we call evolution? . . . Revolution means complete change and we want complete change. I am sorry most of our non-cooperators are still enamoured of parliamentary government. I do not want the sort of Swaraj which will be for the middle class alone.... I want Swaraj for the masses, not for the classes. I don't care for the bourgeoisie. How few are they?"[6]

Roy expected that C. R. Das, who presided over the 1922 Congress session at Gaya, would give a radical orientation to Congress policies. A message sent by the Comintern to this Gaya session declared: "British rule in India was established by force and is maintained by force; therefore it can and will be overthrown only by a violent revolution. We are not in favour of resorting to violence if it can be helped, but for self-defence, the people of India must adopt violent means, without which the foreign domination based upon violence cannot be ended. The economic, social, and cultural progress of the Indian people demands the complete separation of India from imperialist Britain. To realize this separation is the goal of revolutionary nationalism. This goal, however, cannot be attained by negotiation nor by peaceful means."[7]

Whereas the Comintern declared that British rule could not be overthrown except through violent revolution, Gandhi, who was then the leader of the Congress, believed in pursuing a policy of nonviolent non-cooperation for terminating British rule in India. Roy looked upon Gandhi's policy of nonviolence with utter abhorrence. In December 1922 he declared: "We have repeatedly said and still say that a premature resort to violent tactics may be playing into the hands of the enemy. But it is altogether erroneous to think that there can be such a thing as a nonviolent revolution, no matter how peculiar and abnormal the situation in India may be. The cult of nonviolence is inseparable from an anti-revolutionary spirit. Those who do not want a revolution in India can pin their hope on nonviolent methods. Strictly nonviolent methods are hardly distinguishable from constitutional agitation, and no people on the face of the earth has ever made a revolution by constitutional methods."[8]

In 1922 Gandhi called off the non-cooperation movement on account of the eruption of violence at Chauri Chaura. Roy regarded this as a gross betrayal of the revolutionary movement. He complained that a national uprising, which the government had feared, was checked and thrown into rout by the good offices of Gandhi himself. Deriding the "incorrigible pacifism" of Gandhi, Roy said: "What government repression in all its varied forms had failed to accomplish, the agonized appeal of the Mahatma was able to effectuate.... That which arrests, tortures, floggings, imprisonments, massacres, fines, and police-zoolums could not quell—the blind struggles of a starving nation to save itself from utter annihilation—Mr Gandhi by the simple magic of love and nonviolence, reduced to impotence and inactivity. ... The Congress had committed suicide by repudiating the revolutionary action of its own followers. A powerful revolutionary movement had been sacrificed on the altar of Gandhism."[9]

C. R. Das, on whom Roy had pinned his hopes for giving a radical orientation to Congress policies, did not, however, accept Roy's views on the justification and inevitability of violent revolution. Not only did C. R. Das reject the path of violent revolution; in his presidential address at the 1922 Gaya Congress, he even declared that he believed in nonviolence on principle. "I cannot refuse," he said, "to acknowledge that there is a body of Indian opinion within the country as well as outside according to which nonviolence is an ideal abstraction incapable of realization and that the only way in which *Swaraj* can ever be attained is by the application of force and violence. I do not for a moment question the courage, sacrifice, and patriotism of those who hold this view. I know that some of them have suffered for the cause which they believe to be true. But may I be permitted to point out that apart from any question of principle, history has proved over and over again the utter futility of revolutions brought about by force and violence. I am one of those who hold to nonviolence on principle."[10]

The proceedings of the Gaya Congress were a disappointment for Roy. He felt that, in the circumstances, the organization of a party of the workers and peasants of India was indispensable, and that unless such a party was organized the Indian National Congress could not be radicalized. Preparations were set afoot in 1923 for organizing a Workers' and Peasants' Party. In a message sent by the Executive Committee of the Communist International to the projected Workers' and Peasants' Party, it was stated: "It is clear that the workers and peasants on whose shoulders fall the greatest part of the burden of imperialist exploitation, can no longer remain an adjunct to bourgeois nationalism to act or keep quiet at its bidding ... the working class must come forward as an independent political force and take up the leadership."[11]

Though Roy continued to be critical of Gandhi, after the first civil disobedience movement of 1922 and after seeing the tremendous hold that Gandhi had on the Indian masses and the way he had energized them, Roy modified his approach to Gandhi to a certain extent. In *One Year of Non-cooperation,* published in 1923, Roy acknowledged the role that Gandhi had played in rousing the masses. Roy also paid glowing tributes to the personality of Gandhi and compared him with St Thomas Aquinas, Savanorala, and St Francis of Assissi. Yet Roy continued to criticize Gandhi saying that his economics was antiquated and that he was mixing religion with politics. Roy described Gandhi's economics of *Charka* as being reactionary, and charged that Gandhi lacked a clear-cut economic ideology. Moreover, Gandhi's attempts to unite the landlords and the capitalists on the one hand and the workers and peasants on the other in a nationalist movement did not appeal to Roy. Roy also quarrelled with Gandhi's political methods. Roy condemned Gandhi's interviews and negotiations with the Viceroy and asserted that this showed that Gandhi was not a believer in revolution but in "weak and watery reformism."[12]

According to Roy's over-optimistic assessment, in the twenties of this century revolutionary forces were increasingly gaining ground in India. Even as early as 1924 Roy had written: "The masses are very restive. The peasantry is a veritable inflammable material, while the city proletariat demonstrates its revolutionary zeal whenever there is an opportunity. The process of uniting all these revolutionary elements into an anti-imperialist army is going on steadily.... The people will see that the reformist programme of the bourgeoisie does not lead anywhere. The centre of gravity of the nationalist movement will be shifted back to its proper place—namely, mass action. As soon as the rank and file of the nationalist forces are freed from the reformist leadership of the bourgeoisie, they will begin to follow the standard of revolution."[13]

At the Fifth Congress of the Comintern convened on 17 June 1924 a resolution was passed advocating the establishment of direct contact between the Comintern and the Indian National Congress. This Roy opposed. He claimed that such a resolution would run counter to the thesis passed at the Second Congress of the Comintern. Roy argued that instead of establishing direct contact with the Indian National Congress, the Comintern should exclusively encourage the formation of a communist movement in India. Roy told the Comintern delegates: "I must first point out that in the resolution on the report of the Executive, there is a clause which does not correspond with the theses passed in the Second Congress. My amendment was rejected on the ground that it was not in accord with these same theses, but I want to prove that it is the resolution which does not correspond with the theses, and which is totally mistaken when considered in the light of the events that have taken place since the Second Congress. The resolution says that in order to win over the people of colonial and semi-colonial countries, there must be a 'further direct development of the direct contact of the Executive with the national movements for emancipation'. It is true that we must always have a connection with these national movements, but it seems to have been overlooked that these connections have not always been successful."[14]

In 1924 an attempt was made to form a legal Communist party in India by Satya Bhakta. Maulana Hazrat Mohani, a well-known Congressman and president of Muslim League, was requested to act as Chairman of the Reception Committee of the Conference convened for forming this new party. It was originally intended that the conference would be held at the *pandal* set up for the annual session of the Congress. But permission to hold such a meeting in the Congress *pandal* was refused and a separate location for the meeting had to be found. Maulana Hazrat Mohani emphasized that the new party was not connected with the Communist International and was purely an Indian organization.[15] Singaravelu Chettiar was still more emphatic. He said: "Indian Communism is not Bolshevism, for Bolshevism is a form of communism which the Russians have adopted in their country. We are not Russians. Bolsheviks and Bolshevism may not be needed in India. . . . We are one with the world communists but not with Bolsheviks."[16] Here one can trace the beginnings of modern polycentrism in the international communist movement.

The declaration that the new party would be an Indian party and would have no link with the Communist International was wholly unacceptable to M. N. Roy. Roy could not imagine a communist movement in India growing up which had disassociated itself from the world communist movement. He wrote: "Nothing can be more non-communistic than to say that the Indian working class will play its historic role in the struggle for national freedom and work out its own salvation independently of the international proletarian movement. Those who maintain and propagate this point of view are far from being communists, they are veritable enemies of the Indian working class."[17]

Since 1924 the Communist Party of Great Britain began to take a leading part in organizing the communist movement in India. The Communist Party of Great Britain thus posed a challenge to Roy's leadership of the Indian communist movement. Roy, however, continued to send, through secret channels, literature and money from Berlin to develop the communist movement in India and to retain his control over it.

In 1926 Roy wrote *The Aftermath of Non-Cooperation* in which he analysed the reasons for the failure of the non-cooperation movement. Roy attributed such failure to the fact that the Indian bourgeoisie was "too afraid, too hesitating to follow a revolutionary channel." Roy argued that due to the partial relaxation of the old British policy of holding India in industrial backwardness, and due to the grant of certain political and economic concessions by the British imperialists to the Indian bourgeoisie, a section of the Indian bourgeoisie had been won over by the British imperialists and had become their allies.[18] In these circumstances the proletariat alone could conduct an uncompromising struggle against imperialism. The proletariat, however, were asked to wage this struggle in "a close fighting alliance with the forces of national revolution."[19]

In *The Future of Indian Politics* (1926), Roy advocated the organization of a broad-based People's Party which would stand for a programme of revolutionary nationalism and would organize all exploited sections of Indian society, namely, the proletariat, the peasantry, and the petty bourgeois intellectual.[20] Roy considered that the petty bourgeois intellectuals, who were generally regarded as vacillating allies in communist theory, had an important part to play in the organization and leadership of the People's Party pledged to a programme of revolutionary nationalism. The big bourgeoisie, Roy observed, had been practically eliminated from the struggle for national liberation, so reliance had to be placed on the petty bourgeoisie, namely, the small traders, artisans, employees, students, and petty intellectuals.[21]

Roy wanted the class struggle to be intensified along with the development of the national liberation movement. Henceforth the fight for national freedom in India, wrote Roy, "becomes a class-struggle approximating to the final stage."[22] This class struggle was to be intensified not only by the Communist Party, which will contain only the dedicated communists, but also by the more broad-based People's Party which will contain the "democratic allies" of the proletariat. "The people's fight for freedom," wrote Roy, "must be led by the party of the people —a party organization which will be broad enough for all the forces of national revolution. The proletariat will be in it, but it will not be a proletarian party, nominally or essentially. In this party the proletariat will stand side by side with the petty bourgeois and peasant masses, as the most advanced democratic class."[23]

Roy recognized that Indian politics would for some time be dominated by students, small traders, and petty intellectuals and others, but then Roy claimed that the petty intellectuals had been thoroughly proletarianized. Roy wanted the Indian revolutionaries to transform these classes into proper instruments of a national revolution. In *The Future of Indian Politics* Roy condemned the Swarajya Party which was led by C. R. Das and Motilal Nehru, and characterized the party as a defender of capitalism and landlordism.[24] According to Roy, the Swarajya Party "glorified the land-owning classes as the pillars of Indian society and culture."[25] Roy believed in the development of a democratic party consisting of peasants, workers, and the petty bourgeoisie which will have a radical programme of agrarian reforms and a political programme of complete independence.[26]

At about the time when *The Future of Indian Politics* was published, R. Palme Dutt wrote his book *Modern India* which was first published in India in 1926 and then in Great Britain in 1927. "The fight for national liberation," Dutt wrote, "is a fight of many social strata—of workers, of peasants, of the lower middle class, of the intelligentsia and even of a section of the bourgeoisie."[27] Dutt did not call for the formation of a new

People's Party outside the Congress as Roy had done in *The Future of Indian Politics.* Dutt believed that the left nationalistic forces could find some organization and expression within the Congress and Swarajya Party.[28]

In the preface to the English edition of *Modern India*, Dutt, however, assailed the Indian bourgeoisie and spoke of the formation of a new national movement in India. "The Indian bourgeoisie," wrote Dutt in the Preface, "is today a counter-revolutionary force. They fear the social revolution that would follow on national independence more than they desire independence; and therefore they have made their terms with the imperialists and are all supporters of the Empire." Accordingly, a new national movement, based on the workers and peasants and having a radical political and social programme, alone could bring new life to the nation.[29]

Since the writing of *Modern India*, Dutt, a leading member of the British Communist Party, played an important part in guiding the communist movement in India. In fact, British communists played a significant role in the development of the communist movement in India during the early years. In April 1926 the Red International Labour Union sent George Allison— a coal miner and a member of the British Communist Party—to India, to organize the trade union movement. Allison came to India under a forged passport in the name of Donald Campbell. But he was arrested by the police in Calcutta in January 1927 and was later deported.

A month before Allison's arrest, the Communist Party of Great Britain had sent another emissary, Philip Spratt, to organize the communist movement in India. "It was not as an expert that I was sent to India," Spratt later recorded in his memoirs. "I was chosen because I was unknown to the police and my job was to be that of a messenger and reporter."[30] Spratt came to India to organize a Workers' and Peasants' Party and in this connection he contacted Muzaffar Ahmed, S. V. Ghate, and other Indian communists.

On 31 May 1927 a conference of the Indian communists was held in Bombay. This was attended by S. A. Dange, Muzaffar Ahmed, S. V. Ghate, and other Indian communists. This conference passed a resolution stating that the Communist Party of India looked up to the Communist Parties of the world and to the Communist International for guidance. Some time prior to this conference Dange had, however, declared that he was an Indian communist and not a Bolshevik. Roy found the idea of an Indian version of communism utterly repugnant. In July 1927 he wrote in *Masses of India*: "A communist movement in a country must be a national section of the international communist movement, otherwise it cannot be communist and may degenerate into anything. . . . It is absurd to seek for a special Indian variety of communism. An Indian who calls himself a communist must be a communist like the others in the rest of the world."[31]

Spratt was later joined by Benjamin F. Bradley, a member of the British Communist Party. During the greater part of 1927, when Spratt and Bradley were organizing the communist movement in India, Roy was in China. Roy's absence from Europe helped the British communists to gain ascendancy over the Indian communist movement, and during this time Spratt and Bradley became its virtual leaders.

Since 1925 Roy's rivals in Europe had been planning to hold an Oriental Conference. This conference, later called the Congress of Oppressed Nationalities, was eventually held in 1927. Roy never welcomed the holding of such a conference, but the Comintern did. Jawaharlal Nehru attended this conference. In his *Autobiography* Nehru recorded that towards the end of 1926 when he was in Berlin, he learnt of this forthcoming Congress of Oppressed Nationalities at Brussels, and he suggested that the Indian National Congress should take official part in the Brussels Congress. This suggestion was accepted and Nehru was appointed the Indian Congress representative to this conference.[32]

The holding of the Congress of Oppressed Nationalities in Brussels in 1927, which was dominated by Roy's rivals, undermined Roy's position in Europe. Furthermore, in 1927 the *de facto* leadership of the Indian communist movement had also passed into the hands of British communists. Roy's position in Russia was further undermined when Soumyendranath Tagore, a leader of the Bengal Workers' and Peasants' Party, arrived at Moscow in June 1927 with a long bill of indictment against Roy. Tagore met Piatnitsky, the General Secretary of the Central Committee of the Comintern. Piatnitsky was under the impression that there were hundreds of communists in India, but Tagore told him that the number of communists in India did not exceed a dozen. "Piatnitsky," records Tagore, "was quite taken aback. He said that it seemed unbelievable, as Roy had reported the existence of hundreds of communists in India." The Comintern had given large sums to Roy for financing the communist movement in India. Tagore complained to Piatnitsky "that hardly any money had been received in India and the growth of the communist movement was tremendously handicapped due to the lack of money and literature."[33] Tagore charged that Roy had misutilized the funds provided to him by the Comintern, and that as a result the growth of the communist movement in India had been seriously impeded.

At the time of Tagore's visit to Moscow, Roy was in China, where his mission also ended in failure. The Chinese communists had, on the instructions of the Comintern, sought to work in cooperation with the Kuomintang, but eventually the Kuomintang and Chiang Kai-shek turned against the Chinese communists and gave them a shattering blow. Roy had always distrusted the national bourgeoisie and had urged that a fetish should not be made of alliance with the Kuomintang. As the representative of the Comintern in China, Roy had, however, sought to implement, against his own inclination, the Comintern policy of cooperation with the Kuomintang, but when the Kuomintang turned against the Chinese communists, Roy had to bear responsibility for the failure of Comintern policy in China.

The seventh plenum of the Executive Committee of Comintern held at Moscow between November and December 1926, had recommended, notwithstanding Roy's opposition, the continuance of the policy of cooperation with the Kuomintang. It had stated: "The point of view that the Communist Party must leave the Kuomintang is incorrect. The whole process of the development of the Chinese revolution, its character and perspectives demand that the communists must stay in the Kuomintang and intensify their work in it."[34]

On Roy's return to Berlin after the failure of his China mission, there appeared in the *Masses of India* an article, apparently written by Roy, on "The Lesson of the Chinese Revolution." It stated: "The lessons of these revolutionary and counter-revolutionary events in China are that the nationalist bourgeoisie in the colonial and semi-colonial countries are essentially counter-revolutionary; that the national revolution to be successful must be an agrarian revolution; that not only the big bourgeoisie, but even the petty bourgeoisie, in spite of their radical phrases, cannot, and will not lead the agrarian revolution; that the petty bourgeoisie when placed in power by the support of the workers and peasants do not share and defend this power with the working class, but hand it over to the counter-revolutionary bourgeoisie; and that the working class operating through their independent political party is the only guarantee for the success of national revolution."[35]

On his return to Berlin, Roy found that Trotsky had already been expelled from the Russian Communist Party. Roy, like Trotsky, had advocated a policy of militant international communism and of uncompromising hostility to the national bourgeoisie. In the struggle between Stalin and Trotsky, Roy, however, sided with Stalin.

On 30 December 1927 Roy issued a letter to the Indian communists about the policy and tactics they should follow. An intercepted copy of this letter was read in the Indian Legislative Assembly, and the letter came to be known as the Assembly letter. In this letter Roy advocated the continuance of an illegal Communist Party and of a broad-based, open and legal Workers' and Peasants' Party. Inasmuch as the Communist Party aimed at the overthrow of the British Empire in India by force, it could not function as a legal party. Such a party pledged to waging war against the King Emperor could secure legality only at the expense of its very *raison d'être*. The communists would be secretly organized in the Communist Party and would function as the conscious vanguard of the working class and be the driving force behind the Workers' and Peasants' Party. But the Workers' and Peasants' Party should not, in the public mind, be associated with the communists or the Communist Party for, in that event, the fear of communism might repel many leftist and democratic elements who could otherwise have been induced to join the Workers' and Peasants' Party.[36]

In the Assembly letter Roy suggested that the Workers' and Peasants' Party should be affiliated with the League Against Imperialism. In that event it could not be said that the party was controlled from Moscow. The illegal Communist Party, on the other hand, should function as a section of the Comintern. Roy also referred to the role of the British comrades in the Indian communist movement. He knew that the leadership of the Indian communist movement was passing away from him into the hands of the British communists. Roy said that the centres at Berlin and Paris were the agencies of the Comintern for looking after Indian affairs, and that the Communist Party of India should maintain its relations with the Comintern through these centres and not through London or the British Communist Party. Roy stated that no British communist had a superior right to manage the affairs of the Indian Communist Party, and that the Comintern had so far not sent any of its representatives to India. It was clear that this portion of the Assembly letter was an attack on Spratt and Bradley, the emissaries sent by the British Communist Party to India, who had, by then, become the *de facto* leaders of the Indian communist movement.

The Sixth Congress of Comintern met at Moscow between July and September 1928. By this time Roy had developed his theory of decolonization and had moved to the right. But, at this Sixth Congress, the Comintern moved to the left and advocated a policy of uncompromising hostility towards the national bourgeoisie, a policy which Roy had been preaching since the Second Congress of 1920, but which he had then just abandoned.

According to Roy, decolonization arises out of the crisis in imperialism and the decay of capitalism. With the accumulation of capital in imperial metropolitan countries, which cannot be profitably invested at home, imperialists seek fields of investment of such capital in the colonies. In order to invest, the policy of holding the colonies in industrial backwardness had to be abandoned and imperial countries were forced, reluctantly but by the compulsion of events, to grant concessions to the colonies and to permit them to industrialize themselves. This process of industrialization of the colonies leads to decolonization, and sets in motion a process which eventually leads to the transfer of power from the imperialist bourgeoisie to the nationalist bourgeoisie in the colonies.

The Sixth Congress rejected the decolonization theory altogether. It branded the national bourgeoisie as a counter-revolutionary force. The bitter experience of betrayal by the Chinese bourgeoisie induced the communists at the Sixth Congress to accept an extremist militant policy of uncompromising hostility to the bourgeoisie. The Sixth Congress not only rejected the decolonization theory of Roy but also the formulations of the British communists, whose spokesman R. Palme Dutt had asserted that though the bourgeoisie was becoming counter-revolutionary it still had a vestigial anti-imperialist role to play. In June 1928 R. Palme Dutt had written in *The Labour Monthly*: "But if we turn to the rank and the file of the Nationalist Movement, representing in the main the various elements of the petty-bourgeoisie, the sharpening of opposition [to imperialist forces] is much more conspicuous. Here an actual process of revolutionization is at work among a considerable section following on the disillusionment after the collapse of Gandhi and Non-Cooperation, and on the economic hardships of the present period."[37]

The Sixth Congress declared that the bourgeoisie was no longer a revolutionary force. The trading bourgeoisie directly served the interests of imperialist capitalists and, like the comprador bourgeoisie of China, fully collaborated with the imperialists and were, therefore, a class enemy of the proletariat. It is only the poor peasantry and certain sections of the poor urban petty-bourgeoisie and the petty-bourgeois intelligentsia who could be brought under the influence of active revolutionary forces and act as allies of the proletariat. But though there could be temporary agreements or temporary unions with these petty-bourgeois elements, the Communist Parties were exhorted to "demarcate themselves in the most clear-cut fashion, both politically and organizationally, from all the petty-bourgeois groups and parties." The communists were called upon to criticize the "half-heartedness and vacillation of the petty-bourgeois groups," including the left wing of the Indian National Congress.[38]

The Sixth Congress declared that the Workers' and Peasants' Parties could easily be converted into ordinary petty-bourgeois parties. The communists could not aspire to build up a proper organization on the basis of the fusion of these two classes, namely, the workers and the peasants, and they were asked not to organize such parties. On the contrary, the supreme task of the communists should be to organize all communist groups and individuals scattered throughout the country into a single unified, and illegal Communist Party. The Indian communists

had devoted much of their energies to organizing workers'
and peasants' parties and they continued to do so for some time
even after the Sixth Congress. This is because the edict of the
Sixth Congress to liquidate such parties did not reach the
Indian communists till G. M. Adhikari arrived from Europe in
December 1928, about three months after the end of the Sixth
Congress.[39]

With the rejection of Roy's theory of decolonization by the
Sixth Congress, Roy's position in the Comintern became pre-
carious. After the Sixth Congress, Roy lived and worked for
another year in Germany where he wrote *Revolution and
Counter-Revolution in China*. But since the Sixth Congress Roy,
as he put it later, was "standing before the 'sacred Guillotine'."[40]
Eventually at the tenth plenum held in Moscow in July 1929
Roy was expelled from the Comintern. At this plenum it was
stated that Roy was no longer a comrade of the communists but
was rather the comrade of Gandhi, or, at least, the comrade of
Brandler and Thalheimer.

Roy considered that his expulsion from the Comintern was
the result of a conspiracy. "I was the victim," he wrote, "of
some internal intrigue, the history of which had better not yet
be written publicly. The desire of the Communist Party of Great
Britain to establish its protectorate over the Indian Communist
movement had a good deal to do with it. The internal struggle
of the Russian Communist party also contributed to my victimi-
zation. One fact may be mentioned here. For the first time in
the history of the Communist International there appeared an
Indian delegation in the Sixth World Congress. Previously in
spite of repeated efforts, no bona fide communist from India
could reach Moscow. The object of the first Indian delegation
to the Communist International was to denounce me, obviously
in accordance with a previously laid plan. Corroborating the
reports of some British communists, who had previously paid
flying visits to India, the mysterious delegation told the Congress of the Communist International that I was a person completely unknown in India, having no connection whatsoever with
the revolutionary movement. The interesting fact, however, is
that only one member of the delegation was allowed to return
to India. It is reported that the rest were presently suspected of
being British spies and dealt with as such. The one who returned

to India has dropped out of politics altogether."[41]

Roy had been sent to China by the Communist International in 1926. He went to China with Borodin and Blucher and stayed there till the middle of 1927. But Roy's mission in China was not successful, and it was this ill-fated mission combined with his controversial decolonization theory and the activities of his Indian critics, such as Soumyendranath Tagore, that undermined Roy's position and eventually led to his expulsion from the Comintern. Soumyendranath Tagore asserted that Roy was expelled from the Comintern not primarily because of his political differences with Stalin or Stalinism, but because of grave charges, such as misutilization of funds.

After his expulsion from the Comintern, Roy returned to India in December 1930 travelling under a forged passport in the name of Dr Mahmud. Roy got in touch with various trade union leaders and communists in India and, at the invitation of Nehru, attended the 1931 Karachi Congress, where the Congress adopted the now famous resolution on Fundamental Rights and Economic Policy advocating the nationalization of key industries and services. In July 1931 Roy was arrested in connection with an old conspiracy case.

After his arrest Roy asserted in a statement, which he had intended to make at the trial but was not allowed to make, that he had acted only as a pioneer of the Indian revolution. He claimed that he had not created the liberation movement, but had simply perceived it earlier than others. He claimed too that he tried to organize a working-class party because it was necessary for the liberation of the people from political slavery, economic exploitation, and social degradation, and that such a party was a historic necessity and had a historically revolutionary mission, and the British king, as well as any other power, that stood in the way of such a party would have to go.[42]

Roy asserted that any reasonable economic programme for the amelioration of the masses was bound to strike at the roots of imperialism and the capitalistic structure on which it was based. "In reality," Roy wrote in that statement, "the Government is against the most harmless economic programme, for its enforcement would mean loss to imperialism and its Indian allies, the princes, big landlords, and capitalists. Therefore, the realization of the programme will necessarily mean violation of the

11

laws of the imperialist government. The function of the laws is to hold the masses on the starvation level so that foreign imperialism and its native allies can grow rich, and to suppress the attempts of the masses to rise above the present conditions.... I have not preached violent revolution. I have maintained that revolution is a historic necessity. From time to time, surging forces of social progress reach the period of a violent outburst. This is caused by the resistance of the old to the new. An impending revolution produces its pioneers who force events and herald the maturing of the conflict. The task of the revolutionary vanguard is to expedite the historical process caused by objective necessity. They consciously organize the forces of the revolution and lead them to victory. I have acted as a pioneer of the Indian revolution; but the revolution itself is not my invention. It grows out of the historical conditions of the country. I have simply been one who perceived it earlier than others."[43]

According to Roy, he was merely an instrument of historical forces, and the cause of the revolution was to be found not in what he had preached but in what was inherent in the imperialistic system itself which generated forces of national revolution in opposition to it. "So," claimed Roy, "I am not responsible for the revolution, nor is the Communist International. Imperialism is responsible for it. My punishment, therefore, will not stop the revolution. Imperialism has created its own grave-digger, namely, the forces of national revolution. These will continue operating till their historic task is accomplished."[44]

In connection with the Cawnpore Conspiracy Case, Roy was sentenced to imprisonment in 1931 and was released in 1936. After spending six years in prison in India and after having spent about 16 years in exile away from India, Roy was now in a position actively to participate in Indian politics.

On his release from prison Roy joined the Indian National Congress. By this time Roy's breach with the Comintern was complete and irrevocable. Roy had now come to believe in the necessity of a close association between the national bourgeoisie and the leftists, and he no longer subscribed to the view that the proletariat alone could act as the vanguard of the revolution. In fact, Roy no longer believed that class struggle was the only reality or that the proletariat alone could bring about a revolution. Roy had lost his faith in the proletariat, and he asserted that the nonproletarian classes also could bring about a revolution in the same manner as they had, in the past, brought about the bourgeois revolution which replaced feudalism.[45]

In April 1937 Roy founded his weekly *Independent India*, in which he continued his attack on Gandhi and his methods. Gandhi was denounced as a social reactionary and his doctrine of *ahimsa*, Roy claimed, was a subtle intellectual device to conceal the reality of the capitalist exploitation of the country and to induce the workers and peasants to remain contented with their lot. Roy criticized Gandhi's belief in social harmony and national unity saying that the interests of the capitalists and the workers could never harmonize. Furthermore, Roy considered Gandhi's emphasis on nonviolence as a fetter in the way of the development of the revolutionary movement of the Indian people. Most of all, Roy condemned Gandhi's economics and his introduction of religion into politics. Roy was especially critical of Gandhi's faith in the *charka* or the spinning wheel and he said that Gandhi was seeking to convert a political organization like the Congress into a Spinners' Association.[46] In November 1939 Roy wrote to Gandhi accusing him of seeking to elevate nonviolence into a creed or dogma, and asserted that no political organization like the Congress could ever adopt nonviolence as a creed.[47]

In June 1939 Roy formed The League of Radical Congressmen in order to propagate his ideals and to influence the policies of the Congress. Roy also contested the presidential election of the Indian National Congress in 1940 against Maulana Abul Kalam Azad, the official candidate, but was overwhelmingly defeated.

II. ROY AS A CRUSADER AGAINST FASCISM

When World War II broke out Roy considered that it was an international civil war in which the forces of democracy and fascism were ranged against each other. Roy supported the war-effort against Germany. After the fall of France, Roy pleaded that unconditional support should be lent to the Allies so that the Allies may score a decisive victory over fascism.[48] Roy condemned the pursuit of any policy which would in any way embarrass the Allied war-effort. So far as the independence of India was concerned, Roy was convinced that it was bound to come and the end of the War would bring India freedom, so that it was not necessary to wage a liberation movement during the War to hasten Indian independence. In arriving at the conclusion that the end of the War would find India free and independent, Roy relied on his decolonization theory. Economic decolonization, which had begun in India, was bound to have political repercussions, and this process of economic decolonization, Roy believed, would compel the British bourgeoisie to leave India and to transfer power to their Indian counterparts.

Such was Roy's repugnance to fascism that he failed to realize, or did not care to recognize, the feelings of resentment and anger that were then seething in the country against British rule. In 1942 the Congress started the Quit India movement. Roy condemned this movement altogether. He asserted that this movement sprang from feelings of morbid racial animosity against the British and that the Congress had failed to take into account the dangers that were involved in weakening the British war-effort, and necessarily the Allied cause, in a combat against fascism.[49] Roy was supremely unconcerned about the fact that by opposing the Quit India movement he had completely alienated himself from the mainstream of the nationalist movement of the time. Despite popular opposition to his policies, Roy continued to criticize the Congress and dubbed the Congress leaders as the representatives of nascent Indian fascism.[50] He charged that the Quit India movement had been "organized by the industrial and financial patrons of the Congress."[51]

The anti-fascist front which developed during the course of the War, which comprised a larger section of the people than the working class, led to a new alignment of revolutionary forces.[52] Roy was now convinced that the working class was no longer the only revolutionary force. In fact, Roy now came to believe that it was the middle class, and not the working class, which would play a prominent role in bringing about revolutions in the future. Accordingly Roy characterized the theory of the dictatorship of the proletariat as an outworn dogma.

Though Roy had come to recognize the middle class as a revolutionary force, he, by opposing the Quit India Movement, contraposed himself to the Congress, which was dominated by the middle class. Roy persuaded himself to believe that the Congress did not stand for democracy but for fascism, and that the transfer of power to the Congress would lead to the establishment of a fascist dictatorship in India.[53] During this period Roy even asserted that the transfer of power to the Congress "would set India on the path of Petainism."[54]

During World War II and immediately thereafter Roy denounced not only fascism on the one hand and the nationalism of the Congress on the other, but also certain basic tenets of Marxism and communism. In 1946 he said that "radicalism need no longer sail under false colours, either of a particular brand of nationalism or of communism."[55] In the 1940s, rejecting both the nationalism of the Congress and the Marxism of the communists, Roy gradually developed an individualistic political philosophy.

During the War Roy acted in close cooperation with the British authorities in India and even accepted financial assistance from them to carry on propaganda on the labour front. It is no wonder, therefore, that Roy laid himself open to the charge, made by Jayaprakash Narayan, that Roy had become a hireling of Maxwell,[56] who was the Home Member of the Government of India during the Quit India movement. During this period Roy went to the extent of saying that the Indian leaders should be put behind prison bars. For Roy the Congress leaders had only a nuisance value. At a time the world was engaged in a crusade against fascism they had adopted a policy of "cheap martyrdom."[57] During this period Roy's criticism of Gandhi was unrestrained. Gandhi was described as the chief symbol of the backwardness and obscurantism of the Indian people and as one who was responsible for "whipping up forces which undermined the Indian home front."[58]

Roy had always condemned the intrusion of religion or spirituality into politics and he criticized Gandhi, and the Congress that Gandhi dominated, for introducing religion into politics and, in the manner of Jinnah, Roy asserted that the nationalist movement of the Congress was impregnated with Hindu ideals, myths, legends, and tradition.[59] He considered that Gandhi represented fascist irrationalism and that his gospel of nonviolence was merely a device for lulling the people into a spirit of acquiescence with their lot. For Roy Gandhi was the champion of national capitalism. Jawaharlal Nehru, who declared himself to be a socialist and who followed Gandhi's political leadership, also came in for Roy's criticism. While Gandhi was condemned as the champion of national capitalism, Roy claimed that Nehru was the apologist of national socialism and that they complemented each other.[60]

Y. B. Chavan, who later became the Chief Minister of Bombay and thereafter the Defence Minister and then Home Minister and later the Finance Minister of India, had, while he was in jail for the second time at the age of eighteen, come in close contact with the writings of M. N. Roy and had been impressed by them, but he could not obviously welcome M. N. Roy's stand during World War II. "It took a long time for me to make a rational analysis of the whole thing," he told Welles Hangen, author of *After Nehru, Who?*, and added: "It was said that Hitler's Nazism was the greatest danger to human rights in their democratic form. But at the same time we could not make much of a distinction between British and German imperialism. I felt it was intellectual romanticism to say we should support British imperialism against German imperialism. This struggle within myself went on for a long time."[61] After taking a decision in the matter Chavan plunged into the Quit India movement of 1942 and became one of its heroes.

During the War and thereafter Roy waged a relentless polemical warfare against fascism. For Roy fascism represented not merely the methods and tactics of certain aggressive states but also a complete philosophy of retrogression which, if pursued, would result in the debasement of human personality and the complete annihilation of man's moral nature. Fascism was the last defence of capitalism, and it represented a revolt against all modern trends and the turning of the clock back to mediaevalism. Its aim was to bolster up capitalism and imperialism, and ideologically it represented a retreat from reason. To save capitalism, fascism, claimed Roy, dragged Germany into mediaevalism.[62]

A capitalist society leads to atomization of the individual, so that the individual becomes lonely, and it is to rescue the individual from this devastating loneliness that the fascist exalted the totalitarian state and gave the individual something to cling to.[63] In order to escape the solitude and loneliness of an atomistic capitalistic society, the individual sought dependence on something greater than himself. In seeking such dependence the individual sought refuge in the totalitarian state, but it is this totalitarian state which eventually devoured the individual.[64]

III. ROY'S DENUNCIATION OF INDIAN SPIRITUALITY

Along with his attack on fascism, Roy also continued his attacks on Gandhi and the Indian philosophical tradition. Roy denounced Vedantic idealism. He claimed that Sankara and Ramanuja represented mental dogmatism, mediaevalism, and scholasticism. Sankara was for Roy the Brahmanical counterpoise to the liberating forces of the Buddhist movement. Buddha represented a spirit of revolt against Brahmanical ecclesiasticism and against parasitic luxury.[65] Roy regarded Buddhism as a revolutionary force which was making drastic inroads into Brahmanical scholasticism and priestcraft, but the Brahmanical counter-reformation, relying on a policy of superstition and fanaticism eventually overwhelmed the Buddhist spirit of revolt and its attack against the caste system.

Roy was never enamoured of Indian spiritualism. The concept of Indian spiritualism which finds such a prominent place in the writings of Vivekananda, Aurobindo, and even Gandhi, Roy condemned with all the strength that he could command. Roy lashed out against the belief that the West was declining or was losing faith and that it was hungering for Indian spirituality. The advocacy of Indian spiritualism was for him merely an attempt to revive the backward pre-capitalist social conditions of India. The spiritual aspect of Indian civilization that was considered most abiding and changeless by others Roy wanted most to change. Roy said: "The decline of the West being in reality only the decline of capitalism, the crisis of Western civilization means only disintegration of the bourgeois social order. In that context, India's 'spiritual mission' appears to be a mission with a mundane purpose, namely, to sabotage a social system based upon the love of lucre and lust for power.... It indicates an attachment to pre-capitalist social conditions, which are idealized. Objectively, it is therefore the token of a reactionary social outlook. Indian spiritualism is not different from the Western kind."[66]

Roy did not consider that India was ahead of the West in the richness, subtlety, and variety of its philosophical background or ideological heritage. He assailed the preachers of India's "world mission" saying that Indian idealism was no different from, and certainly not superior to, Western idealism. "While the emotional aspect of Indian speculation is well matched, if not surpassed, by Christian mysticism," said Roy, "intellectually it can hardly claim superiority to Western idealism, either modern or ancient. As regards transcendental fantasies, the Western mind has been no less fertile. The great sages of Athens, the seers of Alexandria, the saints of early Christianity, the monks of the Middle Ages—that is a record which can proudly meet any competition. On the question of moral doctrines, Christianity stands unbeaten on the solid ground of the Jewish, Socratic, and Stoic traditions.... The claim that the Indian people as a whole are morally less corrupt, emotionally purer, idealistically less worldly, in short, spiritually more elevated, than the bulk of the Western society, is based upon a wanton disregard for reality.[67]

India was not spiritually superior to the West. In fact, most Indians were merely engrossed with the problems of worldly life but, being culturally backward, they thought in terms of religion. And Gandhi, because he justified the economic backwardness of the Indians, could, claimed Roy, become their idol and exploit the veneration reserved in India for all religious leaders. In "the moralizing mysticism of Gandhi" Roy found little of coordinated thought or philosophy. Gandhism was to him only "a mass of platitudes and hopeless self-contradictions." "The fact that even in the twentieth century India is swayed," said Roy, "by the naive doctrines of Gandhi speaks for the cultural backwardness of the masses of her people. The subtlety of the Hindu philosophy is not the measure of the intellectual level of the Indian people as a whole. It was the brain-child of a pampered intellectual élite sharing power and privileges with the temporal ruling classes. It still remains confined to the comparatively small circle of intellectuals who try to put on a thin veneer of modernism and represents nothing more than a nostalgia. The popularity of Gandhi and the uncritical acceptance of his antics as the highest of human wisdom knock the bottom off the doctrine that the Indian people as a whole are morally and spiritually superior to the Western. The fact is that the great bulk of the Indian people are steeped in religious superstitions. Otherwise, Gandhism would have no social background and disappear before long.... Gandhism ... sways the mass mind, not as a moral philosophy, but as a religion. It is neither a philosopher nor a moralist who has become the idol of the Indian people. The masses pay their homage to a Mahatma —a source of revealed wisdom and agency of supernatural power. The social basis of Gandhism is cultural backwardness; its intellectual mainstay, superstition.... The Gandhist utopia ..: is a static society—a state of absolute social stagnation."[68]

For Roy, Gandhi's philosophy was merely an attempt to preserve the status quo, to prevent the people from rising up in a violent revolution against the established economic order and by securing the nonviolent nonresistance of the people to the social order, to ensure that the holders of power would not have to use force or violence, to any considerable extent, to keep down a people, who by the acceptance of a quietist philosophy generally slumbered in a state of inactive *ahimsa*. But Roy pointed out that no society could eschew force or violence altogether and he doubted whether Gandhians would ever be able to put their theory of absolute nonviolence into practice or to proclaim the absoluteness of nonviolence under all circumstances even as a theory. "Neither the preachers nor the proselytes of Gandhism, however," claimed Roy, "would have the consistency of carrying their cult to the nihilistic extreme. There would be a certain macabre majesty in such a boldness. But with all the absoluteness of its standards, Gandhism remains on the ground of the relative. After all, it prescribes a practical cure for the evils of the world. Philosophically, it is pragmatic. And the remedy suggested is the reactionary programme of forcibly keeping society in a relatively static condition. Gandhism offers this programme because it is the quintessence of an ideology which developed on the background of a static society."

IV. RADICAL HUMANIST CRITIQUE OF MARXISM

Roy was at once a revolutionary and an intellectual. As an intellectual Roy had a zest for new ideas. He accepted Marxism in 1919 in Mexico, but he did not remain a Marxist to the end. In July 1929 Roy was expelled from the Comintern. Since then he gradually veered away from orthodox Marxism. In 1940 Roy began a journey away from Marxism towards Radicalism. As a Radical, Roy proclaimed his critique of the Marxist method of social revolution. Roy considered Marx to be a humanist and a lover of freedom but he regarded the ethical foundations of Marxism to be weak. Roy also considered the Marxian economic interpretation of history as defective for having made inadequate allowances for the role of mental activity in the historical process.

The transition from Marxism to Radicalism has been described by Roy himself in the Preface to his book *Scientific Politics.* "Seven years ago," he wrote, "I still spoke as an orthodox Marxist criticizing deviation from, or faulty understanding of, the pure creed. Nevertheless, the tendency to look beyond Communism was already there in a germinal form. While still speaking in terms of class struggle, I laid emphasis on the cohesive factor in social organization. Already then I appreciated Marxism as something greater than the ideology of a class. I understood it as the positive outcome of earlier intellectual efforts to evolve a philosophy which could harmonize the processes of physical nature, social evolution and the will and emotions of individual man."[69] Roy, who had been a consistent advocate of class struggle and who had often derided Gandhi for not believing in or preaching class conflict, now began to emphasize "the cohesive factor in social organization" as distinct from class struggle.

Between 1940 and 1947 Roy considered himself a Radical and not an orthodox Marxist. Later, Roy changed from Radicalism to what he called integral scientific humanism or New Humanism. A change similar to the radical transformation from Marxism to New Humanism, which took place in the case of Roy, also took place in the case of certain other Indian leaders at about the same time—such as the transition of Jayaprakash Narayan from socialism to Sarvodaya,[70] of M. R. Masani from socialism to liberalism,[71] but, on the other hand, E. M. S. Namboodiripad and many others "took the 'leap' from Gandhism to Marxism–Leninism."[72]

In August 1947 in the manifesto of New Humanism, Roy expounded his political views as being founded on reason and morality and not on any dogma. He rejected Marxism or any other creed which it was sought to elevate into a dogma. He sought in the secular humanism of the European renaissance, enriched by all the discoveries of present-day science, the basis of a new social order. The political method he advocated laid stress on the adoption of right means for the attainment of just ends, a doctrine which Gandhi had preached for long. In the manifesto of New Humanism, Roy said: "Must revolutionary political practice be guided by the jesuitic dictum—the end justifies the means? The final sanction of revolution being its moral appeal—the appeal for social justice—logically the answer to the latter question must be in the negative. It is very doubtful if a moral object can ever be attained by immoral means. In critical moments, when larger issues are involved and greater things are at stake some temporary compromise in behaviour may be permissible. But when practices repugnant to ethical principles and traditional human values are stabilized as the permanent features of the revolutionary régime, the means defeat the end. Therefore, communist political practice has not taken the world, not even the working class, anywhere near a new order of freedom and social justice. On the contrary, it has plunged the army of revolution—proletarian as well as non-proletarian—in an intellectual confusion, spiritual chaos, emotional frustration, and a general demoralization."[73] These words were reminiscent of Gandhi whom Roy had denounced for the greater part of his life.

But though Roy adopted Gandhi's doctrine of the purity of means, the social order he envisaged was very different from Gandhi's *Ram Rajya*. For deriving inspiration for the new social order that was to be established Roy did not go back to indigenous Indian institutions in which Gandhi believed and which he partly idealized, but to the European tradition of liberalism and humanism. He pleaded for the application to the study of man and society of the principles and methods of the physical sciences and for the adoption of the humanist approach of the nineteenth-century Radicals.[74]

Such a humanist conception was necessarily cosmopolitan. It could think not in terms of the nation or a class but only in terms of man. Such a conception could be the foundation of a "New Humanism, new, because it is Humanism enriched, reinforced and elaborated by scientific knowledge and social experience gained during the centuries of modern civilization."[75] Such a humanistic society would be a spiritual community, not limited by the boundaries of national states—capitalist, fascist, or of any other kind.

As a Radical Humanist, Roy's philosophical approach was individualistic. The individual should not be subordinated either to a nation or to a class. Roy rejected both the nationalism of Congressmen and the theory of class struggle of the communists. He said: "Radicalism thinks in terms neither of nation nor of class; its concern is man; it conceives freedom as freedom of the individual."[76] The individual should not lose his identity in the collective ego of the nation or of the class. "The Nation-State, in practice," wrote Roy, "makes no greater concession to the concept of individual freedom than the class-state of the Communists, and also of the Socialists. And no modern democratic state has as yet outgrown nationalist collectivism."[77]

Roy harked back to the rationalism of the eighteenth century and sought to place the individual at the centre of the universe. Roy lamented that the Marxian theory of class struggle had subordinated individual consciousness to class consciousness. Roy also assailed Marxism because of the pre-eminent position it gave to the working class. Further, the polarization of capitalist society into two classes—the exploiting class and the working class—as envisaged in Marxist theory did not take place, and the middle class did not disappear. It is the middle class which produced revolutionaries. Lenin had recognized this and had given a special role in the communist party organization to professional revolutionaries drawn from the middle class. Yet, in the opinion of Roy, Lenin did not recognize the revolutionary significance of the middle class as a class.[78]

As a Radical Humanist, Roy ceased to believe in the Marxian theory of the class struggle. Society could not survive without some kind of social cohesive force and, accordingly, class struggle could not be the only reality.[79] Linked with this theory of social cohesiveness was Roy's emphasis on the role of the middle class as the most progressive class in modern society. Whereas in Marxian theory the working class has a special place, in these later formulations of Roy the middle class had a special status. Roy emphasized the individual and not class, but when he spoke in class terms, he gave pride of place to the middle class and not to the proletariat, whom Roy characterized as the "most backward stratum of society."[80]

As a Radical Humanist, Roy denounced the theories of class struggle and of the dictatorship of the proletariat. In fact, Roy wanted to emphasize the individual more than the class, whether it be the working class or the middle class. Roy envisaged the conflict of the present age as "between totalitarianism and democracy, between the all-devouring collective ego—nation or class—and the individual struggling for freedom.[81]

Roy asserted that the Marxian emphasis on revolution and on the dictatorship of the proletariat would lead to totalitarianism. He warned against the harbouring of romantic illusions about revolutions. Revolutions could not bring about miracles. What was needed was a judicious synthesis of rationalism and romanticism. Roy did not discard the word "revolution" from his political vocabulary but, as a Radical Humanist, he came to believe that a revolution should be brought about not through class struggle or armed violence but through education.

The word education Roy used in a comprehensive sense as including all modes of persuasion of the masses. But change brought about by education could only be slow and gradual and not revolutionary, in the sense that the word is ordinarily understood. The method of education that Roy advocated for bringing about the Radical Humanist revolution was not very different from the constitutional method that the early moderates and liberals of India, such as Dadabhai Naoroji, M. G. Ranade, Surendranath Banerjea, and Gopal Krishna Gokhale, had advocated. These early liberals of India also believed in the method of persuasion and they pinned all their hopes on the education of the masses. It is a curious irony of history that Roy, who started life as a militant nationalist and who later embraced the Marxian doctrine of revolution, came eventually to believe in the gradual and constitutional method which the early liberals pursued. It is interesting to observe that the latter half of the nineteenth century in India, which produced the early liberals of India, was later characterized by Roy as the golden age of Indian history. "I believe," he wrote, on 5 December 1954, "that, if there ever was a Golden Age in the history of India, it was the latter half of the nineteenth century, a historical past about which we can make no mistake."[82]

As a Radical Humanist, Roy's faith in rationalism was accompained by an equally strong belief in individualism and in the role of individuals. Such was his belief in the importance of the individual that, towards the end of his life, he even lost faith in political parties and in organized democracy. Roy sought to revive democracy from the grass roots and wanted that people should be chosen to govern only on the basis of fitness. But he did not answer the question as to who would decide about the fitness of an individual to govern and by what process.

Roy envisaged the elimination of parties from political life. But here, again, he did not answer the question as to how a modern democracy could be run in the absence of political parties. Roy's experience of organized political parties had not been altogether happy. In his youth he had joined the Indian terrorist or revolutionary movement but had failed to smuggle from abroad any significant quantity of arms or money into India for the purposes of the Indian revolution. After his conversion from nationalism to communism, he secured some encouragement from Lenin, and for a number of years was an important member of the Comintern, but in 1929 he was expelled from the Comintern. Thereafter, returning to India Roy spent six long years in prison. After release from prison Roy joined the Indian National Congress, but he could not secure any position of influence within that organization. Roy lived dangerously and with courage, but met with many frustrations in his political life. Such was Roy's disillusionment with politics that towards the end of his life he came to enunciate the theory that political parties should be eliminated from political life altogether. Roy had a massive intellect and was an intrepid revolutionary, but he could not attain any secure position in the political field and, in the end, he died a recluse in the Renaissance Institute at Dehra Dun.

As a Radical Humanist, Roy made certain fundamental criticisms of Marxism. He claimed that the Marxist theory had failed to recognize that the non-proletarian classes could also act as the vanguard of a revolution. As the bourgeoisie had, in the past, played a revolutionary role in overthrowing feudalism, similarly in the twentieth century another non-proletarian class, namely, the middle class, was playing a revolutionary role. The Marxian polarization of classes did not lead to the formation of only two classes in modern industrial society and did not lead to the disappearance of the middle class. And it is this middle class, Roy believed, that would increasingly play a progressive role in modern society.

In criticizing Marxism and in evolving the philosophy of Radical Humanism, Roy did not, however, reject Marxism altogether. He was too much impregnated with Marxism to be able to free himself completely from the Marxist influence. Even as a Radical Humanist, Roy asserted that Marxism was "the positive outcome of early intellectual efforts to evolve a philosophy which could harmonize the processes of physical nature, social evolution and the will and emotions of individual men."[83]

Notwithstanding his attachment to Marxism, as a Radical Humanist Roy no longer believed in the economic interpretation of history. He was greatly influenced by materialism and the Marxist theory that existence determined consciousness, but he yet asserted that the theory of the economic interpretation of history did not follow necessarily as a corollary from materialist philosophy.[84] The biological struggle for existence could not be equated with the economic impulse to earn a livelihood. Roy observed: "The point of departure of the Marxist historiology was the mistake of confounding physical urge with economic motive."[85] For Roy the biological urge of self-preservation preceded the economic motive of earning a livelihood, in the same manner as the idea of the means of production preceded the development of the means of production themselves.

Roy also could not give his wholehearted allegiance to the Marxian doctrine of dialectics. Dialectics as a process of logic or as a method of enquiry was acceptable to Roy. But logic could not be confused with ontology and the laws of thought could not be taken as a description of the processes of nature or the content of reality. Roy criticized Marxian dialectics saying that the subject matter of a branch of metaphysical enquiry was being confounded with the instrument of conducting that enquiry.[86] Though men may think dialectically, the processes of nature or the processes of history were not always or necessarily dialectical. The concept of substance as discovered by modern physics did not support the theory of dialectics in the realm of ontology nor did, Roy asserted, the evolution of democracy to socialism, which was a continuous and not a dialectical process, support the theory of dialectics.[87] Roy wanted to confine the theory of dialectics to the domain of logic and methodology, and felt that such a theory did not necessarily correspond either with the processes of nature or with the processes of history.

Though Roy did not accept in their entirety Marxian materialism and Marxian dialectics, he was a true follower of Marx in his criticisms of theology and religion. Roy was a believer in reason and an enemy of tradition and theology. In fact, he sought to explain away theology by tracing it to its anthropological roots in the same manner as Feuerbach.

Roy also made certain criticisms of the Marxian theory of surplus value and class struggle. Roy did not regard surplus value as a peculiar characteristic of capitalism. In fact, no society could progress and there could be no capital formation unless there was a surplus of production over consumption and unless this surplus was employed as capital for increasing production still further. There could be no accumulation of capital without the creation of surplus value, and there could be no economic progress without the accumulation of capital. Accumulation of capital in a capitalist society was not a condemnation of that society. On the contrary, Roy asserted that such a capitalist society, which helped in the accumulation of capital, was economically a more advanced type of society than a feudal society, which produced for consumption and not for the market and which created no surplus value and, therefore, no capital.[88]

Capitalist society, which involved the creation of surplus value and led to the accumulation of capital, was more progressive than a feudal society. "Capitalism grows out of the exploitation of labour, but at the same time," observed Roy, "capitalist economy raises the entire society to a higher level; in so far as the working class is a part of society, in spite of all antagonism and exploitation in the beginning, its interest is identical with that of the capitalists."[89] The creation of surplus value and the accumulation of capital were also necessary in a socialist society. The only difference between a socialist society and a capitalist society was that in a socialist society, unlike in a capitalist society, the surplus value was not appropriated by a particular class.

Roy did not condemn capitalism or bourgeois culture altogether, and did not subscribe to the view that bourgeois culture was utterly vitiated by a class bias. Roy believed not in the relativity but in the timelessness of all cultural values. "If we do not accept such values we deny," argued Roy, "all higher human values. Otherwise, whatever had been created under feudalism would have had to be destroyed with feudalism. If that were a condition of social progress, we would now live in a period darker even than the middle ages." Roy, therefore, rejected any theory which sought to explain history on the basis of the conflict of classes alone, or which sought to glorify such class conflict or struggle.

With the rejection of the Marxian theory of the class struggle, one would have expected also the rejection of the Marxian theory of revolution. Roy, however, did not discard the word "revolution" altogether. Even as a Radical Humanist, Roy continued to speak of a Radical Humanist revolution. But it was clear that he was using the word "revolution" in a sense very different from that of the Marxist. Roy's revolution involved no sudden change. His radical humanistic revolution was to be achieved, not by violence or armed insurrection, but through the slow process of education.

Further, as a Radical Humanist Roy was averse to state ownership of the means of production. In place of state ownership Roy recommended cooperative ownership. Economic planning, which is an essential feature of socialist or communist reconstruction of society, Roy did not reject altogether, but he came to believe in planning based on voluntary cooperation.

In the end Roy came to believe more and more in individualism and liberalism. Roy who had embraced Marxism in Mexico, ended not as a Marxist but as a revisionist who came ultimately to espouse and propagate the basic ideas of liberalism, and who sought to present the same with a flavour of eighteenth century rationalism. Roy asserted that the task of the fighter for a new humanistic world would be to make every individual conscious of his innate rationality and to find his unity with others in a cosmopolitan commonwealth of free men and women. He declared his final faith thus: "Man did not appear on the earth out of nowhere. He rose out of the background of the physical universe, through the long process of biological evolution. The umbilical cord was never broken: man, with his mind, intelli-

12

gence, will, remain an integral part of the physical universe. The latter is a cosmos—a law-governed system. Therefore, man's being and becoming, his emotions, will, ideas are also determined; man is essentially rational. The reason in man is an echo of the harmony of the universe. Morality must be referred back to man's innate rationality. . . . The innate rationality of man is the only guarantee of a harmonious order, which will also be a moral order, because morality is a rational function. Therefore, the purpose of all social endeavour should be to make man increasingly conscious of his innate rationality."[90]

NOTES AND REFERENCES

1. *M. N. Roy's Memoirs*, pp. 219-20.
2. "Lenin-Roy Controversy on Revolution Strategy," *New Age*, 22 February 1970.
3. M. N. Roy, *India in Transition*, p. 205.
4. *M. N. Roy's Memoirs*, 1964, p. 543.
5. Ibid., p. 544.
6. *Tribune*, 4 November 1922.
7. Overstreet & Windmiller, *Communism in India*, 1960, p. 56.
8. Ibid., p. 55.
9. M. N. Roy & Ellen Roy, *One Year of Non-Cooperation*, 1923, pp. 40-41.
10. P. C. Roy, *Life and Times of C. R. Das*, pp. 267-68.
11. Overstreet & Windmiller, *Communism In India*, 1960, p. 65.
12. M. N. Roy & Ellen Roy, op. cit., pp. 56-60.
13. M. N. Roy, "Anti-Imperialist Struggle in India," in *The Communist International*, No. 6 (1924), pp. 92-93.
14. Ibid., pp. 70-71.
15. *Indian Annual Register*, 1925, II, p. 367.
16. Ibid., p. 371.
17. Overstreet & Windmiller, op, cit., p. 79.
18. M. N. Roy, *The Aftermath of Non-cooperation*, 1926, p. 13.
19. Ibid., p. 14.
20. M. N. Roy, *The Future of Indian Politics*, pp. 98, 117.
21. Ibid., p. 90.
22. Ibid., p. 95.
23. Ibid., p. 114.
24. M. N. Roy, Ibid., p. 85.
25. M. N. Roy, *Fragments of a Prisoner's Diary*, Vol. II, p. 114.
26. M. N. Roy, *The Future of Indian Politics*, p. 17.
27. R. Palme Dutt, *Modern India*, London, 1927, p. 129.

28. Ibid., p. 148.
29. Ibid., pp. 17-18.
30. Spratt, *Blowing Up India*, p. 29.
31. Overstreet & Windmiller, op. cit., p. 89.
32. Jawaharlal Nehru, *An Autobiography*, 1942, p. 161.
33. Soumyendranath Tagore, *Historical Development of the Communist Movement in India*, 1944, pp. 10-11.
34. Overstreet & Windmiller, op. cit., p. 92.
35. Ibid., p. 102.
36. Ibid., pp. 104-5.
37. R. Palme Dutt, "Notes of the Month," in *Labour Monthly*, June 1928, p. 335.
38. Overstreet & Windmiller, op. cit., pp. 119-20.
39. Philip Spratt, *Blowing up India*, 1955, p. 42.
40. M. N. Roy, *Our Difference*, Calcutta, 1938, p. 25.
41. Ibid., p. *ii*.
42. M. N. Roy, *I Accuse*, 1932, pp. 26-29.
43. Ibid.
44. Ibid.
45. M. N. Roy, *Scientific Politics*, p. 189.
46. M. N. Roy, *The Alternative*, Bombay, 1940, pp. 16-17.
47. Ibid., pp. 78-79.
48. M. N. Roy, *War and Revolution*, 1942, p. 20.
49. M. N. Roy, *Jawaharlal Nehru*, Delhi, 1945, pp. 28-29.
50. M. N. Roy, *War and Revolution*, p. 101.
51. Ibid., p. 96.
52. M. N. Roy, *The Communist International*, 1943, p. 4.
53. M. N. Roy, *National Government or Peoples' Government*, 1946, pp. *viii-x*.
54. M. N. Roy, *Nationalism and Democracy*, 1942, p. 5.
55. M. N. Roy, *Scientific Politics*, 1947, pp. *v-vii*.
56. Jayaprakash Narayan, *Socialism, Sarvodaya And Democracy*, 1964, p. 40.
57. M. N. Roy, *Freedom or Fascism*, December 1942, pp. 103-4.
58. Ibid., p. 105.
59. M. N. Roy, *National Government or Peoples' Government*, 1943, p. 49.
60. M. N. Roy, *The Problem of Freedom*, pp. 39-46.
61. Welles Hangen, *After Nehru, Who?*, London, 1963, p. 137.
62. M. N. Roy, *The Communist International*, p. 60.
63. M. N. Roy, *War and Revolution*, 1942, p. 13.
64. M. N. Roy, *The Problem of Freedom*, pp. 22-27.
65. M. N. Roy, *From Savagery to Civilization*, Calcutta, 1940, p. 15.
66. M. N. Roy, *India's Message (Fragments of a Prisoner's Diary, II)*, Calcutta, 1950, pp. 190-218.
67. Ibid.
68. Ibid.

69. M N. Roy, *Scientific Politics*, 2nd Edition, 1947, p. *viii*.
70. Jayaprakash Narayan, *Socialism, Sarvodaya And Democracy*, ed. Bimla Prasad, 1964.
71. M. R. Masani, *Congress Misrule and the Swatantra Alternative*, 1966, pp. 159-69.
72. E. M. S. Namboodiripad, *The Mahatma And the Ism*, 2nd ed., 1959, Introduction, p. *vii*.
73. M. N. Roy, *New Humanism : A Manifesto*, Calcutta, 1947, pp. 34-47.
74. Ibid.
75. Ibid.
76. M. N. Roy, *New Humanism*, p. 36.
77. M. N. Roy, *Radical Humanism*, 1952, p. 21.
78. M. N. Roy, *New Humanism*, pp. 28-29.
79. Ibid., p. 26.
80. Ibid., p. 31.
81. Ibid., p. 33.
82. *The Radical Humanist*, 5 December 1954.
83. M. N. Roy, *Scientific Politics*, p. *vii*.
84. M. N. Roy, *Materialism*, 1951, p. 198.
85. M. N. Roy, *Reason, Romanticism and Revolution*, Vol. II, p. 217.
86. M. N. Roy, *Materialism*, p. 199.
87. M. N. Roy, *Reason, Romanticism and Revolution*, Vol. II, p. 194.
88. M. N. Roy, *New Humanism*, pp. 23-26.
89. M. N. Roy, *Scientific Politics*, p. 83.
90. M. N. Roy, *New Humanism : A Manifesto*, Calcutta, 1947, pp. 34-47.

CHAPTER FIVE

Nehru on Socialism

I. NEHRU'S FAITH IN SCIENTIFIC SOCIALISM

Jawaharlal Nehru, the son of the eminent lawyer–politician Motilal Nehru, was born in the midst of wealth. Prosperity in the family was so pronounced that Jawaharlal in later life said: "I am a typical bourgeois, brought up in bourgeois surroundings with all the early prejudice that this training has given me."[1]

Of the leaders of all-India stature, Jawaharlal Nehru was the most outspoken champion of socialism in the thirties and forties of this century. As a student in England, Nehru had merely toyed with Fabian socialism. In his *Autobiography*, he described his position in 1917 thus: "I was a pure nationalist, my vague socialist ideas of college days having sunk into the background."[2]

In connection with his wife's ill-health Nehru went to Europe in 1926, where he met many socialists and communists and also attended the Congress of the League of Oppressed Peoples at Brussels in 1927. His experiences in Europe convinced Nehru that the principal international conflict was between capitalist imperialism and anti-capitalist socialism.

At the Brussels Congress, Nehru came into contact with many ardent communists, and later in November 1927 he visited Moscow to attend the tenth anniversary celebrations of the Russian revolution. This visit made him a great admirer of the Soviet Union. Nehru was impressed by the progress in education, female emancipation, and improvement in the lot of the peasants that had been effected in Russia, and these he noted in a book *Soviet Russia* written by him in 1928. In this book he said that the Russian experiment was of great interest to Indians because conditions there were not very dissimilar from conditions in India. Both were vast agricultural countries, having only the beginnings of industrialization, and both had to face poverty and illiteracy. If Russia could find a way to solve the problem of poverty and illiteracy, that was bound to help India.

As a result of this visit to Russia, Nehru also developed the firm conviction that the Soviet union was a great champion of anti-imperialism, and that Russia and India had a common interest in opposing British imperialism.[3] It is interesting to note that Nehru was later expelled by the League Against Imperialism because of his part in the Delhi Truce between the Congress and the Indian government. He was amused by this expulsion and wrote in his *Autobiography*: "In 1931, because of my part in the Delhi Truce between the Congress and the Government of India, it [League Against Imperialism] grew exceedingly angry with me, and excommunicated me with bell, book and candle— or to be more accurate, expelled me by some kind of resolution. I must confess that it had great provocation, but it might have given me some chance of explaining my position."[4]

Nehru's coming in contact with many communists at the League of Oppressed Peoples at Brussels in 1927 and his visit to Russia attracted him to communism, and on returning to India in an address at the Labour Session of the 1929 Indian National Congress, Nehru avowed that he was a socialist and a republican and not a believer in kings and princes. In 1929 Nehru also presided over the Trade Union Congress, and hoped to bring labour closer to the nationalist movement as also to make the Congress more socialistic. In *Whither India*, written in 1933, Nehru again spoke of his belief in socialism and stated that the Indian struggle was linked with the world struggle against capitalism and imperialism.

In 1933 Nehru said that nationalism was not enough and that an ideology of social revolution was necessary. Nehru felt that a purely nationalist ideology, which had no economic or social content, could not fit in with the needs of the modern world. Indian nationalists had to be imbued and guided by a progressive ideology of social revolution, only then could India take an effective part in the nationalist struggle as well as the economic and social struggle for freedom, which was being waged throughout the world.[5]

By the thirties Nehru came to believe in socialism not in a humanitarian sense but in an economic sense; or in, what is sometimes called, "scientific" socialism. Gandhi and many Congress leaders were in the habit of using the word socialism in a purely humanitarian sense. Nehru took exception to this and on 13 August 1934, he wrote to Gandhi in this connection saying that socialism had "a clearly defined meaning in the English language." Gandhi replied: "I have looked up the dictionary meaning of socialism. It takes me no further than where I was before I read the definition. What will you have me to read to know its full content?"

In 1933 Nehru wrote to his daughter Indira, future Prime Minister of India, explaining what he understood by socialism. "Socialism, I have told you," wrote Nehru, "is of many kinds. There is general agreement, however, that it aims at the 'control by the state' of the means of production; that is, land and mines and factories and the like, and the means of distribution, like railways, etc. and also banks and similar institutions. The idea is that the individual should not be allowed to exploit any of these methods or institutions, or the labour of others, to their own personal advantage."[6]

In his 1936 Congress presidential address Nehru frankly declared his allegiance to socialism. He said that the world was divided into two vast groups, namely, the imperialist and fascist on the one side, and the socialist and nationalist on the other, and Indian nationalists inevitably sided with those forces of the world which were ranged against fascism and imperialism.[7] "Capitalism, in its difficulties," claimed Nehru, "took to Fascism with all its brutal suppression of what Western civilization had apparently stood for; it became, even in some of its homelands, what its imperialist counterpart had long been in the subject colonial countries. Fascism and imperialism thus stood out as the two faces...of...decaying capitalism....Socialism in the West and the rising nationalism of the Eastern and other dependent countries opposed this combination of Fascism and Imperialism. Nationalism in the East, it must be remembered, was essentially different from the new and terribly narrow nationalism of Fascist countries; the former was the historical urge to freedom, the latter the last refuge of reaction."[8]

Nehru, however, realized that his profession of the socialist faith as the leader of a nationalist organization in a subject country might give rise to controversies. In his 1936 Congress presidential address Nehru said that he was going a little beyond the usual beat of a Congress president in preaching the cause of socialism. This he was doing so that he might not be accepted under any false pretences. Nehru made it clear that he felt that the only key to the solution of the world's problems, and of India's problems, lay in socialism. "When I use this word," he said, "I do so not in a vague humanitarian way but in the scientific economic sense. Socialism is, however, something even more than an economic doctrine, it is a philosophy of life and as such also it appeals to me. I see no way of ending the poverty, the vast unemployment, the degradation, and the subjection of the Indian people except through socialism. That involves vast and revolutionary changes in our political and social structure, the ending of vested interests in land and industry, as well as the feudal and autocratic Indian states system. That means the ending of private property except in a restricted sense, and the replacement of the present profit system by a higher ideal of cooperative service. It means ultimately a change in our instincts, habits, and desires. In short, it means a new civilization, radically different from the present capitalist order."[9]

Though in 1936—speaking as the president of the Congress —Nehru had advocated the ending of vested interests in land and industry and a revolutionary change in the political and social structure for the establishment of socialism, from 1947, when he became the Prime Minister of India, Nehru, though not abandoning altogether his earlier beliefs, sought to follow an evolutionary policy, and to establish a mixed economy in the country so that both the public and private sectors could function, and economic changes could be effected peacefully and not by the adoption of any revolutionary means.

In the thirties of this century Nehru often said that he wanted to be precise with regard to his definition of socialism. But in 1939 Nehru himself was criticized by Subhas Bose as being somewhat vague with regard to his definition of socialism. Nehru answered: "Am I a socialist or an individualist? Is there a necessary contradiction in the two terms? ... I suppose I am temperamentally and by training an individualist, and intellectually a socialist. ... I hope that socialism does not kill or suppress individuality; indeed I am attracted to it because it will release innumerable individuals from economic and cultural bondage."[10]

It is this mixture of individualism and socialism in Nehru, and the faith in democracy as also in social and economic justice, that eventually made him adopt a pragmatic attitude towards socialism when he became the Prime Minister of India and had to decide whether the principle of the socialization of the means of production should be put into practice at once and without any qualification. It is interesting to recall in this connection that speaking about nationalization, Indira Gandhi, who succeeded Shastri as the third Prime Minister of independent India, and who nationalized the 14 major commercial banks of India, similarly told the author of *After Nehru, Who?*: "It depends on nationalization of what. If something is running well in private hands, why disturb it simply for the sake of nationalization? But if they are making a mess of it or have monopoly control, then go ahead and nationalize."[11]

II. THE 1936 CONGRESS CRISIS OVER NEHRU'S SOCIALISM

In his presidential address to the 1936 Congress Nehru had said that he was going outside the usual beat of a Congress president in advocating socialism. This was quite correct because socialism was not then the avowed goal of the Congress. Nehru's espousal of socialism gave rise to a crisis in the Congress in 1936 soon after he became its president. But the crisis did not lead to a split. The split in the Congress came eventually in 1969, but by that time the avowed goal of the Congress had become the establishment of a socialist pattern of society and a socialist state. The split came when Indira Gandhi, Nehru's daughter, was the Prime Minister of India, and Indira Gandhi ascribed the split to the fact that some Congressmen were not fully committed to the Congress ideal of socialism and secularism.

After being elected as Congress president in 1936, Nehru had included three prominent socialists in the Congress Working Committee. But soon Nehru clashed with the orthodox Gandhites in the Congress Working Committee and towards the end of June 1936, seven members of the Working Committee headed by Rajendra Prasad, Vallabhbhai Patel, C. Rajagopalachari, and J. B. Kripalani resigned. The resignations were later withdrawn through the intervention of Gandhi, but the correspondence that passed at that time was frank and revealing, and throws considerable light on the fundamental differences in the approach of Nehru and his seven colleagues in the Working Committee to the question of socialism.

On 29 June 1936 these seven members wrote to Nehru saying that when he appointed them members of the Working Committee, in spite of known differences of opinion and outlook, they had hoped that it would be possible to evolve a common line of action and to work cooperatively, keeping in the background the differences and concentrating on the points of agreement. They had tried their best to accommodate themselves, but they found that it was not possible to adjust the two differing points of view, or to work harmoniously. They felt that the preaching of, and emphasis on, socialism—particularly by the president of the Congress and other socialist members of the Congress Working Committee at a time when the Congress had not adopted it as its goal—was prejudicial to the best interests of the country and to the success of the national struggle for freedom. In the circumstances, they had no alternative but to resign. In doing so they said: "You also appear to feel and have even expressed that the Working Committee as it is constituted is not of your choice but forced on you and that you accepted it against your own better judgment."[12]

Subsequently, on 1 July 1936, Rajendra Prasad wrote a personal letter to Nehru complaining that by the propagation of socialism, which had not been adopted by the Congress as its creed, Nehru, the Congress president, was acting merely as the mouthpiece of a minority group. "It may be, as you tell us," wrote Rajendra Prasad, "that only that portion of your speeches is published which deals with socialism and the rest is not given prominence in the press as it is supposed to have less news value. There is a regular continuous campaign against treating us as persons whose time is over, who represent and stand for ideas that are worn out and that have no present value, who are only obstructing the progress of the country and who deserve to be cast out of the position which they underservedly hold."[13]

Nehru bitterly complained about this letter to Gandhi on 5 July 1936, saying that Rajendra Prasad's letter, though it did not contain specific charges against him, was yet a formidable indictment. It suggested that Nehru's activities were harmful to the Congress cause. The matter, therefore, could not be glossed over. Nehru stated: "For, however tenderly the fact may be stated, it amounts to this: That I am an intolerable nuisance and the very qualities I possess—a measure of ability, energy, earnestness, some personality which has a vague appeal—have become dangerous for they are harnessed to a wrong chariot. The conclusion from all this is obvious. . . . When I reached Bombay this time many people stared hard at me finding it difficult to believe how I had survived. It seemed to me common knowledge there [as reported in the *Times of India*] that a peaceful end awaited me—politically, of course. All had been fixed up except the cremation."[14]

Gandhi sought to resolve the differences between Nehru and his colleagues. In a letter to Nehru dated 15 July 1936, Gandhi said that Nehru's colleagues had lacked courage and frankness. They should have spoken freely and frankly to Nehru before. In fact, Gandhi had advised them previously to do this. "But having lacked the courage, whenever they have spoken," wrote Gandhi, "they have done it clumsily and you have felt irritated. I tell you they have dreaded you, because of your irritability and impatience of them. They have chafed under your rebukes and magisterial manner and above all your arrogation of what has appeared to them your infallibility and superior knowledge. They feel that you have treated them with scant courtesy and never defended them from socialists' ridicule and even misrepresentation."[15]

III. CONFLICTING PULLS OF GANDHISM AND COMMUNISM

Gandhi sought to bridge the differences that separated the socialist Nehru from the majority of his colleagues in the Congress Working Committee of 1936. Though ideologically he differed considerably from Gandhi, Nehru recognized that politically Gandhi was a revolutionary, and, therefore, he often followed Gandhi's advice, even though, left to himself, he might have acted differently. About Gandhi, Nehru wrote in his *Autobiography* that ideologically Gandhi was sometimes amazingly backward, but in action he has been the greatest revolutionary of modern India. Because Gandhi was a unique personality, it was difficult to classify or label him, but politically he was unquestionably a revolutionary who was pledged to obtaining independence for India. As such he was bound to play an uncompromising role till such independence was attained. "And in this very process he would release tremendous mass energies and would himself, I half-hoped," said Nehru, "advance step by step towards the social goal."[16]

There was always a deep bond of affection between the Westernized, socialistically oriented, and agnostic Nehru and the God-fearing, oriental Gandhi. In a telegram sent to Gandhi in May 1933, at a time when Gandhi was about to embark on his twenty-one-day fast, Nehru wrote: "I feel lost in a strange country where you are the only familiar landmark and I try to grope my way in dark but I stumble. Whatever happens my love and thoughts will be with you."

Nehru, the socialist, was distressed by Gandhi's mixing of religion with politics and by the revivalist movement which was encouraged by Gandhi's methods and utterances. Lamenting Gandhi's revivalism, Nehru wrote: "Gandhiji, indeed, was continually laying stress on the religious and spiritual side of the movement... the whole movement was strongly influenced by this and took on a revivalist character so far as the masses were concerned.... I used to be troubled sometimes at the growth of this religious element in our politics, both on the Hindu and the Muslim side.... Their history and sociology and economics appeared to me all wrong, and the religious twist that was given to everything prevented all clear thinking. Even some of Gandhi's phrases sometimes jarred upon me—thus his frequent reference to Rama Raj as golden age which was to return."[17]

There were considerable differences in the approach and outlook of the religious Gandhi and the agnostic Nehru. But Gandhi said: "While Jawaharlal always says he does not believe in God, he is nearer to God than many who profess to be His worshippers." Nehru believed in ethics, but not in traditional religion or in a personal God. In *Discovery of India*, Nehru wrote: "Often as I look at this world, I have a sense of mysteries, of unknown depths. What the mysterious is I do not know. I do not call it God because God has come to mean much that I do not believe in. I find myself incapable of thinking of a deity or of any unknown supreme power in anthropomorphic terms...

Any idea of a personal God seems very odd to me. Intellectually,
I can appreciate to some extent the conception of monism, and
I have been attracted towards the *Advaita* philosophy of Vedanta.
...At the same time the Vedanta, as well as other similar
approaches, rather frighten me with their vague formless incur-
sions into infinity. The diversity and fullness of nature stir me
and produce a harmony of the spirit, and I can imagine myself
feeling at home in the old Indian or Greek pagan and pantheistic
atmosphere, but minus the conception of God or gods that was
attached to it."[18]

Nehru had no desire to mix religion with politics, and he did
not believe that the mass of the people would be able to rise to
the level which Gandhi wanted them to do. Gandhi's faith was
in truth, Nehru's faith was in socialism. "For a hungry man,"
Nehru said on 3 January 1947, "... truth has little meaning, he
wants food; for a hungry man God has no meaning, he wants
food, and India is a hungry, starving country...."[19] The differences between the traditional and religious-minded Gandhi
and Nehru, the agnostic and socialist, were so great that once
in January 1928 Gandhi wrote to Nehru saying: "The differences
between you and me appear to me to be so vast and so radical
that there seems to be no meeting-ground between us...."[20]

But considering Gandhi to be a revolutionary so far as political
action was concerned, as distinguished from economic ideology,
Nehru accepted Gandhi as his leader and put his faith in Gandhi
and gave him a *carte blanche*. Referring to Gandhi's leadership
of the non-cooperation movement, Nehru wrote: "We felt that
we knew him quite well enough to realize that he was a great
and unique man and a glorious leader, and having put our faith
in him, we gave him an almost blank cheque, for the time being
at least." The non-cooperation movement "offered me," wrote
Nehru, "what I wanted—the goal of national freedom and (as
I thought) the ending of the exploitation of the underdog, and
the means which satisfied my moral sense and gave me a sense
of personal freedom."

While working under Gandhi's banner in the political movement, Nehru was attracted by Gandhi's insistence on the purity
of means, and he sought to reconcile the Gandhian emphasis on
purity of the means and nonviolence with the end or objective
of socialism. This attempt at reconciliation or synthesis, however,

satisfied neither socialists nor Gandhites. In the result, Nehru often used to shock socialists by preaching Gandhism to them, and bewildered Gandhites by seeking to convert them to socialism.

The truth of the matter was that while remaining a socialist at heart, Nehru was attracted to certain aspects of Gandhism, such as its emphasis on the purity of means. Nehru sought to bridge the growing gap between socialism and Gandhism, and said: "In a way I represented a link between various sets of ideas and so I helped somewhat in toning down the difference and emphasizing the essential unity of our struggle against imperialism."[21]

Nehru knew that it might not be possible for the Congress to adopt a fully socialistic programme immediately, but he made no secret of the fact that he was a socialist and a republican, and "no believer in kings or princes or in the order which produced the modern kings of industry." He believed that socialism was bound to come to India as, indeed, throughout the world, "and almost the only points in dispute are the pace and the methods of advance to its full realization." Poverty and inequality could not be ended except through socialism, though in achieving socialism, India "may evolve her own methods and may adapt the ideal to the genius of her race."[22]

Nehru believed in a classless society, and in his *Autobiography* he stated that such a society should be established peacefully, if possible, but forcibly, if necessary. This statement of Nehru has often been hailed by the socialists and communists. Nehru said that the aim should be the establishment of a classless society with equal economic justice and opportunity for all, a society which would be conducive to the cultivation of the spiritual values of cooperation, unselfishness, goodwill and love. "Everything that comes in the way will have to be removed, gently if possible, forcibly, if necessary. And there seems to be little doubt that coercion will often be necessary."[23]

But though in his *Autobiography* Nehru spoke of a classless society and of the use of force, if necessary, he was no communist, and did not and could not accept the communist doctrines in their entirety. Nehru admitted that he was far from being a communist, that his roots were still in the nineteenth century, and that he had been too much influenced by the humanist liberal tradition to get out of it completely. "This bourgeois background," said Nehru, "follows me about and is naturally a source of irritation to many communists."[24]

Nehru did not believe wholeheartedly in the Marxist or materialistic interpretation of history, but he felt that the economic interpretation of history contained a larger measure of truth than any other alternative theory. The study of Marx and Lenin produced a powerful impact on Nehru, and as a result of these studies he came to see history and current affairs in a new light. He came to believe that history had a meaning and that the establishment of socialism was consonant with the laws of history. In this connection, he particularly referred to the Russian revolution. "I had no doubt," he said, "that the Soviet Revolution had advanced society by a great leap and had lit a bright flame which could not be smothered, and that it had laid the foundations for that new civilization towards which the world could advance."[25]

Nehru visited Soviet Russia for a short time in 1927 and came back vastly impressed by what he had seen there. He saw glimpses of the new civilization in the territories of the USSR. Nehru confessed that much that had happened there pained him greatly, but yet he said: "I look upon that great and fascinating unfolding of a new order and a new civilization as the most promising feature of our dismal age. If the future is full of hope it is largely because of Soviet Russia and what it has done, and I am convinced that, if some world catastrophe does not intervene, this new civilization will spread to other lands and put an end to the wars and conflicts which capitalism feeds."

Nehru was attracted to the Marxist approach to history. What impressed him most was the scientific, anti-theological and anti-religious orientation of Marxism, though he did not give his absolute allegiance to it. There was much in the Marxist philosophical outlook which he could easily accept, namely, its monism and nonduality of mind and matter, the dynamics of matter and the dialectic of continuous change by evolution as well as leap, through thesis, antithesis, and synthesis. But the Marxist philosophical approach did not answer all Nehru's questions. Sometimes a vague idealist approach, akin to the Vedantic approach, crept into his mind. Again, Nehru doubted whether Marxism or communism could satisfy all his ethical yearnings. "I did not like," said Nehru, "the frequent divorce in communist, as in other, practice between action and these basic urges or principles ... the general Marxist approach, fitting in as it more or less did with the present state of scientific knowledge, seemed to me to offer considerable help. ... Marx's general analysis of social development seems to have been remarkably correct, and yet many developments took place later which did not fit in with his outlook for the immediate future."[26]

The Marxist economic interpretation of history led Nehru to believe that the communal problem in India was not a problem of great importance, and that economic divisions would transcend the divisions among the Hindus and Muslims on the basis of religion. But eventually the growth of separatist politics, coupled with the demand for a separate state, both based on religious differences troubled and distressed Nehru and made him more conscious of the qualifications and reservations of a purely economic interpretation of history and of the processes of politics.

Though he was attracted to the Marxist economic interpretation of history, Nehru was too much of an individualist to regard it as a dogma or to consider it as an all-comprehensive theory. But he certainly considered it to be a more comprehensive theory than any other. Further, the world economic crisis of 1929-32 seemed to confirm the correctness of the Marxist analysis. Most important of all, the anti-imperialist character of Marxist thought appealed to Nehru and he accepted the Marxist interpretation of the close connection between capitalism and imperialism.

But Nehru, who was also much influenced by Gandhi, the apostle of nonviolence, did not believe in the inevitability of violence in transforming the social or economic order, and he condemned the excesses of the Russian Revolution. In his *Autobiography*, he wrote: "In Russia... frequently heresy hunts were organized. That seemed to be deplorable, though it was not difficult to understand in view of the tremendous changes taking place rapidly in the Soviet countries when effective opposition might have resulted in catastrophic failure."[27] But even though Nehru believed that in India, as in Russia, eventually the state must acquire the essential means of production for the establishment of socialism, Nehru did not give up faith in democracy for realizing this objective. Nehru, who was steeped in Western liberal and democratic ideas, retained his faith in democracy and did not become a champion of the dictatorship of proletariat, though he repeatedly stated that political democracy was doomed unless it could lead to the realization of socialism in the economic sphere.

The great progress in the economic and educational field achieved in Soviet Russia filled Nehru with hope and a spirit of emulation. In *The Discovery of India*, Nehru said that Indians looked up to the USA, and even some Eastern countries which were making progress, but, most of all, they were inspired by the Soviet Union "which in two brief decades, full of war and civil strife, and in the face of what appeared to be insurmountable difficulties, had made tremendous progress ... all were fascinated by the advance of the Soviet Union in education and culture and medical care and physical fitness and in the solution of the problem of nationalities—by the amazing and prodigious effort to create a new world out of the dregs of the old."[28]

Increasingly Nehru came to believe that liberalism in India could not mean mere political liberation, for that may amount to substituting the rule of the Indian vested interests for British rule. Indian freedom was necessary to remove the burden on the Indian masses as well as the middle classes, and the value of such freedom could be judged only by the extent to which it enabled this burden to be removed. This burden on the people was imposed by the vested interests, both foreign and national. "If an indigenous government," said Nehru, "took the place of the foreign government and kept all the vested interests intact, this would not even be the shadow of freedom."[29] There would be no freedom or *swaraj* for the masses unless these vested interests were removed.

Nehru repeatedly raised the question whether the aim of the Indian nationalist endeavour was the realization of human welfare or merely the preservation of class privileges, and said that this question must be answered clearly and unequivocally in order that the interests of the dumb millions were preserved and safeguarded. The aim of the Indian nationalist endeavour, Nehru asserted, could only be the ending of all exploitation. Politically, this would mean independence and the severance of the British connection, and economically and socially it would mean the

13

ending of all class privileges and vested interests, that is, the establishment of socialism.[30]

But often it was said that socialism was un–Indian and anti-religious. Nehru scathingly attacked those who were critical of socialism on the ground that it was un–Indian or that it was not spiritual enough, and he took up arms against those who claimed that communism or socialism could not make headway in a religious or spiritual country like India. In 1935 in an article entitled "Orthodoxes of All Religions Unite," Nehru said: "It is an astonishing thing to me that while our millions starve and live like beasts of the field, we ignore their lot and talk of vague metaphysical ideas and the good of their souls; that we shirk the problems of today in futile debate about yesterday, that when thoughtful men and women all over the world are consi-dering problems of human welfare and how to lessen human misery and stupidity, we, who need betterment and raising most, should think complacently of what our ancestors did thousands of years ago and for ourselves should continue to grovel on the ground."[31]

Nehru felt that opposition to socialism sprang either from ignorance or from attachment to vested interests, and warned that ignorant criticism of socialism or communism could only help the emergence of fascism. Nehru declared that the "fear of communism has driven many liberals and other middle groups in Europe to fascism and reaction. . . . In India communism and socialism are understood by relatively very few persons and most people who shout loudest against them are supremely ignorant about them."

Nehru's socialism had an agrarian bias. He realized that in an agricultural country like India, emphasis would have to be laid on the development of peasant organizations. In *Towards Free-dom* (1941), Nehru said that the Indian communists had asso-ciated only with the industrial workers in the big towns and that they had little knowledge of, or contact with, the peasants, but the Congress workers had spread all over the countryside and, "in the ordinary course, the Congress must develop into a vast peasant organization."[32]

IV. DIVERGENT APPROACHES OF NEHRU AND BOSE TO COMMUNISM AND FASCISM

Nehru's faith in socialism was as intense as his antipathy to fascism, and between fascism and communism, Nehru's sympathies were all for communism. Nehru rejected fascism altogether and denounced it as barbaric. In fact, he regarded fascism as a development of and a more dangerous form of imperialism. "We," said Nehru, "looked upon the two as twin brothers which crushed freedom and prevented peace and progress."[33]

In particular, the fascist theory of racialism and the Nazi theory of *Herrenvolk* repelled Nehru. Nehru compared such theories with the doctrine of the master race on which the edifice of the British rule in India was based. In *The Discovery of India* (1946), he wrote that though Hitler had recently talked a great deal about racialism and the Nazi theory of the *Herrenvolk*, Indians had known of racialism in all its forms ever since the commencement of British rule. "The whole ideology of this rule," asserted Nehru, "was that of the *Herrenvolk* and the Master race, and the structure of government was based on it; indeed the idea of a master race is inherent in imperialism. There was no subterfuge about it; it was proclaimed in unambiguous language by those in authority. More powerful than words was the practice that accompanied them, and generation after generation and year after year, India as a nation and Indians as individuals were subjected to insult, humiliation, and contemptuous treatment. The English were an imperial race, we were told, with the God-given right to govern us and keep us in subjection; if we protested we were reminded of the 'tiger' qualities of an imperial race."[34]

Nehru had drawn attention to the dangers of fascism from the very beginning, and warned his countrymen against all forms of fascist ideology. Nehru feared that the association of vague leftist slogans with no clear left ideology may lead to fascism. In a letter to Subhas Bose written on 3 April 1939, he said that the association of vague leftist slogans with no clear leftist ideology had in Europe led to the development of fascism and nothing should be done so that such a thing might happen in India.[35]

Nehru closely watched the rise and growth of fascism in

Europe and saw the retreat from reason, the suppression of individual liberty, and the decline of democracy in some European countries. Nehru visited Spain at the height of the civil war and he was also much concerned with the rise and growth of Nazism and Fascism in Germany and Italy. While Nehru and other Indian nationalists hoped to establish a parliamentary democracy in India, Nehru was distressed to find that fascism, which openly derided democracy, was day by day gaining strength in Western Europe. And though the problems of Indian freedom engaged Nehru's immediate attention, as that of other Indian nationalists, the challenge that freedom and democracy faced in Europe could not but trouble Nehru deeply. "Our problems fill our minds. Yet," wrote Nehru, "the problem of problems today, overshadowing all else, is the growth and triumph of gangsterism in international affairs. The lights go out in Europe and elsewhere, the shadows increase, and in the darkness freedom is butchered and brutal violence reigns. Tragedy envelops us, heart-breaking tragedy, as we see the death of nation after nation, the vast suffering and misery of millions of people crushed by barbarian feet. 'Brother-hood', 'Sister-hood' are bastard creeds, says Signor Mussolini; only the sword counts with him, the sword that kills freedom and democracy and puts an end to the culture and civilization of ages. Spain of the Republic and of freedom is no more, only the bright and imperishable memory of her glorious struggle remains. Czechoslovakia used to be on the map of Europe. It is no more, and Herr Hitler's minions trample on her brave children, betrayed so shamefully by England and France. From day to day we await in suspense what this dictator or that says; anxiously we wonder what the next aggression will be."[36]

Jawaharlal Nehru and Subhas Bose were the idols of the young nationalists of India in the thirties of this century, and both were attracted to socialism, yet their understanding of socialism and their approach to parliamentary democracy and fascism were very different.

Bose started more as a humanitarian than as a "scientific" socialist, which Nehru claimed to be. For Bose, the main appeal of socialism lay in its concern for the uplift of the poor and downtrodden, and in this sense socialism to him was not a new ideology imported from Europe, but the realization in practice of Vivekananda's gospel of *Daridranarayan*. In his presidential address at the Rangpur Political Conference in March 1929, Bose referred to Vivekananda's emphasis on the uplift of the poor or the *Daridranarayan*, and said that this socialism did not derive its birth from the books of Karl Marx, but had its origin in the thought and culture of India. The gospel of democracy that Swami Vivekananda preached manifested itself in the life and work of Deshabandhu Das, who said that *Narayan* lives amongst those who till the land and, prepare our bread by the sweat of their brow. "New ideas of socialism," said Bose, "are now-a-days travelling to India from the West, and they are revolutionizing the thoughts of many, but the idea of socialism is not a novelty in this country. We regard it as such only because we have lost the thread of our own history. It is not proper to take any school of thought as unmistakable and absolute truth. We must not forget that the Russians, the main disciples of Karl Marx, have not blindly followed his ideas. Finding it difficult to apply his theories they have adopted a new economic policy consistent with possession of private property and ownership of business factories. . . . "[37] On another occasion Bose said that communism was not a Western institution, and in this connection he referred to the fact that among the Khasis in Assam private property as an institution did not exist at all.[38]

In 1931 Bose declared that he wanted a Socialist Republic in India. Such a republic alone could usher in "complete, all-round, undiluted freedom."[39] Bose said that he did not believe that the Congress programme could win freedom for India, and that for winning freedom the peasants and workers would have to be organized on a socialistic programme, British goods would have to be boycotted, and the youth and women of the country would also have to be organized.

Both Nehru and Bose welcomed the formation within the Congress of a party called the Congress Socialist Party pledged to the ideal of socialism. In his presidential address at the Hari-pura Congress in 1938, Bose referred to the controversy over the formation of the Congress Socialist Party. He said that though he was not a member of that party he was "in agreement with its general principles and policy from the very beginning." Bose wanted that the leftist elements in the country should organize themselves around a socialistic programme.

During the period of the freedom struggle against an alien rule, when Bose wanted all classes to combine in the freedom movement, socialism could not be a matter of immediate importance. "Socialism is not an immediate problem for us; nevertheless," said Bose, "socialist propaganda can be conducted by a party like the Congress Socialist Party which stands for and believes in socialism."[40]

But though Bose spoke in favour of socialism, he did not believe in any particular brand of socialism. He said that socialism would have to be adjusted to Indian conditions. On 4 July 1931 Bose declared that the salvation of India, as of the world, depended on socialism but India would have to evolve her own methods and her own version of socialism. Socialism had to be applied not dogmatically, but creatively, keeping in mind the peculiarities of Indian history and geography. "India should therefore evolve her own form of socialism. When the whole world is engaged in socialistic experiments, why should we not," asked Bose, "do the same? It may be that the form of socialism which India will evolve will have something new and original about it which will be of benefit to the whole world."[41]

Not only did Bose believe that socialism would have to be harmonized with, and adapted to, Indian environment and traditions, he also believed in a synthesis of the ideals of communism and fascism, and asserted that an experiment that would combine the best elements of communism and fascism might take place in India. Bose had no repugnance either for communism or fascism as such. In fact, Bose admired Hitler, Mussolini, and Stalin as strong rulers. He did so not because he was either a fascist or a communist, but because he believed that to solve the manifold problems of India a strong ruler and an iron rule was necessary.[42] To cope with the manifold problems that plagued India Bose wanted a strong party rule as in Russia or Germany and the enforcement of a strict military discipline.[43] Bose felt that in the conditions prevailing in India, parliamentary democracy in the mid-Victorian sense could not flourish or succeed, and India needed a strong government. Bose also admired Kamal Pasha for the way he had modernized a backward country like Turkey, and like Kamal Pasha, Bose was a nationalist and not a fascist or a communist.

Bose had emotional leanings towards the "strong" ways of

modern dictators. In his book *The Indian Struggle*, written in the thirties of this century, Bose declared that Mussolini was "a man who really counts in the politics of modern Europe." He welcomed Gandhi's visit to Italy and his interview with Mussolini in 1931. "The Mahatma," he wrote, "rendered great public service by his visit to Italy. The only regret is that he did not stay there longer and did not cultivate more personal contacts."[44]

Bose was a political realist. In his *An Indian Pilgrim*, he tells us that while at Cambridge he read Bismarck's *Autobiography*, Metternich's *Memoirs*, and Cavour's letters, and that such studies "helped to rouse my political sense."[45] Again, in his Congress presidential speech at Tripuri in 1939, Bose said that he was speaking as "a cold-blooded realist," and urged that the situation should be viewed in a "thoroughly realistic manner." Bose used to say: "We have to render unto Caesar what is Caesar's."[46] Being a political realist, Bose believed in adopting a strong attitude in the course of political bargaining. He wrote: "The secret of political bargaining is to look more strong than you really are."[47]

Bose's grievance against Gandhi was that he laid all his cards on the table and appeared humble at the Second Round Table Conference in London in 1931. He wrote: "If, on the contrary, the Mahatma would have spoken in the language of Dictator Stalin, or Duce Mussolini or Fuehrer Hitler, John Bull would have understood and would have bowed his head in respect."[48]

In *The Indian Struggle*, Bose stated that the next stage of evolution in India would be a synthesis between the totalitarian ideologies of Europe or between communism and fascism. But so far as fascism is concerned, Nehru had throughout attacked it in unmistakable terms. He had said that the choice between the world lay between some form of communism and some form of fascism. Bose, on the other hand, considered that there were many common traits in fascism and communism, and that a synthesis between these two ideologies was both possible and desirable.

Bose's views on communism and fascism were fundamentally different from Nehru's. In *The Indian Struggle* Bose wrote: "A question which is on everybody's lips in Europe is: 'What is the future of Communism in India?' In this connection it is worth while quoting the expressed opinion of Pandit Jawaharlal Nehru whose popularity in India today is, according to the [present] writer, second only to that of Mahatma Gandhi. In a press statement issued on 18 December 1933, he said: 'I do believe that fundamentally the choice before the world today is one between some form of Communism and some form of Fascism, and I am all for the former, that is Communism. I dislike Fascism intensely and indeed I do not think it is anything more than a crude and brutal effort of the present capitalist order to preserve itself at any cost. There is no middle road between Fascism and Communism. One has to choose between the two and I choose the Communist ideal. In regard to the methods and approach to this ideal, I may not agree with everything that the orthodox Communists have done. I think that these methods will have to adapt themselves to changing conditions and may vary in different countries. But I do think that the basic ideology of communism and its scientific interpretation of history is sound....' The view expressed here is, according to the [present] writer, fundamentally wrong. Unless we are at the end of the process of evolution or unless we deny evolution altogether, there is no reason to hold that our choice is restricted to two alternatives... considering everything, one is inclined to hold that the next phase in world-history will produce a synthesis between Communism and Fascism. And will it be a surprise if that synthesis is produced in India?"[49]

Bose believed that India could learn from what was common in the ideologies of fascism and communism. "Both Communism and Fascism," wrote Bose, "believe in the supremacy of the State over the individual. Both denounce parliamentary democracy. Both believe in party rule. Both believe in the dictatorship of the party and in the ruthless suppression of all dissenting minorities. Both believe in a planned industrial reorganization of the country. These common traits will form the basis of the new synthesis. That synthesis is called by the writer Samyavada, an Indian word, which means literally 'the doctrine of synthesis or equality'. It will be India's task to work out this synthesis."[50] The idea of a synthesis between fascism and communism did not, however, find any wide acceptance in India.

Nehru rejected fascism altogether and denounced it as barbaric. "There are few persons in India, I suppose," said Nehru, "whether they are Indians or Englishmen, who have for years past so consistently raised their voices against Fascism and Nazism as I have done. My whole nature rebelled against them."[51]

Subhas Bose and Jawaharlal Nehru were the leaders of the left forces inside the Congress. The election of Bose as the Congress president in 1938 elated these leftist forces, and when in 1939 Subhas Bose sought re-election as the Congress president, against the express wishes of Gandhi, all the leftist forces inside the Congress united to ensure him victory in his contest with Pattabhi Sitaramyya, whose defeat Gandhi considered and acknowledged to be his own defeat. But soon after Bose's re-election as Congress president at Tripuri in 1939, G. B. Pant moved a resolution that Bose should form the Congress Working Committee with the approval of Gandhi. This resolution was passed, the result was that Bose had to resign.

After resigning as Congress president, Bose formed a Left Consolidation Committee composed of the Congress Socialists, the communists, the members of the Forward Bloc, the followers of M. N. Roy (Royists), and other leftist groups. Bose organized a protest against the decision of the Congress Working Committee which banned local Congress units from conducting mass struggles without the approval of the All India Congress Committee. The Congress High Command then threatened to expel those who sought to defy this ban, and as a result the Royists left the Left Consolidation Committee to be followed, later, by the Congress Socialists and the communists. Bose continued his opposition to the Congress High Command with the support of the Forward Bloc, the RSP, which had by then severed its connection with the CSP, and other small leftist groups.

In 1941, after war had broken out in Europe, Bose dramatically escaped from police surveillance at Calcutta and reached Germany via Afghanistan and Russia to secure outside armed assistance for Indian independence. After Bose left India and established contacts with Hitler in Germany, the British declared Bose to be an enemy agent and the communists in India, who supported the British war-effort after Russia had entered the war, also denounced Bose as a fascist. Bose knew that there was considerable revulsion against fascism in India, and his policy of seeking support from the Axis powers would give rise to grave questionings in India, but he claimed that without foreign armed assistance independence was impossible of attainment, and as such he had no alternative but to seek armed military assistance from the Tripartite Powers. "If the struggle at home had sufficed," declared Bose in Singapore on 9 July 1943, "I would not have been so foolish as to undertake this unnecessary risk and hazard."[52]

While Bose believed that for India's independence, help should be sought from all who could give such help, including the fascist powers, Nehru was wholly opposed to fascism or to any approach to the fascist powers for help. In fact, in 1942, when Gandhi decided to start the Quit India movement, Nehru had serious reservations about launching such a movement against the British at a time when it was engaged in a mortal combat with fascism.

Though both Bose and Nehru were the leaders of the leftist forces inside the Congress, and though Bose often spoke of socialism, it was Nehru who, during the thirties and forties of the century, was the most persistent advocate of socialism and friendship with Russia. Nehru was sometimes distressed about the excesses committed in Russia, but then he often excused the same by saying that they were unavoidable in the circumstances prevailing in Russia. But, throughout, Nehru had considerable reservations as to the communist approach to violence, and with the passage of years and with the growth of Gandhi's influence on him, Nehru's antipathy to violence increased.

The liberal democratic tradition of the West, which Nehru had assimilated as a student, gradually asserted itself and this, as also the influence of Gandhi, was instrumental in lessening Nehru's ardour for communism. The policies that the Communist Party of India pursued during the civil disobedience movements were wholly disapproved of by Nehru, and the support that the Indian communists gave to the British war-effort in 1942, at a time when the Congress had launched the Quit India movement, made Nehru angry and bitter, and he said that this attitude had brought the Communist Party, and the ideology in which it believed, into disrepute.

V. POST-INDEPENDENCE PLANNING AND SOCIALISM

After independence came in 1947 the question arose whether

Nehru, who led the government, would fully implement the socialistic policies which he had so long advocated. In 1948 there developed a crisis in business confidence inasmuch as Nehru, an avowed socialist, had become the Prime Minister of the country and there was a "strike of capital" pending announcement of the industrial policy of the government. Such policy was announced in 1948. This policy contemplated public ownership of munitions, atomic energy, and railways; and in certain other industries, namely, coal, iron and steel, aircrafts manufacturing, ship building, telephonic and telegraphic materials, and minerals, the government reserved the exclusive right to start new ventures, though the existing concerns in those industries were to remain free from governmental control and were not to be nationalized for at least 10 years. The rest of the industrial field was to be left open for free enterprise.

This industrial policy contained no revolutionary programme, and was welcomed by the business community, but denounced by the leftists as a retreat from socialism. The policy represented a compromise between the policies of Nehru and Patel. Patel was utterly opposed to the adoption of full-fledged socialistic measures, and furthermore Nehru realized that a full-fledged policy of revolutionary socialism would not have been acceptable to the party he led.

The 1948 industrial policy of the government has been described as a policy of the "socialization of the vacuum," that is to say, state enterprises were to be set up where private enterprises did not exist, or did not exist to the extent that they could meet the needs of the country adequately. It was felt that in an underdeveloped country like India both public and private sectors had vital roles to play, that it would be wasteful and unwise for the state to interfere with already existing industries in the private sector, but that the state could profitably invest its resources and operate in fields which were unoccupied or were not adequately occupied by private enterprise.

The policy which Nehru followed at this stage was not a policy of rigid socialism, but none the less it laid great emphasis on economic planning. Economic planning was dear to Nehru's heart, and the example of planning in Soviet Russia had enthused him greatly. In fact, in 1938, when Subhas Bose was Congress president, a National Planning Committee had been set up by the Congress to consider in what respects economic development in India could be planned. Nehru had always taken a prominent part in the deliberations of the National Planning Committee, and after India attained independence he was one of the foremost exponents of planning in India.

India's First Five Year Plan (1951–56) was moderate as compared to the subsequent plans. This Plan really integrated into a systematic framework certain specific projects which had been approved by the pre–independence Planning Department and its successor, the Advisory Board on Planning. The First Plan laid stress on agriculture, and about one-third of the total expenditure was to be allocated to it. Another large proportion of expenditure—about 23 per cent—was to be utilized in connection with the development of transport and communication. The outlays on agriculture and on transport and communication were to be made with the object of increasing the food supplies of the country, thereby reducing the pressure on foreign exchange which the importation of food grains from abroad would have entailed. In fact, under the First Plan, about two-thirds of the expenditure of the public sector was allocated for agriculture, community development, irrigation and power projects, and for transport and communications. Only 10 per cent of the expenditure was allocated for industrial development. So far as industry was concerned, it was decided that more emphasis would be given to it under the Second Plan.

The First Plan achieved a reasonable measure of success. National income increased by 18 per cent over the five years covered by the Plan, whereas population increased by 6 per cent. Per capita annual income increased, but not to a great extent, and there was considerable increase in the production of capital and consumer goods. The First Plan succeeded in maintaining the "hope level" and in making the people conscious of the benefits of planning.

In the Second Five Year Plan, Nehru insisted that more importance should be given to industry than to agriculture. The approach to nationalization still remained pragmatic, so that socialization or nationalization of all existing industries was not contemplated or advocated, but what was envisaged was that the state should play an important role in the economic field which was uncovered or not adequately covered by private enterprise.

By 1955, Nehru had persuaded the Congress to accept at its Avadi Session that its goal should be the establishment of a socialistic pattern of society. The resolution passed at Avadi stated: "Planning should take place with a view to the establishment of a socialistic pattern of society, where the principal means of production are under social ownership or control, [and where] production is progressively speeded up and there is equitable distribution of the national wealth. . . . "

But was this socialistic pattern different from socialism? To this question Nehru's answer was in the negative. In April 1956, Nehru said: "Some people seem to make fine distinctions among socialistic pattern, socialist pattern and socialism. They are all exactly the same thing without the slightest difference. But what they are is not such a very easy thing to define. . . . Doctrinaire thinking leads to rigidity . . . leaves us high and dry. This should not mean that we think of a socialist pattern of society in some flabby, goody-goody way, though there are many . . . who think [that] by an expression of goodwill to all and sundry they have done their duty."

Nehru referred to the Karachi resolution of the Congress of 1931 which had stated that the essential industries would be owned and controlled by the state, and claimed that the Avadi resolution of 1955 was merely a continuation of previous policies. It is also possible that Nehru's visit, in the meantime, to China, and the economic progress that he saw there, impressed him about the need of speeding up the rate of economic growth in India. After returning from China, Nehru contrasted the Chinese system with the democratic and parliamentary system of India. He was, however, fully conscious of the fact that the ideologically uncommitted nations of Asia were looking to China and India and were watching whether the rate of economic growth was faster under a democratic system or under a communistic system.

Nehru wanted to introduce a socialistic pattern of society in India through the democratic process and wanted to accelerate the rate of growth in the economic field by means of state planning. In the 1950s Nehru's views on socialism had become more pragmatic than before. Nehru now denounced economic dogmatism of any kind and he wanted to follow the middle path. In 1958, he said: "I do not want State socialism of that extreme kind in which the state is all powerful and governs practically all activities. The State is very powerful politically.... I should, therefore, like decentralization of economic power. We cannot, of course, decentralize iron and steel and locomotives and such other big industries, but you can have small units of industries as far as possible on a cooperative basis, with State control in a general way. I am not at all dogmatic about it. We have to learn from practical experience and proceed in our way.... My idea of socialism is that every individual in the State should have equal opportunity for progress."[53]

The Second Five Year Plan (1956–61) was designed to accelerate the rate of economic growth and to establish a welfare state in India. The object of this Plan was stated to be "a sizeable increase in national income; rapid industrialization with particular emphasis on basic and heavy industries; a large expansion of employment opportunities; and reduction of inequalities in income and wealth and a more even distribution of economic power."[54]

Under the Second Five Year Plan it was expected that the national income would increase by 25 per cent in five years, as compared with a target of 11 per cent under the First Plan. A 25 per cent rise in food production was contemplated, with a 65 per cent net increase in industrial production. The Plan was ambitious, and only about 25 per cent of the planned outlay was to be covered by existing and new taxes, railway profits, etc. Another 25 per cent was to come from loans and small savings. A further 25 per cent was to be met by deficit financing, and the balance 25 per cent from foreign aid and untapped domestic resources. The aim of this ambitious Second Plan was to maintain a fairly high "hope level." Nehru stated in Parliament in September 1956 that the Plan was based on an act of faith, and he had faith in the capacity of the Indian people.

But the Second Plan met with unexpected difficulties. There were widespread floods, hailstorms, and drought in 1956-57 and food production suffered. The programme of industrialization also meant import of costly equipment, and this caused a drain on foreign resources. In the meantime, inflationary trends had developed in India. To check the inflationary trends and cope with the financial crisis and to obtain further funds for development, further tax burdens were imposed by the 1957-58 Budget. By the middle of 1958, the Second Five Year Plan was facing real difficulties, and hence arose the need of slicing or pruning the Plan with the hard core of the plan remaining unaltered, namely, agricultural production, power projects, and the three steel plants, one built with British assistance, the second with Russian assistance, and the third with German assistance.

The Third Plan was much more ambitious, and its targets were more than double those of the Second. In 1957, Nehru had said that if the objectives of the Second Plan were achieved, India would cross the danger barrier which separated an underdeveloped country from a developing country, and once that barrier was crossed, the rate of growth in the economic field would be faster. So far as the Third Plan was concerned its objective had been to take India to a stage where the national economy would be self-sustaining. It cannot be denied, however, that India has not reached the self-sustaining stage, but according to Walt Rostow—whose concepts as to the stages of economic growth have received world-wide attention—India may be considered to be in the "take-off" stage.

Nehru had always been a great exponent of planning, but he insisted that planning in India must be implemented within the framework of a political democracy and should not lead to totalitarianism. Whether a democratic political structure is compatible with the kind of efficient planning that can rapidly raise the standards of living of an underdeveloped country, is one of the great questions that India faces. The Planning Commission that was set up in India stated that India has embarked on an experiment in democratic planning which is perhaps larger and more complex than any in the modern world. "What is on trial," it said, "is, in the last analysis, whether democracy can solve the problems of mass poverty. It is a trial perhaps never before made in such an atmosphere of urgency."[55]

In India most of the institutions of production are in private hands, and the Indian economy has been described as the world's greatest example of functioning anarchy, where a smallish socialized sector has been superimposed atop this anarchical economic structure. But the planners in India, from the very beginning, proceeded on the basis that in India production could be maximized only if the public and private sectors were allowed to coexist. Discussing about the First Five Year Plan in December 1952, the Planning Commission stated: "In a planned economy the distinction between the public and the private sector is one of emphasis. The two sectors are and must function as parts of single organism."[56]

The technics of planning in India have been democratic. Plans have been finalized after considerable discussion in the country. The draft outline of the First Plan was published in July 1951, and this was followed by continuous discussions in Parliament, in the press, and throughout the country, and the final draft was approved only in December 1952. The process of discussion in finalizing the plan which was followed in the case of the First Plan was also followed in the case of the Second and Third Plans.

The composition and functioning of the Planning Commission, however, gave rise to considerable controversy in the country. The Planning Commission was at first envisaged merely as an advisory body, but the association of Prime Minister Nehru and the Finance Minister in the Planning Commission gave it much greater prestige and authority. Many, who were opposed to the radical economic ideas of Nehru, have, therefore, criticized the functioning of the Planning Commission. In 1959 K. M. Munshi asserted that it was not Parliament but a nominated super-cabinet, the Planning Commission—which owed no responsibility to Parliament—that governed India. But the most trenchant criticism of the Planning Commission came from Professor D. R. Gadgil, a leading economist of India, who stated that though the Planning Commission was established only "to assess resources, formulate the plan, define its stages, appraise progress and make related recommendations on policy and administration," it failed in this task because, instead of acting as an advisory body, it engaged itself with the actual process of the formation of public policies even in matters other than development. This happened because of the power complex of the Planning Commission and its members, and led to the needless extension of its activities to many irrelevant fields. "The misdirection has been helped largely," wrote Gadgil, "by membership of the Prime Minister and the Finance Minister of the Planning Commission which appears to have invested the Planning Commission and its decision with an unnatural kind of prestige and importance."[57]

As a result of the criticism that the Planning Commission was tending to become a super-cabinet, certain reforms were made in 1967 when it was decided that the Central Ministers should not generally be associated with the Planning Commission. Accordingly the Planning Commission was considerably reorganized in order to emphasize its advisory character, and it was decided that the Finance Minister should not be its member. The Prime Minister, however, continued to be a member of the Commission.

Whatever the structure or composition of the Planning Commission might have been, Nehru, during his life-time, dominated the Planning Commission as much as he dominated the Congress Party, and even the Indian Parliament. Nehru had a great faith in planning, but he also believed that the private sector and the public sector could peacefully and profitably coexist in India. Nehru believed in a mixed economy in which private enterprises would be controlled but not done away with. On 21 December 1954, Nehru stated in the Lok Sabha: "But it is obvious, in a country as undeveloped as ours, that we cannot progress except by state initiative, except by enlarging the public sector . . . except by controlling the private sector at important points. . . . It is very necessary that the private sector should function under certain broad strategic controls, but otherwise, with freedom and with initiative. The private sector is a part of the Plan, a coordinated part; this is where the strategic controls come in."[58]

VI. THE YEARS OF POWER AND PRAGMATIC SOCIALISM

In 1955 Nehru induced the Congress at its Avadi session to officially accept the socialist pattern of society as its goal. About a decade later, in January 1964, Nehru even persuaded the Congress to pass a resolution at its Bhubaneshwar session approving of the eventual establishment of "a socialist state" in India. Yet, Nehru's views on socialism and his approach to socialism did not remain static over the years, and became more and more pragmatic with the passage of time.

Before independence Nehru had spoken only of the doctrines

14

of socialism, but after independence he was faced with the problem of putting them into practice. The socialist doctrines, which Nehru had previously preached, had to be applied within a particular and existing institutional framework, that is to say, within the framework of political democracy and a constitution which guaranteed certain property rights. In this framework the process for the establishment of socialism could only be peaceful, slow, and evolutionary. It is this evolutionary path that Nehru sought to follow during the years of power.

And perhaps it is for this reason that, in respect of the period after independence, some have described Nehru as a hesitant socialist while Nehru regarded himself as a democratic socialist. Nehru wanted to introduce socialism without violence and without dictatorship. "I believed more and more," he said, "in socialism. More and more even in some parts of communism; not the action, but the theory part of it; a communist society somewhere in the future. But . . . the methods should be peaceful, broadly speaking peaceful, and not wrong. Whether the two can be synchronized or not it is difficult to say. But I am deeply convinced that the methods in certain communist societies, that is too much coercion and suffering, are not the right methods."[59]

In the fifties and sixties of this century, Nehru's position as regards Marxism and communism was considerably different from his previous position. He had then come to believe that the advances since Marx wrote had made Marxism, in the literal nineteenth-century sense, outdated. Moreover, Nehru could never reconcile himself completely to any rigid ideology. Narendra Dev, a leading Indian socialist who knew Nehru well, said that Nehru did not believe "in any particular ism. . . . He believes in some of the fundamental principles of scientific socialism, yet he is not prepared to swear by everything taught by Marx and Lenin. He does not subscribe to any rigid ideology. He considers himself free to examine the claims of every system of ideas . . . and he is always revising his ideas in the light of new experiences gained." In fact, Nehru considered life and reality to be too complex and complicated to be capable of being confined within the four corners of a rigid theory.[60]

Further, one of the major attractions of communism and Marxism for Nehru during the pre-independence days was their anti-imperialistic character. So long as India was a subject country, Nehru could denounce capitalism and imperialism in the same breath, and regard the latter as only a manifestation of the former. The roots of Nehru's socialism undoubtedly lay in his concern for peace and in a revulsion against imperialism, as much as in the hatred of exploitation and love of economic equality and justice. But after imperial rule in India was ended and a political democracy was established, the political and economic perspective necessarily changed. With the elimination of imperialism in India, the question that remained to be solved, so far as Nehru was concerned, was how the ideal of socialism was to be combined with the practice of democracy. The questions that Nehru then had to face were whether capitalism and free enterprise should be abolished altogether or merely controlled, and whether economic changes should be effected in a peaceful manner or by the adoption of violent and revolutionary means.

In 1933, writing to his daughter, who was later to hold the office of Prime Minister which he first held in free India, Nehru defined socialism as the control of the means of production and distribution, that is, land, mines, factories, banks, etc., by the state.[61] While speaking to the Congress as its president in 1936, Nehru again defined socialism as meaning a revolutionary change in the social structure and the ending of vested interests in land and industry.[62] About the same time, in his *Autobiography* (1936), Nehru said that everything that came in the way of such a revolutionary change would have to be removed gently, if possible, and forcibly, if necessary,[63] but in 1947, when he became the first Prime Minister of free India, Nehru had to face the question of how far and with what speed the ideals he had preached, and the methods he had advocated, in the past, could be adopted in the context of a changed and changing India. Being the head of a democratic republic, Nehru did not, and could not, adopt any violent or revolutionary means to achieve socialism.

Nehru's socialism during the years of power was pragmatic rather than rigid, and he has been described by some as an empirical gradualist and by others as a pragmatic socialist. During the years of power, Nehru envisaged that the private sector had a role to play along with the public sector, and he did not speak of the expropriation of private property or of the immediate or wholesale socialization of the means of production. Nehru proclaimed and put into practice his faith in planning, but in the context of, and within the limits of, a democratic polity. This flexible and pragmatic economic policy has been characterized by communists and some of his previous admirers of the left as a retreat from socialism and as a sign of Nehru's "inability to ride the waves of social revolution."[64]

Nehru himself once remarked: "Communists have called me a petty bourgeois with perfect justification. Perhaps they might label me now as one of the 'repentant bourgeoisie'." But in Nehru's socialism there was always an element of individualism and a desire to raise production—and not merely to have equitable distribution—as also a desire to adapt socialism to Indian conditions and to India's peculiar agrarian problems, and to harmonize socialism with democracy. In fact, Nehru was as much the product of socialism as of Western liberalism and Gandhism, and he never gave up his faith in democracy and his belief in the purity of the means.

The influence of Gandhi and his own ingrained belief in democracy increasingly made Nehru suspicious of the doctrine of class struggle and the theory of the desirability of adopting revolutionary means for effecting social and economic changes. Accordingly, Nehru's attitude to socialism and communism in the forties, and more particularly, in the fifties, of this century was considerably different from his attitude of the thirties when he had often talked of "Soviet democracy."

Nehru denounced the role of the communists during the Quit India movement of 1942. Nehru was also a member of the special Congress Committee of 1945 which recommended the expulsion of the communists from the Congress. About a decade later, in November 1954, referring to the communists, Nehru said: "They have no moorings in the land of their birth, but always look to outside countries for inspiration and guidance. They are of the opinion that internecine trouble, violence, and bloodshed are the main things to be pursued."[65]

After independence was attained, the Indian government led by Nehru encountered one of its most serious clashes with the communists when the latter participated in a violent agrarian movement at Telangana in Hyderabad. Nehru denounced this movement, and took effective steps to suppress it. He also denounced any attempt to start a countrywide insurrection on the Chinese pattern, and was not prepared to countenance any revolutionary movement in India which was sustained by Maoist practice.

Further, the riots and communal frenzy that followed independence gave Nehru a horror of violence and made him suspicious of attaining anything through violence. It was one thing to have welcomed or, at least, countenanced, revolutionary communism during the freedom movement in India on the ground that the violence of communism was less offensive than the violence of fascism or capitalism, but it was a different thing altogether to allow or encourage any violent programme or method after India had attained independence and had a framework of political democracy. Nehru's approach to revolutionary methods changed considerably after the experience of the violence and communal frenzy that erupted in India on the eve of, and also as an aftermath to, the partition of the country in 1947.

After India attained independence in 1947, Nehru spoke of India as a bastion of democracy where the people were engaged in a great social experiment to achieve socialism by peaceful, democratic, and evolutionary means. He referred to planning and the economic experiment which was going on in India within the framework of a political democracy, and contrasted it with the Russian experience and the Chinese pattern. India, proclaimed Nehru, would tread the path towards socialism on the basis of democracy, without following the path of revolutionary violence, and without establishing a dictatorship of the proletariat.

In the end, Nehru came to believe in a mixed economy oriented towards socialism and proceeding to that goal peacefully and in a democratic manner. Nehru also condemned the coercion associated with communist planning.[66] There were some who wondered whether the objectives of communism could be achieved without violence, and raised the old question whether Nehru could have Russia's fruit without Russia's blood. But it is in the synchronization and harmonization of socialism and economic planning with peaceful and democratic methods that Nehru eventually rested his faith.[67]

214   SOCIALISM AND COMMUNISM IN INDIA

NOTES AND REFERENCES

1. Jawaharlal Nehru, *An Autobiography*, London, 1955, p. 529.
2. Ibid., p. 35.
3. Ibid., pp. 56-63.
4. Ibid., p. 164.
5. *Nehru on Socialism*, pp. 50-51.
6. Jawaharlal Nehru, *Glimpses of World History*, Vol. II, pp. 851-52.
7. *Important Speeches of Jawaharlal Nehru*, pp. 4-14.
8. Ibid.
9. Ibid.
10. Jawaharlal Nehru, *A Bunch of Old Letters*, 2nd ed., 1960, p. 363.
11. Welles Hangen, *After Nehru, Who?*, London 1963, p. 181.
12. Jawaharlal Nehru, *A Bunch of Old Letters*, 2nd ed., 1960, pp. 188-89.
13. Ibid., p. 192.
14. Ibid., pp. 195-96.
15. Ibid., pp. 203-4.
16. Jawaharlal Nehru, *An Autobiography*, 1955, p. 365.
17. Ibid., p. 72.
18. Jawaharlal Nehru, *The Discovery of India*, p. 12.
19. Jawaharlal Nehru, *Before and After Independence* ed. J. S. Bright, 1950, p. 410.
20. D. G. Tendulkar, *The Mahatma*, 1954, Vol. 8, Appendix on Gandhi-Nehru letters, pp. 289-90.
21. Jawaharlal Nehru, *Eighteen Months In India*, Allahabad, 1938, p. 64.
22. Jawaharlal Nehru, *India and the World*, 1936, pp. 27-28.
23. Jawaharlal Nehru, *An Autobiography*, 1936, pp. 551-52.
24. Ibid., p. 591.
25. Jawarharlal Nehru, *The Discovery of India*, p. 29.
26. Ibid., pp. 13-14.
27. Jawaharlal Nehru, *An Autobiography*, 1936, p. 363.
28. Jawaharlal Nehru, *The Discovery of India*, 1946, p. 394.
29. *Nehru On Socialism*, p. 25.
30. Ibid.
31. Jawaharlal Nehru, "Orthodoxes of All Religions Unite," in *The Modern Review*, December 1935, p. 630.
32. Jawaharlal Nehru, *Towards Freedom*, 1941, p. 235.
33. Jawaharlal Nehru, *The Unity of India*, 1944, pp. 294-95.
34. Jawaharlal Nehru, *The Discovery of India*, 1946, pp. 386-87.
35. Jawaharlal Nehru, *A Bunch of Old Letters*, 1958, p. 347.
36. Jawaharlal Nehru, *The Unity of India*, 1944, pp. 148-49.
37. *Selected Speeches of Subhas Chandra Bose*, 1962, p. 50.
38. Ibid., p. 32.
39. Presidential Address at the Karachi Conference of the All-India Naujawan Bharat Sabha, 27 March 1931 (*Selected Speeches of Subhas Chandra Bose*, 1962, p. 62).
40. *Selected Speeches of Subhas Chandra Bose*, ed. S. A. Aiyer, 1962, p. 91.

41. Presidential address at the All-India Trade Union Congress Session in Calcutta, 4 July 1931, *Selected Speeches of Subhas Chandra Bose*, 1962, p. 69.
42. *Hindustan Times*, 8 March 1946.
43. Subhas Bose, *The Indian Struggle*, pp. 428-29.
44. Ibid., p. 322.
45. Ibid., p. 122.
46. Ibid., p. 409.
47. Ibid., p. 320.
48. Ibid.
49. Ibid., pp. 345-47.
50. Ibid.
51. Jawaharlal Nehru, *The Unity of India*, 1944, p. 397.
52. *Selected Speeches of Subhas Chandra Bose*, ed. S. A. Aiyer, p. 185.
53. Speech to the All India Congress Committee (Michael Brecher, *Nehru: A Political Biography*, paperback edition, p. 204).
54. *Second Five Year Plan*, p. 24.
51. Planning Commission, *The New India: Progress Through Democracy*, 1958, p. 4.
56. Planning Commission, Government of India, *The First Five Year Plan*, New Delhi, 1958, p. 9.
57. D. R. Gadgil, *Indian Planning and the Planning Commission*, Ahmedabad, 1958.
58. *Nehru's Speeches*, Vol. III, pp. 14-15.
59. *Conversations with Nehru*, 1956, pp. 31-32.
60. Narendra Deva, *Socialism And National Revolution*, Bombay, 1946, p. 206.
61. Jawaharlal Nehru, *Glimpses of World History*, Vol. II, pp. 851-52.
62. *Important Speeches of Jawaharlal Nehru*, pp. 4-14.
63. Jawaharlal Nehru, *An Autobiography*, 1936, pp. 551-52.
64. Hiren Mukherjee, *The Gentle Colossus: A Study of Jawaharlal Nehru*, Calcutta, 1964, p. 176.
65. *The Hindu*, 29 November 1954.
66. *Conversations with Mr. Nehru*, 1956, pp. 31-32.
67. Ibid.

CHAPTER SIX

The Congress Split and Socialism

I. POLARIZATION INSIDE THE CONGRESS

After Nehru's death the Congress continued to reiterate its faith in socialism. But it always contained within its fold both rightist as well as leftist elements. During his lifetime, Nehru was the leader and inspirer of the leftist forces inside the Congress, just as Sardar Patel was of the rightist forces. After Nehru's death the importance of any single individual in shaping the policies of the Congress diminished, and power at the top passed to a group of important leaders, that is to say, the era of collective leadership emerged. But the Congress, as before, continued to accommodate within its fold both rightist and leftist forces.

Lal Bahadur Shastri, who succeeded Nehru as the Prime Minister of India, held, more or less, a centrist position within the Congress. Mrs Indira Gandhi, who succeeded Lal Bahadur, also held a centrist position leaning, however, towards the left. Compared to Indira Gandhi, Morarji Desai—who was Deputy Prime Minister and Finance Minister until Indira Gandhi relieved him of his office in July 1969—was a rightist.

After the fourth general elections of 1967, and particularly after the mid-term elections of 1969, there has been much talk of polarization of rightist and leftist forces both inside the Congress as well as outside. The leftists inside the Congress, some of whom are called the Young Turks, were committed to a policy of more rapid nationalization of banks and certain industries. The Young Turks and Chandra Shekhar, in particular, one of their leaders, clashed repeatedly with Morarji Desai on the question of nationalization of banks and on the question of the speed with which socialistic measures should be introduced into India. The Young Turks also clashed with other elder leaders of the Congress, such as S. K. Patil and Atulya Ghosh, as also with Nijalingappa, the Congress President of 1969.

Nijalingappa, in his presidential address at the Faridabad session of the Congress in April 1969, criticized the performance of certain public sector industries. Such criticism immediately gave rise to controversy, and the question was raised whether Nijalingappa was, at heart, a socialist. Stung by such criticism, Nijalingappa declared: "I am a socialist to the core but I am an Indian socialist, not of any other brand." He said that he had no particular love for the private sector, but, at the same time, he did not think that large units should be started in the public sector merely to suit socialist slogans.[1]

At this Faridabad session in April 1969 the theory that there should be a polarization of leftist and rightist forces inside the Congress was criticized, as also the theory that the Congress would not be able to gain a majority at the centre in the fifth general elections to be held in 1972 and that, therefore, the Congress should enter into coalitions with like-minded parties. The panel report prepared by Y. B. Chavan, along with Karan Singh, Hitendra Desai, and others, which was adopted, with minor changes, by the Congress Working Committee at Faridabad in April 1969, deplored any despondency about the future and refused to envisage the contingency of a deadlocked parliament in 1972. The panel report claimed that the Congress ideology of democratic socialism was the only way in which the nation could make rapid progress, and that any attempt at polarization and splitting up of the party on the basis of extreme right or left ideologies would be a disruptive process which would not only weaken the party but also hinder the political and economic development of the country.[2]

In April 1969 Indira Gandhi deprecated any talk of polarization within the Congress, and declared that such talk arose out of the frustration of individuals, rather than from serious political thinking. According to her the Congress was, and should remain, a centrist organization, and should not split itself into rightist and leftist factions. It is significant in this connection that the call given during this time by V. K. Krishna Menon, once a close associate of Nehru who later left the Congress and was eventually returned to Parliament in 1969 from a constituency in Bengal on a Bangla Congress ticket after defeating a Congress candidate, to the "progressives" inside the Congress to leave the Congress and strengthen the leftist and socialist forces outside the Congress, did not find favour even with the Young Turks.

The Young Turks, and particularly Chandra Shekhar, however, asserted that on issues like concentration of economic power—against which there were directives in the Constitution —the Congress could cooperate with the communists, the SSP, and the PSP. Further, Chandra Shekhar strongly pleaded for the nationalization of banks and other financial institutions to bring about a radical change in the credit policy of the country. He criticized Morarji Desai for not nationalizing the banks, and asserted that for about 20 years the Congress had not taken any radical economic measure. He warned that if people's aspirations were not fulfilled then some form of violent revolution may break out.[3]

Chandra Shekhar's criticisms of the economic policies of Desai mingled with personal criticism. Desai resented this and made an issue of it, and Indira Gandhi was entrusted with the task of reprimanding Chandra Shekhar. Though, eventually, the Chandra Shekhar affair was treated as closed, the differences within the Congress Party were not stilled.

During pre–independence period the Congress had been a platform for all those who desired to participate in the freedom movement. To that extent, the Congress was a united front which embraced within it all shades of political opinion. It included conservatives and radicals, respectable members of the bourgeoisie as also fiery socialists, the rightist S. K. Patil, as also the leftist Krishna Menon. During Nehru's time, these differences existed, but were not strong enough to split the organization and, furthermore, all groups within the Congress felt that Nehru was indispensable. When Patel was the Home Minister of free India the differences between the leftist Nehru and the rightist Patel sometimes became very acute, but Gandhi in his lifetime could, in a measure, control both Nehru and Patel and prevent them from falling apart altogether.

After Patel's death, Nehru's authority was unquestioned till the Chinese aggression on India when, under the pressure of public criticism, Nehru had to drop the leftist Menon from the Union Cabinet. Lal Bahadur Shastri succeeded Nehru as Prime Minister. He was a man of the centre and the leftists and rightists inside the Congress could carry on under him. After the Indo–Pak conflict, Shastri emerged as a leader whose authority could not be lightly challenged.

But since the Congress was really a united front which contained within it people holding widely divergent political, social, and economic ideas, it could not indefinitely avoid the conflict between the leftists and rightists which had always existed within it. In the end the split in the Congress took place in November 1969. The roots of the split lay deep in Congress history, but the proximate causes of the split were the decisions taken at the Bangalore session of the All India Congress Committee (AICC) in July 1969—firstly, approving Indira Gandhi's Note on economic policy favouring *inter alia* bank nationalization and, secondly, approving Sanjiva Reddy as the Congress nominee for the presidential election, against the wishes of Indira Gandhi—and the events that succeeded these decisions in a dramatic sequence.

The clash of personalities and the desire to retain power played their part in bringing about the split. But the clash of ideas and attitudes also had much to do with it. Eventually, inside the Congress, Indira Gandhi, Jagjivan Ram, and Fakhruddin Ali Ahmed formed one group, and Nijalingappa, Kamaraj, Atulya Ghosh, and S. K. Patil another. The latter group was generally referred to as the Syndicate. Towards the end of the drama which brought about the split, Morarji Desai was also treated as a part of the Syndicate though he had not originally belonged to it, and though after being divested of the finance portfolio by Indira Gandhi he remarked that he had been the victim of the Syndicate. Chavan had supported Sanjiva Reddy's candidature for the presidency against the wishes of Indira Gandhi but after Reddy lost the election and disciplinary proceedings were contemplated by Nijalingappa against Indira Gandhi, Chavan took the leading part to avoid a split and to cause a unity resolution to be passed by the Congress Working Committee in August 1969. Since then, he supported Indira Gandhi and declared that he would reach the goal of socialism with her.[4]

Indira Gandhi and her supporters saw the conflict within the

Congress as a conflict between those who fully supported the socialistic and secular policies of the Congress and others who were not fully committed to them. Early in November 1969 Indira Gandhi wrote to Nijalingappa that his Faridabad speech as the Congress president in April 1969, where he had denounced the inefficiency of the public sector, was regarded by many as more appropriate to a leader of the Swatantra Party, which was hostile to socialism.

The split in the Congress took place not merely because of a clash of personalities, but even more so because of a clash of ideologies. The differences between Nehru and Patel were certainly not mere differences in temperament, but were primarily differences in outlook, approach and ideology. So also were the differences between Indira Gandhi and Morarji Desai. Though even after the split there continued to be rightists and leftists both inside the old Congress and the new Congress, yet the ideological reasons and causes which led to the split cannot, by any means, be ignored.

The attitude of other political parties to the split within the Congress also showed that the split was not based merely on a clash of personalities. The opposition parties welcomed this split because they could profit by it. But which opposition party supported which particular group within the Congress was also significant. The Swatantra and Jana Sangh generally supported the stand taken by Nijalingappa and his group, and other opposition parties, barring the ssp, which was pledged to a policy of anti-Congressism, supported Indira Gandhi and her group.

When Nehru and Patel differed, the leftists supported Nehru and the rightists stood by Patel. Similarly, when Indira Gandhi clashed with Morarji Desai, the leftists stood by her and the rightists by Morarji Desai. In fact, on 8 November 1968 Balraj Madhok, the Jana Sangh leader, said that if the "split in the Congress led to one of the factions adopting the 'Nehru line' and the other the 'Patel line', it would help polarization of political forces in the country... if Mr Nijalingappa takes the Patel line, my party will be with him.... The split was welcome and good for the country. If Gandhi's will was followed, it would have happened in 1948, leading to the creation of two viable parties, one led by Nehru and the other by Patel. The present split was acting as a catalyst to political polarization. Though the 'tussle appeared to be one of personalities, the ideological over-tones were unmistakable. For example, the resolution adopted by the Congress Working Committee on Rabat is just like what it would have been if Patel was alive."5

After the Congress was split into two parties, namely, the Congress (Requisitionist) and the Congress (Organization), an adjournment motion was moved in the Lok Sabha for censoring the government for having participated in the Rabat Con-ference, which, it was said, was a purely Islamic and, therefore, a religious conference. The voting on this adjournment motion showed how the polarization had taken place in the country. The motion was supported by the Swatantra, Jana Sangh, the Congress (o), the ssp and some independent members and was opposed, amongst others, by the Congress (r), DMK, CPI, CPI(M), and BKD, and was rejected by 306 to 140 votes.6

The CPI and the CPI(M) supported Indira Gandhi on the issue of bank nationalization, as also on the Rabat question, saying that the Swatantra, the Jana Sangh, and the Syndicate, who were utterly anti-communist, had aligned themselves in order to bring about a right take-over at the centre. The CPI, however, was a much more vigorous supporter of Indira Gandhi than the CPI(M).

The CPI had always asserted that there was a progressive section inside the Congress Party, and they now said that Indira Gandhi represented that progressive section. In August 1969 Biswanath Mukherjee, a CPI Minister in the United Front gov-ernment of Bengal, and Dr Ranen Sen, the secretary of the West Bengal unit of the CPI, asked the people to appreciate that the Congress Party was splitting into two not because of mere personal squabbles, but because of the people's movements which had "so scared the rightist forces that they were not prepared to take any chance."7 They referred to the fact that the CPI had been forecasting such a situation in the Congress Party for quite a number of years. "When we spoke of progressives in the Congress some of our comrades laughed, broke away and formed the CPI(M). Today, even those revolutionaries have to hail Mrs Gandhi for nationalizing 14 banks and to acknowledge the existence of ideological differences in the Congress."8 In view of the developing situation it was meaningless to remain allergic to all Congressmen. Rather, every effort should be made, they said, to draw out the progressive elements from the Congress to "fight the reactionary elements in that party who have ganged up with the Swatantra Party and the Jana Sangh."

The CPI(M) also considered that there were some real differences between the two groups inside the Congress, and between the two they decided to support the group led by Indira Gandhi, but the CPI(M) was not prepared to admit that there was a progressive section inside the Congress. In August 1969 Promode Das Gupta, the secretary of the West Bengal unit of the CPI(M), asserted that the opposition of the CPI(M) to Reddy and the support for Giri did not mean that the CPI(M) had, at last, found a "progressive section" in the Congress Party. The Syndicate was only "the open spokesmen of the reactionaries." Both the Syndicate and the group led by Indira Gandhi were interested "in the maintenance of the monopoly of power," but they adopted different tactics. The Syndicate wanted to maintain its exclusive hold in alliance with the Jana Sangh and the Swatantra Party through "the suppression of all democratic forces, and by dislodging the United Front governments and by establishing a police State." The Prime Minister, on the other hand, wanted to retain her position by "resorting to manoeuvres, some concessions and some form of understanding with non–Congress parties."[9] Between "the two evils" the CPI(M) decided to support Giri and the group led by the Prime Minister in the presidential election. The victory of a "Syndicate candidate," according to Promode Das Gupta, would mean that the democratic forces would be immediately threatened and it might have even led to the banning of the CPI(M).

The Jana Sangh and the Swatantra, who opposed Giri, also considered that the presidential election raised ideological questions. According to them the division in the country was between those who thought that the communists posed a threat to India's security and way of life and others who did not think so. In August 1969, A. B. Vajpayee, president of the Jana Sangh, stated that on the question of the presidential election, Indian politics had arrived at a cross-road, and the Congress was bound to be split into two from the highest level to the lowest level, though the split would not be on the basis of economic issues or between leftists and rightists. "The issues at stake are really political, and also personal. The conflict is not between those who believe in nationalization, and those who believe in free enterprise (the Jana Sangh, I stress, does not believe in free enterprise, though we do not subscribe to the creed of socialism either). The conflict really is between those who regard communists as a grave menace to nationalism and democracy and those who fail to recognize them as such."[10] Similarly, referring to Indira Gandhi, M. R. Masani, the Swatantra MP, said in August 1969 that the Prime Minister was coming out "more and more openly in her true colours." "I would describe her accurately as a communist fellow-traveller who in the company of communists has set her foot on the' slippery slope of dictatorship."[11]

Some of those inside the Congress, who were opposed to Indira Gandhi, charged that she was soft to the communists and was even encouraging them. In August 1969, Sucheta Kripalani —Congress MP and former Chief Minister of Uttar Pradesh— asserted that Indira Gandhi was under the influence of persons who were fellow-travellers of the communists.[12] Referring to bank nationalization she said that, though she was not opposed to the measure itself, the Prime Minister had taken the step in a "huff, in anger, and to give an economic face to a political move."[13] Similarly, in August 1969 the former Congress president, Kamaraj said that the communists, whose strategy was to create confusion and then to seize power, were infiltrating into the Congress, and he called upon the' Congress not to fall a prey to communist strategy.[14] Kamaraj felt that it was wrong to brand Congressmen as reactionaries or progressives. Further, critics of Indira Gandhi said that by making a plea for a free vote during the presidential election, Indira Gandhi had broken party discipline and that she was seeking to act as a dictator.

Indira Gandhi charged that those inside the Congress who were opposed to the party's programme of a socialistic pattern of society were carrying on a whispering campaign against her.[15] She lamented that she had been described by certain people as a dictator for having implemented the programme set before the party by its leaders fifteen years ago. "If these people had guts, they should have opposed the programme then. Now when I am trying to implement the programme, I am being labelled a dictator."[16] She asserted that those who had voted for the socialistic programme had no business to say anything against it or against bank nationalization. Referring to the charge that she was trying to promote communism, Indira Gandhi said: "If

I wanted to become a communist nothing could have prevented me from doing so. It does not sound reasonable to say that by implementing Congress programmes and policies I have become a communist."[17] Indira Gandhi asserted that bank nationalization was the beginning of a bitter struggle between the common man on the one side and a few individuals on the other, and that if her critics were "itching for a fight," then the people of India were also prepared for a showdown and she would fight back.[18] She would not retreat from the battle merely because some had dubbed her as a communist. Speaking in Parliament on 7 August 1969 she likened this bogey of communism to McCarthyism: "It is strange to see that McCarthyism, long dead in the place of its birth, should find its foothold across the seas and continents to India. Those who propound this theory show astounding ignorance of political forces at work in our country and the facts of life in the India of 1969."[19]

With the passage of time, the differences between the Congress leaders increased. It was clear that two groups—one led by Indira Gandhi and the other known by the imprecise term, the Syndicate—had emerged inside the Congress and were contending for mastery over that organization. Eventually the confrontation between these two groups led to the Congress split of November 1969.

II. INDIRA GANDHI, BANK NATIONALIZATION AND THE PRESIDENTIAL ELECTION

The proximate causes of the Congress split, as already stated, were the decisions taken at the Bangalore session of the AICC held in July 1969. At this session it came to be known that Indira Gandhi, the Prime Minister, had in a Note favoured the nationalization of the major banks. Those within the Congress fold who call themselves radicals and particularly the Young Turks were working hard to commit the Prime Minister on the issue of bank nationalization. They were naturally happy that the Prime Minister had associated her name with a set of proposals which would give the Congress a more leftward orientation. But as soon as the Prime Minister's Note was read out, S. K. Patil, known for his rightist views, protested against reviving the suggestion for the take-over of the banks, and expressed his fear that a snap decision for nationalization would dislocate the credit structure and disrupt the country's economy.[20] The then Deputy Prime Minister, Morarji Desai, similarly claimed that social control of the banks, which had been brought into force only six months ago, should be given a trial at least for another two years, and that any hasty nationalization of the banks would shake the confidence of the public in the banking system. But Fakhruddin Ali Ahmed came out in support of Indira Gandhi's Note and the former Congress president Kamaraj, who had previously expressed his support for bank nationalization, said that the Note should be approved and forwarded to the government for implementation. Eventually this was done.

On 13 July 1969, the AICC unanimously adopted a resolution endorsing the broad guidelines contained in the Prime Minister's Note. The resolution passed by the AICC stated that the Note of the Prime Minister set out the policies to be pursued for improving the performance of the economy in industry and agriculture and for ensuring that the process of economic development did not lead to concentration of wealth and economic power in a few hands. This resolution was eventually proposed by Morarji Desai, who had previously been a protagonist of social control of banks as an alternative to their nationalization. In seconding the resolution Chavan said that he could not say whether nationalization of banks would be done "today, tomorrow or next year" since that depended upon the party's "political wisdom."[21]

Though Indira Gandhi's proposal on bank nationalization was accepted by the Congress at Bangalore, her suggestions as to who should be the Congress nominee for the office of the president of India in the vacancy caused by the death of Zakir Husain was rejected by the Congress Parliamentary Board. Indira Gandhi had first suggested the name of V. V. Giri, who was the Acting President, and then of Jagjivan Ram. The Board, however, decided in favour of N. Sanjiva Reddy, the then Speaker of the Lok Sabha. On 13 July 1969, Nijalingappa, the Congress President, formally and publicly declared that Sanjiva Reddy was the Congress nominee for the presidency of the Indian Union. Immediately after this announcement was made, V. V. Giri

15

announced that he would be a candidate for the presidency of the Indian Union.

The decision to nominate Reddy was taken by the Congress Parliamentary Board on 12 July 1969 outvoting Indira Gandhi's final nominee, Jagjivan Ram. The eight-member Board comprised Nijalingappa, Indira Gandhi, Jagjivan Ram, S. K. Patil, Fakhruddin Ali Ahmed, Kamaraj, Morarji Desai, and Chavan. Chavan's role was of crucial importance because if he had sided with Indira Gandhi—the other two supporters being Jagjivan Ram and Fakhruddin Ali Ahmed—there would have been a four-to-four tie. In the end the voting was four to two in favour of Reddy. Both Nijalingappa and Jagivan Ram abstained from voting. This was the second time that the Congress Parliamentary Board decided on a candidate against the wishes of the Prime Minister. In 1957 the Board had overruled Nehru's opposition to the renomination of Dr Rajendra Prasad.

Immediately after the Board's decision to nominate Sanjiva Reddy was made known, Indira Gandhi said that the Board's decision in forcing a candidate on her was related to "my view and attitudes and my social and foreign policies. . . . When one holds certain views one expects to be attacked."[22] Indira Gandhi characterized the manner in which the Board decided on Reddy's candidature as "certainly distressing." She said that she had been working on the principle that the office of president was not a party post and had sought to evolve a consensus, and the two names that had emerged in the discussion that she had with others were those of Giri and Jagjivan Ram. Indira Gandhi made it clear that she would fight against her opponents in the organization, and as regards the unity of the organization, she posed the question, "certainly there should be unity, but unity of purpose for what?"[23]

On 16 July 1969, in a dramatic sequence, Indira Gandhi as Prime Minister relieved Morarji Desai of the finance portfolio and the latter resigned from the Cabinet. On that day Indira Gandhi had written to Morarji Desai stating that in view of the mandate from the AICC she would not like to place the burden of implementing the economic programme on him. Within a few hours of the receipt of this letter, Desai sent in his letter of resignation.

Most opposition parties welcomed the exit of Desai from the

Cabinet. They hailed the event because it was bound to sharpen the cleavage in the topmost Congress ranks. Further, the Communist parties had always regarded Desai as a reactionary. S. A. Dange, chairman of the CPI, said: "It is good news in so far as the most outspoken representative of monopoly capital had to resign from the Government.... The democratic masses should celebrate it as the beginning of a new process in which the right reactionaries will suffer a great defeat."[24] The response of the CPI(M) was similar, but more cautious and guarded. P. Ramamurthy, CPI(M) leader and a Member of Parliament, said: "No democrat will shed a tear over the exit of Mr Desai who is known to be one of the staunchest champions of Indian monopoly and foreign collaboration, but whether this foreshadows a radical change in the basic policies of the Congress or is a reflection of factional quarrels only events will unfold. In 1964 too in the wake of the Kamaraj plan, Mr Desai left the Cabinet, but it did not result in any change in Congress policy."[25] The PSP, on the other hand, while regarding Desai's exit as mainly an internal matter for the Congress, asserted that the taking away of Desai's portfolio had direct connexion with the selection of the candidate for the presidentship, and that since the Prime Minister's wishes were turned down by the Congress Parliamentary Board, she chose to fight a battle on ideological grounds.[26]

Desai, on the other hand, found sympathy from the Jana Sangh and the Swatantra leaders. The Jana Sangh suspected that the Prime Minister's action was aimed at pressurizing the party to her views on the presidential election. Madhok, MP and Jana Sangh leader, claimed that Indira Gandhi had "begun to play the Communist game openly," and called upon the nationalist forces inside and outside the Congress "to take concerted steps to foil her designs."[27]

After Desai was divested of his portfolio there was considerable discussion as to whether the Congress would split into rightists and leftists. Indira Gandhi, however, deplored the tendency to label people as leftists or rightists, and also refuted the charge that she was encouraging the communists, saying that nobody interested in freedom could be a communist. She added, however, that the Congress Party had not made an impact on the public that it was a socialist party, or that it was going all out to achieve socialism, and that it was for this reason that the

Congress was losing support. On 19 July 1969, while speaking in support of socialism, Indira Gandhi strongly defended the public sector, some criticisms of which had been made by Nijalingappa in his Faridabad Congress presidential speech in April 1969, and regretted that not enough had been done to counter criticism of the public sector. She asserted that the "sweeping attacks" made on the public sector were misconceived, inasmuch as the public sector ventured into difficult and capital-intensive fields which the private sector had shunned.

On 19 July 1969, Indira Gandhi also called an emergency Cabinet meeting in which a decision was taken to nationalize fourteen major commercial banks of India with deposits of not less than Rs. 50 crores. Accordingly, an Ordinance was issued on the same day nationalizing these fourteen banks. Indira Gandhi referred to the fact that as early as December 1954 the Indian Parliament had taken the decision to frame plans and policies within a socialist pattern of society. Control over the banks or the commanding heights of the economy was necessary particularly in a poor country where it was extremely difficult to mobilize adequate resources for development. "An institution, such as the banking system, which touches—and should touch—the lives of millions, has necessarily," said Indira Gandhi, "to be inspired by a large social purpose and has to subserve national priorities and objectives. That is why there has been widespread demand that major banks should be not only socially controlled but publicly-owned ... this has been the practice even in some countries which do not adhere to socialism. That is also why we nationalized, more than a decade ago, the Life Insurance business and the State Bank, or the Imperial Bank as it was then called."[28]

The decision to nationalize the banks was welcomed by certain Congress leaders outside the Cabinet, such as Kamaraj and Atulya Ghosh, but S. K. Patil, who also declared that he welcomed the step, added: "Although we do not like the hasty manner in which it has been done, ... She had done this to make it appear that her action in dismissing Mr Morarji Desai was justified. ... "[29] But almost all opposition parties, apart from the Swatantra and the Jana Sangh, supported the decision to nationalize the banks.

Divesting Desai of the finance portfolio, however, continued to cause uneasiness to many members of the Congress High

Command. Some senior leaders, such as Nijalingappa and Kamaraj and even Chavan, met Indira Gandhi, in an attempt to ensure that the finance portfolio was restored to Desai. K. D. Malaviya, chairman of the Congress Forum for Socialist Action, on the other hand, claimed that Desai's removal would help in the implementation of a socialist programme. The exit of Desai was welcomed by the radicals inside the Congress and by most opposition parties, including the CPI and CPI(M). The Swatantra and the Jana Sangh, on the other hand, regretted Desai's exit. On 17 July 1969, M. R. Masani said that the Swatantra Party would not help Mrs Gandhi if she sought to support Giri for the presidency, "a candidate whose candidature had been endorsed by the Communists and Mr. Krishna Menon."[30]

But most of the opposition parties came out in support of Giri. The CPI supported Giri and, a little later, the CPI(M) did likewise. P. Ramamurthy, the CPI(M) leader, however, explained that fundamentally the conflict between Indira Gandhi and the Syndicate was of a factional character, but in so far as this represented a split within the Congress leadership, the situation should be exploited by the leftist forces in their favour. According to Ramamurthy, the Syndicate had been conspiring against the Prime Minister for quite some time, and but for the presence of Zakir Husain in the picture, it might have attacked Indira Gandhi earlier and if Sanjiva Reddy was elected as the President, then Indira Gandhi might not be able to continue as Prime Minister for long.[31]

Efforts were made to put up a single opposition candidate for the presidency. This was because of the fact that though Sanjiva Reddy could succeed on the strength of Congress votes alone by a majority of nearly 50,000, his selection and the Prime Minister's distress over the manner of such selection, combined with the state of the Congress Party, created confidence among the opposition parties that their candidate would succeed if the opposition could unite. Karunanidhi, the DMK Chief Minister of Tamil Nadu, did his best to achieve unity among the opposition groups but without success. In the event the Swatantra, the Jana Sangh, and the BKD decided to sponsor C. D. Deshmukh and to cast their first preference votes in his favour. C. D. Deshmukh had hardly any chance of succeeding and the contest between Giri and Reddy was expected to be a close one. In these circumstances, the Jana Sangh and the Swatantra parties decided to cast their second preference votes for Reddy, the Congress candidate, but the BKD members were divided over this question.

The CPI strongly supported Giri. In a statement issued on 23 July 1969, the central secretariat of the CPI accused the Syndicate of trying to throw out Indira Gandhi as Prime Minister and to "take over power at the Centre backed by Jana Sangh and Swatantra parties." Referring to bank nationalization, the statement said that on the political front the Syndicate had lost the first round of battle, but the second and more crucial round was getting crystallized with regard to the presidential election, and that if Reddy was elected it would be the first step "in the process of preparing for a right reactionary take-over of power at the Centre."[32]

According to the CPI, the election of Giri as president would, on the other hand, be the first step in the building up of an all-India leftist and democratic unity "to thwart the plans of reaction." A mass movement had, therefore, to be built up in support of Giri. The CPI claimed that "popular anger" against monopoly interest and "a leftward swing among the masses" enabled Indira Gandhi to nationalize the banks, but it warned that the "bureaucrats and monopolists" would utilize their strategic positions in the administrative apparatus to "sabotage and undermine" the true objectives of nationalization, namely, the utilization of the resources of the banks for priority objectives, like assistance to the peasants and to small-scale and medium industries, development of economically backward regions, and the strengthening and rapid expansion of the public sector.[33] Biswanath Mukherjee, a CPI leader, however, made it clear that the CPI and other leftist forces had chosen to support Giri not because he was a revolutionary, but because he was a liberal "who should be supported to oppose reaction." For the "creation of a new democracy," he said, "the people would have to take the help of any one who agrees to be their ally even if for the time being."[34]

While the Communist parties of India, and particularly the CPI, supported Indira Gandhi in her radical utterances and measures, those belonging to the Syndicate, such as Nijalingappa, Kamaraj and S. K. Patil, were highly critical of Indira Gandhi and of her refusal to issue an appeal to Congressmen to vote for

Sanjiva Reddy. On 11 August 1969, Kamaraj said that any party member who would not vote for Sanjiva Reddy in the coming presidential polls was not a Congressman at all.[35]

In a series of dramatic developments past midnight on 13 August 1969, Indira Gandhi sought the right of free vote for Congress members of Parliament and state assemblies in the impending presidential election. Indira Gandhi's suggestion was contained in her reply to Nijalingappa's letter entreating her to issue a whip to Congress electors to vote for Sanjiva Reddy. This reply was sent after Jagjivan Ram and Fakhruddin Ali Ahmed had written a second letter to the Congress president saying that the Congress president's talk with the Jana Sangh and Swatantra leaders for securing their support for the election of Sanjiva Reddy had disturbed them and other Congressmen greatly, and had raised the question whether the Congress president had entered into an electoral alliance with those parties. In his reply to Indira Gandhi, Nijalingappa said that the rumour that he had talked with the Jana Sangh and the Swatantra Party on a coalition arrangement was an "unadulterated lie."[36]

The Congress was deeply divided over the presidential election that was due to be held on 16 August 1969. In her final reply to the Congress president, Indira Gandhi said that for constitutional and other reasons she was unable to issue a whip to Congress MP's to vote for Sanjiva Reddy. She repeated the charge that electoral arrangements with the Jana Sangh and the Swatantra Party had been sought to be made, and that, therefore, the basis on which Sanjiva Reddy's nomination was decided upon no longer existed. Stating that her two Cabinet colleagues, namely, Jagjivan Ram and Fakhruddin Ali Ahmed, and leading members of the party had been convinced that "attempts are now being made at the highest level in the party to compromise with political parties totally opposed to our principles and accepted programmes," she declared that she was unable to "think of winning elections by clouding principles."[37] Indira Gandhi, therefore, supported the stand taken previously by Jagjivan Ram and Fakhruddin Ali Ahmed for a free vote.

After the plea for a free vote had been made by Congress members, such as Arjuna Arora and K. D. Malaviya and, later, by Jagjivan Ram and Fakhruddin Ali Ahmed, and, finally, by Indira Gandhi, events moved in quick succession. On 13 August

1969 the Kashmir Legislature Congress Party decided to vote against Sanjiva Reddy. Sadiq Ali, the Kashmir Prime Minister, said that it would be against the basic objectives of the Congress if Sanjiva Reddy was elected president with the help of the Jana Sangh and Swatantra parties which were "totally opposed to its economic policies and secular ideals."[38]

On 14 August 1969, Nijalingappa declared that those partymen who would not vote for Sanjiva Reddy in the presidential poll would be committing an act of indiscipline. Desai also opposed the plea for free vote, and said that such a plea was a plea for a candidate supported by communist parties "who neither in their profession nor in their practice are democratic, who believe in violence, who practise violence when it suits them, who are totalitarian and who would finish democracy if they came to power."[39] Desai asked Congressmen as "dutiful children" to vote for Reddy and not to commit "matricide" by voting otherwise. Abid Ali, Congress MP and INTUC leader, described Giri as a defector, and said that genuine Congressmen could not vote for him.[40]

Congress votes were split in the presidential election, and Giri was elected President of the Indian Union. Those who had supported Reddy demanded that immediate action should be taken against those who had flouted the Congress president's directive in the presidential election. A resolution to that effect was passed by the Gujarat Pradesh Congress Committee. S. K. Patil, a member of the Syndicate, dubbed as diabolical the suggestion by the Prime Minister for a free vote which, he said, had twin objectives: one was to defeat the Congress candidate, and the other was to provide protection to defectors against any disciplinary action. Patil said that the Prime Minister and her close colleagues, Jagjivan Ram and Fakhruddin Ali Ahmed, had used the propaganda technique of communists and Hitler, and added that it was as if Dr Goebbels made a fine art of such technique and left it to the Prime Minister and her colleagues to make use of it.[41]

On 17 August 1969, Indira Gandhi said that she had asked for a free vote in the presidential election to "avoid a serious split in the party and preserve its unity."[42] Had she not done so, certain sections of the party at the centre would have got frustrated. Regarding the oft-repeated charge of her being under communist influence, she said that it was not she who was leading the people to communism, but it was the factional attitude of the leadership which was making the people frustrated and forcing them to seek alliance outside the Congress.[43] Further, there was a lot of difference between communist ways and hers; while the communists believed in violence, "we believe in nonviolence and carrying everybody with us," but if there was a clash of interests between the rich and the poor, she naturally would take the side of the poor. As to divesting Morarji Desai of the finance portfolio, Indira Gandhi recalled that Kamaraj had told Chandrajit Yadav at Faridabad: "If this [radical economic policy] is to be implemented why does not she take over the finance portfolio?"[44]

On 18 August 1969, Indira Gandhi sent a letter to all Congress MP's stating that the Congress Party had been going through a period of anguish during the last few weeks, when senior colleagues in the party had taken differing stands with regard to the presidential election, but the differences arose not because of any struggle for power, nor as a result of a clash of personalities, but because of basic differences on policy which had existed for some time. "Unfortunately in the course of the years our organization," she wrote, "has been losing that dynamism and crusading spirit necessary to bring about a change in the attitudes and the thinking of our people. I have a feeling that as a party we are losing contact with the vast masses of our people and especially with the youth. . . . We took a very important step after the Bangalore session in nationalizing the fourteen major banks. This has kindled a sense of hope and confidence in the minds of the common man that there is now a serious intention to tackle the problems of unemployment and of the poverty affecting millions of our countrymen. But this has given the opportunity for some people to cloud the issues by raising the old bogey of communism and communist influence. . . . Any liberal social or economic reform produces a reaction in the vested interests and conservative elements."

Reacting sharply to the notices sent by the Congress president seeking explanations from her, Jagjivan Ram, and Fakhruddin Ali Ahmed, regarding their attitude towards the presidential election, Indira Gandhi questioned the propriety of Nijalingappa's action "over and above the head of the Congress

Parliamentary Party." Indira Gandhi said that discipline could not be maintained by waving whips, but had to be based on common policies and programme. There had been a deviation from party policies which had begun during the last days of Nehru. "I know," she said, "what anguish he [Nehru] suffered during the last years. He saw the Congress going in the direction in which neither he nor Gandhi wanted to go."[45]

On 19 August 1969, Indira Gandhi detailed how she had to swallow insults on many occasions: "I had responsibility of many things but no voice in the shaping of decisions." She referred to the Bangalore episode—"the manner in which the Presidential candidate was chosen was not a chance. Things could not have worked with clock-like precision had there been no pre-planning. Within minutes the news of the Parliamentary Board's decision was out, including the voting break-up. All over the world the impression went round that the Prime Minister was demoted in her own organization. No democracy can function if the head of the government is insulted in the party."[46] She had to retrieve her position "not because I was involved but because the Prime Ministership of India was involved. The Prime Minister must have [pre-eminent] position. Only in the Communist countries, the party's voice is above that of the government. In democracies it is the elected people who matter.... I told the leaders [responsible for the episode] that I will fight back." She also denied the charge that she was developing communistic tendencies. "Am I responsible for bringing communism in West Bengal and Kerala? Results would have been different if my suggestions were carried out. People left the Congress because they were driven to the wall."[47] Indira Gandhi was referring especially to Bengal where Ajoy Mukherji had to leave the Congress because of differences with Atulya Ghosh, who then controlled the organization of the Bengal Congress. It was under Ajoy Mukherji's leadership that a non–Congress United Front government was set up in Bengal first in 1967, and then again in 1969.

Like Indira Gandhi, Jagjivan Ram and Fakhruddin Ali Ahmed questioned the propriety of the action of Nijalingappa in issuing the notices. Jagjivan Ram referred to the "double standards" about discipline adopted by the Congress president who sought to enforce discipline in regard to voting but not against those who violated fundamental Congress policies. Jagjivan Ram wanted the issues arising out of the notices to be taken to the 4,000 delegates of the plenary session. "Let us go back to the delegates who had laid down the party policies. Action should be taken against those who violated the decisions arrived at by the delegates. It is we," said Jagjivan Ram, "who will carry the real Congress with us. People are with us."[48]

During the crisis within the Congress, Chavan emerged as the peacemaker. Chavan suggested a meeting between Indira Gandhi and Nijalingappa. Nijalingappa's reply was characteristic: "The possibility is always there, after our going to the moon." On 22 August 1969, Nijalingappa was not even prepared to repeat his previous assurance, given before the plea for free vote, that Indira Gandhi's position as Prime Minister would not be upset till 1972. "I cannot say. A lot of things have happened since then."[49]

In the mean time a large number of Congress MP's warned the High Command that any action that may be taken against the Prime Minister "will be fully fought back." About 248 of the 436 Congress members of the Indian Parliament gathered at the residence of former Congress president Sanjivayya on 23 August 1969, to pledge their loyalty to Indira Gandhi and to urge the Congress Working Committee to avoid any precipitate action against those who had voted against Sanjiva Reddy.[50]

The day before the Congress Working Committee meeting of 25 August 1969 witnessed intense political activity and rival groups within the Congress made claims and counter-claims. A certain piquancy was added to the situation by the reported remark of Kamaraj to a group of MP's that if the Congress Working Committee did not act with resoluteness, he would leave the Congress Working Committee and head a group of Congress MP's in the Lok Sabha to form a distinct identity.[51]

The grouping within the Congress was generally referred to as being between the Syndicate on the one hand, and the supporters of Indira Gandhi on the other. The Congress president, however, frowned at the word "Syndicate." Nijalingappa said it was the most abused word, and Kamaraj had asked him: "Suppose somebody wants to resign from the Syndicate, to whom does he submit his letter of resignation?" The Congress president declared: "Who are the members of the Syndicate?

When did it take shape? This is Goebbels propaganda. They [the Syndicate members] are supposed to be reactionaries.... The Syndicate is used as a weapon against a few people in the Congress. Is Kamaraj a reactionary? The public is merely fed on this word. What has the Syndicate done?"[52] Later, in October 1969, Nijalingappa said that the term Syndicate started when it was applied to certain senior Congressmen when they met at Tirupati in the early 1960s. "They decided to back Mr Lal Bahadur Shastri for the Prime Ministership. Then it was a good Syndicate.... Mrs Gandhi was backed for the Prime Ministership twice. Then also in a way it was not a bad Syndicate.... Now it has become a bad Syndicate."[53]

On 25 August 1969 the Congress Party stopped short of an open split by agreeing to a patchwork peace, evolved through compromise resolutions primarily drafted by Chavan. But the political victory was distinctly of Indira Gandhi, because, in spite of the notices served on her and two Cabinet Ministers by the Congress president, no action was taken against them.

The Working Committee in a brief resolution also exonerated Nijalingappa of the charge that he had made an electoral understanding with the Jana Sangh and the Swatantra Party: "The allegations made against the president were on wrong assumptions based on information available at that time and therefore they are untenable." The main resolution passed by the Working Committee appealed to Nijalingappa and Indira Gandhi to work harmoniously, described the defection of Congress votes to Giri as "painful and unfortunate," but warned that a split in the party would have incalculable consequences, and declared that "mistakes have been made on all sides in the wake of the conflict of ideas and approaches in the last few weeks." The main resolution stated: "What is needed is that the disease should be treated rather than the symptoms.... Disciplined conduct and behaviour is an essential ingredient for the proper functioning of the party. However, this can be effectively ensured only on the basis of strict adherence to party policies and programmes and internal democracy within the party.... A factor of crucial importance is the need for the two key figures in the organization, the President of the Congress and the leader of the Parliamentary Party, to work harmoniously and with mutual understanding.... They are not rival centres of power.

They have to function in a complementary manner in the interest of the party and the country."

The compromise at the Working Committee became possible in view of the realization on the part of the senior leaders opposed to Indira Gandhi that Chavan would not side with them against the Prime Minister. The unity resolution, however, left some senior members of the party unhappy and discontented. After the unity resolution, Morarji Desai hastened to make it clear that the resolution was not unanimous. Kamaraj's comment on the resolution was: "We have succeeded in deceiving ourselves."

A group of Congress MP's, including Tarakeshwari Sinha, were unreconciled to the compromise resolution passed by the Congress Working Committee, and they said that they would function independently. Tarakeshwari Sinha also disclosed that there had been informal discussions among the Syndicate members before the meeting of the Congress Working Committee on 25 August 1969 on a possible successor to Indira Gandhi, following her contemplated suspension from the party, and Kamaraj wanted a person with a socialist image to replace Mrs Gandhi, his choice being Home Minister Chavan. She said that but for Chavan's role, disciplinary action would have been taken against Mrs Gandhi and two of her Cabinet colleagues. "Before the result of the presidential election was announced," she added, "Mr Chavan remained cooperative with us. Later he became elusive."[54]

After the Congress Working Committee resolutions, dissension came to the surface on the question as to who had adopted a soft line in the Congress Working Committee. The names of Atulya Ghosh and S. K. Patil were suggested in this connection. Patil denied the charge, and claimed: "In fact, I was the only person who roared like a lion."[55] Upset by the reported criticism of his role by Kamaraj and Morarji Desai, Patil asked what prevented the two leaders from taking a hard line. "After all, I am not the leader of the Syndicate."

On 28 August 1969, the Congress president Nijalingappa declared that in spite of the Working Committee resolutions on unity, the Morarji Desai issue was still open and he would discuss it with the Prime Minister.[56] He also warned against the "mischievous and sophisticated tendency of personality cult" developing in the country, which may lead to dictatorship.[57] He said that some people were trying to make use of "catchy phrases and slogans" to achieve their own ulterior ends. On 4 September 1969, Nijalingappa said that communists had infiltrated into the Congress organization at all levels, and he was thinking of some sort of screening process for weeding them out.[58]

In September 1969, Morarji Desai also spoke of the danger to the country if the Congress was split. Though the communists appeared to be the happiest about the political crisis within the Congress, they would, Desai prophesied, never be able to come to power in the country, for in spite of their "apparent strength" in Kerala and West Bengal, the ancient culture and independent spirit of the people would resist communism.[59] Desai referred to the growing indiscipline in the Congress party, and said: "Let the Prime Minister stop indiscipline first. Then only there is a meaning in enforcing discipline among the rank and file."[60]

Speaking about discipline, Indira Gandhi said that party discipline was broken for the first time by Gandhi in 1919, when he gave a new turn to the Congress and transformed it into a fighting machine. She claimed that by her recent acts the Congress has taken a similar turn, and that it was for Congressmen to make the best use of it.

But on the question of discipline some opposition leaders, such as J. B. Kripalani and H. V. Kamath, criticized Indira Gandhi. Kripalani contended that there could be no conscience voting if political parties were to survive, and charged that the Prime Minister had launched on "an adventurist political career" in making a plea for free vote.[61] Similarly, H. V. Kamath, PSP leader, said in August 1969 that there would be chaos and dictatorship in the country if political parties functioned without discipline. He said that the power of the Prime Minister "has increased, was increasing and must be diminished."[62]

In view of the deep divisions within the Congress Party J. P. Narayan, the Sarvodaya leader, said on 7 September 1969 that the time had come when the Congress should split. Such a split was necessary so that a proper coalition government could be formed at the centre in 1972. Such a split would give rise to a healthy polarization, otherwise there would be only an anti–

Congress coalition, but mere anti–Congressism was no ideology.[63]

While people talked of polarization and a split within the Congress, Indira Gandhi gave a call to all those who believed in secularism, democracy, and socialism to join the Congress. This appeal was interpreted to be directed to groups led by Charan Singh in Uttar Pradesh, Harekrishna Mahatab in Orissa and even Ajoy Mukherji in Bengal. After Indira Gandhi's call to secular, socialistic, and democratic forces to join the Congress, Nijalingappa also gave a similar call. He explained that he would welcome J. B. Kripalani—who, incidentally, was a most persistent critic of Indira Gandhi—to rejoin the Congress.[64]

Bank nationalization created considerable enthusiasm among the people. This measure also increased Indira Gandhi's popularity in the country. Further, Chavan, who acted as the peacemaker to avert a split at the Congress Working Committee on 25 August 1969, later unreservedly came out in support of Indira Gandhi. On 18 September 1969, Chavan said that Indira Gandhi was "the leader of the nation and I shall follow her. She has given a lead to implement the socialist programmes and as a loyal worker of the Congress committed to its social ideals ...I shall strive hard to achieve the goal with the Prime Minister."[65]

Chavan's unambiguous commitment to follow Indira Gandhi's leadership removed the misunderstanding that had grown up between them since the Bangalore session of the AICC, where Chavan had opposed the nominees suggested by Indira Gandhi for the presidency of the Indian Union. In explaining his stand to follow Mrs Gandhi, Chavan recalled that he had twice supported her for the Prime Ministership at the cost of incurring the displeasure. of many "big friends" in the country. At one time, Chavan claimed, he was the one against all in supporting her for the leadership of the Congress Parliamentary Party. Chavan disagreed with Indira Gandhi's critics that she had nationalized banks because of political motives, saying that all major decisions were political, and there was nothing wrong if she had taken the step of taking over the banks to politically outwit her opponents.[66]

In September 1969, Chavan also unambiguously declared that he had no ambition of becoming the Prime Minister. Chavan said that some people in the country characterized him as a very shrewd person, and thought that he had an eye on the Prime Ministership, but that was not so.[67] Referring to the unity resolution passed by the Congress Working Committee on 25 August 1969, Chavan declared that both sides had made mistakes, and that it would have been better had the consensus method been followed in deciding on the presidential nomination.[68]

While Chavan came out as an unqualified supporter of the Prime Minister, Morarji Desai, who had been relieved of the finance portfolio, increasingly became her bitter critic. On 13 September 1969, Morarji Desai declared that he would undertake a *satyagraha* of the Gandhian type to compel the Prime Minister and her colleagues to repent for breaking party discipline.[69] S. K. Patil also criticized Indira Gandhi, and said that she was making radical promises to the people which would be difficult to fulfil, and when it was found out that the promises could not be fulfilled, then "the very people who are showering flowers on Mrs Gandhi will throw stones at her."[70]

Answering Desai's criticism, who had wondered whether rickshaw-wallahs and others who attended the meetings before the Prime Minister's residence to congratulate her on bank nationalization knew anything about the significance of that measure, Indira Gandhi said: "Many people say that the rickshaw-wallahs, cobblers, and others who came to my residence, do not know anything about banks or nationalization. What I would like to know is that when we go out and seek their votes do we say that they do not know anything about democracy?"[71] The controversy over bank nationalization had shown not only what people think, but "what some think of the people."

Indira Gandhi called upon the people to actively participate in the country's march towards socialism. The nationalization of the major banks was the first step in this direction, and had brought the country to the threshold of a new economic era of opportunity. She charged that a few individuals had created a controversy over bank nationalization only to divert the attention of the people from their freedom struggle—the struggle to gain economic freedom.[72] She said: "Many people, especially of the upper strata, are not happy over bank nationalization. There is widespread propaganda that I have become a communist. But I tell you that if you do not work for peaceful progress the people will not wait."[73]

Indira Gandhi lamented that the Congress had, to some extent, strayed away from the common people. The party's Bhubaneswar resolution, which directly advocated the cause of socialism, was not given serious consideration. It was for this reason that over the past few years the people's enthusiasm had lagged, and a spirit of alienation between the people and the government had developed. To restore people's faith in the government, "we have to take big steps."[74] Bank nationalization was one such step.

The Congress should never be conceived as a party of the privileged but as a party of the masses. In September 1969, in a message to the Maharashtra Pradesh Congress Committee, Indira Gandhi said: "The denigration of the poor and illiterate masses which has been indulged in of late by some people runs counter to the democratic traditions taught to us by Mahatma Gandhi and Jawaharlal Nehru.... The recent nationalization of banks, although primarily an economic and social measure, has become a dynamic symbol of the paramountcy of the people. That is why it has released the latent enthusiasm of the people to such an extent. More than any other decision that we have taken in independent India, it proclaims that the few cannot constitute themselves into the managing agents or arbiters of the destinies and fortunes of the many. The forces that have been released by bank nationalization are forces which strengthen the spirit as well as the process of democracy in our country.[75]

Apart from nationalizing the banks, Indira Gandhi decided to set up a judicial commission to inquire into alleged irregularities by the Birla group of industries. Bank natonalization and inquiry into Birla affairs had been two of major demands of Chandra Shekhar and the Young Turks.[76] These demands Morarji Desai had persistently resisted, and over these demands Desai and Chandra Shekhar had clashed openly and publicly. Some leftists had criticized the Congress government at the centre as being a government which was dominated by monopolists and capitalists, and particularly by the Birlas. In this context the decision to have an inquiry over Birla affairs was

16

hailed by some as a measure of even greater significance than bank nationalization.

Indira Gandhi went on a tour of various parts of the country to mobilize public support for the policies and programme that her government was pursuing. In Bengal, Siddhartha Sankar Ray, the leader of the Congress Legislature Party, arranged a meeting at the Calcutta Maidan which she was to address. In order to show that the Congress had been freed from the influence of the Syndicate, Atulya Ghosh, one of the leaders of the Syndicate, was not invited to this meeting and P. C. Sen, former Chief Minister of Bengal, did not attend the meeting because of this. The meeting that was held at the Maidan in Calcutta was, however, one of the biggest, and Indira Gandhi gave a call to the people to join the march to socialism.

Later, before Indira Gandhi's visit to Tamil Nadu, disputes arose between C. Subramaniam—the president of the Tamil Nadu Congress and a supporter of the plea for free vote—and the group led by Kamaraj. On 27 September 1969, Subramaniam announced his resignation as the president of the Tamil Nadu Congress in the face of a massive revolt against his leadership by supporters of Kamaraj. While resigning Subramaniam also disclosed that Kamaraj had offered Chavan the Prime Ministership during the crisis in the Congress Party about the presidential election.[77] Subramaniam said that when differences within the Congress became acute, following the letters of Jagjivan Ram and Fakhruddin Ali Ahmed to the Congress president, the Congress Working Committee should have been in continuous session to resolve the differences, but Kamaraj was opposed to calling a meeting of the Congress Working Committee, obviously because he and his group were then confident that Sanjiva Reddy would win and that thereafter disciplinary action could be taken against Indira Gandhi to throw her out of office.[78]

Subramaniam had been elected to the Congress Working Committee from the AICC of which he had become an ex-officio member by virtue of his being the Tamil Nadu Congress chief. After he resigned from that office, Nijalingappa raised the question as to whether Subramaniam could retain his membership of the Working Committee as he had ceased to be a member of the AICC. On 8 October 1969, charging that Nijalingappa had removed Subramaniam from the Congress Working Committee,

Indira Gandhi, Chavan, Jagjivan Ram, Fakhruddin Ali Ahmed, Uma Shankar Dixit, and Subramaniam wrote a joint letter to Nijalingappa warning him that his action would "aggravate the situation and make the implementation of the unity resolution more difficult."[79] The fact that Chavan was a signatory to this letter showed that he was now firmly behind Indira Gandhi. Nijalingappa replied saying that he was only intending to write to Subramaniam to point out the constitutional difficulty in his continuance as a Working Committee member after his resignation from the post of the Pradesh Congress chief, but that he had not removed Subramaniam from the Working Committee.

In spite of the unity resolution of the Congress Working Committee, it was clear that the differences between those who supported Indira Gandhi and her policies and those who were aligned with Nijalingappa, Kamaraj, and Morarji Desai were increasing. On 18 October 1969, a requisition was signed by several senior leaders including Chavan, Fakhruddin Ali Ahmed, Jagjivan Ram, and Uma Shankar Dixit, whereby the Congress Working Committee was requested to convene a session of the AICC as early as possible to facilitate the election of a new party president before the end of 1969. The requisitionists stated that the acceptance by the Bangalore session of the AICC of the Prime Minister's Note embodying a radical economic programme, and the steps taken by her to nationalize the major banks, created a sense of confidence in the masses that the progressive and socialist policies of the Congress would be fully carried out, that the resolution of the Working Committee passed on 25 August 1969 generated the hope that the unity necessary for the effective implementation of the said policies and programme would be brought about, but that, unfortunately, this wind of change that was welcomed widely by the nation, generated tensions within the party and threatened the execution of those basic policies to which the Congress was committed. The requisitionists stated that it was, therefore, necessary to elect a new Congress president so that the declared policies of the Congress could be fully implemented.

On the eve of the Congress Working Committee meeting scheduled for 1 November 1969, Nijalingappa in a dramatic move dropped Fakhruddin Ali Ahmed from the Working Committee on the ground that he had lost confidence in him, and disqualified Subramaniam from membership of the Committee on the ground that, having ceased to be the president of the Tamil Nadu Congress, he had also ceased to enjoy the privileges of being a Working Committee member.

Indira Gandhi and her supporters in the Congress Working Committee decided to boycott the Working Committee meeting of 1 November 1969 as a protest against these steps taken by Nijalingappa. A separate meeting was held at Indira Gandhi's residence which was attended by those members of the Congress Working Committee who supported the requisition to elect a new Congress president.

The first of November 1969 was a turning-point in Indian political history. On that day two meetings were held: one at the AICC office under the presidentship of Nijalingappa, and the other at Indira Gandhi's residence. The Congress Working Committee meeting presided over by Nijalingappa decided that the requisition by 405 AICC members calling for the election of a new president amounted to a vote of no-confidence in Nijalingappa, who had been elected by the plenary session and not the AICC, and was out of order, and, further, that the next meeting of the AICC in the "normal course" would be held in Gujarat in the second half of December 1969.

The meeting at the residence of Indira Gandhi decided that a special session of the AICC would be convened in Delhi on 22 and 23 November 1969 on the basis of the requisition of 405 AICC members. (The AICC had 708 members with voting rights.)

Out of 21 members of the Working Committee, 10 members each were present at the respective meetings held under the chairmanship of the Congress president and Indira Gandhi. The remaining member K. C. Abraham, president of the Kerala Congress, first participated in the meeting held at Indira Gandhi's residence, and then attended the meeting at the AICC office under the chairmanship of Nijalingappa. Abraham said he was trying to bring about unity, but was with the organization men.

The holding of parallel meetings of the Congress Working Committee, one under the presidentship of Nijalingappa and the other under the chairmanship of Indira Gandhi, and the calling of parallel AICC meetings, virtually split the Congress organization which was founded in 1885, which had fought for and won Indian independence, and had ruled at the centre for 22 years.

On 2 November 1969, the Congress Working Committee meeting held under the chairmanship of Nijalingappa passed a resolution declaring that those who would participate at the parallel meeting of the AICC at Delhi on 22 and 23 November 1969, "must be prepared to face the constitutional consequences" thereof. This meeting also passed another resolution blaming the Congress government at the centre for compromising India's position in the world by participating in "a purely Islamic summit at Rabat." Later, at a meeting of 10 members of the Working Committee held under the chairmanship of Indira Gandhi, a resolution was passed charging that the Congress president had wrongfully dropped certain members of the Working Committee and was himself the main cause for bringing about dissension and disunity within the party.

The split in the Congress was complete on 12 November 1969, when the Congress Working Committee, meeting under the presidentship of Nijalingappa, which meeting had been boycotted by Indira Gandhi and her supporters, passed a resolution expelling Indira Gandhi, the Prime Minister, from the party and called upon the Congress Parliamentary Party to elect a new leader. Indira Gandhi had, however, overwhelming support in the Congress Parliamentary Party, which reaffirmed its faith in her leadership but a minority group in the Congress Parliamentary Party elected Ram Subhag Singh as the leader of the Congress Party (o) in the Lok Sabha, and S. N. Misra as the leader in the Rajya Sabha, and Morarji Desai as the chairman. At this time, those who were in favour of Indira Gandhi claimed that they had the support of 210 members in the Lok Sabha and 104 members in the Rajya Sabha, whereas the other group claimed they had the support of 65 members in the Lok Sabha and 46 in the Rajya Sabha.[80]

Though the overwhelming majority of the Congress Parliamentary Party supported Indira Gandhi, the formation of another group under Ram Subhag Singh meant that the Congress Party lost its absolute majority in Parliament. At the first session of Parliament, after the Congress split, the Congress Party (Organization) voted against the ruling Congress Party on an adjournment motion seeking to condemn the government for participating in the Rabat Conference, but the motion was overwhelmingly defeated.

Towards the end of November 1969, the requisitioned meeting of the AICC opposed to the Nijalingappa group, met at New Delhi and removed Nijalingappa as Congress president, and appointed in his place Subramaniam as interim Congress president till the plenary session that was convened for December 1969 at Bombay. At this Bombay Session, Jagjivan Ram was elected the president. The Congress party led by Nijalingappa also held a plenary session at Gandhinagar at Ahmedabad.

The question arose as to whether the Congress Party (Organization) would follow the old Congress policy or go back on it. In an economic policy statement issued by the Congress Party (Organization), it was stated that the party was pledged to democracy, socialism, and secularism, that these goals were interdependent so that an exclusive dependence on just one of them to the neglect of others would be fatal, and that the party would guard against any attempt to subvert democracy by authoritarian socialism.[81] On foreign policy the party reiterated the ideal of nonalignment, but complained that certain distortions had crept in the matter of the implementation of that policy, and in this connection referred to the failure of the government of India to condemn the Soviet intervention in Czechoslovakia.[82] The party charged that there was a pro-Soviet bias in Indian foreign policy.[83] Leaders of the party also continued to attack Indira Gandhi; Nijalingappa asserted that the government was taking the country towards communism under the influence of "some fellow-travellers and ex-card-holders,"[84] and Kamaraj charged that Indira Gandhi was committing a fraud on socialism.[85] Taunting the CPI and the DMK for the support they gave to Indira Gandhi, Kamaraj suggested that these parties should rename themselves as "Indira Communist Party" and "Dravida Munnetra Congress" respectively.[86] Kamaraj even argued that the Syndicate, which was opposed by Indira Gandhi, had been founded at the instance of Nehru. But this was contradicted by Atulya Ghosh, who said that the term "Syndicate" had been coined by a leftist weekly "at the behest of Nehru."[87]

The requisitionists' Congress of which Subramaniam was elected the interim president, claimed that it was the real

Congress, both because it had the support of the majority of
the members of the AICC and of the plenary session and, further,
because it was the party which really accepted the Congress
ideal of democracy, secularism, and socialism and wanted to
put these ideals into practice. At the requisitioned AICC meeting
held at New Delhi, T. T. Krishnamachari was present. Krishnamachari's speech did not please the Young Turks, and their
leader Chandra Shekhar said that listening to Krishnamachari's
interpretation of socialism he wondered whether he was listening to Morarji Desai.[88]

When Subramaniam formed the Congress Working Committee, in which Chandra Shekhar was not included as a member
but was given the status of a permanent invitee, and in which
Nandini Satpati, Chandrajit Yadav, and K. R. Ganesh were
included, it gave rise to a controversy. A section criticized the
inclusion of Nandini Satpati, Chandrajit Yadav, and K. R. Ganesh
on the ground of their alleged communist background. In
protest, these three members offered to resign, but their resignations were not accepted. Later, when Jagjivan Ram was elected
the president of the party at its Bombay Session, Chandra
Shekhar was taken in as a member.

At this Bombay session, Indira Gandhi denied that Indian
foreign policy had any pro-Soviet bias, or that India was leaning
towards communism. Nehru used to describe the policy of the
Congress as being left of centre. It is this policy, Indira Gandhi
said, that she would pursue. At this Bombay session, the Congress under the leadership of Indira Gandhi decided to abolish
privy purses, to nationalize the bulk of the import trade, to take
steps for the early nationalization of general insurance, and to
implement land reforms statutes by 1970-71. The question of
imposing a ceiling on urban property also came up for discussion at this session, but considering the complexity of the question, no specific proposal was adopted. The question of exclud-
ing the right to hold property from the chapter on Fundamental
Rights in the Indian Constitution was raised by the Young
Turks, but again no decision was taken on this question.

The question of amending the Constitution came up for consideration after the Supreme Court had, by a majority decision,
declared that the Act for the nationalization of the 14 major
banks was *ultra vires*, both on the ground that it was discrimina-

tory, as well as on the ground that the compensation provided for therein was not in accordance with the Constitution. Some radicals inside the Congress and the CPI[89] and the CPI(M)[90] generally claimed that the Supreme Court was standing in the way of social progress, and that the fundamental rights of holding property[91] and carrying on trade had become fetters in the path of enacting progressive legislation. It was said that the Supreme Court decision made it clear that the chapter on Fundamental Rights in the Constitution, which guaranteed the right to hold property, would have to be abrogated before socialistic measures could be enacted lawfully. However, in view of the Supreme Court decision, the government brought another bill in Parliament for the nationalization of the fourteen banks. In this bill provision was made for the grant of more liberal compensation, and there were other safeguards so that the bill, when enacted, may not be struck down either on the ground of discrimination or on the ground that the compensation provided was illusory.

III.   THE CPI, THE CPI(M) AND THE CONGRESS SPLIT

In the struggle that Indira Gandhi waged with the Syndicate, the sympathies of the CPI were wholly with her, for the CPI considered that Indira Gandhi led the progressive forces inside the Congress, and believed that the victory of Giri heralded a fresh realignment of social and political forces in India. The CPI attributed this victory to the "dismissal" of Morarji Desai from the government, the nationalization of the banks, and the open confrontation between Indira Gandhi and the Syndicate, and claimed that it had been correct all along in stressing the existence of a progressive section within the Congress. To accelerate the process of radicalization of Indian politics, which had already commenced, the CPI emphasized the need for forging a national democratic front. Such a front was later to form the national democratic government at the centre, consisting of the CPI and other leftist parties, and was to draw into its ranks "not only the masses following the Congress but also its progressive sections."[92] The approach of the CPI(M) to Indira Gandhi and the Congress was somewhat different. Namboodiripad, the

CPI(M) leader, said the CPI's contention that the conflict in the Congress was a struggle between national bourgeoisie, led by Indira Gandhi, and the big monopoly capitalists, represented by the Syndicate, "was contrary to facts and was not, therefore, a useful approach." It may be noted here that the Chinese analysis of the Indian situation was that the struggle inside the Congress was an attempt to exploit the masses by two sections of "monopoly capitalists" one led by the USA, and the other by the Soviet Union; the Syndicate was in alliance with the USA, while the Prime Minister was in league with the Soviet Union, and, accordingly, the revolutionary forces of the country could not take sides with either of these two groups. Though the CPI(M) did not accept this Chinese analysis, they also did not agree with the CPI that there was a progressive section within the Congress. None the less the CPI(M) decided to support Indira Gandhi in her fight against the Syndicate.

In August 1969, the CPI(M) general secretary, Sundarayya, said that his party would oppose any conspiracy by the Jana Sangh, the Swatantra Party, and similar groups to topple Indira Gandhi's government.[93] But there was no question of forming any kind of United Front with Indira Gandhi or the participation of the CPI(M) in a government headed by her. The CPI(M) could enter a government only when it had enough power to mould the policies of such a government. It is for this reason that the CPI(M) had refused to join United Front governments in Bihar and Uttar Pradesh, but had participated in those which had been formed in West Bengal and Kerala. But the CPI(M) gave its support to bank nationalization, and was agreeable to support any other progressive measure that Indira Gandhi might bring.

The politbureau of the CPI(M) considered that the Syndicate was the most aggressive representative of extreme political reaction, but the other section headed by Indira Gandhi was prepared to sponsor certain radical measures, like nationalization of banks, in order to regain the lost image of the Congress among the people. The CPI(M) was, however, not prepared to characterize the rival groups within the Congress as representing monopolists and anti-monopolists. Such a characterization would only disarm the anti-Congress democratic forces, breed "unwarranted illusions" among the people, and reduce the anti-

Congress democratic forces to the position of camp-followers of one particular section within the Congress. Besides, one or two measures like bank nationalization could not transform the government from "a bourgeois-landlord government" led by the big bourgeoisie.

The attempts at restoring unity among the contending Congress sections after the defeat of the Syndicate in the presidential contest was viewed with uneasiness by the CPI(M). If such unity was restored, it would mean that the promises and pledges made by Indira Gandhi and her group would not be kept. The CPI(M) therefore, warned all democratic-minded Congressmen to awaken to "the conspiratorial move of unity" and scotch it.

The unity resolution passed at the Congress Working Committee meeting on 25 August 1969 was also regarded by the CPI as an "uneasy truce." It considered, however, that the Congress Syndicate had been routed, as was proved by the failure of the Congress Working Committee to censure the Prime Minister. The decision on bank nationalization and the victory of Giri were other instances of the defeat of the reactionary forces within the Congress. N. Krishnan, a member of the Central Secretariat of the CPI, said that the Syndicate, along with other rightist forces outside the Congress, wanted to take over power at the centre, but the Congress Working Committee resolutions had temporarily frustrated that effort. The rightist forces, now reduced to a minority, would, however, try to regroup themselves and strike again. They would work for sabotaging any further radical economic measures that may be taken by the government and would, for this purpose, also utilize their strength in the bureaucracy. Krishnan feared that the "reactionary, pro-West elements" among the officers of the fourteen nationalized banks would attempt to sabotage this progressive measure, and that would lead to a situation where the people would get disillusioned and this might enable the rightists to stage a come-back.

In September 1969, the National Council of the CPI decided that it would launch a mass campaign to make the government implement radical measures, and to defeat decisively the Syndicate and its allies. The CPI, however, made it clear that it did not want the present government at the centre to be toppled by the rightists. On the contrary, it denounced the SSP which was pledged to a policy of pure anti-Congressism. Krishnan claimed that the ssp theory that all opposition parties should always combine to topple the Congress at the centre had been completely exploded by the march of events.[94]

While the cpi held that "the Syndicate–Jana Sangh–Swatantra combine" represented the capitalist monopolists, foreign capitalists, and semi-feudal landlords, it regarded the rest of the opposition, including sections of the bourgeoisie, as part of the popular forces. The resolution of the National Council of the cpi in September 1969 said that the division in the Congress was broadly a political one between the rightists on the one hand and the democratic forces on the other.[95]

The main bone of contention between the cpi and cpi(m) was whether there was any progressive or democratic section inside the Congress. In September 1969 the cpi(m) leader, Promode Das Gupta, said that the Syndicate and Indira Gandhi were just two faces of the Congress, and Indira Gandhi was no less a Congressite than Nijalingappa or Morarji Desai. The Syndicate wanted to form a coalition with the Jana Sangh and the Swatantra Party, but Indira Gandhi did not want such a thing for fear of being isolated from the scheduled castes and minorities. Promode Das Gupta said that the support that the cpi(m) had given to Indira Gandhi during the presidential election was nothing but "the support of the hangman's noose to the condemned convict."[96]

On 13 September 1969, B. T. Ranadive, a member of the cpi(m) politbureau, said that Indira Gandhi's love for socialism as reflected in the nationalization of fourteen major banks was "a big hoax"; she had no special love for socialism, and had taken that extreme step only to consolidate her position within the Congress Party. If President Zakir Husain had not passed away, the power struggle in the party would not have come into the open and Indira Gandhi, said Ranadive, would not have nationalized the major banks. One swallow could not make a summer; similarly, one significant action of Indira Gandhi would not usher in socialism, he said.[97]

In September 1969, Basavapunniah criticized the efforts of the cpi to discover one "so-called progressive Congress leader after another"; in the past the cpi had asked the people to rally behind Nehru against Patel, and, after Nehru's death, behind Lal Bahadur

Shastri. "It was now seeking to create similar illusions about Mrs Indira Gandhi."[98] Basavapunniah said that though the conflict between the Syndicate and the Indira group in the Congress could not be dismissed as a factional quarrel, at the same time it would be wrong to consider the conflict as representing a clear division between monopolists and non-monopolists.[99]

The approach to Indira Gandhi and her policies continued to be a crucial point of difference between the CPI and CPI(M). Rebutting the charge of the CPI(M) that the CPI suffered from "pro-Indira emotions," Biswanath Mukherjee, the CPI leader from Bengal, said that it was true that his party had supported some of the actions of Indira Gandhi, such as the nationalization of banks and opposition to the rightist candidate, Sanjiva Reddy, in the presidential poll, but then the CPI(M) had also supported these actions of Indira Gandhi. That party had declared that it would defend Indira Gandhi's government against any attempt to topple it. Biswanath Mukherjee said: "They [CPI(M)] want to leave the initiative with Mrs Gandhi. We want the Communists and other Leftists and democratic forces to seize the initiative by uniting and developing a countrywide movement for progressive measures and against the extreme Right reaction. We believe that such a united Left and democratic movement will strengthen democratic trends within the Congress also and completely isolate all reactionary conspiracies. . . . The CPI(M) has refused to respond to our call for Left and democratic unity on a national plane and for closer cooperation between the two Communist parties. Instead, it has chosen this moment to launch a vicious campaign against the CPI in order to cover its sectarian and opportunistic policy."[100]

In September 1969, the West Bengal CPI's Council passed a resolution stating that the CPI(M) had engaged itself in a new crusade against the CPI by accusing the latter of pro-Indira emotions, although the CPI(M) itself had followed the same policy as the CPI as regards bank nationalization, support for Giri during the presidential election, and opposition to SSP's no-confidence motion in Parliament against Indira Gandhi. This crusade was necessary to hide "the CPI(M)'s own contradiction between its current practices and past profession."[101] Reiterating the belief that the Congress Party would split and a group from that party would join the democratic front breaking away from "the reactionary clique," the CPI said that the contemporary task of leftists was to intensify mass movements, and through this to develop a leftist democratic front on an all-India basis.[102]

The question whether Congress contained a progressive section became a matter of considerable importance for some of the constituent parties of the United Front in West Bengal, particularly in the context of Indira Gandhi's call to all progressive elements who had left the Congress to rejoin it. Ajoy Mukherji, the Bangla Congress leader, however, said that there could be no question whatsoever of his rejoining the Congress.

Further, many of the West Bengal United Front parties were not prepared to recognize Indira Gandhi as a progressive leader despite the nationalization of fourteen major Indian banks and her determined opposition to the Congress leadership identified with the Syndicate.[103] Most of the United Front parties of Bengal, except the Bangla Congress and the CPI, were critical of Indira Gandhi. In its public stance, however, the Bangla Congress maintained that the factional quarrel within the Congress was the party's internal affair and did not concern the Bangla Congress. The CPI, as already stated, fully supported Indira Gandhi in her fight with the Syndicate, whereas the support of the CPI(M) was, as stated by Promode Das Gupta, "the support of the hangman's noose to the condemned convict."

The comments of the West Bengal United Front parties, apart from the Bangla Congress and the CPI, on the policies of Indira Gandhi, though not always as critical as that of the CPI(M), was only a little less so. The chairman of the West Bengal Forward Bloc, Nalini Guha, said that nationalization of banks was an intelligent device to save the Congress, which was fast losing its popularity: "The Forward Bloc does not think that by taking this measure Mrs Gandhi has become a progressive overnight."[104] In a similar vein, Nikhil Das, the RSP leader, said that the Congress was a capitalist organization, and Indira Gandhi had taken recourse to "left manoeuvring" to save the "moribund Congress and crisis-ridden capitalism." He remarked: "Mrs Gandhi is as reactionary as any other Congress leader and nobody should be misled by her so-called leftist pronouncements."[105] Likewise, the Socialist Unity Centre (SUC) thought that the conflict inside the Congress between the Syndicate and Indira group was not a struggle between monopolists collaborating with imperialism on the one hand, and the so-called progressive national bourgeoisie on the other, or between reaction and progress; it was a reflection of the contradiction between the conservative section of the bourgeoisie representing individual interests of monopolists, and the so-called radical section of the bourgeoisie representing the aggregate interest of capitalism. It would be for the leftists to take advantage of this contradiction for developing a mighty mass movement. Similarly, Bibhuti Dasgupta, the leader of the Lok Sevak Sangh, said that the Congress was a reactionary capitalist organization dominated by vested interests. Indira Gandhi, who was part of it, could not be called a progressive, but circumstances had compelled her to nationalize banks in order to fight the Syndicate. But mere nationalization of banks could not transform the Congress into a progressive organization. "In the past, when insurance companies were nationalized, we did not call the Congress a progressive organization,"[106] he said. Bidyut Bose of the PSP (Dissidents), using the language of Ranadive of the CPI(M), said that nationalization of banks was a hoax, and Indira Gandhi had taken this measure to maintain her office and influence, and not to bring about the economic emancipation of the masses.[107]

The SSP—which did not join the United Front Cabinet in West Bengal, though it was a constituent of the United Front —was no less critical of Indira Gandhi.[108] The SSP was wedded to a policy of anti–Congressism. Following the legacy of Ram Manohar Lohia, it sought to maintain a policy of equidistance between the Congress and the communists, both of whom it denounced. In the presidential poll of 1969, the SSP discerned an alliance between two of its enemies, namely, the pro–Indira Congress and the communists. On 13 September 1969, Madhu Limaye, MP and SSP leader, said that the presidential election had become an occasion which made the "Indira faction of the Congress" and the Communist Party "strange bedfellows" for the purpose of wreaking joint vengeance on the Congress Syndicate.[109] Limaye taunted the communists, who were hounded out of Kerala in 1959, and from West Bengal in 1967 by the Congress government, for having aligned themselves with the "pro–Indira" Congress.

The CPI, on the other hand, considered that the SSP policy was only helping the rightists. In September 1969, C. Rajeshwar

Rao, general secretary of the CPI, vigorously assailed SSP's policy of "non–Congressism." He accused the SSP leaders of playing the game of the rightist forces, consciously or unconsciously, and called upon the SSP to fall in line with the democratic forces who were resisting any attempt to topple Indira Gandhi from power.[110] The PSP also condemned the SSP policy of pure anti-Congressism, and it opposed the SSP policy of seeking to topple the Indira Gandhi government at the centre.

Prior to the split inside the Congress and thereafter, the CPI has openly given considerable support to Indira Gandhi. At the first session of Parliament after the Congress split when the Congress (o) and certain other parties opposed to Indira Gandhi, such as the Jana Sangh and the Swatantra, moved a censure motion against her government the CPI firmly stood behind her. The CPI (M) also opposed the censure motion, but its approach to the government of Indira Gandhi was very different from that of the CPI. For example, when in 1969 Indira Gandhi nationalized the fourteen major commercial banks the CPI supported this measure enthusiastically while the CPI(M), even though it supported the measure, commented that she had introduced it not because of her faith in socialism but in order to retain her position and to rehabilitate the Congress image in the public eye. Later in 1970, when she brought a bill in the Lok Sabha for abolishing the privy purses and privileges attached to the princely rulers of India, the support that the CPI gave her was again much more enthusiastic than that of the CPI(M).

The abolition of privy purses had been one of the objectives of the undivided Congress. But the Congress (o) was opposed to the manner in which such legislation was introduced and it, along with the Jana Sangh, Swatantra and BKD members of the Lok Sabha, voted against the bill in the Lok Sabha. But the bill was passed by the Lok Sabha. It was supported by the CPI and the CPI(M) and even the SSP, which was generally pledged to a policy of anti–Congressism, supported the bill. But the bill could not secure the requisite majority in the Rajya Sabha and was defeated there. Thereupon the government decided to derecognize the princes by executive action and this was done. Most of the left parties welcomed this step.

Soon after such derecognition of the princes, in September

1970 a mid-term poll was held in Kerala. The success that the Congress (R) achieved in this poll by entering into an electoral understanding with the CPI and the eventual instalment in October 1970 of a mini-front government in Kerala under the leadership of Achutha Menon, the CPI leader, but with the support of Congress (R), brought the Congress (R) and the CPI closer than ever before and the idea of repeating the Kerala-type electoral understanding between the Congress (R) and the CPI at the national level and throughout the country gained support among many within the Congress (R) and the CPI.

In October 1970 the CPI passed a resolution favouring an electoral understanding with the Congress (R) at the national level and denouncing "the obsolete concept of non-Congressism". The resolution was passed in the context of the fact that for the Kerala mid-term poll held in September 1970 there had been an electoral understanding between the CPI and the Congress (R) and that this had given the mini-front, led by the CPI, and the Congress (R) taken together an absolute majority in the Kerala legislature. By this alliance the CPI(M) was electorally contained in Kerala and the resolution that the National Council of the CPI passed in October 1970 envisaged the formation of a Kerala-type anti–CPI(M) front throughout India in order that the CPI(M) may be contained throughout the country.

The CPI passed this resolution on the basis of its assessment that the CPI(M) regarded the rightist forces in the country, such as the Congress (O), Jana Sangh and Swatantra, to be somewhat weak and, therefore, it had directed its main fire and was waging its main political battle against the CPI and the Congress (R). The CPI also was opposed to the Congress (O), Jana Sangh, and Swatantra, all of whom it described as the right reactionaries, but it was still more antagonistic to CPI(M), which it considered as disruptionist. Accordingly, the resolution of October 1970 of the CPI stated: "What has become extremely urgent in West Bengal is the need to bring into existence a broad front against the CPI(M) disruption and right reaction, at least to meet their challenge in elections." But the plea that there should be an understanding or alliance with the Congress (R) did not find favour with the other partners of the CPI in the Eight-Party Combination and particularly with the Forward Bloc, SUC and PSP (Dissidents). The Patna session of the Congress held in October 1970, soon after this resolution of the CPI was passed, also did not favour the move, which the Young Turks had supported, of entering into an understanding with the CPI at the national level. This Patna session decided that the Congress should enter into local adjustments with such parties as may appear beneficial to it.

NOTES AND REFERENCES

1. *The Statesman*, 29 April 1969.
2. *The Statesman*, 27 April 1969.
3. *The Statesman*, 26 May 1969.
4. *The Statesman*, 19 September 1969.
5. *The Statesman*, 9 November 1969.
6. *The Statesman*, 18 November 1969.
7. *The Statesman*, 11 August 1969.
8. Ibid.
9. *The Statesman*, 16 August 1969.
10. Ibid.
11. *The Statesman*, 14 August 1969.
12. *The Statesman*, 11 August 1969.
13. Ibid.
14. *The Statesman*, 12 August 1969.
15. *The Statesman*, 5 August 1969.
16. Ibid.
17. Ibid.
18. *The Statesman*, 6 August 1969.
19. *The Statesman*, 8 August 1969.
20. *The Statesman*, 13 July 1969.
21. Ibid.
22. *The Statesman*, 13 July 1969.
23. Ibid.
24. *The Statesman*, 17 July 1969.
25. Ibid.
26. Ibid.
27. Ibid.
28. *The Statesman*, 20 July 1969.
29. Ibid.
30. *The Statesman*, 18 July 1969.
31. Ibid.
32. *The Statesman*, 24 July 1969.
33. Ibid.
34. *The Statesman*, 11 August 1969.

17

35. *The Statesman*, 12 August 1969.
36. *The Statesman*, 13 August 1969.
37. *The Statesman*, 14 August 1969.
38. Ibid.
39. *The Statesman*, 15 August 1969.
40. *The Statesman*, 16 August 1969.
41. *The Statesman*, 19 August 1969.
42. *The Statesman*, 18 August 1969.
43. Ibid.
44. Ibid.
45. *The Statesman*, 20 August 1969.
46. Ibid.
47. Ibid.
48. Ibid.
49. *The Statesman*, 23 August 1969.
50. *The Statesman*, 24 August 1969.
51. Ibid.
52. *The Statesman*, 26 August 1969.
53. *The Tribune*, 17 October 1969.
54. *The Statesman*, 26 August 1969.
55. *The Statesman*, 1 September 1969.
56. *The Statesman*, 29 August 1969.
57. *The Statesman*, 28 August 1969.
58. *The Statesman*, 5 September 1969.
59. *The Statesman*, 7 September 1969.
60. *The Statesman*, 8 September 1969.
61. Ibid.
62. *The Statesman*, 7 September 1969.
63. *The Statesman*, 8 September 1969.
64. Ibid.
65. *The Statesman*, 19 September 1969.
66. Ibid.
67. *The Statesman*, 21 September 1969.
68. Ibid.
69. *The Statesman*, 14 September 1969.
70. Ibid.
71. *The Statesman*, 10 September 1969.
72. Ibid.
73. *The Statesman*, 14 September 1969.
74. Ibid.
75. *The Statesman*, 17 September 1969.
76. *The Statesman*, 8 September 1969.
77. *The Statesman*, 28 September 1969.
78. Ibid.
79. *The Statesman*, 10 October 1969.
80. *Hindustan Times*, 17 November 1969.
81. *The Statesman*, 21 November 1969.

82. *The Statesman,* 1 December 1969.

83. *The Statesman,* 22 December 1969.

84. *The Statesman,* 10 December 1969.

85. *The Statesman,* 11 December 1969.

86. *The Statesman,* 8 December 1969.

87. *The Statesman,* 13 December 1969.

88. *The Statesman,* 25 November 1969.

89. "Supreme Court Has Its Say, Now People Speaking Up", *New Age,* Central Organ of the Communist Party of India, 22 February 1970.

90. "Polit Bureau on Supreme Court Verdict on Bank Nationalization," *People's Democracy,* 22 February 1970. P. Ramamurthy, "Amend Constitution," *People's Democracy,* Organ of the Communist Party of India (Marxist), 19 April 1970, pp. 4, 7.

91. "Remove This Clause from The Indian Constitution", *New Age,* 8 February 1970.

92. *The Statesman,* 26 August 1969.

93. *The Statesman,* 23 August 1969.

94. Ibid.

95. *The Statesman,* 3 September 1969.

96. *The Statesman,* 14 September 1969.

97. Ibid.

98. Ibid. See also Basavapunniah's article "Nothing New In Indira Gandhi's 'New Deal'," in *People's Democracy,* 28 December 1969.

99. For a CPI criticism of this view see Mohit Sen's article "Basavapunniah's Balancing Trick," *New Age,* 21 December 1969, p. 3.

100. *The Statesman,* 17 September 1969.

101. *The Statesman,* 15 September 1969.

102. Ibid.

103. *The Statesman,* 14 September 1969.

104. *The Statesman,* 17 September 1969.

105. Ibid.

106. Ibid.

107. Ibid.

108. Ibid.

109. *The Statesman,* 14 September 1969.

110. *The Statesman,* 17 September 1969.

CHAPTER SEVEN

The Indian Socialists

I. THE SOCIALISTS, CLASS STRUGGLE AND NATIONALIZATION

Socialist groups sprang up in various parts of the country during the thirties of this century. Of the leaders of all–India stature, Jawaharlal Nehru was one of the first to be attracted to socialism. Nehru was elected president of the Indian National Congress in 1929. At the Labour Session of the Indian National Congress in 1929, he said: "I must frankly confess that I am a socialist and a republican, and am no believer in King and princes, or in the order which produces the modern kings of industry, who have greater power over the lives and fortunes of men than even the Kings of old, and whose methods are as predatory, as those of the old feudal aristocracy."[1]

At the instance of Nehru, the 1929 All India Congress Committee at Bombay passed a resolution which bore the imprint of his socialistic ideas. The resolution ascribed the poverty of India not merely to foreign rule, but also to economic exploitation. To remove poverty and exploitation and to ameliorate the condition of the Indian masses it was essential to make revolutionary changes in the economic and social structure of society.[2]

In 1929 Nehru, in addition to being the president of the Indian National Congress, was also elected president of the Trade Union Congress. It was somewhat unusual for the same person to preside over both the Indian National Congress and the Trade Union Congress within a few weeks of each other. Nehru said that he would seek to utilize his special position to bring these two organizations closer to each other, to make the Indian National Congress more socialistic and more proletarian, and to induce organized labour to join the national struggle under the leadership of the Indian National Congress.[3]

The Indian National Congress at its Karachi Session of 1931 passed a resolution on Fundamental Rights and Economic Policy, which stated: "The State shall own or control key industries and services, mineral resources, railways, waterways, shipping and other means of public transport."[4] But the 1931 resolution on Fundamental Rights and Economic Policy of the Congress did not satisfy the socialists who were in the Congress, who wanted not merely the nationalization of the key industries, but also the nationalization of the essential means of production.

Early in the thirties the Indian socialists began to organize themselves. In May 1934, Jayaprakash Narayan organized an All India Socialist Conference at Patna. Those prominent in the socialist movement at that time were Jayaprakash Narayan, Achyut Patwardhan, Asoka Mehta, M. R. Masani, N. G. Goray, S. M. Joshi, and M. L. Dantwala. In fact all these persons had been in prison in Nasik Jail during the second civil disobedience movement of 1932, and it is in the discussions that took place there that the foundations of the Congress Socialist Party were really laid.

Early in the thirties, the socialists, and particularly the communists, began to propound theories of class war and confiscation of private property. The Indian National Congress, which was then dominated by Gandhi and those belonging to the Swarajya Party, disapproved of class war and all talk of confiscation of private property. On 18 June 1934 the Congress Working Committee passed a resolution condemning the "loose talk about confiscation of private property and necessity of class war."[5] The resolution stated that the 1931 Karachi resolution of the Congress on Fundamental Rights and Economic Policy did not envisage either confiscation of private property or class war. The Congress Working Committee resolution further declared that the concept of class war and the doctrine of the confiscation of private property were contrary to the principles of nonviolence.

The socialists within the Congress were dissatisfied with this resolution of the Congress Working Committee. In October 1934, at a conference in Bombay the socialists declared that their policy was the socialization of the key and principal industries with a view to achieving the progressive socialization of all the instruments of production, distribution, and exchange, the deve-

lopment of the economic life of the country on the basis of
planning by the state, the elimination of princes and landlords,
and the redistribution of land to the peasants. Explaining the
objectives of this resolution, Jayaprakash Narayan, the socialist
leader, claimed that the Congress policies were contrary to the
spirit of the Karachi resolution of the 1931 Congress, and that
the Congress socialists were endeavouring to remove the discre-
pancy between the objectives of the Karachi resolution of the
1931 Congress and the actual policies that the Congress sought
to pursue.[6]

Jayaprakash regretted that the Congress was not seeking a
revolution of the Indian economic structure. He said that, far
from working for a revolution, the Congress wanted to leave
the economic structure of society intact, to permit private individuals to own the means of production—except in the sphere
of key industries—and to preserve the economic system based
on the exploitation of the poor and middle class. All these
showed that the "preamble and substance of the Karachi Resolution are at wide variance with each other."[7] Jayaprakash
declared that if the ultimate objective was to make the masses
politically and economically free, then "socialism becomes a
goal to which one must irresistibly be drawn. If, again, the
objective is to take hold of the chaotic and conflicting forces
of society, to fashion the latter according to the ideal of utmost
social good, to harness all conscious directives of human intelligence in the service of the common wealth, then, again, socialism
becomes an inescapable destination."[8]

In 1935 Jayaprakash declared that the policy of the Congress
Socialist Party was not to convert the Congress into a full-
fledged socialist party, which was not possible in the circumstances then prevailing, but to make it a true anti–imperialist
body. He said: "It is not our purpose, as sometimes it has been
misunderstood to be, to convert the whole Congress into a
full-fledged socialist party. All we seek to do is to change the
content and policy of that organization, [so] that it comes
truly to represent the masses having the object of emancipating
them both from the foreign power and the native system of
exploitation."[9]

Like the communists, the Congress socialists also believed in
the theory of class struggle, though not with the same intensity.

The latter, however, hoped that the class struggle that was going on would make the Indian nationalist movement more broad-based. In his presidential address at the first session of the All-India Socialist Conference at Patna in May 1934, Narendra Deva said that "the process of intensive differentiation amongst the various classes of society has been going on in the country with greater and greater rapidity, cutting more and more layers of the upper and middle classes from the national movement. New classes are being formed and are being separated from the great mass of the people. . . . Instead of wailing over unity for which no basis exists, it is our duty to find out methods that will intensify the national struggle which has so far been a predominantly middle class movement. I feel that the only way to do it is to broaden the basis of the movement by organizing the masses on an economic and class-conscious basis. The two instruments which can make a class self-conscious are propaganda and organization."[10]

Though differing from the economic policy of the Congress, the Congress Socialist Party did not want to wreck the Congress, but wanted to make it more revolutionary and more socialistic. In 1934 Acharya Narendra Deva, Jayaprakash Narayan, and others had founded the Congress Socialist Party as an integral part of the Congress. Narendra Deva, Jayaprakash Narayan, and other leaders who founded this party were already in the Congress, but they felt that for the growth and development of socialism in India, the leftist forces should be united under the banner of the Congress Socialist Party.

These socialists, such as Jayaprakash Narayan, had been closely associated with Gandhi; in fact, the formation of the Congress Socialist Party marked the transition, for many nationalists, from Gandhism to socialism. Socialist leaders like Jayaprakash Narayan were attracted by Gandhi's emphasis on economic equality and simplicity and his passion for social justice, but they felt that Marxism provided a truer diagnosis of the economic ills of society, and that the Marxian science of revolution offered a surer and quicker way of social and economic transformation than the technique of Gandhi.

During the second civil disobedience movement initiated by Gandhi in the year 1932, Jayaprakash was the acting general secretary of the Congress, and after other Congress leaders had been imprisoned Jayaprakash organized an underground resistance movement, but was later himself arrested and sent to Nasik prison. The Indian communists did not participate in this civil disobedience movement. On the contrary, some of them denounced the nationalist struggle as a movement which was being waged in the interests of the bourgeoisie. Socialists, like Jayaprakash and Narendra Deva, felt that the Indian communists acted under the guidance of the Comintern, and did not appreciate the revolutionary character of a nationalist resistance movement in a subject country like India. In order to organize the socialist forces, as also to strengthen the nationalist movement, and to give it a revolutionary rather than a constitutional character, the Congress Socialist Party was formed in the year 1934.

The formation of the Congress Socialist Party was welcomed both by Jawaharlal Nehru and Subhas Bose. In 1936 when Nehru was elected the Congress president he openly avowed his faith in socialism and appointed three prominent socialists—Jayaprakash Narayan, Narendra Deva, and Achyut Patwardhan—to the Congress Working Committee. Nehru continued as the president of the Congress for the following year, and was succeeded in 1938 by Subhas Bose who had leftist leanings, and who had also blessed the formation of the Congress Socialist Party.

The socialists who joined the Congress Socialist Party believed in what was called scientific socialism, and not in any humanitarian kind of socialism. In 1936 the Congress Socialist Party published a pamphlet written by Jayaprakash entitled *Why Socialism*. In this pamphlet, he sought to define the kind of socialism that the Congress socialists believed in. He conceded that there had been different schools of socialism, and mutually conflicting socialist parties, but claimed that, latterly, and particularly as a result of the impact of the world crisis and the rise of fascism, there had been a growing unity in socialist thought, so that "today more than ever before it is possible to say that there is only one type, one theory of socialism—Marxism."[11]

In fact, the greater part of the differences between various groups of socialists were not so much about the nature and definition of socialism, but about the method and tactics that had to be adopted for transforming the capitalist society into a socialist one. "So far only communists have vindicated their theory of tactics," said Jayaprakash, "by their great and remarkable success in Russia. The proponents of the other methods are today everywhere in the trough of failure."[12]

Socialists in India, as in other parts of the world, insisted that socialism was not merely "a code of personal conduct; it is not something which you and I can practise,"[13] but a system of social reconstruction and an ideology for the reorganization of the entire economic and social life of the country including its farms, factories, and schools. It is because socialism meant not merely individual reform but social reconstruction that socialists were interested in power and in the manner as to how the coercive power of the state could be utilized to transform society and economy. In order to transform society, the socialists sought to capture power and the entire apparatus of the state machinery. Jayaprakash wrote: "Whether it is a constitutionalist party, like the Labour Party of England, a revolutionary party, like the Bolshevik Party of Russia, a fascist party like that of Hitler in Germany, it seeks in every case to capture the State. When the State is in your hands, you can legislate, you can use the whole magnificent apparatus of propaganda and education that modern science has made available; you can enforce your will. And if there is resistance, you can use the coercive arm of the State—the police and the army—to crush it. . . . No Party in the world of today can build up Socialism unless it has the machinery of the State in its hands: whether it has come to acquire it through the will of the electorate or by a *coup d'état*."

But the socialists explained that after the acquisition of state power by them the introduction of socialism could not be achieved by shooting the exploiters and "pot-bellied capitalists" or by blowing talukdars and zamindars to pieces or by distributing the treasures of the *rajas* and the *mahajans* among the people. They explained that after seizing state power the socialists would concentrate on the acquisition by the state of the means of production in order to eliminate economic inequality and to ensure to each citizen equality of opportunity in the economic field.

What distressed the socialists most was the lack of opportunities and the inequalities that existed in Indian society. They referred to the fact that for the great majority of the people

there was poverty, hunger, filth, disease, and ignorance but for
the minority there was comfort, luxury, culture, position, and
power. The extremes of inequality and the absence of equal
opportunities of development in present-day society, the socialists claimed, were entirely due to the existence of the capitalist
system.

The central problem of our society, declared Jayaprakash,
was the fact of inequality and its brood of social consequences.
The best minds of the world in all ages had directed their efforts
to this problem and had sought a solution of the problem of
inequality. But the socialists claimed that the usual solutions of
this problem that had been advocated in the past, such as
"charity, philanthropy, utopias, appeals to the more fortunate
to be kind to the less fortunate, denunciation of the rich and
exaltation of poverty, curtailment of wants,"[14] were wholly
inadequate and antiquated. The socialists denounced Gandhi's
theory of trusteeship and said that it would be futile to except
that the rich would act as the trustees of the poor.

The socialists pointed out that sometimes a rich man earned a
thousand times more than a poor man, but an "individual, no
matter how clever, cannot possibly produce, at any stage of
productivity, thousands of times more than others who are
using the same means of production."[15] They claimed that the
great riches of the rich were not the result of their own production, but the result of exploitation.

The Indian socialists urged, like their counterparts in the
West, that the enormous wealth that had accumulated in the
hands of those who owned the means of production had so
accumulated by virtue of their exploitation of the labour of
the workmen. The rich, they claimed, accumulated their wealth
not because they created it, but because they diverted to themselves a larger share of the national produce than what they
actually produced, that is to say, they exploited others.

In the ownership of the instruments of production in private
hands the socialists found the real cause of the inequality of
present-day society. They claimed that in the earliest times the
sources and instruments of production passed into private hands
through force, that "the surplus wealth thus accumulated in the
hands of those who were able to use force went on multiplying
through the ages through the institution of slavery and inden-

tured labour, till the loot from India and the inventions of certain German–Englishmen combined to usher in the Industrial Revolution. "This," said Jayaprakash, "became *par excellence* the age of exploitation, because it made the employment of unheard of masses of labourers in single manufactures possible."[16]

As the cause of inequality, in socialist thought, was the private ownership of the means of production, the means of removing such inequality was the social ownership of the means of production. To develop a socialist movement in India pledged to the policy of socialization of the means of production, the socialists believed that they could profitably unite with all leftist forces, including the communists and Royists.

During the thirties when the Indian Communist Party was illegal, many communists were allowed to become members of the Congress Socialist Party, and thereby to influence Congress policy. But so far as the approach of the socialists and the communists to Gandhi and the official leadership of the Congress was concerned, there were significant differences. The communists had serious reservations about Gandhi and the official Congress leadership, which they considered to be reactionary, but the socialists considered that, in the circumstances prevailing in India, a mass movement could be initiated only under the leadership of Gandhi. Accordingly it was "madness to attack the leadership, to seek to discredit it, to weaken it."[17] Further, the Indian socialists said that a "capitalist democracy is any day preferable to serfdom and subjection to alien rule,"[18] and accordingly asserted that Gandhi's movements against alien rule should be strengthened and supported.

Though the communists were allowed to join the Congress Socialist Party, the discovery of a circular of the communists by Jayaprakash Narayan in August 1937, and of another circular by M. R. Masani[19] in September 1938, convinced the socialists that the communists had no faith whatever in the Congress Socialist Party, which they had joined. Eventually the communists were expelled from the party in 1940. Referring to the second circular discovered by Masani in September 1938, Jayaprakash later said: "For many comrades that circular was the last straw. Yet, the Executive again held its hand and allowed things to drift. Now it was no longer the ideal or hope of unity that decided the Executive. It was just reluctance to face an

unpleasant task. Those were dark days for the Party, when lack
of decision created a good deal of confusion and weakness. The
enemies of the Party did not fail to profit fully by it. . . . This
policy of drift which was daily delivering the Party into the
hands of the Communist Party drove some of the leading
members of the Executive to resign. This produced great con-
sternation in the ranks of the Congress Socialist Party, though it
was welcomed by the Communist Party and its 'Trojan Horses'
and stooges."[20]

II. THE SOCIALISTS, MARXISM AND DEMOCRACY

The socialists and the communists differed not only in their
tactics and methods but also in their attitudes and beliefs. So
far as the communists were concerned they relied greatly, if not
exclusively, on Marx, Engels, and Lenin. The socialists too
relied on Marxism and regarded it as a form of scientific socialism, as distinguished from utopian socialism or social revisionism,
but they had also other sources of inspiration. Acharya Narendra
Deva, one of the leaders of the Indian socialists, declared: "We
can perform the task before us only if we try to comprehend
the principles and purposes of socialism and to understand the
dialectical method propounded by Marx for the correct understanding of the situation and make that understanding the basis
of true action. We must take our stand on scientific socialism
and steer clear of utopian socialism or social reformism. . . .
Nothing short of a revolutionary transformation of the existing
social order can meet the needs of the situation."[21]

But though the Indian socialists were influenced by Marxism
they were also, to a certain extent, influenced by Gandhism and,
more particularly, by the ideas of Western democracy. The
socialists were not whole-hearted Marxists. They thought that
the communists had converted Marxism into a dogma, and
there always existed revisionist tendencies among the Indian
socialists. Further, the Indian socialists gave their own interpretation to Marxism to show that it was not opposed to democracy,
and some of them also claimed that the Marxist interpretation
of history did not leave out or ignore the noneconomic causes
and forces altogether. Acharya Narendra Deva said: "All that

Marx means to say is that an idea can influence the course of history only when it realizes itself in fact and thus becomes a thing. He has nowhere considered the question of the relative importance of mind and matter. Both are equally important. Man cannot create anything independently of the objective situation, nor can a given objective situation by itself produce a result desired by man without his active participation. He only used the expression to distinguish his method from the idealism of Hegel who denied the reality of the world of experience and only recognized an Absolute Idea. Marx does hold that many causes operate in the evolution of history.... Marx has always held that what was originally derivative had the power of becoming an independent cause. Therefore, it is wrong to say that Marx recognized only one single cause of historical evolution."[22]

Though the Gandhian creed of nonviolence was not wholly acceptable to the socialists, the method of *satyagraha* formulated by Gandhi appealed to them. They wanted to avoid violence and dictatorship, and also wanted to combine socialism with democracy. The socialists felt that in the conditions prevailing in India it might be possible to come to power through the democratic processes. It is true that they believed in the need of state power and in the need to utilize the coercive apparatus of the state for effecting an economic regeneration of the country, but they felt that it may be possible to attain state power without violence.

In their belief in the necessity of state power and in the need to utilize the entire coercive apparatus of the state for effecting economic changes, the socialists differed fundamentally from Gandhi, who believed in individual effort and in a decentralized economy, and who subscribed to the doctrine that that state was best which governed the least. Gandhi felt that real changes could come only through change in the character of men, and not by a mere change in the power of the state, or by a change of the persons who wielded that power. But, unlike Gandhi, the socialists were concerned not so much with changing men individually, as with changing institutions so that men could have proper opportunity to develop themselves. They claimed that socialism was not a code of personal conduct, but an economic ideology on the basis of which state power was to be captured for effecting an economic transformation of society. Jayaprakash said: "Those who desire to construct a socialist society should have the power and the requisite sanction behind them to do so. . . . Behind every piece of legislation lies the State's power to persuade and, ultimately, to coerce."[23]

To remedy the inequalities and lack of opportunity prevailing in a capitalistic society, said Jayaprakash, there could be two solutions. Either there could be a society in which each individual cultivated his own land without making any payment of rent or royalty to anyone else, worked his own tools in his own workshop for his own use, and did not possess large means of production; or, alternatively, the basic means of production could be owned by a socialist state. But a society in which each individual only produced for himself would be a primitive society where there would be no large-scale production, and where it would not be possible to have railways, telephones, and other big industries. Such a society would be economically vulnerable. Further, to have such a society, it would involve the confiscation of the properties held by existing owners and the distribution thereof to small producers, but to bring about such a situation it would have been necessary to install a ruthless dictatorship whereas, in fact, as Jayaprakash stated, for such a dictatorship of the small producers "there is no social basis in society."[24]

Indian socialists urged that the only solution for existing inequalities and exploitation was the abolition of private property and the establishment of social ownership of the means of production. This would result in "the eradication of economic exploitation, the ending of economic inequalities, in other words, the removal of the basic curse of the present society. The source of accumulation of wealth in private hands is the exploitation of labour. . . . With social ownership established people no longer work for others. They work for themselves, not individually but collectively; and what they produce is not for the profit of the manufacturer, but for their own consumption. Social ownership means that all wealth is held in common and shared equitably, the basis of distribution being initially, the amount and character of work done, and finally, the needs of the individual; only that part of the produce being withheld from distribution which is necessary for defence and administration, for schools and hospitals, for economic development, and for other common purposes."[25]

The socialists claimed that in order to establish socialism in India complete political freedom had first to be attained, and only thereafter the privileges of the princes and zamindars could be abolished and the land redistributed to the people. So far as agriculture was concerned, the Indian socialists, such as Jayaprakash, considered that one would have to pass through two stages: the stage of cooperative farming and then the stage of collective farming.[26] After the zamindary system was abolished, there would be a redistribution of land with the object of breaking up the big holdings and making the smaller holdings economic. Upon such redistribution of land no peasant would have more than a certain maximum acreage of land, perhaps not exceeding thirty acres. No one would be allowed to own any land who did not reside in the village and who did not actually till the land. The unit of agricultural economy would be the village. The village panchayat would have the power to settle the lands among individual peasants considering their needs. The peasants would thus have a kind of proprietary right over the lands settled with them. Under this scheme no peasant would be allowed to sell land to anyone except to the village panchayat. The system described above can broadly be called the cooperative stage of socialist farming. The next stage would be the collectivistic stage, in which no individual proprietary rights in agricultural lands would be recognized. A collective farmer may, as in Russia, be allowed to own privately about three acres of land around his homestead for kitchen, gardening, raising poultry, and other similar purposes, but otherwise at the stage of collective farming all lands pertaining to a village shall be owned and run by village collectives.[27]

Jayaprakash sounded a note of warning as regards the collectivist methods employed in Russia. He, like other Indian socialists, felt that too much violence had been employed in Russia to implement a policy of collectivization. It is in their criticisms of the Russian methods and in their renunciation of the method of violence that the Indian socialists differed most from the Indian communists. "In Russia," said Jayaprakash in 1946, "collectivization was pushed through at great human cost and under a ruthless dictatorship. Estimates run up to as high a figure as twenty millions of those who had to be 'liquidated' in order to make collectivization a success. I do not favour such a colossal repression of the toiling peasant masses, nor does socialist theory permit it. Abolition of landlordism, redistribution of land, and breaking up of big holdings would require state coercion to be used against fifteen to twenty per cent of the agricultural population perhaps. But collectivization might require sixty to seventy per cent of that population to be repressed. I do not find any justification for any political party, speaking and acting in the name of the toiling masses, to indulge in such wholesale repression. Twenty per cent may be coerced in the interest of the remaining eighty per cent, but there is no justification for repressing seventy per cent of the peasants even 'for their own good'. Cooperative farming itself would require a good measure of coercion.... Collectivization on the other hand would require a degree of wholesale repression that is repugnant to socialism."28

It is this approach of the socialists that distinguishes them from the communists. The socialists condemned violence and certain features of the Russian experiment which involved the excessive use of violence. The socialists considered that the road to socialism lay not through revolutionary violence only, and that it was possible to achieve socialism in certain countries without violence and through the instrumentality of the democratic machinery alone.

Further, the socialists claimed that in order to apply Marxism in India, socialists would have to take into account not only all the developments that have taken place since Marx wrote but also the special conditions prevailing in India, and that socialism in India would have to adapt itself to Indian conditions. Accordingly, Marxism would have to be applied in India not dogmatically but creatively. "Marxism," said Jayaprakash, "is a science of society and a scientific method of social change that includes social revolution. As such there can be no room for dogmatism or fundamentalism in Marxist thought. Those who on the one hand call Marxism scientific and on the other introduce dogmatism into it do it great disservice. In science there is no such thing as final truth. Science progresses by progressive elimination of untruth from human knowledge. If Marxism is a science, Marx could not have expounded ultimate truths, but only made approximations to them. Today with a vastly developed store of human knowledge and vastly greater experience and observation of capitalist society, we are in a position to make far greater approximations to the truth than Marx."[29]

The socialists referred to Marx's theory that in certain countries labour may come to power through democratic means and argued that Marxism should not necessarily lead to a belief in dictatorship. About six months before India became independent, in an article written in *Janata*, Jayaprakash referred to the fact that at the Hague Convention of the First International in 1872, Marx, speaking on tactics, had observed: "The worker must one day capture political power in order to found the new organization of labour.... But we do not assert that the way to reach this goal is the same everywhere. We know that the institutions, the manners, and the customs of the various countries must be considered, and we do not deny that there are countries like England and America, and, if I understood your arrangements better, I might even add Holland, where the worker may attain his object by peaceful means. But not in all countries is this the case." Marx, therefore, clearly conceived two ways of achieving socialism, one peaceful, the other violent. Which of these two ways should be adopted would depend on the conditions prevailing in a particular country. "In Russia," said Jayaprakash, "there was no democracy, so Lenin took the path of violent revolution though it may be doubtful today how far was Lenin justified in disbanding the Constituent Assembly when he had no majority in it. There is democracy in England, and its scope has developed greatly since Marx's days. Accordingly, we find British Labour installed in Government by a democratic process and putting socialist schemes into practice in a democratic fashion. Not even the blindest fanatic would dream of the possibility or necessity of a violent revolution in Great Britain today."[30]

The Indian socialists said that if a political democracy was established in India after India became independent, then on the basis of the prognostications of Marx and Lenin, the bourgeois class would assume control of the state. But that did not mean that the working class and the city and rural poor would not be able to displace the bourgeoisie and establish socialism through the democratic process and without resort to a violent revolu-

18

tion. They conceded that the method of the violent revolution and dictatorship might conceivably lead to a socialist democracy; but in the USSR, such a method, said Jayaprakash, "led to something very different, i.e. to a bureaucratic State, in which democracy does not exist." If the socialist movement in India had no freedom or opportunity to use the democratic method, there could certainly be no other way of destroying bourgeois society and bourgeois rule than by a violent revolution and dictatorship. But if a full democratic state was established in India, then why could not socialism be achieved peacefully? Even at a time when political democracy had not risen to its full height, Marx himself had visualized the possibility of a peaceful transition to socialism. Since the days of Marx, political democracy had become a more powerful and potent instrument of social change. Further, the economic, political, and ideological forces of capitalism had been weakened and the power of labour and the strength of socialist parties had greatly increased. In these circumstances, the possibility of the peaceful transition to socialism was even greater than in the times of Marx.

The Indian socialists say that it is a grave mistake to assume that there must be a dictatorship of the proletariat in a socialist state.[31] They claim that such an assumption is really against the teachings of Marx. The dictatorship of the proletariat in Marxist theory had a place only for the transitional period from capitalism to socialism, and that also only for some countries, for Marx himself had visualized that in a capitalist state, such as England —where political democracy was greatly developed and where there was no large standing army—progress towards socialism could be achieved through the democratic path. Further, Indian socialists point out that the concept of the dictatorship of the proletariat should not degenerate into a dictatorship of a single party. The dictatorship of the proletariat in Marxist theory does not mean the dictatorship of a single party, but the dictatorship of a class, such as the working class or, in industrially backward countries such as India or post–Tsarist Russia, of a combination of the toiling classes, such as workers, peasants, and the lower middle class. The dictatorship of the proletariat, therefore, never meant or could mean that parties of the working class or other toilers would be suppressed; it meant only the suppression of the ruling class and their political and economic institutions.

Indian socialists have to a certain extent been influenced by Fabian socialism and Western parliamentarianism. They say that Marxism is only a method, and accordingly the statements and theories of Marx on political democracy or the dictatorship of the proletariat cannot be taken as the last word in socialism. And some of them have even put forward the explanation that inasmuch as Marxism as a philosophy was born before the democratic age Marxists have felt difficulties to adjust themselves to the concept of the political democracy. Asoka Mehta remarked: "The Marxists . . . have never been happy with democracy. To deny it and where necessary to disrupt it becomes their instinctive approach. In Asian countries where democracy is struggling for strength it is easy to adopt the traditional Marxist stance, but it is far more necessary to explore revisionist re-statement where socialism becomes integral to democracy."[32] Mehta pleaded for an Asian socialism which would be revisionist, democratic, and pacific. He wrote: "Somerset Maugham has said somewhere: 'Prose is rococo art; poetry is baroque'. One might say likewise that revolutionary socialism which is elemental, massive, mystical, tragic, is baroque; revisionist socialism, which, as it were, prefers accomplishment to power, stability to intransigence, vigour to grandeur, is rococo. In the free countries of Asia a shift is desired from the baroque to the rococo."[33]

Apart from proclaiming their faith in democracy, the socialists in India have often given expression to the thought that in an underdeveloped country like India, with its poverty and ever growing population, the problem of production is no less, if not more, important than the problem of distribution, and they said that the primary aim of Indian socialism should be to complete or telescope in India within a short period the economic progress made in industrially advanced European countries over a long period. They felt that in an underdeveloped country like India it was essential that the rate in the increase of production should be high, so that the problem of poverty could be satisfactorily tackled. They warned that the poor would not be satisfied with political democracy for long, unless such a democracy could act fast enough and plan sufficiency well and raise production adequately in order to cope with the problem of poverty. "It is therefore clear," said Asoka Mehta, "that unless development gathers speed early enough, growing population can retard further development. Again, if after thirty years' development efforts, the pre-consumer income remains virtually unchanged, can stability be maintained? Only a rapid tempo of development can maintain an accelerating momentum, check fertility, raise level of living and uphold democracy."[34]

The Congress socialists envisaged the establishment of socialism in free India by a victory through the polls.[35] On the eve of independence, when a Constituent Assembly was set up in India, the question arose whether the Congress socialists would seek to orient that Assembly to a socialist goal. But the Cabinet Mission Plan on the basis of which the Constituent Assembly was set up had been rejected by the Congress socialists, who believed that Britain did not intend to part with power and was merely seeking to lead nationalist India up the garden path. The Congress socialists boycotted the Constituent Assembly. But by July 1947 the Congress socialists reconsidered their position and their attitude to the Constituent Assembly. On 3 July 1947, Jayaprakash wrote to Nehru stating that considering the changed circumstances the Congress socialists would join the Assembly, if invited. Jayaprakash said that he was "too occupied" and should not be invited, but he suggested the names of other Congress socialist leaders who may be invited. On 5 July 1947, Nehru wrote back saying that the Congress would welcome the persons suggested in Jayaprakash's letter and "we shall try to get them in." Eventually, however, nothing materialized and by May 1948, the non-cooperationist wing of the Congress Socialist Party gained ascendancy within the party so that the party not only refused to send delegates to the Constituent Assembly, but passed a resolution calling for the dissolution of the Assembly and its reconstitution on the basis of adult suffrage.

III. THE SOCIALISTS, GANDHISM AND LIBERALISM

In 1948 the Congress socialists severed their connection with the Congress. Since 1934 the Congress socialists had functioned within the Congress but in 1948, after Gandhi had been assassinated, the rightist group within the Congress led by Sardar Patel caused a resolution to be passed which outlawed the formation of political parties within the Congress. Accordingly, the social-ists had to choose between disbanding their organization within the Congress, or of leaving the Congress altogether and setting up an independent political party. The socialists chose the latter alternative at the Nasik Congress held in March 1948 and there-after an independent Socialist Party outside the Congress was formed.

The attainment of independence brought to the forefront the question of the method that the socialists should pursue in free India. In accordance with their previously declared beliefs, the Indian socialists decided that they would pursue peaceful methods and would not resort to revolutionary violence. In fact, one of the founders of the Congress socialist movement, Jaya-prakash Narayan, had by this time been so thoroughly imbued with Gandhism and Gandhi's doctrine of the purity of means that he insisted that the socialists must pursue not only democra-tic and peaceful methods, but must also ensure that only right and pure means and methods were used for the attainment of their ideals. At the Nasik Conference of the Socialist Party held in March 1948, Jayaprakash said: "There are many things that Mahatma Gandhi taught us. But the greatest thing he taught was that means are ends, that evil means can never lead to good ends and that fair ends require fair means. Some of us may have been sceptical of this truth but recent world events and events at home have convinced me that nothing but good means will enable us to reach the goal of a good society, which is socialism."

The communal frenzy that flared up in India following inde-pendence and the formation of Pakistan on the basis of religious differences had shattered Jayaprakash's faith in the economic interpretation of history and he said: "Is everything due to economic inequalities? Is Capitalism the only evil? Can we entirely depend upon class struggle? I do not think so. Economic approach cannot be the only approach. We have been preach-ing all this all these years. I feel that our approach has a limited appeal. If ours was the only method, class struggle the only weapon, economic approach the only attitude, then India would not have been partitioned."

The change that came over Jayaprakash's views gradually led him from socialism to Gandhism and *sarvodaya*, so that Jaya-prakash pleaded that there should be no suspicion or hatred between the forces of democratic socialism and Gandhism, and that the names of Marx and Gandhi should not act as barriers between the socialists. Jayaprakash's emphasis on the purity of means also led him to emphasize a policy of decentralization of the sources of power. Advocating a policy of economic and political decentralization, Jayaprakash wrote in 1951: "Ordinarily, in leftist circles this is characterized as antediluvian. But those socialists who do not equate their own power with a workers' democracy, who are aware of the disastrous consequences of centralization of economic and political power must carefully and sympathetically consider this aspect of Gandhism. Economic decentralization does not necessarily mean rejection of modern science and technology; though it does mean that the modern techniques of production are neither used as a means of exploitation, nor as a means of domination, of man by man. The need of decentralized industry in a backward economy like India's where production must be labour-intensive instead of capital-intensive, further underlines the nearness of Gandhian thought on this matter with socialist reconstruction in India. Political decentralization neither means a weak State nor absence of planned life."[36] Jayaprakash wanted to build socialism from below and from the villages, and as his belief in *sarvodaya* increased, he gradually retired from the active political field.

Jayaprakash's transition from socialism to Gandhism and *sarvodaya* resulted mainly from the belief, which he eventually came to cherish, that the ends alone could not justify the adoption of undesirable means, and that the invocation of the name of revolution alone could not sanction the use of violence. In this respect the transition of Jayaprakash—who during the Quit India movement of 1942 had said that violence could be used to subvert a foreign rule, and who had been one of the heroes of the underground resistance movement of 1942—is in some respects similar to the transition of M. N. Roy, the revolutionary communist, from Marxism to Radicalism and then to Humanism. Explaining the change that came over him, Roy had said that he had come to reject the Jesuitic belief that the end could justify the means—any means—or that the cause of revolution could always justify the adoption of the methods of violence and coercion.[37]

Further, both Jayaprakash and Roy felt that the experience

of the revolution in Russia did not justify the hopes it had first aroused, and that, in fact, no revolution could justify the adoption of any means, or the divorce of ethics from politics. In 1951, Jayaprakash wrote: "The first aspect of Gandhism that must interest the socialist is its moral or ethical basis, its insistence on values. Russian or Stalinist interpretation of socialist philosophy has reduced it to a cross Machiavellian code of conduct utterly devoid of any sense of right or wrong, good or evil. The end justifies the means; and when the end is power—personal and group power—there is no limit to the depths to which the means will sink to secure the objective. The struggle for power in every communist country—not against the old order but amongst communist power-seekers themselves—has led to a totalitarian society which is so different from what was proclaimed by the fathers of Socialism as the goal of the social revolution. To the horrors of this unscrupulous, amoral, political philosophy, Gandhism offers a corrective that socialists would overlook only at the cost of the very substance of their creed. The values of individual and social life that Socialism strives to achieve and make the basis of new civilization also constitute the foundation stone of a Gandhian society. It is true that philosophically Gandhism has a nonsecular and religious or supernatural foundation, whereas socialist philosophy is wholly secular and natural or material. But translated in terms of the practices of life, the values are not different...."[38]

Another prominent member of the Congress Socialist Party who later radically changed his views as regards socialism was M. R. Masani. Though both Jayaprakash and Masani were socialists, Masani had been more attracted to the Western liberal tradition as Jayaprakash had been to Marxist thought. Eventually, Masani became an advocate of liberalism and an opponent of the socialist theory of the socialization of all the means of production.[39] According to Masani, socialism is on the way out, and in support of this proposition he relies on the experience of various European countries. In 1959, he wrote: "The Dutch Labour Party adopted in 1959 a new programme which defines socialism in terms of a set of social and ethical values. Specifically rejecting 'State Socialism and the bureaucratic assumption of power', it declares that 'ownership of the means of production should be made subservient to the well-being of the nation.

... It is desirable for different forms of publicly-owned and privately-owned undertakings to exist side by side. ... Public control must be exercised over the privately-owned undertakings if this should prove to be necessary in the interests of the community.' ... The Swedish Social Democratic Party will have before it at a Party Conference in June 1960 a new programme prepared by the Prime Minister of Sweden and some of his colleagues. According to this draft, 'Social democracy supports the demand for public ownership or public control ... to the extent that this is necessary in order to safeguard important public interests ... [it] wants to stimulate private enterprise in those provinces where it shows that it can combine efficiency and progressive thought with responsibility towards consumers, employees, and the community'. ... The Swiss Social Democratic Party adopted a new programme in June 1959 which declares that 'in the case of monopolistic enterprises, we must either establish the conditions necessary for fair competition or place them under public control or actually transfer them to public ownership' .... The Austrian Socialist Party, historically the most Marxist in Europe, states in its new programme adopted in May 1959 that 'the aim of socialists is an order of society which has for its objective the free development of the human personality.' On the question of ownership, it declares that 'the only test as to which undertakings are to be taken into public ownership will be the public interest ... large sectors will, even in the future, remain reserved for private enterprise.' ... The new German Social Democratic Manifesto adopted at a special convention last November makes clear the direction in which enlightened and progressive socialist thought is moving when it says: 'Free choice of consumer goods and services, free choice of working place, freedom for employers to exercise their initiative and free competition are essential conditions of a Social Democratic economic polity. The autonomy of trade unions and employers' associations in collective bargaining is an important feature of a free society. Totalitarian control of the economy destroys freedom. The Social Democratic Party therefore favours a free market wherever free competition really exists. Where a market is dominated by individuals or groups, however, all manner of steps must be taken to protect freedom in the economic sphere. As much competition as possible—as much planning as necessary.' "[40]

According to Masani the rate of growth in a free capitalistic economy is higher than in a socialist or communist economy. Masani claims that the march of events in the century that followed the publication of Karl Marx's *Communist Manifesto* falsified all the prophecies of the nineteenth century prophet, so that in countries undergoing the process of industrialization the poor have not become poorer. On the contrary, the bulk of the workers in countries, such as the United States and Canada, in the democracies of Western Europe, and in Australia and New Zealand have become more and more prosperous under what is called the capitalist system. The workers in these countries have acquired an important place in society through the power of their trade unions. "All this has been gained," wrote Masani, "without the bloody civil wars and revolutions forecast by Karl Marx. In the field of agriculture, phenomenal yields of food grains and other raw materials have been attained by small peasant farmers cultivating their own plots of land in countries as far apart as England and Denmark on the one hand and Japan on the other. . . . On the other hand, the last half century has seen the defeat of the effort made by those led by Lenin who claimed to be Karl Marx's followers to establish a free and equal society by Marxist means." Masani recognized that the Soviet Union made striking progress in the production of steel and the development of armaments, but, he asserted, "even its Sixth Five Year Plan has failed to give the Russian people a materially higher standard of life than before the Revolution or anything approximating a free and equal society. In the field of agriculture, the yields per acre of Soviet collective farms are among the lowest in the world. After forty long years, it is Man that has withered, not the State." It is for all these reasons, claimed Masani, that public opinion in the democratic countries of the world have "moved slowly but consistently away from the shibboleths of state socialism and communism and back to the fundamental values of liberty and' people's enterprise. The State is being recognized to be the most dangerous source of concentration of power and to offer the biggest single threat to human freedom and advance. Before this Leviathan, all other monsters pale into insignificance."[41]

Another leader of democratic socialism in India, but one who retained his faith in democratic socialism till the end, was Acharya Narendra Deva (1889–1956). Narendra Deva believed in a classless society, but he felt that Indian socialists must remain wedded to the ideal of democracy and to the policy of effecting changes peacefully for the establishment of a new economic and social order. Narendra Deva did not accept Gandhi's doctrine of nonviolence as a creed, but felt that Gandhi's method of *satyagraha* was the right method to be pursued for the attainment of desired ends, and that such a method was permissible even after independence was attained.

Other socialists who felt that a policy of violence should be eschewed were also attracted to the Gandhian technique of *satyagraha* and civil disobedience, and they said that even after independence it would be open to socialists to resort to a policy of civil disobedience against unjust laws. Ram Manohar Lohia, one of the socialist leaders, said: "It is not necessary for a people suffering from starvation . . . to depend on parliament or to wait expectantly for another general election. They have this price-less, matchless weapon of civil disobedience in their hands. When injustice and oppression go beyond bearable bounds, when constitutional methods have proved incapable of achieving redress, it should be open for the people to violate unjust laws, and wrongs and injustices that are inflicted upon them. To violate laws, to court imprisonment, to invite punishment by authority even to the extent of death . . . is the only satisfactory way of effecting change . . . in any case this is specific contribution [to] political action which Gandhiji made. . . . "[42]

Indian socialists have derived inspiration not only from Marx but also from Gandhi. They derived their faith in classless society from Marx, but their belief in the possibility of effecting peaceful changes through *satyagraha* or civil disobedience from Gandhi. They felt that by evolving the method of *satyagraha* Gandhi had made a unique contribution to revolutionary technology. Before Gandhi, the peaceful means that the exploited could adopt to fight the oppressor were generally limited to agitation, and, in the case of industrial labour, to strike and general strike. Beyond these limits the struggle was powerless to go except in a violent direction. In such circumstances, the struggle for social justice could not express itself adequately, but in Gandhi's method of civil disobedience and *satyagraha* the exploited found a new weapon to carry forward the struggle.[43] The Indian socialists deriving inspiration from the Western democratic tradition as also from Gandhism believed in the achievement of socialism through the polling booths, if possible, and by the adoption of the Gandhian method of civil disobedience, if necessary.

IV. FRAGMENTATION OF SOCIAL FORCES IN INDIA

The history of the socialist parties in India has been somewhat chequered. At a conference held at Cawnpore after the release of the Congress socialist leaders from prison in 1945-46, the Congress Socialist Party decided to drop the appellation "Congress" from its name, but the Socialist Party still continued to function within the Congress till the year 1948, when at the Nasik Conference it decided to sever altogether its connection with the Congress.

The Patna conference of the party in 1949 adopted a new constitution for the party in order to give it a wider base. The more militant section of the party opposed the adoption of this new constitution, and they argued that the new constitution will let in the middle class within the party who will be able to dominate it and deprive it of its revolutionary character. However, Jayaprakash Narayan, Asoka Mehta, Ram Manohar Lohia, and the elder leaders supported the adoption of the new constitution, and this was done.

In May 1951, Acharya Kripalani formed the Kisan Mazdoor Praja Party (KMPP), mainly with persons who had seceded from the Congress. Jayaprakash Narayan sought to persuade Acharya Kripalani to join the Socialist Party, but failed. Later, after the 1952 elections, in August 1952 the Socialist Party and the KMPP merged, and the new party formed as a result of such merger was called the Praja Socialist Party (PSP). The 1952 elections had shown the need for the combination of the leftist forces if any effective opposition to the Congress was to develop, and both the Socialist Party and KMPP welcomed the merger so that an anti–Congress noncommunist leftist opposition could emerge.

In February 1953 there were certain talks, which eventually proved unsuccessful, between Jayaprakash Narayan and Jawaharlal Nehru to consider the prospects of cooperation between the Congress and the PSP both within and outside the government. This plea of cooperation between the PSP and the Congress was opposed by Acharya Narendra Deva and particularly by Dr Ram Manohar Lohia. These differences within the party eventually led to the election of Dr Lohia, the stormy petrel, as the general secretary of the party.

Soon thereafter a further crisis developed within the PSP. In Travancore–Cochin, where the Ministry was headed by a PSP Chief Minister, Pattom Thanu Pillai, police had to fire on certain demonstrators. Deploring that firing had taken place under a socialist government, Dr Lohia, the general secretary of the PSP, sent a cable to the Chief Minister asking him to resign after instituting a judicial inquiry into the firing. The Chief Minister did not resign. Dr Lohia then resigned from the general secretaryship of the party in protest. The National Executive and a special convention of the party supported the Chief Minister, but there was a sharp division within the party over the question of firing. After the voting at the national convention the chairman of the party, Acharya Kripalani, also resigned.

Further difficulties were in store for the party. After the Congress at its Avadi session in 1955 declared its support for a socialist pattern of society, the Bombay group of the party issued a statement that the party's policy of non-cooperation with the Congress had become obsolete. Madhu Limaye, who was close to Dr Lohia and was then a young member of the party, but who was later to make his mark in the Indian Parliament, charged that Asoka Mehta had inspired this statement. The then party chairman, Acharya Narendra Deva, asked Limaye to withdraw this charge. Limaye did not withdraw the charge but repeated it. Limaye was then suspended by the executive of the Bombay city PSP. Later, Dr Lohia was also suspended.

Dr Lohia left the PSP and sought to revive the old Socialist Party. This weakened the PSP, and the party was further weakened when Jayaprakash Narayan left politics and dedicated himself to *bhoodan* movement and *sarvodaya*. The death of Acharya Narendra Deva in 1956 was another blow to the party.

The PSP fared badly in the 1957 general elections. Thereafter Jayaprakash Narayan attempted twice to bring about a rapprochement with Dr Lohia and his party, but without success.

In the 1962 elections both the PSP and the Socialist Party fared badly. After the 1962 elections, the PSP expelled Asoka Mehta, who by this time had come to feel that the PSP had no future. Asoka Mehta became a Cabinet Minister in the Congress government at the centre, in defiance of a directive to the contrary given by the party.

Later, in March 1964, Dr Lohia spoke in favour of the merger of the Socialist Party with the PSP, and as a result of the merger which took place in June 1964, the Samyukta Socialist Party (SSP) was formed. But, in spite of the merger, the old members of the PSP and the Socialist Party could not work together, and in January 1965 most of the PSP members and leaders, except S. M. Joshi, left the SSP. The PSP and SSP today exist and function as two separate socialist parties of India.

Apart from the SSP and PSP, which are the big socialist parties of India, there are other parties, such as the Forward Bloc, the Revolutionary Socialist Party (RSP), and divers other small parties who are all pledged to socialism.

The Forward Bloc was founded by Subhas Bose in 1939. Soon thereafter, Subhas Bose left India for Germany in order to secure outside assistance for Indian independence. Early in 1942, during World War II, the party was banned for advocating armed revolt against the British, and most of its leaders went underground or were in jail. In June 1946 the Working Committee of the All India Forward Bloc approved of a new manifesto for the party declaring itself to be a socialist party pledged to a militant class struggle. In December 1948 there was a split inside the party and the anti–Marxist section met at a convention in Calcutta while the pro-Marxist section met at Chandernagore. The non-Marxist Forward Bloc was not prepared to adopt communist revolutionary methods in their entirety, but it did not also believe that socialism could be attained by parliamentary and constitutional methods alone. The Marxist Forward Bloc, on the other hand, unequivocally declared itself in favour of a revolutionary seizure of power by the peasants and the workers in the fields and factories.[44] Later, after the elections of 1952, and the merger of the Socialist Party and the KMPP into the new Praja Socialist Party (PSP), the non-Marxist Forward Bloc also merged with the PSP. The other wing of the Forward Bloc continues to function, and is pledged to the ideal of a socialist transformation of society.

The RSP is a noncommunist Marxist Party, and it developed out of the revolutionary Anushilan group of Bengal. The RSP believes in a classless society and regards the proletariat as the only consistently revolutionary class.[45] In 1940, the RSP declared that World War II was an imperialist war, and even after Germany attacked Soviet Russia the party, unlike the communists, did not change its stand. In 1941, it claimed that only a free and Soviet India could help Soviet Russia.[46] The RSP had, in the early years, functioned as an organized group within the Congress Socialist Party (CSP), but in 1940 the RSP came to believe that the CSP had become pseudo–Marxist and had deviated from Marxism–Leninism to, what it called, social–Gandhism. Accordingly, the RSP formed itself into a separate party from the Congress socialists. Since then, the RSP has functioned as a separate party pledged to socialism. In a thesis published in 1950, the RSP declared its adherence to the revolutionary socialist way propounded by Marx, Engels, and Lenin and opposed the "new fangled China way of Mao Tse-tung and Cominform."[47]

The Socialist Unity Centre (SUC) is a small party which broke off from the RSP. The SUC came into prominence during the time of the first United Front government in Bengal in 1967 when the party and particularly its leader, Subodh Bannerjee, who was the Labour Minister in the first United Front government, advocated *inter alia* a policy of *gherao* (confinement) of the employers by workers in order to bring pressure on the employers so that the demands of the workers were conceded. Subodh Bannerjee supported this policy on the plea that in a capitalist society law lagged behind developing social consciousness so that even though *gherao* may be illegal it was not immoral or unethical, and that it was in fact a proper weapon which the workers could use for advancing their cause.

There are various other small leftist or socialist parties in India. Most of these parties believe that parliamentary methods alone would not suffice for the development of a socialist consciousness in India, and that work on the labour front, and among the *kisans* or peasants, and mass demonstrations, rallies, and other modes of agitation and protest including hartals, strikes, and civil disobedience movements are essential for the growth of socialist consciousness among the masses. Furthermore, each of these parties has its thesis or manifesto which enunciates a comprehensive social philosophy. Most of these parties are committed to a policy of nationalization of industry, confiscation of land without compensation, and the distribution thereof to the tillers, as also to a comprehensive policy of planning for ushering in a socialistic and egalitarian society in India.

The question of the consolidation of the leftist socialistic forces in India has often been considered. But in June 1969 the Standing Committee of the SSP came to the conclusion that a coming together of parties of either the right or the left was neither politically feasible, nor could such coalitions by themselves displace the Congress at the centre. In a thesis released in June 1969, in respect of the Jana Sangh–Swatantra–BKD merger talks, which had failed, the SSP said that the main cause of the failure of such unity talks was the total lack of a clear purpose and aim among the participants. If these parties set removal of the Congress as their main aim and sought to pursue this aim single-mindedly, they could have discovered some ground for action, if not outright merger, but the hatred that each of these parties harboured against the other and the "attachment to their sectarian outlook and dogma" and to their leadership and group interests were greater than their dislike of the Congress.

The SSP, therefore, virtually decided to go it alone. It was agreeable to the formation of united fronts on specific issues, but sought to preserve the independent role of the party with a view to projecting its distinctive image before the public. The SSP was sceptical of alliance with other parties because "people know that just at present [June 1969] socialist parties by themselves cannot provide a viable alternative to the Congress at national level."

The SSP was particularly critical of the PSP which continuously called for unity and merger talks: "The PSP talks interminably of a socialist alternative and merger sometimes with the Bihar LCD and sometimes with Mr Charan Singh's BKD, but it will never merge its identity in a larger grouping. These merger talks are not sincere but a cheap publicity stunt. While the PSP mouths high-sounding moral principles and denounces the ssp's militancy and policy of cooperation with political parties on specific issues and concrete and time-bound programmes as blind anti–Congressism, it openly allies with a fascist movement like the Shiv Sena in Bombay and privately condemns it in Mysore."[48]

The PSP, however, continues to speak of unity of leftist forces opposed both to communism and communalism. The need for political parties believing in nationalism, democracy, and socialism to form a united front even with the left-wing of the Congress was asserted by Nishith Nath Kundu, chairman of the West Bengal PSP, in June 1969. Such a front was necessary to counter the activities of communal, capitalist, and communist parties.[49]

The PSP was highly critical of the United Fronts both in Bengal and Kerala. In fact, N. G. Goray, national chairman of the PSP, said that there was little difference between the United Fronts of West Bengal and Kerala on the one hand, and the Congress on the other, which was also a kind of united front. "For after all what is common between Mrs Indira Gandhi and Morarji Desai?" asked Goray. Again, in June 1969, N. G. Goray said that the in-fighting among constituent parties of the United Front in West Bengal would either bring down the government or help in the emergence of the CPI(M) as a much stronger party. In that event the CPI(M) might come out of the government and seek election alone. If that happened the smaller left parties might be absorbed by the CPI(M). He also warned that the adventurist activities on the part of some militant parties in the United Front might, on the other hand, help consolidate the reactionary forces, and bring about a revival of the Congress Party in West Bengal.[50]

In June 1969—Goray gave a call to the parties believing. in socialism and democracy to come together before the 1972 general elections. As for the PSP, it was ready to start coalition talks with such "like-minded parties" as the SSP, BKD, Lok Tantrik Dal, and the Janata Parishad. Without such a coalition and consolidation of left forces there was little likelihood, he felt, of a split inside the Congress, but the moment such a consolidation among like-minded opposition parties was achieved, polarization. would take place within the Congress.[51] Goray was unduly pessimistic, for even without such a consolidation of the left forces, the Congress party split in November 1969.

Even before November 1969, the Congress was on the verge of a split in August 1969. The split was averted by the resolution on unity dated 25 August 1969, passed by the Congress Working Committee. Disturbed by this unity resolution, Goray proposed a meeting of "like-minded parties," such as the SSP, DMK, BKD, the LCD of Bihar, the Janata Paskha of Mysore, and the Indian Socialist Party of Kerala, to bring about a "socialist consolidation." For Goray the Congress working Committee resolution had come as "an anticlimax, once again putting up the same old facade of unity behind which the bitter struggle for power could indefinitely be continued."[52] This development in the Congress was dangerous from every point of view: "Not only will it work as an impediment to social transformation but it will also prevent healthy natural political trends from emerging by encouraging unprincipled defections, secret deals, and questionable alliances. Mrs. Gandhi will have to agree to soft-pedal her programme while the traditionalists and the reactionaries in the Congress would use her image as they used to do her father's. If the Birlas, the Syndicate, and the Indicate can remain united for the sake of power, is it not necessary for us to think of coming together to save democratic socialism from being either totally suppressed or vulgarized beyond recognition?"[53]

Similarly, in September 1969, the PSP general secretary, Prem Bhasin, spoke of a combination of non–Congress, non-communist parties to fight reaction and yet remain positively committed to social changes. Such a combination would eschew communalism and conservatism and thus leave out parties like the Jana Sangh and the Swatantra.[54] The parties who could come together in such a combination of democratic socialist forces were, according to Bhasin, the PSP, SSP, Lok Tantrik Dal of Bihar, Bangla Congress and Forward Bloc of West Bengal, Peasants' and Workers' Party of Maharashtra.

Bhasin did not include either the CPI or the CPI(M) in such a combination of anti–Congress democratic socialist forces. The CPI, according to Bhasin, was no longer anti–Congress, and the CPI(M) was not democratic. The CPI no longer believed in a left front as an alternative to the Congress, for, in the opinion of that party, the supreme task of all democrats was to defeat

19

every manoeuvre of the right reaction to topple Indira Gandhi's government. That is why they were extending almost unqualified support to the Congress in the hope that it would enable Indira Gandhi to capture the entire Congress machinery, when they would be able to put pressure on her to go ahead with more radical reform proposals so as to transform the Congress into the main instrument for bringing about social changes. While the CPI could not form part of such a left democratic consolidation of parties due to its "pro–Indira emotions," the CPI(M) also could have no place in such a consolidation because the CPI(M), said Bhasin, was committed to undemocratic means for bringing about social changes.[55] An anti-Congress democratic socialist front could, therefore, include neither the CPI(M) nor the CPI.

Though most of the socialist parties of India do not consider the Congress as a socialist party and are generally pledged to a policy of anti–Congressism, the question has begun to be raised —particularly after the Congress split of 1969—whether such a policy of pure anti–Congressism fits in with the changing realities of the Indian political scene. The SSP is still committed to a policy of unmitigated anti–Congressism.[56] Most left parties, apart from the SSP, however, supported the Congress led by Indira Gandhi on the policy of bank nationalization and in her confrontation with the Syndicate which eventually led to the Congress split in November 1969.

NOTES AND REFERENCES

1. Jawaharlal, Nehru, *India and the World*, p. 27.
2. Jawaharlal Nehru, *Eighteen Months in India, 1936-37*, pp. 34-35.
3. Jawaharlal Nehru, *India and the World*, p. 27.
4. P. C. Lakhanpal, *History of the Congress Socialist Party*, p. 30.
5. *The Indian National Congress, 1934-36*, p. 21.
6. Jayaprakash Narayan, *Towards Struggle*, p. 100.
7. Ibid., p. 99.
8. Ibid.
9. Ibid., 130.
10. Narendra Deva, *Socialism and the National Revolution*, Bombay, 1946, pp. 6-7.

11. Jayaprakash Narayan, *Socialism, Sarvodaya and Democracy*, ed. Bimla Prasad, 1964, p. 3.
12. Ibid.
13. Ibid.
14. Ibid., p. 5.
15. Ibid., p. 9.
16. Ibid., pp. 12-13.
17. Jayaprakash Narayan, *Towards Struggle*, p. 141.
18. Narendra Deva's Presidential Address at Patna Conference on 17 May 1934, *The Indian Annual Register*, 1934, Vol. 1, p. 341.
19. M. R. Masani, *The Communist Party of India*, London, 1954, pp. 69-70.
20. Jayaprakash Narayan, *Socialist Unity and the Congress Socialist Party*, 1941, p. 26.
21. Narendra Deva, *Socialism and the National Revolution*, pp. 24-25.
22. Ibid., pp. 20-21.
23. Jayaprakash Narayan, *Socialism, Sarvodaya and Democracy*, ed. Bimla Prasad, 1964, pp. 3-4.
24. Ibid., p. 13.
25. Ibid., p. 14.
26. Ibid., pp. 43-44.
27. Ibid.
28. Ibid., pp. 44-45.
29. Ibid., p. 41.
30. Ibid., pp. 49-50.
31. Ibid., pp. 50 51.
32. Asoka Mehta, *Studies in Asian Socialism*, Bombay, 1969, p. 200.
33. Ibid., p. 165.
34. Ibid., p. 229.
35. Jayaprakash Narayan, *Socialism, Sarvodaya, and Democracy*, ed. Bimla Prasad, 1964, p. 52.
36. Ibid., p. 95.
37. M. N. Roy, *New Humanism : A Manifesto*, Calcutta, 1947, pp. 34-47.
38. Jayaprakash Narayan, *Socialism, Sarvodaya and Democracy*, p. 94.
39. M. R. Masani, *Congress Misrule and the Swatantra Alternative*.
40. Ibid., pp. 164-65.
41. Ibid., p. 167.
42. Ram Manohar Lohia, *Marx, Gandhi and Socialism*, Hyderabad, 1963, p. 127.
43. Jayaprakash Narayan, *Socialism, Sarvodaya and Democracy*, p. 95.
44. *From Arrah to Chandernagore—A March Towards Social Revolution*, Calcutta.
45. *The Thesis and Platform of Action of the Revolutionary Socialist Party of India—What Revolutionary Socialism Stands For*, Calcutta, p. 7.
46. *Thesis of the RSP on the Russo-German War*, Calcutta, 1941, p. 18.
47. *The Leninist Way*, Calcutta, Revolutionary Socialist Party, 1950.

48. *The Statesman*, 13 June 1969.
49. *The Statesman*, 14 June 1969.
50. *The Statesman*, 15 June 1969.
51. Ibid.
52. *The Statesman*, 28 August 1969.
53. Ibid.
54. *The Statesman*, 12 September 1969.
55. Ibid.
56. S. M. Joshi of the SSP, however, urged that such a policy should be changed. (S. M. Joshi, "Choice Before Socialists," *New Age*, 28 December 1969, p. 13.)

CHAPTER EIGHT

The Indian Communists

I. THE EARLY YEARS

The early period of the communist movement in India, up to the time of the commencement of the Meerut Conspiracy Case, has already been dealt with in detail in Chapter Three under the heading "The Communist Critique of Gandhi." Here we shall deal only very briefly with some general aspects and features of that early period.

Muzaffar Ahmed—one of the veteran communists of India and who was an accused in the Meerut Conspiracy Case of 1929 —claims that the Communist Party of India was founded abroad and was affiliated in 1921 with the Communist International. According to him, the Communist Party of India was formed towards the end of 1920 at the Tashkent Military School.[1] A Communist Party publication also states: "The first ever attempt made by the Communist International to form an Indian Communist Party (from among Indian revolutionaries who had migrated from the country to Europe and America on the eve of and during the first world war) was in 1920. The first appeal issued by that party to India was to the session of the Indian National Congress held at Ahmedabad at the end of 1921."[2]

One of the early communists of India was S. A. Dange, who published a small book *Gandhi and Lenin* in 1921. Dange founded a library for the dissemination of Marxist literature and caused translations to be made of Marxist classics. Dange also established a Marathi daily and an English weekly, the *Socialist*, for the propagation of Marxist views. Among the other pioneers of the communist movement in India at that time were Muzaffar Ahmed from Bengal and Shaukat Osmani from the United Provinces.

One of the first Indians to become a communist was M. N.

Roy. Roy was one of the founding fathers of the Mexican Communist Party, and he attended the Second Congress of the Communist International in 1920 as a delegate from Mexico. At the Second Congress, Roy submitted a thesis disagreeing with Lenin on the attitude to be adopted by communists to national liberation movements.

Roy prepared this thesis on the assumption that in all dependent countries there were two distinct movements: one was the bourgeois national movement with a programme of political freedom, and the other the mass movement of the peasants and the workers for their liberation from exploitation. It was because Roy entertained the romantic belief that from the outset there existed in India a movement of the peasants and the workers that he unequivocally denounced Gandhi and the Congress Party which he led, and argued that if from the outset the leadership of the liberation movement in the colonies was in the hands of a communist vanguard, then the revolutionary masses would not be led astray. But in 1920 there was hardly any communist in India, not to speak of an organized revolutionary party in close touch with the working masses, as Roy fondly believed. In such circumstances "how on earth was a Communist Party in a subject country to secure the leadership of its freedom movement from the outset?" later asked Sardesai, a leading member of the CPI.[3]

In his *Memoirs*, Roy gave an account of his differences with Lenin at the Second Congress. The differences related to the attitude that the communist parties should adopt towards the national movements in the subject countries, and to the role of Gandhi in the Indian national movement. Lenin considered Gandhi to be a progressive, while Roy considered Gandhi as a medieval reactionary. Lenin considered that historically the national-liberation movements had the significance of bourgeois-democratic revolutions, and that the communists should help the colonial liberation movements under the leadership of the nationalist bourgeoisie, regarding the latter as an objectively revolutionary force. Roy argued that Gandhi might travel the way of Russian Social Revolutionaries, who were characterized by Plekhanov as politically revolutionary and socially reactionary. "As a disciple seeking light from the master, I enquired," wrote Roy, "whether an anti-imperialist movement inspired by reactionary social ideas and burdened with obscurantist religious beliefs, could be politically revolutionary. Lenin saw the force of my doubt and agreed to differ for the moment. ... "[4]

Lenin considered the Indian nationalist movement as a democratic movement. After there had been a strike in Bombay in protest against Tilak's sentence and imprisonment in 1908, Lenin wrote that popular India was "beginning to stand up in defence of her political leaders" and against the "infamous sentence pronounced by the British jackals against the Indian democrat Tilak." Lenin made a distinction between the role of the bourgeoisie in free European countries and in dependent Asian countries. So far as the bourgeoisie in dependent countries, who struggled against foreign domination, were concerned, Lenin considered them to be democratic. In his famous article "Backward Europe and Advanced Asia" written in May 1913, Lenin said: "Everywhere in Asia a mighty democratic movement is growing, spreading and gaining strength. There the bourgeoisie is still siding with the people against reaction. Hundreds of millions of people are awakening to life, light, and freedom."

Considering the liberation movements of the bourgeoisie in subject countries as democratic movements, in the Preliminary Draft Theses on the National and Colonial Questions prepared for the Second Congress of the Communist International, Lenin stated: "With regard to the more backward states and nations in which feudal or patriarchal and patriarchal-peasant relations predominate, it is particularly important to bear in mind: first, that all communist parties must assist the bourgeois-democratic liberation movement in these countries and that the duty of rendering the most active assistance rests primarily with the workers of the country upon which the backward nation is dependent colonially or financially."[5]

Roy objected to the use of the expression "the bourgeois-democratic liberation movement." Alfred Rosmer, who attended the Second Congress of the Communist International, in his memoirs entitled *In Moscow in Lenin's Days: 1920-21*, gave his version of Lenin's reactions to Roy's objection. Rosmer wrote: "Patiently Lenin replied to Roy explaining that for a longer or shorter period of time the Indian Communist Party would be a small party with but few members, having only weak resources incapable of reaching, on the basis of its programme and by means of its own activity, a substantial number of peasants and workers. On the other hand, on the basis of demands for national independence, it would become possible to mobilize large masses —experience had already demonstrated that amply—and it was only in the course of this struggle that the Indian Communist Party would forge and develop its organization to the point where it would be in a position, once the national demands were satisfied, to attack the Indian bourgeoisie." But so far as the manifesto of the Second Congress of the Communist International is concerned, the words "bourgeois-democratic liberation movement" were, after taking into account Roy's objection, replaced by the words "national revolutionary movement."

In spite of Lenin's advice that the Indian communists should cooperate with the national liberal movement, they did not in fact do so. The Indian communists later said that they had failed to adopt the correct approach to the national liberation movement in India and had also failed to recognize that Gandhi, in launching the civil disobedience movements against British rule, was playing a progressive role. An official Communist Party of India publication (August 1967) stated: "There is no doubt that if Indian communists in the early thirties had studied and grasped Lenin's opinion on this question the Communist Party of India would have been saved the extremely costly mistakes it made in the Civil Disobedience movement between 1930 to 1934, and would have emerged as a powerful national force in the course of it."[6]

In 1922, Roy made an attempt to orient the 1922 Gaya Congress towards communism, and in 1923 the communists in India sought to organize a Workers' and Peasants' Party which was intended to be a mass party whose nucleus was to be the members of an illegal Communist Party.

In the meantime the British Indian government was keeping a keen watch on the growth of the communist movement in India and the part that the Comintern and its emissaries were playing in that connection. A memorandum of the British government of May 1923 mentioned that amongst the most useful bases for Russian anti–British propaganda was the area which comprises Persia, Afghanistan, and the Indian border, that the Russian Minister at Tehran had been the most tireless

—though not always the most successful—operator in this field, that he had housed Indian seditionists within his hospitable walls, and had sped them on to their mission in India. It was claimed that the government knew the exact sums which had been sent to the Russian Minister of Tehran from time to time by the Russian government primarily for the purpose of anti–British intrigue. The Indian government was also aware of the fact that in November 1922, seven Indians, who had been trained as communist agitators at Tashkent, had travelled to India under the charge of Russian civil and military officials by a circuitous and very difficult route in order to avoid detection. To stop the spread of communism, in 1924 the Indian government launched the Cawnpore Conspiracy Case in which certain communists were tried for sedition.

In December 1925 a conference of the Communist Party of India was convened. One Satya Bhakta took a leading part in the formation of this party, but shortly after its formation, he left it and founded a separate "National Communist Party." Another person connected with the formation of the Communist Party of India was Singaravellu Chettiar. He declared that Indian communism was not Bolshevism and that the Indian communists were "with the world communists but not with Bolsheviks."[7] But the idea that an Indian communist party could grow up which would have no connection with the Russian communists or with the Comintern was abhorrent to M. N. Roy, and he condemned this idea altogether.[8]

Early in the twenties the British Communist Party and its members took an active part in inspiring and developing the communist movement in India. In 1926 one of the founders of the British Communist Party, R. P. Dutt, wrote a book *Modern India* in which he explained the method and tactics that the communists in India should adopt. Dutt's thesis was that the Indian bourgeoisie were cooperating with the British capitalists and that British capitalists were penetrating into the Indian economy so that it was a dangerous delusion to think that the capitalist development in India was a national development. The interests of the Indian bourgeoisie coincided with the interests of the British bourgeoisie and, therefore, the Indian national struggle had to be a struggle of the working masses against the political and economic exploitation of the British capitalists as

also of the Indian bourgeoisie, who had entered into a partner-
ship with the former, that is to say, "the struggle of the Indian
people must be ultimately a struggle for social liberation."[9]

R. P. Dutt recognized that Gandhi had given a mass base to
the national movement and that he had put before the masses a
policy of action. But Dutt was not enamoured of Gandhian
methods, and he had no faith either in nonviolence or in the
spirituality of Gandhi. "There is no question of a gentle per-
suasive spiritual argument. it is a question of power," wrote
R. P. Dutt. Dutt also attacked Gandhi's belief that in the
nationalist movement there could be a reconciliation of the
interests of the bourgeoisie on the one hand and the workers
and peasants on the other, or that they could combine in a
movement of nonviolent non-cooperation. Dutt said: "All
parasitic and propertied classes have to weave around themselves
a fog of confused language, superstition, traditions, religion,
reverence, etc. in order to hide from the masses the fact of their
exploitation. ... From this class alignment inevitably follows his
[Gandhi's] cooperation with the imperialist Government."[10]

R. P. Dutt pleaded for paying greater attention to the workers
and peasants and for organizing them for the purpose of the
liberation movement. In order to energize the workers and
peasants he felt that a distinct economic ideology would have
to be placed before the masses and Swaraj was not to be treated
as an "indefinable mystery" but as meaning liberation from
imperialistic dominion. Such liberation was to be not merely
political but also social and economic, that is to say, a liberation
which was to end class divisions and exploitation by "the common entry of the whole people into the possession of their
country ... [and] into the wealth and means of livelihood,
into the common sharing of work and the return on work."[11]
Swaraj or liberation, as defined by Dutt, was economic Swaraj
which would usher in a classless society. For parliamentary democracy of the Western type, Dutt had nothing but
contempt. Such democracy he characterized as "a mockery of
popular representation and whose so-called liberties are an
obvious sham."[12]

Though R. P. Dutt had at one time thought that, in the early
stages, the leadership of the Indian national movement might,
to some extent, be progressive, by 1926 his faith in such leader-

ship had been shaken. In the preface written in December 1926 to the English edition of his book *Modern India,* he characterized the Indian bourgeoisie as a counter-revolutionary force and claimed that conditions were ripe for the organization of a new national movement based on workers and peasants. He wrote: "The Indian bourgeoisie is today a counter-revolutionary force, they fear the social revolution that would follow national independence more than they desire independence and therefore they have made their terms with the imperialists and are all supporters of the Empire."[13] Therefore, he suggested: "Only a new national movement based on the workers and peasants, and with a political and social programme expressing the interests of the masses can bring new life. The conditions for this are ripe."[14]

By June 1928, however, there came over a change in the views of R. P. Dutt towards the nationalist movement. Dutt still regarded the nationalist movement and the bourgeois leaders, who led it, as being counter-revolutionary, but he had by then come to believe that the petty bourgeoisie in India would increasingly play a revolutionary role. In June 1928, in the *Labour Monthly,* he wrote: "In general and on all fundamental questions, the role of the Indian bourgeoisie since the collapse of the Non-Cooperation movement has evolved in the direction of becoming more and more clearly counter-revolutionary.... But at the same time, within this general framework of capitulation, there takes place a process of friction and antagonism which has recently grown sharper.... Thus the role of the bourgeoisie in the national struggle is not yet exhausted, and may even extend under certain conditions, but it remains permanently limited in scope by its fear and hostility towards any wider mass revolutionary movement and, therefore, very dangerous to the real struggle against imperialism. It becomes the task of the mass movement to exploit to the maximum the opportunities presented by bourgeois resistance as in the boycott of the Simon Commission, but under independent leadership." Having no faith in the bourgeois leadership, Dutt, however, found some hope in the future role of the petty bourgeoisie and it is to them that he turned for injecting a revolutionary spirit in the nationalist movement. But this formulation of Dutt that the bourgeoisie in India had still a vestigial anti-imperialist role to play was not accepted by the Sixth Congress

of the Communist International which met in September 1928.
The Sixth Congress of the Communist International denounced
the national bourgeoisie altogether. It asked the communists to
adopt a militant uncompromising role and advocated a policy
which was considerably at variance with the policy of cooperating with the national bourgeoisie in the national liberation
movement that Lenin had suggested at the Second Congress.
The Sixth Congress passed a resolution asking the communists
to unmask all national reformist movements, such as the Swarajist movement and Gandhism. It urged the communist parties
in colonial countries to emancipate themselves from the influence
of the bourgeois parties, and not to form any kind of bloc with
national reformist opposition parties, though they could enter
into temporary agreements with them. The resolution claimed
that in all colonies and semi-colonies, such as in China and India,
the development of productive forces and the socialization of
labour stood at a comparatively low level, and in these countries the task of the revolutionary movement should be the
emancipation of the country from the yoke of imperialism and
the establishment of the dictatorship of the proletariat and
peasantry, the consolidation of the hegemony of the proletariat,
the strengthening of the Communist Party and its assumption
of a leading position among the toiling masses. The resolution
stated: "The bourgeoisie of China, India and Egypt ... attempts
by means of empty nationalist phrases and gestures to keep the
petty-bourgeois masses under its influence and to induce
imperialism to grant certain concessions.... Without the liberation of the toiling masses from the influence of the bourgeoisie
and of national-reformism, the basic strategical aim of the
Communist movement in the bourgeois-democratic revolution ...
cannot be achieved.... In India, Egypt ... etc ... it is necessary
to carry through much work in the building up and consolidation of the Communist Party and trade union organizations of
the proletariat ... in winning over the masses and their liberation from the influence of national-reformist bourgeoisie.... It
is necessary by means of correct communist tactics, adapted to
the conditions of the present stage, to help the toiling masses in
India, Egypt, Indonesia and such colonies to emancipate themselves from the influence of the bourgeois parties ... [Swarajists,
Wafdists, etc.]"

Alluding to India, the resolution specifically stated: "The communists must unmask the national reformism of the Indian National Congress and oppose all the phrases of the Swarajists, Gandhists, etc. about passive resistance.... It must be remembered that under no circumstances can the communists relinquish their right to open criticism of the opportunist and reformist tactics of the leadership of those mass organizations in which they work."

In view of the extremist line laid down by the Sixth Congress, it was not possible for the Indian communists to work inside the Indian National Congress or to work in cooperation with the national bourgeois liberation movement. This extremist, militant policy laid down by the Sixth Congress continued to guide the Indian communists till 1935, when the Seventh Congress of the Comintern reversed this policy by advocating the formation of popular or broad national fronts against imperialism in all colonial and semi-colonial countries.

II. THE MEERUT CONSPIRACY CASE

Towards the end of the twenties there took place many strikes in the big cities of India. The British government in India felt that Russian gold and Russian money were encouraging strikes and were helping in the spread of communism in India. On 29 January 1929, while opening the Legislative Assembly, Lord Irwin, the Viceroy, said that the spread of the methods of communism was causing anxiety to the government. "Not only have communist agents from abroad promoted a series of strikes in the industrial world, but," he said, "the programme which they have openly set before themselves includes undisguised attack on the whole economic structure of society. All classes alike are threatened by the spread of these doctrines, and no Government can afford to ignore this insidious danger.... We have watched in the great city of Bombay the industrial labouring population brought into a state of great unsettlement, excited, prone to violence and often deaf to reason, while in Calcutta we have seen a strike, which appears to have no clearly reasoned basis, indefinitely prolonged."[15]

The Indian government was resolved to take stern measures

to check the influx of Russian money into India, to prevent the entry into India of communist agents from abroad, and to stop the spread of communism. Eventually, in March 1929, the Indian government brought certain communists to trial in a case which came to be known as the Meerut Conspiracy Case. Philip Spratt, Benjamin Francis Bradley and another Englishman and certain Indian communist leaders, such as S. A. Dange, Shaukat Usmani, and Muzaffar Ahmed stood trial in that case. The prosecution case was that the accused had conspired with the help of the Third International to deprive the King Emperor of the sovereignty of India and to set up a government in India on the Soviet model. The Meerut Conspiracy Case, which can be said to have commenced with the police raids in Bombay, United Provinces, and Punjab in March 1929, when eight persons were arrested, continued for a number of years and, in fact, dragged on till August 1933.

The charge in the Meerut Communist Conspiracy Case of 1929 stated that there existed in Russia an organization called the Communist International which aimed, by the creation of armed revolution, to overthrow all the existing forms of government throughout the world and to replace them by Soviet Republics subordinate to, and controlled by, the Central Soviet administration in Moscow; that in the year 1921 the Communist International had decided to establish a branch organization in British India; that Sripad Amrit Dange, Shaukat Usmani, and Muzaffar Ahmed had entered into a conspiracy with certain other persons to establish such a branch organization with a view to depriving the King Emperor of his soverignty of British India; and that thereafter various persons, including Philip Spratt and Benjamin Francis Bradley were sent to India by the Communist International through the medium of one of its branches or organizations, with the object of furthering the aims of the Communist International.[16]

The Meerut Conspiracy Case created a sensation. Labour leaders in India claimed that on the pretext of checking the spread of communism and subversion, the government really wanted to destroy all labour movements in India. Foremost among those who protested against this trial was Jawaharlal Nehru, the then president of All India Trade Union Congress. Nehru had attended the Congress of the Oppressed Peoples at

Brussels in 1927 where he had come in contact with many communists. He visited Russia thereafter and he came back to India as an admirer of the communist experiment in Russia.

On 22 June 1929 Nehru sent a cablegram to Walter Citrine, secretary of the British Trade Union Congress General Council, claiming that the government was seeking to break the labour movement in India and to hamper trade union organization by repressive legislation. Nehru sought the support of the British Trade Union Congress against these governmental actions,[17] and followed up this cable with a letter of the same date to Walter Citrine claiming that the trial was part of an offensive which the government had started against the Indian labour movement. "There is a lot of shouting about communists and communism in India. Undoubtedly there are some communists in India," said Nehru, "but it is equally certain that this cry of communism is meant to cover a multitude of sins of the Government. Of the 31 accused in the Meerut case, now 32 since Hutchinson's arrest, the majority knew little about communism. People connected with any kind of labour or peasant activity have been arrested and are being tried."[18] The All India Congress Committee sanctioned Rs. 1,500 as legal aid for the defence of the accused persons in the case. Motilal Nehru presided over a Committee for the defence of such accused persons, and Mahatma Gandhi interviewed many of them in prison.

The judgment delivered in the Meerut Conspiracy Case is interesting.[19] It was held that it had been conclusively proved that throughout the period under consideration there had been in existence in Russia an organization known as the Communist International, which had as its aim the bringing about throughout the world a revolution or revolutions for the overthrowal, by armed uprisings, of existing governments and the establishment in their place of Soviet Republics similar to that established in Russia. The evidence established that soon after the Communist Conspiracy Case of 1924 the Communist International had sought to bring about a revolutionary situation in India by assisting and instigating communists in India to active revolutionary work, and that it had also functioned through various agencies in England and also in Europe. Through these agencies literature, advice, instructions, and financial help had been sent to India. In addition, the Communist Party of Great Britain had sent a number of agents to work in India, for example, Glading, Allison, Spratt, Bradley, and others, who had been guided in their work by members of the Foreign Bureau, particularly M. N. Roy and C. P. Dutt.[20]

Notwithstanding the judgment in the Meerut Conspiracy Case, the attraction of communism increased rather than diminished by reason of the publicity that the case received. That case became one of the landmarks in the history of the communist movement in India. M. N. Roy, Dange, and Muzaffar Ahmed, whose names came into prominence, instead of being hounded out of public life, were regarded as heroes. M. N. Roy acquired great prominence as a Marxist theorist, and Dange and Muzaffar Ahmed later became communist leaders of India. Among the Englishmen whose names acquired prominence during the Meerut Conspiracy Case were Benjamin Francis Bradley and Philip Spratt. Bradley was later associated with the famous Dutt–Bradley thesis of 1936. So far as Spratt is concerned he, however, later became one of the secretaries of the Indian Committee for Cultural Freedom.

III. THE LEFT MILITANT PHASE

Some time prior to the Meerut Conspiracy Case, the Comintern had in its Sixth Congress held in September 1928 formulated the militant policy that the Indian communists should pursue. The Indian communists were called upon to develop a militant communist party, to energize the masses and to look upon the Congress led by Gandhi as a counter-revolutionary organization. In particular, warnings were given against the policy of left reformism pursued by Jawaharlal Nehru and Subhas Bose.

An important document of this ultra-left period was the Draft Platform of Action of the Communist Party of India, which was published in the Comintern's International Press Correspondence (Inprecor) in December 1930. In this document, the extremist line laid down by the Sixth Congress of the Comintern was reaffirmed and further developed. The fire was directed not only against the national bourgeoisie and its leadership, but, even more so, against the leftist non-communist elements in that leadership. It is the exposure of these left elements that was to be the primary task of the communists. This document stated: "The greatest threat to the victory of the Indian revolution is the fact that great masses of our people still harbour illusions about the National Congress and have not realized that it represents a class organization of the capitalists working against the fundamental interests of the toiling masses of our country. . . . The National Congress, and particularly its 'left' wing, have done and are doing all in their power to restrain the struggle of the masses within the framework of the British imperialist constitution and legislation. . . . The most harmful and dangerous obstacle to victory of the Indian revolution is the agitation carried on by 'left' elements of the National Congress led by Jawaharlal Nehru, Bose, Ginwala and others. . . . The exposure of the 'left' Congress leaders, who may once again undertake to set up a new Party or organization like the former League of Independence, in order once again to bamboozle the mass of workers is the primary task of our Party. Ruthless war on the 'left' national reformists is an essential condition if we are to isolate the latter from the workers and mass of the peasantry and mobilize the latter under the banner of the Communist Party and the anti-imperialist agrarian revolution of India."

This document gave a call for revolutionary armed insurrection around the banner of the Communist Party of India and advocated a policy of confiscation of land without compensation and the handing over of the same to the toiling peasantry. The Indian communists continued to follow the policy laid down in this document, and prior thereto, by the Sixth Congress in September 1928, and endeavoured to build up a revolutionary movement in India free from the influence of the Congress, Gandhi, Nehru, and Bose, who were all denounced as bourgeois and counter-revolutionary.

The first criticism of this ultra-left policy pursued by the CPI was made in 1932 in an "Open Letter to the Indian Communists" written by the Central Committees of the Communist Parties of China, Great Britain, and Germany. This Open Letter criticized the Indian communists for having alienated themselves from the liberation movement that the people were waging against British imperialism. It pointed out that though the bourgeoisie was continuing its policy of "counter-revolutionary compromise with British imperialism," the bourgeois National Congress still had a great influence over the Indian masses, and that the Indian communists should not alienate themselves completely from the national movement against British imperialism, but they should, while exposing the National Congress and its left wing, be in the forefront of all demonstrations and activities of the toiling masses against the British imperialists.

The Open Letter gave a call for the formation of a militant mass Indian Communist Party which would emulate the organization and iron discipline of the Communist Party of the Soviet Union and which would not be a peaceful party, but a militant, bold and revolutionary party. The Open Letter stated: "It must be thoroughly realized (and this will determine how seriously and consistently the communists stand by the illegal party and the revolutionary struggle) that the leading cadres of the party and the kernel of its organization must be in an illegal position and that mixing the conspiratorial and open apparatus of the Party organization is fatal for the Party and plays into the hands of the Government provocation. While developing the illegal organization in every way, measures must be taken for preserving and strengthening the conspirative kernel of the party organization. For this purpose all kinds of open activity (in the press, meetings, leagues, trade unions, etc.), special groups and commissions, etc. should be formed which, working under the leadership of the party committees, should under no circumstances injure the existence of the illegal nuclei. . . . To sum up, the slogan of an all–India centralized Communist Party, ideologically and organizationally united, a true section of the Comintern, fighting for the Platform of Action of the Communist Party of India and the programme of the Communist International, must become the central slogan for gathering and forming the Party and for the struggle against the waverings, against a tendency of keeping to isolated circles, against toning down the struggle against national reformism and opportunist sectarianism, all of which hinder the victory of the working class."

The attack on Gandhi and the Indian nationalist leaders alienated many Indians from the communist movement and proved to be a tactical error for the Indian communists. During the thirties and forties of this century the attention of many young men in India had been drawn to communism and Russia; and the writings and utterances of Nehru and Tagore, both of whom hailed the Russian experiment, helped in that direction. But there was a feeling that the Indian communists wanted to break completely with the past, and, further, that the revolutionary methods that were adopted in Russia were marked by avoidable violence and excesses. These excesses distressed Tagore and Nehru and they often referred to them. It is these excesses which Khrushchev later denounced in the famous Twentieth Congress of CPSU in 1956. A publication of 1967 of the Indian Communist Party states: "It has to be conceded, in the light of later revelations made at the 20th Congress of the CPSU that such criticism and disapproval expressed by Nehru and others, whose basic sympathies for the Soviet Union were beyond dispute, had a certain grounding in reality. It was neither anti-Soviet nor entirely based on a lack of realization of the necessity of revolutionary violence for the suppression of counter-revolutionary terror."[21]

Nehru helped greatly to attract Indian young men to communism. Referring to Nehru's stand on Soviet Russia, the Communist Party publication referred to above stated: "Halting in many respects, never mustering the strength for a decisive break with liberalism and Gandhism, its immense contribution lay in this that it stood firmly by the side of progress, democracy, and freedom against imperialism, fascism, and internal Indian obscurantism, and that it clearly asserted that Marxism was the one social philosophy which interpreted history scientifically and made life meaningful. . . . It is thus that he [Nehru] helped thousands upon thousands of Indian youth to bridge their own transition from the limitations of Gandhism and nationalism to socialism."[22]

To many Indian intellectuals who might otherwise have been attracted to communism, it appeared that the Indian communists wanted to write on a clean slate altogether and to make a complete break with the past, and this repelled some of them from the Indian Communist Party. "It has also to be admitted," states the said Communist Party publication, "that the Communist Party of India, in that period [the thirties of this century], with all its valuable contribution to the development of the contemporary communist movement did not really make any such effort. We built an independent working-class and peasant movement, we strove to integrate it with the national freedom movement. But there was hardly any effort to present the growing Indian communist movement as a continuity of the progressive, radical, and revolutionary thought currents and popular movements in India going back to centuries and, indeed, thousands of years.... India has no dearth of such traditions, and that, too, in every sphere of life and activity—social, political, scientific, cultural, and philosophical. But we neglected studying and bringing them out."[23]

IV. THE POLICY OF THE UNITED FRONT

From 1933 the Comintern decided to pursue a less militant or leftist policy. During this time fascism was rising in Germany, and the Soviet leadership was considering the desirability of having a united front against fascism. A new policy was announced at the Seventh Congress of the Comintern in 1935. The main spokesman of this new policy was Wang Ming, the Chinese leader, who rebuked the Indian communists for their "left sectarian errors" which had prevented them from participating in the mass demonstrations organized by the Congress. "Our Indian comrades can serve as an example of how not to carry on the tactics of the anti-imperialist united front," he said.

The policy of denunciation of Gandhi, the Congress, and the nationalist movement was partly changed as a result of the adoption of the policy of the United Front as advocated by the Communist International in 1935. The report on colonial countries that was presented at this meeting of the Communist International at Moscow stated: "India is a classical colonial country with a relatively numerous proletariat and a considerably advanced demarcation of classes.... Our comrades in India have suffered for a long time from 'left' sectarian errors; they did not participate in all the mass demonstrations organized by the National Congress or organizations affiliated with it. At the same time the Indian communists did not possess sufficient forces independently to organize a powerful and mass anti-imperialist movement. Therefore, the Indian communists, until very recently, were to a considerable extent isolated from the mass of the people [and] from the mass anti-imperialist struggle. The toiling masses of India could not be convinced of the fact that the communists not only really desire to struggle themselves, but can also lead the millions in a struggle against the principal mortal enemy of the Indian people—British imperialism. In this connection, for a long time the small scattered groups of communists could not become a united, mass all–India Communist Party. By their sectarian policy and isolation from the mass anti–imperialist movement, these small communist groups objectively helped to retain the influence of Gandhism (the theory of Gandhi, who preaches passive resistance to British imperialism and who is [the] actual leader of the National Congress in India) and national reformism over the masses. . . . It was only recently that the all–India Communist Party, which has already taken shape, began to rid itself of its sectarian errors and made the first step towards the creation of an anti-imperialist united front. Nevertheless, our young Indian comrades, having taken this road showed a great lack of understanding of the United Front tactics. This may be borne out even by the fact that our Indian comrades in attempting to establish a united anti-imperialist front with the National Congress in December of last year put before the latter such demands as 'the establishment of an Indian Workers' and Peasants' Soviet Republic', 'confiscation of all lands that belong to the zamindars without compensation', 'a general strike as the only effective programme of action', etc. . . . Such demands on the part of our Indian comrades can serve as an example of how not to carry on the tactics of the anti-imperialist United Front. True, the Indian communists somewhat corrected their line later on and achieved, on the one hand, the unification of the revolutionary and reformist trade unions and, on the other hand, an agreement with the so-called Congress Socialists for a struggle against the new slavish constitution. . . . The Indian communists should in no case disregard work within the National Congress and the national revolutionary and national-reformist organizations affiliated with it, maintaining at the same time their complete political and organizational independence. Both within and without National Congress, the Indian communists must consolidate all the genuine anti-imperialist forces of the country."

This new Comintern line was further clarified and developed

by R. Palme Dutt and Bradley, the British communists, in an
article entitled "The Anti-Imperialist People's Front in India"
published in February 1936. This article was known as the
famous Dutt–Bradley thesis. Dutt and Bradley felt that the
Indian National Congress could play a role in the work of
organizing an anti-imperialist people's front in India. Their thesis
stated: "Every Indian patriot will recognize that the first need
for the powerful advance of the Indian national struggle, the
key need of the present situation is the common struggle. This
is the indispensable condition for the successful fight against the
existing and ever sharpening reaction and oppression. . . . It is
evident that all elements, including from among the Liberals,
who are prepared to break with . . . imperialism and accept the
programme of the national struggle, are welcome to the common front."[24] So far as the National Congress was concerned
this thesis specifically stated that the Congress can play a great
and the foremost role in the work of realizing the Anti-
Imperialist People's Front. "It is even possible," the thesis stated,
"that the National Congress, by the further transformation of its
organization and programme, may become the forum of realization of the Anti-Imperialist People's Front; for it is the reality
that matters not the name."

. The Dutt–Bradley thesis changed the previous communist line
of total antipathy to the Congress. The ideas adumbrated in
"The Anti-Imperialist People's Front in India" found eventual
acceptance with the Indian Communist Party. The Politbureau
of the Indian Communist Party stated: "No political document
has created so much stir in recent times as Dutt and Bradley's
article *The Anti-Imperialist People's Front in India*. No political document has evoked such unanimous and enthusiastic response from all the anti-imperialist elements. . . . Comrade Dutt
and Bradley's article successfully applies to the actual circumstances prevalent in India the policy of united front adopted
at the Seventh Congress of the Communist International and the
decisions arrived at in that World Congress. It is generally
recognized that the Seventh Congress was no mere Party Conference of the communists alone but one which had blazoned
the path of heroic struggle and certain victory for the entire
world revolutionary movement of today. The concrete application to the present stage of the anti-imperialist movement in our

country of the line of the Seventh Congress is a historic affair."[25]

The Dutt–Bradley thesis cleared the way for the Indian communists to join the Congress Socialist Party and thereby to influence Congress policy. Dutt and Bradley suggested that the communists, leftists, Congressmen, Congress socialists and trade unionists should all join this united front. Their thesis stated: "Congress Socialists, Trade Unionists, Communists, and Left Congressmen should all be able to unite on the essentials of a minimum programme of anti-imperialist struggle for complete independence, of organization of the masses and development of mass struggle, and of the fight for changes in the Congress Constitution, policy, organization, and leadership to forward these aims. The Congress Socialist Party can play an especially important part in this as the grouping of all the radical elements in the existing Congress. It is of the greatest importance that every effort should be made to clarify questions of programme and tactics in the Congress Socialist Party."

In January 1936 the Congress Socialist Party, on the recommendation of its general secretary, Jayaprakash Narayan, decided to admit the communists to its membership. As the CPI was then an illegal party, this decision was naturally not given any publicity. As a result of this decision Indian communists joined the Congress Socialist Party, and thereby gained admittance into the Indian National Congress.

Though there were basic differences between the Congress socialists and the Indian communists, these differences were not brought to the forefront in 1936, and for a few years thereafter, and the communists had a ready admittance and a cordial welcome into the Congress Socialist Party. The Congress socialists also wanted to transform the Congress into a revolutionary anti-imperialist body, and in this respect their policy had certain common features with those of the communists. The Congress socialists felt that the Indian National Congress, as then constituted, could not hold on together for very long and that with the sharpening of the class struggle the Congress would split,[26] and, therefore, they welcomed all leftist elements within the Congress Socialist Party.

Though since 1935 the policy of the United Front was advocated by the Indian communists, it was made clear that the Govern-

ment of India Act, 1935 was a "slave" constitution and could not
be accepted. In December 1936 the Central Committee of the
Communist Party of India published a pamphlet entitled *Transform the Elections into Mighty Anti-Imperialist Demonstrations*,
which declared: "Today the focal point of imperialist attack on
India is the new constitution. To free ourselves from the new
bondage should be the main flank of our political struggle. To
concentrate all our forces, to mobilize all our energy to fight the
slave constitution, that is the task which confronts us....
Transform the elections into a weapon to forge an anti-imperialist United Front! Form the United National Front against
imperialism! Smash the New Constitution!"

According to M. N. Roy—who by this time had severed his
connection with the Comintern—the alternative to this "slave"
constitution was the setting up of a free Constituent Assembly in
India. But R. P. Dutt and Bradley felt that the correct slogan
should be the slogan of Soviet power. In a leaflet they issued
along with Harry Pollitt it was stated: "There can be no question of substituting the slogan of Constituent Assembly for the
slogan of Soviet Power. It was Roy who advanced the slogan
of Constituent Assembly against Soviets, against revolution....
Roy counterposes the slogan of Constituent Assembly to Soviets
instead of counterposing it to the present slave Constitution,
raising the illusion that the Constituent Assembly can fulfil the
task of the Soviets."

In 1936 a significant development took place in Congress
politics which was hailed by the communists. Jawaharlal Nehru,
who was the Congress president that year, declared in his presidential address that he was a socialist. In an article entitled "For
the Anti-Imperialist People's Front: Long Live Soviet Hindustan" it was stated: "The bourgeois leadership is no longer united in
its reformism, it is disintegrating. In his Presidential address Nehru's
anti-imperialist voice stammered on some vital points, yet it
was full throated on several others, it was a clearer anti-imperialist call than had ever been made from the Congress chair. Nehru's
was an approach which stood in opposition to all that the orthodox Indian National Congress leadership has stood for so far."[27]

The Communist Party of India had been banned by the
British Government in July 1934. In 1935 there were only about
a thousand members of the party. In 1936 the Communist Party

decided that its members should join the Congress and attempt to give it a revolutionary direction and that they should also cooperate with the Congress Socialist Party. During 1937 to 1939, when there were Congress Ministries in the provinces, the Communist Party was able to function semi-legally and in January 1938 it started its first all–India weekly journal, the *National Front*.

The Indian communists, who joined the Congress Socialist Party after the policy of the United Front was adopted, could not continue in that party for long. For, in August 1937, Jayaprakash Narayan and, again, in September 1938, M. R. Masani,[28] lighted upon certain communist documents which showed that the Indian communists did not consider the Congress Socialist Party as a socialist party at all. Jayaprakash Narayan stated that the secret document found by him stated in substance that "the Congress Socialist Party was not a socialist party and that the Communist Party would never tolerate a rival party. It went on to say that the Communist Party was the only real socialist party, and that the Congress Socialist Party was to be developed merely into a platform of left unity."[29]

Accordingly, in December 1939 Jayaprakash Narayan issued a "war circular" stating that the communists had "left nothing undone" to destroy unity within the Congress Socialist Party. He was convinced that the Indian communists were the "sworn enemy" of the Congress socialists.[30] In spite of the issue of the "war circular" by Jayaprakash Narayan in December 1939, no action was taken against the communists immediately. When eventually in March 1940 the National Executive of the Congress Socialist Party resolved to expel the communists, the communists had consolidated their position in the party and had captured a large part of the party organization.

The period of cooperation between the Congress socialists and the Indian communists had been most advantageous to the communists. Jayaprakash Narayan said: "During this united front period, the communists made big strides at the cost of the socialists with the help of the csp [Congress Socialist Party]. They managed to capture important posts in the Indian National Congress, in the AITUC, the All India Kisan Sabha, and the Students' Federation. The policy of collaboration all but finished the csp. The havoc was specially great in South India. The National

Executive had allowed the control of party organizations in Andhra, Tamilnad, and Kerala to pass into the hands of communists. These branches went over to the communists *en bloc.*"

After being expelled from the Congress Socialist Party, the Indian communists gave a call for a political general strike in the major industries, and the government countered this with severe repressive measures. In the meantime, world events were moving fast and World War II was declared in Europe.

V. THE PEOPLE'S WAR

When World War II broke out, the Indian communists declared that it was an imperialist war. Russia was not involved in the War when it first broke out. But later Germany attacked Russia, and the attack was denounced by the Indian communists as also by the Congress Working Committee. The latter condemned this attack saying: "The Soviet Union has stood for certain human, cultural, and social values which are of great importance to the growth and progress of humanity. The Working Committee consider that it would be a tragedy if the cataclysm of war involved the destruction of this endeavour and achievement. They have admired the astonishing self-sacrifice and heroic course of the Soviet people in defence of their country and freedom and send to them their warm sympathy."[31] But, none the less, the Congress did not consider that because Russia had been attacked the very character of the war had changed, or that India should support the Allied war-effort without any guarantee of freedom for India.

With the entry of Russia into the war most communist parties in Europe, however, declared that the war had become a people's war. But the Indian Communist Party evidently was not in effective contact with the Comintern some years prior to its dissolution in 1943, and for about six months after Hitler had invaded Russia, Indian communists were still opposed to Indian participation in it. Later, however, the Communist Party of India issued a manifesto declaring that the war had become a people's war and called upon the Indian people to support the Allied cause. This manifesto stated: "The Soviet entry into the war isolated Fascism as the main enemy of mankind. It flung

the non-Fascist imperialists into the people's camp by creating
the basis for the international front against Fascism and for
Freedom. It transformed the war of the imperialists into a war
of the peoples and opened the gate to a world-wide people's
unity. We opposed the imperialist war for all we were worth,
we must go into the people's war for all we are worth. We had
nothing to gain and everything to lose by supporting the
imperialist war. We have nothing to lose and everything to gain
by going into the people's war.... This war is India's great
opportunity to fight for her national liberation, no more in isolation, no more single-handed, but as part of the battle for world
liberation. It is the war of the Soviet people, whom we pledged
support against an imperialist attack. It is the war of the heroic
Chinese people, whose five years of lone struggle we have admired
with veneration. It is the war of the British people, with whom
we have preached friendliness and cooperation despite the British
imperial domination over us. It is the war of the enslaved peoples
of Europe, for whom our hearts bleed. It is an All–People's War
against Fascism and for freedom. It is the Indian people's war no
less than the war of all the rest of the peoples of the world....
The People's camp is blessed with an incomparable leader in the
great USSR, Its mighty Red Army, its wise Soviet Government,
and its leader, Stalin. Never before in human history has any
struggling people, any enslaved nation, had such powerful support guaranteed to it."[32]

Russia was the ally of England during World War II, but
England still retained her imperial hold on India. Most Indian
nationalists felt that they could not support the British war-
effort simply because Russia had joined the war, particularly
when the freedom of India was none of Britain's war aims. But
when Stalin called upon his countrymen to rally round their
fatherland the Indian communists began to support the British
war-effort. This act was construed in nationalist circles in India
as putting the interests of the Soviet state above the interests
of the country. A Communist Party publication states: "There is
not the remotest doubt that the overwhelming majority of Indian
patriotic opinion thought that when the country was fighting
for independence 'the communists were on the other side'. We
paid very dearly for this in the years to come.... The plain and

simple fact remained that national defence minus the people is reduced to absurdity."[33]

After the Indian communists decided to support the Allied war-effort, the Indian government began to release the Indian communists from prison and announced that the CPI had become a legal party. Not only this, the Indian government accepted the offer of the Indian communists to bear arms in support of the Allied war-effort and organized a programme for training a guerrilla army composed largely of communist volunteers.

During the Quit India movement, most of the Congress leaders and the leaders of the left parties, other than the communists, were in jail or had gone underground. During this period the communists functioned effectively in various trade unions, peasant, and student organizations and came to dominate the All India Trade Union Congress (AITUC), the All India Kisan Sabha, and the All India Students' Federation. The AITUC had been formed in Bombay in 1920 and had close connection with the Indian National Congress. In 1929 there had been a split in the AITUC and the communists left the organization to form the Red Trade Union Congress. After a few years the communists returned to the AITUC and obtained considerable influence over this organization. The AITUC contained Congressmen, socialists, communists, and members of other political parties, but during World War II, when the Congress and socialist leaders were in prison or had gone underground, the communists came to dominate the AITUC. After political and trade union leaders were released from prison in 1945, they found that the communists had come to control the AITUC. In these circumstances, most of the Congress members withdrew from the AITUC, and in 1947 formed the Indian National Trade Union Congress (INTUC). The socialists, who remained within the AITUC, also came into conflict with the communists, and eventually in 1948 the socialists left the AITUC and formed the Hind Mazdoor Panchayat.

After coming out of prison Congress leaders began to criticize the communists for their role in supporting the British during the Quit India movement. On 23 October 1945, at a public meeting, Nehru said: "When lakhs of Indians staked their all for the country's cause the communists were in the opposite camp, which cannot be forgotten. The common man associates the Communist Party with Russia and Communism. But the action of the Communist Party of India has prejudiced both Russia and Communism."[34] Nehru further said: "When the Second Great War started, the Congress agreed to join hands with the anti-Fascist forces, provided the national freedom of the country was assured. This demand was not a bargain, because as the situation stood, neither the Congress nor its biggest leaders could have organized the national forces against Fascism without the assurance of National Independence. The Communist Party was the one party that tried to do what the Congress could not do, namely, organize the national forces without the assurance of Independence, and it failed.... For the Congress, National Independence was the prime objective, while the communists gave primary importance to other issues."[35]

VI. THE MULTI-NATIONAL THEORY AND PAKISTAN

As a protest against the attitude of the Congress to the communists, the Communist Party asked all communists, with the exception of the communist members of the AICC, to resign from the Congress. One of the reasons given for taking this action by P. C. Joshi, the then general secretary of the party, was that the Congress was determined to fight the Muslim League, and had denied the right of self-determination to a section of their countrymen by opposing the demand of the Muslim League for the partition of the country. Because the Congress did not support the demand of the Muslim League for self-determination, P. C. Joshi charged that it was guilty of "sectarian arrogance." "Their declaration of fight against the Muslim League," said P. C. Joshi, "will only unleash forces of civil war, not forge the future Indian Union. To glorify the strength of the Congress and deny that of the League is to be blind. To demand self-determination from the British and to deny it to a section of our own countrymen is plain injustice."[36]

The Communist Party formulated a multi-national theory for India and supported the demand for Pakistan. In August 1942, B. T. Ranadive, the communist leader, wrote in the *People's Age* : "What is the progressive essence of the Pakistan demand? The application of the principle of self-determination to certain nationalities in India. Muslims in certain areas do form a distinct nationality bound together by common culture, history, and tradition. In consonance with the demands of justice and fair play, they must have the completest liberty to build their own life and liberty sanctioned by the right to form a separate State if and when they choose."

In September 1942 the Communist Party passed a resolution which spoke of the multi-national character of the Indian sub-continent and of the right of the various nationalities, which constituted the Indian Union, to secede from it if they so desired. This resolution stated that every section of the Indian people which had a contiguous territory as its home-land, common historical tradition, common language, culture, psychological make-up, and common economic life should "be recognized as a distinct nationality with the right to exist as an autonomous state within the free Indian Union or federation and will have the right to secede from it if it may so desire." Accordingly, the free India of the future would be "a federation or union of autonomous states of the various nationalities such as the Pathans, Western Punjabis (dominantly Muslims), Sikhs, Sindhis, Hindusthanis, Rajasthanis, Gujaratis, Bengalis, Assamese, Biharis, Oriyas, Andhras, Tamils, Karnatakis, Maharashtrians, Keralas, etc." A. N. Dyakov, the Soviet expert on India, in his *New Stage in India's Liberation Struggle,* claimed that it was only the Communist Party of India which had put forward the slogan of democratic solution of the national question, namely, "the right of all the nationalities of India to self-determination, including the right to secession and the formation of independent States."

The Communist Party considered that the demand for Pakistan was justified on the basis of the principle of self-determination. On 15 October 1944, the *People's War,* a Communist Party organ, wrote that the rational kernel of the Pakistan demand was that wherever people of the Muslim faith lived together in a territorial unit, they formed a nationality and had a right to autonomous state existence just like other nationalities in India, such as Andhras, Karnatakis, Marathis, and Bengalis.[37]

As a logical corollary of the multi-national theory of India, the Communist Party was prepared to give the right of secession and the right to form independent states to Andhras,

Karnatakis, Maharashtrians, etc. In August 1942, in an editorial the *People's War* stated that the fears of a minority which distrusted the majority could not be allayed unless it was "given the right to secession, the right to form an independent state. ... To look upon the right of secession as the special fad of Jinnah, as the conspiracy of a few communists to divide India in the interests of British imperialism, is to ignore the new Muslim awakening, as also of other nationalities, e.g. Andhras, Karnatakis, Maharashtrians, etc., the awakening of a distinct nationality to new life, individual national consciousness."[38]

From 1942 the CPI began openly to support the Muslim League demand for partition of the country on the basis of the principle of self-determination. Sajjad Zaheer, a Muslim and a member of the Central Committee of the CPI who later, after the formation of Pakistan, became the first secretary of the Communist Party of Pakistan, thought that it was a good and fine thing, a happy augury, for Indian Muslims and for Indians generally that the Muslim League continued to grow, for it was in the capacity of the League to move the Muslim masses that the possibility of Congress–League unity lay. Sajjad Zaheer admonished Congressmen for their failure "to see the anti-imperialist, liberationist role of the Muslim League," and to recognize "that the demand of Muslim self-determination or Pakistan is a just, progressive, and national demand, and is the positive expression of the very freedom and democracy for which Congressmen have striven and undergone so much suffering all these years."[39]

The condemnation of the Quit India movement by the communists and the promulgation of the theory of the multinational nature of the Indian subcontinent, widened the gulf that separated the Indian National Congress from the Communist Party of India. Referring to the multi-national theory of the Indian communists and their role during the Quit India movement, Nehru later said that he was "greatly surprised at the treacherous attitude of the Indian communists, who want to create a dozen or perhaps more divisions of India. The part the Communist Party has played during recent years has no relation with communism, and if there is any party which has done the maximum harm to the cause of communism, it is the Communist Party of India which has by its treacherous policy isolated itself from the masses."[40]

In 1946 R. P. Dutt endeavoured to bridge the gulf that separated Congressmen from the communists. In this connection, Dutt suggested that the Communist Party should not support the Muslim League demand for Pakistan. He said that the sharp division between the Congress and the Communist Party had to be bridged in order that both could march forward for the achievement of full independence and for the implementation of the economic and social demands of the people, namely, land reform, nationalization, and planned industrial development.[41] But Dutt's efforts to lessen the sharp divergence that existed between the Congress and the Communist Party, on the basis *inter alia* of the Communist Party dropping its support for the demand for Pakistan, did not succeed.

VII. RANADIVE AND THE INSURRECTIONARY METHOD

In the middle of 1947 the Soviet theoreticians began to criticize Nehru and the Indian National Congress openly. At a discussion held at a special session of the Academy of Sciences in Soviet Russia in June 1947, Dyakov and Balabushevich declared that it was true that the Nehru government represented not only the big bourgeoisie but the middle bourgeoisie as well, but then the middle bourgeoisie had also turned reactionary. According to this analysis, the Indian bourgeoisie and the leadership of the National Congress had gone over completely to the camp of reaction and imperialism. In July 1947 the Soviet leaders decided to denounce Nehru outright. E. Zhukov, a leading Soviet authority on Asia, said that Nehru was supporting the reactionary clique and had capitulated to imperialism. The Soviet leaders attacked the Mountbatten Plan as a betrayal of the nationalist cause, but, at about the same time, the CPI in India had declared that the plan was a step ahead and pledged its support to the Nehru government.[42]

When independence came the CPI at first welcomed it and wanted to strengthen the hands of the leftist Nehru against the rightist Patel, but later its views about the Nehru government became as critical as that of Zhukov and Dyakov. In the *New*

Stage In India's Liberation Struggle, written by Dyakov and published by the Academy of Sciences of the USSR, it was stated: "In June 1947, the Communist Party of India also was not able to give a correct evaluation of the Mountbatten Plan and characterized it not as an imperialist manoeuvre but as a certain step forward. It did not immediately understand the treachery of the leadership of the National Congress and counterposed its Right to its Left wing as though the latter was a progressive one. Therefore, it called upon the masses to rally round Nehru and assist him to get rid of Patel. All this shows that illusions about the unity of national interests and the influence of the Congress were still strong not only among the backward peasantry and the petty bourgeois masses, but also among a certain section of the working class and that the Right opportunist mistakes had not been overcome within the Communist Party. . . . It was only in December 1947, that the Communist Party of India gave a correct estimate of the Mountbatten Plan as a new imperialist manoeuvre and characterized the Nehru Government as a whole as a government of the Indian big bourgeoisie, which had entered into an agreement with British imperialism and formed an alliance with the Indian princes and landlords."

During this time the radicals inside the CPI were getting restive under the moderate leadership of P. C. Joshi, the then general secretary of the party. Later, the radicals found support for their militant policy in the speech delivered by Zhdanov in the Cominform meeting held in Poland in September 1947. Kardelj, in another militant speech, advocated that the democratic and socialist revolutions must be intertwined and that, accordingly, the communists must attack the bourgeoisie as a whole.

The militant policy advocated at the Cominform meeting in September 1947 had its repercussion on the Indian communists. The Central Committee of the CPI, meeting at Bombay in December 1947, adopted a radical line attacking the bourgeoisie as a whole. It denounced as opportunistic Joshi's thesis that the Nehru government could be influenced by popular pressure and that it might be reorganized to include the leftist forces.

The Second Congress of the Communist Party of India held at Calcutta in February 1948 adopted the tough Zhdanov line and deprecated any betrayal of the revolution. It stated that "though the bourgeois leadership parade the story that indepen-

21

dence has been won, the fact is that the freedom struggle has been betrayed and the national leadership has struck a treacherous deal behind the back of the starving people, betraying every slogan of the democratic revolution." Further, the Second Congress denounced the Indian socialists for harbouring "the illusion that socialism may be achieved by constitutional means."

At this Second Congress, P. C. Joshi, who had been the general secretary of the party, was replaced by B. T. Ranadive. Ranadive represented the radical element of the party, and supported the violent Telengana movement. The movement at Telengana in Hyderabad (now part of Andhra Pradesh) was accompanied by violent peasant uprisings and a state of incipient civil war developed. The aim was to create in Telengana a Yenan—the communist stronghold in China from where the Chinese Communist Party eventually gained control of the entire country.

After Ranadive assumed the leadership of the party the communists embarked on a policy of armed insurrection, and the government of India and the different state governments retaliated with severe repressive measures. In March 1948 Kiron Sankar Roy, the Home Minister of Bengal, announced that the police had seized arms from the communists and, invoking powers under the Public Safety Act, he banned the party in Bengal. The party was also declared illegal in certain other parts of the country. The official newspapers of the party in West Bengal, Kerala, and Andhra Pradesh were also banned and many leading communists, such as S. A. Dange, Jyoti Basu, and Muzaffar Ahmed were arrested.

In his public utterances Ranadive denied that the party was engaged in collecting arms for organizing a violent uprising. But in August 1948 Ranadive addressed a secret letter to party members saying that within six months there would be a general strike and a large-scale peasant uprising in the country. The communists wanted to organize a railway strike throughout the country, but a settlement was reached between the government and Jayaprakash Narayan, the president of the All India Railway Federation, and the strike was called off. Notwithstanding this settlement, the communists proceeded to organize the strike but did not succeed.

During this period the communists took part in divers violent activities. In February 1949 Nehru denounced the communists for having indulged in "murders, arson, looting as well as acts of sabotage."[43] Nehru accused the party of seeking to create a chaos in the country by sabotaging the railway and communication system. During this period the police raided different communist centres in the country and seized arms. The police unearthed communist literature which contained detailed instructions as to the use of small arms and hand grenades. In the raids made by the police various documents were discovered which advocated "the raiding of the police stations, zamindar or jotedar houses; ambushing police parties ... sabotaging the enemy communication lines, cutting of telephone and telegraph lines for isolating the enemy."[44] Among the documents seized by the Bengal police were leaflets which advocated attack on the houses of Congress agents and of turning the guns and bayonets against the "Congress fascists." In these leaflets the people were exhorted to take up arms for storming "the Congress Bastilles."[45]

Ranadive considered that the Indian government under Nehru was tied to the apron-strings of Anglo–American imperialists and had to be overthrown by force and violence. In October 1949 Ranadive, as the general secretary of the Indian Communist Party, wrote to Mao Tse-tung thus: "I wish to assure you and through you the people of China that the Nehru Government which pursues a policy of hostility to the Chinese people and still combines its recognition of the bankrupt Kuomintang Government, does not represent the wishes and the will of the people of India. The overwhelming majority of the Indian people decisively stand for friendship and cooperation with the great Chinese people. The Nehru Government on the other hand follows the dictates of the Anglo–American imperialists, who wish to build India as a bastion of reaction against China. The Anglo–American imperialists carry on their nefarious conspiracies in Nepal and Tibet under the cover offered by the Nehru Government. Thus the Nehru Government is directly advancing the game of the enemies of the Chinese people. ... I wish to assure you and through you the people of China that the Communist Party of India will unmask all the anti–Chinese intrigues that the Nehru Government might hatch under the dictates of the American imperialists and rally the people to defeat them."[46]

The Indian communists under Ranadive's leadership indulged

in violent activities in the belief that India was on the verge of a revolution. But this assessment of the Indian situation was contrary to facts. In June 1948 Dyakov in an article in *New Times* spoke of the deep disappointment of the people with government policies, but he did not say that India was on the verge of a revolutionary upsurge.[47] The articles that appeared in Soviet Russia at this time showed that, according to the Soviet theoreticians, India was not then on the verge of a revolution, so that the pursuit of an all-out anti-capitalist, anti-bourgeois policy and the adoption of violent methods were not yet appropriate in India.

Within the Indian party itself discontent was brewing over Ranadive's ultra-leftist policies. Ajoy Ghosh, who was in prison since the middle of 1948, accused Ranadive of pursuing the policy of a petty bourgeois revolutionary. Ranadive, on the other hand, threatened Ajoy Ghosh with expulsion. But Ajoy Ghosh was supported by S. A. Dange, the trade unionist leader, who felt that the militant extremist policy pursued by Ranadive would undermine and destroy the position that the communists had gained in the trade union movement. P. C. Joshi, likewise, thought that Ranadive was pursuing an adventurist Trotskyite policy.[48]

In the meantime, the communists in Telengana were following Ranadive's insurrectionary methods. Within a few months hundreds of village Soviets had been set up, land had been seized, and many landlords and government officials had been liquidated. A guerrilla army took control of Nalgonda and Warangal districts in Hyderabad. The communists in Hyderabad were supported by their comrades in the neighbouring state of Andhra.

VIII. MAO'S NEW DEMOCRACY AND THE ANDHRA COMMUNISTS

Curiously, it is among the Andhra communists themselves that Ranadive found the most serious opponents of his policy. The Andhra communists believed in an agrarian revolution and derived inspiration not from Russian but from Chinese sources. In June 1948 the Andhra communists asserted that Mao's concept of New Democracy should be followed in India. According to this concept, the only enemies of the revolution were the big bourgeoisie and the landlords. The entire peasantry, including the middle peasantry, could be won over to the cause of the revolution. The rich peasantry, even though a vacillating ally, could also support the revolution up to a point. The Andhra communists stated: "Our revolution in many respects differs from the classical Russian Revolution; and is to a great extent similar to that of the Chinese Revolution. The perspective is like not that of general strikes and general rising leading to the liberation of the rural side; but the dogged resistance and prolonged civil war in the form of an agrarian revolution culminating in the capture of political power by a democratic front."

The Andhra communists had been impressed by Mao's New Democracy and they challenged Ranadive's assumption that the revolution in India must follow the Russian model. They felt that in an agrarian country like India the Chinese communist experience had greater validity than the Russian experience, that the revolution in India would start in the villages, not the cities, and that the revolutionary pockets that would develop in the rural areas would eventually encircle the cities. Further, they held that the revolution in India would come as the culmination of a protracted civil war, as in China.

Here, then, were the beginnings of the polarization between those in the Communist Party who felt that Indian communism must follow Marxist doctrine and the Russian experience, and others who derived sustenance from Maoist practice and the Chinese experience. These and other differences were eventually to split the Communist Party of India.

P. C. Joshi, who had opposed Ranadive's policy, also found himself in disagreement with the Andhra communists. He felt that whereas Ranadive sought to follow the Russian example dogmatically, the Andhra communists sought to follow the Chinese example blindly. He complained that "the swing-over from ignorant, insolent slandering to blind and servile idol-worship comes very naturally and easily to the Indian intellectuals with our traditional outlook determined by the caste-ridden and Brahmin-dominated feudal society."[49]

Ranadive's differences with the Andhra communists were fundamental. He attacked the Maoist theory, which the Andhra communists supported, namely, that the rich peasantry could be allies of the revolution. He regarded the strategy of the

Andhra communists of including the rural bourgeoisie as allies of the revolution as a "shame-faced theory of class collaboration" and as amounting to "reformism in its most naked and gross form." Further, in Ranadive's criticisms the suggestion was implicit that the Andhra communists supported such a theory because they were members of the rural bourgeoisie and were sons of rich and middle peasants.

In any event, Ranadive was not prepared to accept Mao as a source of communist theory. He said: "Firstly, we must state emphatically that the Communist Party of India has accepted Marx, Engels, Lenin, and Stalin as the authoritative sources of Marxism. It has not discovered new sources of Marxism beyond these. Nor for the matter of that is there any Communist Party which declares adherence to the so-called theory of new democracy alleged to be propounded by Mao and declares it to be a new addition to Marxism." Ranadive added: "Some of Mao's formulations are such that no communist can accept them. They are in contradiction to the world understanding of the Communist Parties. . . . Why do the Chinese have to go through the protracted civil war? Just because the leadership of the Chinese Communist Party at times failed to fight for the hegemony of the proletariat."

In September 1948 the Indian army marched into Hyderabad. The communists proclaimed an Azad Hyderabad. Resistance in Hyderabad was offered to the Indian army by the communists as also by the Rajakars, a private army of Muslim extremists who were loyal to the Nizam of Hyderabad. The resistance of the Rajakars was crushed. The communists, however, continued their resistance adopting hit-and-run tactics and guerrilla methods.

In June 1949 Soviet academicians reviewed the Indian situation and approved of the pursuit of a policy of people's democracy for Asian countries. Zhukov stated: "In the struggle for People's Democracy in the colonies and semi-colonies are united not only the workers, the peasants, the petty bourgeoisie, the intelligentsia, but even certain sections of the middle bourgeoisie which is interested in saving itself from cut-throat foreign competition and imperialist oppression." Zhukov welcomed the armed struggles in divers colonial and dependent countries, such as Indonesia, Indochina, Malaya, and Burma as also the peasants' uprisings in India. Similarly, Dyakov in his *Crisis of the Colonial System* stated that peasants' struggles, sometimes taking the form of violent uprisings, were the most characteristic features of the Indian revolution. It was clear that Dyakov was approving the Chinese method of peasants' uprisings for Asian and colonial countries.

The Chinese method of struggle found powerful support at a Trade Union Conference of Asian and Australasian countries which met in Peking in November 1949. At this Conference Liu Shao-Chi, the Chinese leader, declared that the path taken by the Chinese revolution should be followed by the peoples of colonial and semi-colonial countries. This would involve the acceptance of the four-class strategy of the Chinese revolution and the waging of an armed struggle, whenever possible. There were appreciative references to the civil wars in Vietnam, Indonesia, Burma, Malaya, and the Philippines, and it was declared that the method of armed struggle is "the main form of struggle" in many Asian countries. Liu Shao-Chi said: "The path taken by the Chinese people . . . is the path that should be taken by the people of many colonial and dependent countries in their struggle for national independence and People's Democracy. . . . The mass movement of the peoples in the colonies and semi colonies, the movement that unfolded after the war and developed into an armed struggle, forced the British imperialists to make a tactical retreat. A sham independence was bestowed on India. But the interests of British imperialism remain 'sacred and inviolable'. The Mountbattens have departed but British imperialism remains and, octopus-like, grips India in its bloody tentacles. . . . In these conditions, the task of the Indian communists drawing on the experience of national liberation movement in China and other countries is naturally to strengthen the alliance of the working class with all the peasantry, to fight for the introduction of urgently needed agrarian reforms and— on the basis of common struggle for freedom and national independence of their country, against the Anglo–American imperialists oppressing it and against the reactionary big bourgeoisie and feudal princes collaborating with them—to unite all classes, parties, groups and organizations willing to defend the national independence and freedom of India."

In January 1950 an article "For a Lasting Peace" appeared in the *Cominform* which generally approved of the Chinese form of struggle for Asian countries, though it did not state, as Liu Shao-Chi had stated in November 1949, that the Chinese path was universally applicable in Asian and colonial countries.

After this *Cominform* article, Ranadive who had previously criticized the Chinese path, openly admitted that he had been guilty of "certain errors in dogmatist and sectarian directions." But dissatisfaction with Ranadive's policy had developed within the party to a critical point and in May 1950 Ranadive was replaced as the secretary of the party by C. Rajeswar Rao, an Andhra communist, and a new Central Committee of the party consisting of nine members was elected of which four were from Andhra. The editorial board of the party journal *Communist* was reconstituted, and in an article[50] in the next issue of the journal Ranadive was accused of having been the initiator, executor, and dogged defender of a left-sectarian Trotskyite line. It was also stated that the communist parties in the colonial countries were "looking upon the Communist Party of China as their model."

The CPI under the leadership of Rajeswar Rao adopted the Chinese programme of having a united national front which would include not merely the middle bourgeoisie but also the rich peasantry. It asserted that armed struggle was a necessary concomitant of the Chinese path of revolution, that the struggle had to be waged by means of armed guerilla warfare in the countryside by the formation of liberation bases and liberation armies, and that the struggle would culminate with the seizure of power all over the country. At this time the Indian communists believed that India was on the verge of a revolution and they, therefore, prepared for an armed agrarian struggle throughout India.

IX. REJECTION OF ADVENTURISM

This analysis that India was ripe for a revolution was challenged by P. C. Joshi, who had previously also opposed the radical policy of Ranadive. The new Chinese line of agrarian armed revolution, advocated mainly by the Andhra communists, was also opposed by the communists in the trade union field and mainly by S. A. Dange. In July 1950 Dange issued a statement saying that "the ill-planned behaviour of some sections of the leadership of the Communist Party" had given rise to the unfortunate impression that the CPI was planning an armed revolt and he added that there were conflicting views about this matter in the party. The party press immediately issued a statement saying that Dange had spoken only for himself and not for the party.

Dange was firm in his conviction that at this time the party was pursuing an adventurist policy. As early as April 1950 Dange had prepared for circulation inside the party "Some Notes on the Roots of Our Mistakes after Calcutta." It was pointed out therein that the pursuit of an extremist policy had resulted in a sharp drop in the membership of the party and had seriously jeopardized the communist position in the trade union movement. Dange, who had earlier opposed the militant policy pursued by Ranadive, now opposed the extremist policy of armed agrarian revolt adumbrated by Rajeswar Rao.

Ajoy Ghosh, a centrist, broadly shared Dange's views. Dissensions within the party reached such a stage that a journal called *PHQ* [Party Head Quarters] *Open Forum* was published which contained the opposition view within the party. In October 1950 the journal reported a speech by Ajoy Ghosh, who had said: "Today the reality is that nobody in the Indian Party can solve this crisis. It was the international comrades who pointed out our mistakes. Since we are not agreed on the interpretation, only they can help us. We must, therefore, contact the international leaders. None of us is clear what the *Lasting Peace* editorial means. If anybody claims he is correct, it is arrogance on his part."

In October 1950 a confidential letter was sent by the Political Committee of the British Communist Party to the Central Committee of CPI stating that the *Cominform* article of January 1950 *For a Lasting Peace* had been misinterpreted to mean that the method of armed struggle was the only method appropriate for India. Though the method of armed revolution was a permissible method, when the situation was ripe for it, it was essential that the Indian communists should not pursue an ultra-revolutionary Trotskyite line, but should utilize all opportunities for carrying on legal modes of struggle including participation in elections.

At about this time R. Palme Dutt also declared[51] that the situation in India was not such as called for an immediate resort to armed struggle. On the contrary, the communists should seek to forge a broad united democratic front in India so that the Indian government, which contained two divergent groups, one led by Patel and the other by Nehru, and which therefore vacillated in the pursuit of an anti-imperialist policy, could, by the pressure of popular movements, be made to follow a more anti-imperialist policy. Nehru, it was pointed out, was pursuing an anti-imperialist peace policy though in a hesitant way. The task of the Indian communists would be to compel the Indian government to pursue a more consistent peace policy and to disentangle India from the imperialist camp altogether. To bring pressure on the Indian government a broad united democratic front consisting of the four classes had to be formed. The aim of this front was to be the establishment of a people's democracy or a new democracy.

The idea that Nehru was not a mere lackey of imperialism but was pursuing a peace policy, though in a hesitant and vacillating manner, was somewhat new. The acceptance of such an idea, as also the idea of forging a broad united democratic front, would have necessitated significant changes in the policy of the CPI. These changes were only partly reflected in the election manifesto of the CPI for the first general elections held in India in 1951. The CPI pointed out that though socialism was its goal, considering the circumstances in India, it was not demanding the immediate establishment of socialism. For the time being, it was reconciled to a mixed economy under governmental regulation and even to the development of certain private industries in India which could replace the foreign industrialists. Further, the CPI desired to protect not merely the interests of the proletariat, peasantry, and petty bourgeoisie but also of the middle bourgeoisie.[52] The CPI, however, did not hesitate to express its reservations about Nehru's foreign policy. The CPI exhorted the people to wage a struggle against imperialism, and warned that the Nehru government was tied to the imperialists and that its peace policy was largely spurious.[53] To pursue a policy of peace, India would have to break its link with the Commonwealth and to disentangle herself from "the war camp, led by the USA."

Before the first general elections were held in India in 1951, there had developed within the Communist Party of India what may be called the rightist section and a leftist opposition. The rightist section was led by S. A. Dange and P. C. Joshi who felt that conditions in India were not ripe for a revolution on the Chinese pattern. Joshi had been expelled from the party temporarily in December 1949 and in a pamphlet called *Views*, he wrote: "I think my comrade holding the present situation to be a revolutionary situation is not only unable to use the evidence of his own eyes and ears but is guilty of repudiating Lenin's own definition of the same. . . . Of all our sectarian mistakes this has been the most disastrous, for it has led to the adoption of tactics suited to an insurrectionary or semi-insurrectionary situation. The result has been that the masses have not responded to our calls and our comrades have landed themselves into the terrorist mire."

In 1951 the centrists within the party came to power. On 1 July 1951 Rajeswar Rao was replaced by Ajoy Ghosh, a man of the centre, as general secretary of the party. Ajoy Ghosh believed that the country was not yet ready for armed insurrection and that the party should concentrate on constitutional opposition to the policies of the Nehru government. In 1951 the Politbureau also issued a policy statement saying: "The tradition of our party, especially since the 'People's War' period, has been to swing like pendulum from one extreme to another. . . . We woke up suddenly like Rip Van Winkle at the end of 1947 to jump into left sectarianism which has brought the party and the mass movement to the present plight of total disruption."

Ajoy Ghosh, P. C. Joshi, and S. A. Dange felt that the importance of parliamentary or constitutional methods in strengthening the communist movement should not be underestimated. Eventually, the Communist Party session at Madurai in 1953 exhorted its members not to neglect the lawful activities that the party could pursue through the legislature and other democratic institutions provided under the Indian Constitution.

In an article entitled *For Lasting Peace and People's Democracy* which was published on 8 October 1954, R. P. Dutt asked the Indian communists to support the peace policy of Nehru and said that the anti-imperialist and anti-colonial struggles of the colonial peoples were closely linked with the fight for peace.

Dutt also advocated the adoption of a policy of a united national front and said that the communists should seek to build up "the united national front of the urban petty bourgeoisie, and the national bourgeoisie for the victory of the democratic, anti-feudal, anti-imperialist revolution, and for the establishment of a new type of State or People's Democracy upon this basis."

Dutt's article gave rise to a great debate inside the Communist Party and the question arose whether the article could be fully reconciled with the 1953 Madurai resolutions of the party. But support for Dutt's thesis that Nehru's peace policy should be supported also came from Russia. On 26 January 1956 an editorial appeared in *Pravda* praising Nehru's foreign policy and even some of his domestic policies. The article of Dutt and the editorial in *Pravda* and certain other writings emanating from Russia gave rise to questionings inside the Communist Party, and in the fourth Congress of the Communist Party held in Palghat in Kerala in April 1956, the entire question was reviewed and many delegates gave vent to the feeling that unless the policy of the party was clarified there would be no party centre worth the name.

At Palghat the Communist Party decided that the party would not attack the Congress indiscriminately but would distinguish the reactionary forces from the anti-imperialist and democratic forces inside the Congress and would support the latter against the former. At Palghat it was, therefore, declared: "Although the political party of the bourgeoisie which has taken many land-lords in its fold, the Congress has, among its members, a vast number of democratic elements. It has an anti-imperialist and democratic tradition. Among millions it evokes deep sentiments connected with many of the heroic episodes of our national liberation movement, episodes that are still fresh in public memory. Recent measures of the Government and its promises have helped the Congress to rehabilitate its position even among some sections that were moving away from it. Simultaneously there has been a growth of radical and democratic sentiments inside the Congress and among many masses following the Congress. Our approach towards the Congress and the methods of criticism of its policies have to be such as will take into account all these factors. They have to be such as do not repel the honest Congressmen but draw them towards unity. They have

to be such as strengthen the fight for democratic policies inside
the Congress itself, strengthen the forces that, however haltingly,
are taking a relatively more progressive stand."

But at Palghat it was also made clear that ceaseless efforts
should be made to explain to the people the achievements of
the USSR and China and to point out that these achievements
were the result of the overthrow of the bourgeois-landlord rule.
"It is essential," declared the policy statement adopted at Palghat,
"to popularize the great role the USSR is playing in defence of
peace. It is essential to bring before our people the great advance
registered by China. . . . It has to show also that the consistent
championship of the cause of peace by USSR, its massive achievements in every sphere, its utilization of the atomic energy for
peaceful purposes, the gigantic advance made by China in every
sphere—all these are not accidental. They have resulted from
the fact that these countries overthrew bourgeois-landlord rule
and took to the path of socialism."

At this Palghat session the Communist Party had also to take
into account the startling disclosures that Khrushchev had made
at the Twentieth Congress of the Communist Party of the Soviet
Union in 1956 about the repressive policies that had been pursued
by Stalin. At this session it was decided that the members of
the Communist Party of India would consider the disclosures
made at the Twentieth Congress of the Communist Party of the
Soviet Union along with an editorial in *People's Daily*, a journal
of the Chinese Communist Party, which had supported many
of the actions of Stalin. However, as a result of the deliberations
that took place and the resolutions that were passed at the Palghat Congress, the Communist Party began to support the peace
policy of the Nehru government in the international field.

An unauthorized text of Khrushchev's attack on Stalin was
published by the State Department of the USA on 4 June 1956.
In July 1956 the Central Committee of the CPI published a
resolution stating: "It is evident that Comrade Stalin was mainly
responsible for the distortions of Soviet democracy and for the
violation of inner-party norms. It is also incontestable that in
the later period of his life, the cult of the individual assumed
enormous proportions. While fully recognizing the negative
features and grave defects that developed in Stalin's method of
leadership, the Central Committee of the Communist Party of

India considers that a one-sided appraisal of his role during the last twenty years of his life, years of mighty developments in the USSR and the world Communist movement, causes bewilderment among the masses and can be utilized by enemies of communism to confuse them.... It is evident that a system in which such violations and distortions were inherent could not have unleashed the creative energies of hundreds of millions on a scale never known before and brought about such unprecedented social transformations."

Khrushchev's denunciation of Stalin was eagerly seized upon by all opponents of Soviet Russia and, accordingly, later criticisms of Stalin by the communists became more guarded. On 23 December 1956 Ajoy Ghosh, the general secretary of the CPI, in an article in the *New Age,* while acknowledging that serious mistakes had been committed by Stalin, wrote: "Nevertheless, notwithstanding these mistakes, the name of Stalin will always be cherished by mankind as one of the greatest Marxists of all times, as a towering personality and a titan of thought and action, as a man who dedicated his life to the service of the working people and to the cause of socialism."[54]

During this period certain developments that took place in the international field also helped the Indian communists to adopt a less militant and more constitutional approach. In Russia there had been a process of de-Stalinization and liberalization. Further, there had been a lessening of tensions in the international field. All these strengthened the hands of the rightist section of the Communist Party who had always urged that the importance of a policy of constitutionalism or parliamentary communism should not be underestimated. Eventually, the first communist government under the Indian Constitution was established in the state of Kerala in 1957, and at the extraordinary Congress of the party held at Amritsar in April 1958 the party constitution was amended to provide that the party shall strive to achieve democracy and socialism by peaceful means and by winning a majority in Parliament.

X. THE COMMUNISTS AND PARLIAMENTARY INSTITUTIONS

During pre-independence days the communists did not participate in the legislative assemblies set up by the British. When elections were held under the Government of India Act, 1935 the CPI was an illegal party and the communists could not, in any event, participate in such elections. Moreover, the 1935 Act was regarded as a slave constitution by the communists. Accordingly, they were not prepared to accept office in order "to join the ranks of the slave masters." They were only prepared to support those candidates who were willing to work for wrecking the legislative assemblies set up under the 1935 Act, and to replace them by a Constituent Assembly elected by the people.

In 1937 the Politbureau of the CPI declared that the right wing of the Congress was seeking to divert the national movement to mere parliamentarianism. "We must explain," the resolution stated, "to the masses that Congress ministries do not mean a people's government. Not a single demand can ever be enforced until the people are prepared to organize and to fight against imperialism."[55]

In 1940 after the communists declared that the war had become a people's war, the British Indian government lifted the ban on the party so that it became a legal party. For the first time in 1945–46 the party participated in the elections and won 8 seats in the provincial assemblies and even succeeded in securing the election of one of its leaders, Somnath Lahiri, to the Constituent Assembly set up in terms of the Cabinet Mission Plan.

Somnath Lahiri attended the Constituent Assembly with the Leninist object of dispelling the illusions of the people about that Assembly. He regretted that the Congress had cooperated with the British by participating in the Assembly, and said that India could not secure independence through the Constituent Assembly. This was because independence could be secured only through action and by the revolutionary seizure of power and not through negotiation.[56]

Later Somnath Lahiri moved a draft resolution calling upon the Constituent Assembly to declare independence, and to convene a new Constituent Assembly based on universal adult franchise. The resolution, which amounted to a vote of no-confidence in the existing Constituent Assembly, was ruled out of order by the Chairman of the Assembly.[57]

The Constituent Assembly promulgated a new Constitution

which came into effect on 26 January 1950. This Constitution was denounced outright by the communists who, at that time, were engaged in armed resistance at Telengana. The new Constitution was described as a slave constitution, a constitution which was born out of the conspiracy between the Indian capitalist class and British imperialists and which, instead of conferring freedom, had committed a fraud on the Indian people.[58] Declaring that the new constitution was a constitution of fascist tyranny, the Central Committee of the CPI called upon the people to carry forward their struggle for framing a people's constitution. The Soviet Press also anathematized the new Constitution as one which in the garb of conferring some kind of bourgeois democracy perpetuated the right of private property and restricted the right of the working people to fight against exploitation.

The CPI, however, participated in the first general elections held under the new Constitution in 1951 and it fared well. It secured 16 seats in the Lok Sabha, whereas the Socialist Party secured only 12 seats. The Congress obtained an overwhelming majority by securing 364 seats in the Lok Sabha, but the communists emerged as the largest single opposition party in Parliament. Later, at the party session at Madurai in 1953, the Communist Party exhorted its members not to neglect the lawful activities that the party could pursue through the legislatures and other democratic institutions provided by the Constitution.

In the second general elections held in 1957 the communists were able to establish a government in Kerala. Further, they secured more than double their popular votes in the centre as compared to the 1952 figures. In the second general elections in India in 1957 the Communist Party considerably improved its position in the centre as also in the states as would appear from the figures in Table 1.

So far as the Lok Sabha is concerned, in the 1957 general elections the communists secured 9.8 per cent of the popular votes. The results of the 1957 general elections to the Lok Sabha were as set out in Table 2.

At the extraordinary Congress of the Communist Party of India held at Amritsar in April 1958 certain significant changes were made in the policy of the party. It was now felt that though the party's policy should continue to be based on the philosophy

Table 1

COMMUNIST POSITION IN THE STATE ASSEMBLIES

State	Election Year	
	% 1951–1952	% 1957
Kerala	17.5	35.3
West Bengal	10.4	17.8
Andhra Pradesh	22.8	29.5
Orissa	5.7	8.4
Madras	9.8	7.4
Punjab	6.2	13.6
Bihar	1.1	5.2
Assam	2.4	8.1
Maharashtra	2.5	6.3
Uttar Pradesh	0.9	3.8
Rajasthan	0.6	3.0
Mysore	1.4	1.9
Madhya Pradesh	0.7	1.6
Gujarat	2.5	0.8

COMMUNIST POSITION IN PARLIAMENT

	Votes polled	Seats secured
1952	3,484,401	16
1957	10,754,075	27

Table 2

1957 ELECTION RESULTS—LOK SABHA
(494 SEATS)

	Seats won	Percentage of popular vote
Congress	366	46.5
Communists	29	9.8
Praja Socialists	18	10.5
Lohia Socialists	6	5.0
Scheduled Castes Federation	7	4.0
Jana Sangh	4	6.0
Others	58	18.2

22

of Marxism and Leninism, conscious efforts would have to be made to integrate it with Indian history and Indian experience and that the role of constitutionalism in advancing the communist movement in India should not be underestimated. The preamble of the new party constitution adopted at Amritsar mentioned that the goal of Communist Party would be to strive "to unite and lead all patriotic and democratic forces in the country in the struggle for defence and consolidation of national freedom." No reference was made to the inevitability of revolution or the necessity of the dictatorship of the proletariat but it was stated that the party would seek to apply "the theory of Marxism–Leninism to the realities of the Indian situation" and to "organize itself in accordance with the principles of democratic centralism."

At this Congress a new clause was added to the party constitution which provided: "The Communist Party of India strives to achieve full democracy and Socialism by peaceful means. It considers that by developing a powerful mass movement, by winning a majority in Parliament and by backing it with mass sanctions, the working class and its allies can overcome the resistance of the forces of reaction and ensure that Parliament becomes an instrument of people's will for effecting fundamental changes in the economic, social, and State structure."

In the third general elections held in 1962 the party improved its position still further. The figures relating to the percentage of votes that the communists secured in the different states in the 1962 elections are given in Table 3, except that the figures for Kerala and Orissa are the figures of the mid-term elections which took place in Kerala in February 1960 and in Orissa in June 1961.

Mid-term elections took place in February 1960 in Kerala after the dismissal of the Namboodiripad ministry. In the mid-term elections the non–communists presented a united front, and though the communists were reduced to a minority, they increased their total number of votes. The non–communist ministry remained in power for two years but eventually fell due to internal dissensions. In the fresh elections that took place, the communists obtained a clear majority and the Congress was reduced to a minority.

In the 1962 elections the communists secured 10 per cent of

the popular votes in the elections to the Lok Sabha. The results of the 1962 elections to the Lok Sabha were as set out in Table 4.

By the time the fourth general elections were held in 1967 the split within the Communist Party had taken place. In the fourth general elections, the CPI secured 4.8 per cent of votes for the Lok Sabha and the CPI(M) secured 4.3 per cent of such

TABLE 3

PERCENTAGE OF COMMUNIST VOTES IN THE STATES IN 1962 ELECTION

States	Percentage of votes polled
Kerala	39.1
West Bengal	25.0
Andhra Pradesh	19.3
Orissa	8.0
Madras	7.8
Punjab	7.1
Bihar	6.3
Assam	6.3
Maharashtra	6.0
Uttar Pradesh	5.4
Rajasthan	5.4
Mysore	2.3
Madhya Pradesh	2.0
Gujarat	0.2

TABLE 4

1962 ELECTION RESULTS—LOK SABHA (516 SEATS)

	Seats won	Percentage of popular vote
Congress	355	48
Communists	29	10
Swatantra and Ganatantra Parishad	22	7
Jana Sangh	14	6
Praja Socialists	12	7
Lohia Socialists	5	6
Others	57	16

votes. The results of the 1967 general elections for the Lok
Sabha were as set out in Table 5.

So far as the State assemblies are concerned, in the 1967
general elections the CPI secured 4.2 per cent of the popular
votes and the CPI(M) secured 4.6 per cent of such votes as would
appear from Table 6.

In the United Front governments that were formed in Kerala
and West Bengal after the fourth general elections in 1967, the
CPI(M) was the leading and the CPI was an important constituent.
The functioning of the United Fronts in Kerala and West Bengal
have been discussed in greater detail in Chapter Nine.

Though the communists participated in all the elections held
after the Constitution came into force in 1950, the Naxalites,
who broke away from the CPI(M), gave a call in 1967 to boycott the elections and to shun the parliamentary path altogether.
Both the CPI and the CPI(M) chided the Naxalites for this and
charged that the Naxalites were guilty of left sectarian errors.
They said that Parliament could be utilized for advancing the

TABLE 5

1967 ELECTION RESULTS—LOK SABHA
(520 SEATS)

	Seats won	Percentage of popular vote
Congress	275	39.6
Swatantra	44	8.3
Jana Sangh	35	8.9
Dravida Munnetra Kazhagam	25	3.7
Lohia Socialists (SSP)	23	8.6
CPI	22	4.8
CPI(M)	19	4.3
Praja Socialists	13	3.0
Muslim League	3	0.4
Akali Dal	3	0.6
Forward Bloc	2	0.4
Revolutionary Socialists	2	0.7
Republicans	1	0.2
Other parties	13	2.2
Independents	25	11.6

TABLE 6

1967 ELECTION RESULTS—STATE ASSEMBLIES

	Seats won	Percentage of popular vote
Congress	1,690	40.1
Jana Sangh	264	8.7
Swatantra	255	6.8
Lohia Socialists (SSP)	176	5.1
Dravida Munnetra Kazhagam	138	4.4
CPI (M)	127	4.6
CPI	121	4.2
Praja Socialists	106	3.3
Bangla Congress	34	0.9
Jana Congress	28	0.5
Jana Kranti Dal	26	0.7
Akali Dal (Sant Fateh Singh)	24	0.6
Republicans	23	1.5
Progressive Workers	19	0.7
Muslim League	17	0.4
Hill Peoples	9	0.08
Kerala Congress	5	0.3
Mahagujarat Janatantra Parishad	2	0.2
Akali Dal (Master Tara Singh)	2	0.1
Other parties	43	1.2
Independents	310	15.3

people's struggle and that in refusing to tread the parliamentary path altogether the Naxalites were departing from the teachings of Lenin, who had asked communists to make a skilful use of parliamentary and extra-parliamentary methods for advancing the cause of the revolution.

The question as to what attitude the communists should take to the institution of parliamentary democracy has, however, been a vexed one. Lenin considered parliamentary institutions as bourgeois institutions, but yet asserted that the communists should participate in such institutions to dispel the people's illusions about them and to prove that these institutions were politically obsolete. He said: "Precisely because the backward masses of the workers and—to an even greater degree—of the small peasants are in Western Europe much more imbued with bourgeois-democratic and parliamentary prejudices than they were in Russia, precisely because of that, it is only from within such institutions as bourgeois parliaments that communists can (and must) wage a long and persistent struggle, undaunted by any difficulties, to expose, dissipate and overcome these prejudices."[59]

According to the communists the basic malaise of political democracy has been its inability, in the context of capitalist property relations, to bring about rapid and effective economic advancement of the common man. But it was on the basis that the parliamentary system should not be judged only by what it was but also by what it could be transformed into, that the Indian communists claimed that they contested the parliamentary elections.[60] The communists said that they entered Parliament not for giving a performance of "the foam-at-the mouth and tub-thumping variety" but to use Parliament as an instrument of power to bring about changes beneficial to the common man. Parliament and parliamentary procedures were generally unfamiliar to the Indian communists, but then they[61] referred to Lenin's saying: "Communists must not stew in their own juice, but learn how to penetrate into prohibited premises where the representatives of the bourgeoisie exercise influence over the workers; they must not hesitate to make certain sacrifices and not be afraid to make mistakes, which are inevitable in every new and difficult undertaking."

The fact that the communists entered the "prohibited premises where the representatives of the bourgeoisie exercise influence" raised the question whether the experience of Parliament, and all that it involved, would have a mellowing effect on Indian communists. Reference was also made to the observation of the French wit that there was more in common between two deputies, one of whom was a revolutionary and the other not, than there was between two revolutionaries one of whom was a deputy and the other not.[62] But the communists maintain that they entered Parliament not to be mellowed by it or even to accept that a parliamentary opposition was a necessary concomitant of democratic government, but to transform Parliament into an instrument of people's will for effecting a socialist reconstruction of society.

It was said that in certain sets of circumstances, as during the modern period of British history, "there might well be a regular see-saw of political power between two major parties, the government in its turn yielding to the opposition and vice versa" but this could not be elevated into a universal principle of political life. From time to time revolutions have taken place in England and elsewhere, and the experience of revolutions have shown that the new system established by a revolution is to a certain extent authoritarian, and cannot afford to have an opposition which is pledged to subvert the gains of the revolution and restore the status quo. "When, for example, a socialist system requires to be set up ... an opposition, wedded to capitalism and therefore to the desirability of its restoration, can hardly be tolerated. In independent India, a party or group aiming at and working for the return of subjection to the foreigner will be deemed traitorous and will undoubtedly be suppressed with a stern hand. When the country has really made up its mind about socialism, it will hardly be possible to permit the active functioning, in Parliament and elsewhere, of parties and groups that fear socialism. ... Toleration of opposing views may be, normally speaking, a good thing, but in certain circumstances, specially when fundamental socio-economic changes are being effected, it becomes a dangerous luxury, an invitation to disaster."[63]

Democracy and capitalism grew up together in the nineteenth century but while democracy laid stress on the power of the many, capitalism sometimes confined and limited that power in the economic field to the few so that political democracy without economic equality, claimed the Indian communists, was a mere sham. Communists advocated the overthrowal of capitalist democracy and urged its replacement by the dictatorship of the proletariat or by a socialist economy.

They said that backward India could economically raise herself quickly only by implementing a vigorous national economic plan and that such a plan could only be implemented by a strong socialist centre. Communists urged that in order to build socialism the capitalists would have to be suppressed, as otherwise the progress of the plan would be slowed down and the life of the plan and the hope of bringing prosperity to the common man would be imperilled. To implement a national economic plan and to change and transform a backward economy rapidly, a strong and powerful dictatorship committed to the ideal of socialism was essential. They urged that when society had a · purpose and an economic plan to implement, a centralized control of the entire economic life of the country was unavoidable, and that the alternative to socialist or communist control was capitalist or fascist despotism. They said that a communist-controlled state would represent the interests of the many while any other rule would embody the vested interests of a minority. The protection of minorities is the essence of democratic freedom, but their protection at the expense of the interests of the workers and the peasantry, who constitute the majority, implies, the communists argue, that the majority have no firm faith in their own interests and were not, therefore, sufficiently democratic. If society had a dominant economic purpose, then about such purpose, failing unanimity, a decision had to be arrived at by the majority, and the opposition of the minority to such a purpose, could be made ineffective only by the establishment of a strong socialist government which was prepared to suppress all opposition to socialism.

When society reaches a sort of equilibrium and basic questions regarding the organization and character of society are not in doubt or dispute, then a two-party parliamentary system, as exists in Britain, say the communists, may be possible. In such times there is an agreement on fundamentals between the opposition and the government, and a change of government does not lead to any radical social or economic change, as in Britain when a Conservative government is replaced by a Labour government, or in the United States when the Democrats take over the reins of governmental power from the Republicans or vice versa. But during a time of national crisis or when the unity of national will and endeavour is essential then an opposition ceases to exist. This is why during World War II there was a national government in England when His Majesty's Opposition hardly existed.

Similarly, if a war on a national scale is waged against poverty and inequality then an effective opposition can be allowed to exist no more than it existed in England during World War II. When socialism has to be built and defended against its enemies, who may resort to last-ditch battles for its overthrow, when support of the generality of the people is essentially required for the task of socialistic construction, then an opposition, opposed to the principles of socialism, can have no place in the political life of the country. Accordingly, the fact that a state like the Soviet Union does not have a parliamentary opposition of the kind that exists in Britain does not mean, argue the communists, that the Soviet government is necessarily despotic.

The right communists hope that they will be able to gain control of the Indian Parliament with the backing of the Indian people so that they will be in a position to effect a socialist regeneration of Indian society. They point out that Marx did not envisage that violent methods must necessarily be used to attain the objectives of socialism. On the contrary, he had said that if the working class in England or the United States obtained a majority in Parliament or the Congress, as the case may be, then they would be able to abolish those laws which stood in the way of their development. In August 1852 he had even said that "universal suffrage is equivalent of political power for the working class of England."

Marx exhorted the working class to endeavour to secure majority support in the country. To secure such a majority the working class should work in conjunction with, and not in opposition to, other sections in society who also suffered under the capitalist system. To obtain a majority and, through it, state power, the workers should cooperate with other exploited sections of the people. If a majority could be secured then there would neither be any necessity nor any justification for resort to violence. In support of this conclusion the communists quote Lenin who said: "In order to obtain the power of the State the class-conscious workers must win the majority to their side. As long as no violence is used against the masses, there is no other road to power. We are not blanquists, we are not in favour of the seizure of power by a minority."

According to present-day communist theory, as enunciated by the CPI, violence is not a necessary part of socialist strategy but, on the contrary, it is the ruling classes who resort to violence in order to defeat the democratic rights of the people. Violence was unavoidable in the conditions prevailing in Russia prior to the revolution, but the Indian communists and particularly the supporters of the CPI, say that the Russian experience is not necessarily a model for the achievement of socialism in every country. They quote Lenin who said that Marxism was not a dogma but a guide to action, and Stalin who said that the strategy of the communists can never be fixed or permanent but it must change "to meet historical turns, historical shifts."

The Marxists apprehend, however, that when, through the exercise of the machinery of political or parliamentary democracy, the people would attempt to bring about economic democracy, then the holders of power, instead of peacefully surrendering power, would fight for retaining it and the structure of the old, acquisitive, and inequalitarian society. Harold Laski in many of his writings had propounded this view. Laski considered that the ruling class will fight to preserve their power and privilege not because of any conscious selfish motives but because, by being long accustomed to power and privilege under the existing system, they regard that system as essentially just not only to them but also to those who seek to overthrow that system. "Those who benefit by the inequality are so wedded to its righteousness," wrote Laski, "that they tend to prefer to fight for it rather than surrender its advantages." The experience of history, Laski felt, did not warrant the conclusion that the holders of economic power would allow a political democracy to be transformed into an economic and social democracy without fight and without seeking to overthrow the constitutional system which endangered their economic power. Laski's writings had a great influence on Indians and have been hailed by Indian socialists and communists alike. It has even been said that Laski had a nation of followers.[64]

The change from capitalist society to socialist society is such a revolutionary change and such a fundamental breach of the old economic order that it would be unrealistic, say the communists, to expect that such a change can be effected at all times and everywhere altogether in a peaceful manner. After World War II, from which time socialistic régimes came to hold sway over more than a third of the world's population and after the strength of the working classes had vastly increased, the communists felt that it might be possible to utilize the parliamentary machinery as part of a social struggle to achieve economic equality. In fact, at the Twentieth Congress of the Communist Party of the Soviet Union in 1956, and also in the declaration issued by the Conference of the Communist and Workers' Parties held at Moscow in November 1957, the path of the peaceful transition to socialism or the attainment of socialist revolution by peaceful means was advocated. Again, the 1960 Conference of 81 Parties held in Moscow reaffirmed the faith in peaceful transition to socialism. Since the concept of peaceful transition to socialism was formulated, communists in various countries of the world, particularly where a system of political democracy prevails, began to give greater importance to constitutional communism. The CPI welcomed this theory, but the CPI(M) consider that it is not fully in consonance with Marxist–Leninist doctrines. The approaches of the CPI and the CPI(M) to parliamentary democracy and to the theory of peaceful transition to socialism have been further considered in Chapters Ten and Eleven respectively.

XI. THE COMMUNIST SPLIT OF 1964

For more than a decade there had existed within the Communist Party a rightist section which, while not abandoning its ultimate faith in revolution, did not give up hope of making substantial gains for the communist movement through constitutional methods. Against this was a leftist section which leaned more towards a policy of revolution. Gradually there developed a split in the field of international communism as a result of differences between Russia and China on the questions of war, nuclear warfare, policy of revolution, and other matters. These differences had repercussions on members of the Communist Party of India, and ultimately Chinese aggression on India in October 1962 aggravated and crystallized these differences.

Since the destalinization process started in Russia, and with the growth of ideological and other differences between Russia and China, there took place a split in the international communist movement. The Communist Party of India was split in two in 1964 with an official Communist Party (CPI), which was ideologically closer to the Russian communists, and the group which seceded from it and formed the Communist Party of India (Marxist) or the CPI(M), which originally was ideologically closer to the Chinese communists. But, later, and particularly since the Naxalbari incidents in Bengal in 1967, the Chinese communists felt that the CPI(M) has become a revisionist party while the CPI(M), in its turn, denounced the dogmatism and left-sectarianism of the Chinese communists.

Differences between the right and left communists had existed within the Communist Party of India for more than a decade. The differences between the extremist militant wing and the moderate rightist section became acute during 1948–50. The crucial difference related to the appraisal of the role of the Indian bourgeoisie and centred round the question whether the bourgeoisie could still play an anti-imperialist and anti-feudal role, or whether they had gone over completely to counter-revolution. If the bourgeoisie had a vestigial anti-imperialist and anti-feudal role, then they could be supported, up to a point, but if the bourgeoisie and the Congress government at the centre had become completely counter-revolutionary, then a war had to be waged against the bourgeoisie by following the Russian method of country-wide insurrection that Ranadive had preached, or by pursuing guerrilla insurrectionary methods on the Chinese style as Rajeswar Rao later advocated.

These differences were temporarily resolved at a special conference of the party held in 1951. At this conference it was decided that India need not follow blindly either the Russian method of country-wide insurrection or the Chinese method of partisan war of the peasantry but, bearing in mind both the Russian and Chinese experiences, the Indian communists should seek to follow the path, consistent with Leninism and Marxism, that was best suited for India.[65] The 1951 conference of the CPI, while not abandoning the path of armed revolution altogether, counselled the communists to follow a pragmatic and more moderate policy.

The differences again came to the forefront at the Fourth Congress of the party at Palghat in 1956. Prior to this the Indian National Congress had at its Avadi Session (1955) acknowledged the establishment of a socialistic pattern of society as its goal. The Congress government had also published the draft of the Second Five Year Plan and was generally pursuing a policy of peace and nonalignment in international affairs. The question, therefore, arose as to what approach the communists should adopt towards the national bourgeoisie which was being split into a monopoly section that sought collaboration with imperialism and another section, led by Nehru, which was opposed to imperialism and feudalism.

Believing that Nehru wanted to pursue an anti-imperialist, anti-feudal progressive policy, Bhowani Sen presented a draft at the Fourth Congress of the Party suggesting that Nehru and his policies should be supported. He stated: "The Nehru government, representing the progressive section of Indian big business, in the main, abandoned collaboration with imperialism and embraced the policy of peaceful coexistence and established cooperation with socialist States." He also said that the pro-imperialist and pro-feudal sections amongst the big bourgeoisie and in the government were not interested in India's independent capitalist development, that they feared the people more than the imperialists and they knew that Nehru's policies would "ultimately strengthen the popular forces and hit themselves."[66]

Bhowani Sen suggested that Nehru's hands in pursuing a policy of liquidating feudalism and semi-colonialism in India and of pursuing a policy of peace in international affairs should be strengthened. P. C. Joshi and certain other rightist leaders were also of the same opinion. In a note submitted at the Fourth Congress, they said: "In our opinion the slogan of a national democratic coalition government will in the present circumstances most effectively enable the Party to defeat and isolate the pro-imperialist and pro-feudal reactionaries, forge an alliance with national bourgeois elements and help realize the hegemony of the proletariat over the national movement."

Believing that by supporting Nehru and his progressive policies an alternative government of national unity could be brought into existence, P. C. Joshi, C. Rajeshwar Rao, Bhowani Sen, Somnath Lahiri, Ramesh Chandra, and others moved an alternative resolution at this Fourth Congress. This resolution stated: "The CPI believes that as a result of the development of national unity and on the basis of the changed correlation of forces in favour of the progressive forces, an alternative government of national unity can be brought into being." But this resolution was defeated.

Though the pro–Nehru resolution was rejected by the party, those within the party who had sponsored such a resolution found some support for their views when in July and August

1956 Modeste Rubinstein published two articles in the *New Times*, an English journal published from Moscow, where he cited with approbation the fact that in January 1955 the Congress had at its Avadi session accepted the socialistic pattern of society as its goal, and where he also argued that the Nehru government had embarked upon the path of noncapitalistic development towards socialism.

The rightists within the party wanted that the Palghat thesis of the party should be reviewed in the light of Rubinstein's articles. But the Central Committee of the party rejected this demand and Ajoy Ghosh, general secretary of the party, summed up the situation thus: "To conclude: there undoubtedly exists a noncapitalist path for underdeveloped countries like India. But it would be an illusion to think that the present government, headed by the bourgeoisie, can advance on that path. The Communist Party of India does not suffer from such illusions. Therefore while fully recognizing certain possibilities of advance in the existing situation and while fully supporting all measures of the government which help to realize these possibilities and strengthen the cause of peace, national freedom, and national economy, the Communist Party simultaneously strives to strengthen the force of democracy and socialism in our country so that power passes into the hands of the democratic masses, led by the working class. That alone can complete the tasks of the democratic revolution with the utmost rapidity and advance the country towards socialism."

The second general elections were held in India in 1957. Certain rightist and communal parties improved their position as a result of the elections. Within the Communist Party, the question again arose as to whether, in view of the strengthening of the forces of right reaction, the communists should concentrate their energies in fighting these forces and support the Nehru government at the centre, or whether they should simultaneously give battle to the forces of right reaction as also to the Congress government at the centre. The Fifth Congress of the party held at Amritsar in 1958 decided in favour of a policy of giving simultaneous battle against the forces of right reaction as also against the Congress government.

Differences within the party, which were temporarily resolved at Amritsar, again came to the surface when members of the party differed in their reactions to the events culminating in the Red Army marching into Hungary. The leftists within the party supported the Soviet intervention in Hungary saying that the Red Army had marched in to crush counter-revolutionary forces in Hungary. But the rightists within the party led by S. A. Dange regarded the happenings in Hungary as a national upsurge of the Hungarian people. Achutha Menon, who was then a member of the Central Committee, resigned not only from the Central Committee but also from the party saying that events in Hungary had shattered his faith in the world communist movement. Achutha Menon later joined the party and in October 1969 he became the Chief Minister of a non-Congress non–CPI(M) government in Kerala.

Disputes within the party also developed on the question of language and of regional nationalism. In 1957 the Maharashtra Committee of the party under the guidance of S. A. Dange had decided to demand that Belgaum district should be separated from Karnatak and should form part of Maharashtra, and in 1958 it was decided that a *satyagraha* movement should be started to support this demand. In 1958 the National Council of the party at its Madras meeting countermanded this decision to launch a *satyagraha* movement. The National Council took this decision in the absence of Dange, who was then in Europe.

In 1959 clashes took place on the Indo–China border. Dange supported the stand of the Indian government, and at the Meerut session of the National Council of the party, he was reprimanded for this. The National Council observed that the border question between India and China was very much a disputed matter. But the Meerut session could not still the disputes within the party regarding the divergent approaches to the Indo–China border question. Those who supported the stand of the Indian government accused the leftists within the party of being antinational and pro-Chinese, whereas the leftists characterized the rightists as chauvinists.

There were also differences within the party on the policy to be adopted as regards foreign capital. In May 1960 when the National Council of the party met at Calcutta, the draft resolution of the Executive Committee could not be considered because it was opposed *inter alia* by Dange on the ground that it over-estimated the penetration of foreign capital, and particularly

US capital, in the Indian economy. Due to this opposition the general secretary of the party did not move the draft resolution that had been previously adopted by the Executive Committee.

In the latter part of 1960 ideological and other differences came to the surface in the world communist movement. To resolve these differences a conference of the communist parties of the world was held in Moscow. This conference issued the now famous 81 Parties' Statement. But this policy statement also could not resolve all the differences within the Indian communist movement.

Prior to the meeting of National Council of the party early in 1961 the governments of India and China had published their reports on the Indo-China border clashes. On the basis of these reports M. N. Govindan Nair, a right Communist and a member of the Indian Parliament, declared that India's case had been proved. The National Council of the party meeting, however, took no sides and counselled a political settlement at the highest level.

On the eve of the Sixth Party Congress at Vijayawada in 1961, S. A. Dange, P. C. Joshi, and G. Adhikari produced a draft party programme, which the leftists inside the party criticized as being a revisionist programme and as one which underestimated the danger of the penetration of foreign capital into the Indian economy. The leftists were totally opposed to India receiving any foreign aid from the USA, whereas the rightists retorted: "Why do you see only the dollars coming? See also the roubles in the till." The rightists felt that the flow of foreign capital into India would not necessarily endanger Indian independence. The programme drafted by Dange, Joshi, and Adhikari accordingly stated: "In its eagerness for rapid development of the Indian economy, it [the Indian government] underestimates the danger of the penetration of Anglo–American capital into strategic lines of India's development. It feels confident to contain the poison, because it thinks imperialism can take away a few crores from the country, but it cannot take away our independence and freedom. It uses the existence of the socialist camp as a ready help on call, as the basis of its tactics and confidence."

The draft programme prepared by Dange, Joshi, and Adhikari did not satisfy the leftists within the party and gave rise to acute dissension. When the question of elections to the National Council came up, the gulf that separated the rightists from the leftists became all too clear, but a split was avoided through some kind of patch-work solution. At the next meeting of the National Council, the Executive was elected, but leftists like P. Sundarayya, Jyoti Basu, and Harkishan Singh Surjeet were not included in the Executive.

In spite of manifold internal differences, the party faced the third general elections of 1962 as a united party. After the elections the National Council met in April 1962. By this time Ajoy Ghosh, the general secretary, had died. Ajoy Ghosh was a centrist and was acceptable to both the rightist and leftist wings of the party, and his death created further problems for the party.

The differences inside the party again came to the surface when divergent drafts were prepared as to the political implications of the results of the third general elections. P. C. Joshi suggested that the communists should cooperate with the Congress to fight the rightist parties who had made significant gains in the third general elections. P. C. Joshi stated: "The Congress losses to the parties of the right also create the preconditions for building better and more friendly relations between the communists and Congress leaders as also their cadres. The initiative for achieving this new shift cannot obviously come from inside the Congress. It has to be unfolded by the Party. The Party cannot afford to remain sunk in the mire of sectarianism for the simple reason that the discontent against the Congress which during the first and second general elections was going left and mostly towards our Party is now going towards the right. The Party, therefore, has to make a new turn for its sheer survival and the sooner it makes the turn the stronger it will grow." Joshi discerned a growing polarization inside the Congress between the rightists and leftists and he wanted to strengthen the hands of the leftist Nehru.

Bhupesh Gupta, on the other hand, suggested that the communists should continue to give simultaneous battle against right reaction as also against the Congress government and warned that support of the Congress government would only reduce the party to the pursuit of a policy of tailism behind the national bourgeoisie. Bhupesh Gupta said: "While there must be no

23

underestimation of the communal and right reaction, there need be no exaggerated or alarmist appraisal either. The first may lead to sectarianism and the neglect of the task of drawing all secular and progressive forces in the struggle against right reaction, the other may lead to tailism behind the Congress and bourgeois leaders."

The Central Executive of the party did not approve of Joshi's policy of supporting the Nehru leadership or of forming a United Front with the Congress. It assailed the growing forces of right reaction, communalism, and separatism but observed that the Congress leadership itself was partly responsible for generating these forces. It stated: "While the situation demanded the most determined efforts to prevent the growth of reactionary and communal forces or separatist trends in the various parts of the country, the Congress is, however, by its policies, facilitating their rise and growth.... The Council, therefore, came to the conclusion that the general line of the Sixth Congress of our Party of striving to build the unity of all democratic and popular forces in the struggle against right reaction and of directing into popular channels the discontent of the masses against the policies of the government which hit the people, rather than allow the forces of right reaction to take advantage of this to consolidate themselves, should be carried forward."

The death of Ajoy Ghosh also raised the question of leadership and the manner in which the leftist and rightist groups should be accommodated in the highest policy-making bodies of the party. To accommodate both the sections, the rightist Dange was elected chairman, the leftist Namboodiripad was made general secretary, and a composite Secretariat was set up. The Central Executive Committee was expanded to include leftists, such as P. Sundarayya, Jyoti Basu, and Harkishan Singh Surjeet, but three others, who were supporters of Dange, were also included.

In the meantime the situation on the Indo–China border was deteriorating and members of the party were faced with the question whether they would support the nationalistic policies of the government of India or whether they would support the Chinese stand in the name of proletarian internationalism. Meeting at Hyderabad in 1962 the National Council passed a resolution pledging its support to "the policy of the Prime Minister of India, Pandit Jawaharlal Nehru, of making all efforts to bring about a peaceful negotiated settlement of the border question even while taking necessary measures for the defence of the borders of the country."

Indo–Chinese relations deteriorated considerably after the Hyderabad session of the National Council of the party. The party was now seriously divided on the question whether it should condemn China and thereby accept the position that a communist country like China could be guilty of aggression. Eventually in the middle of October 1962 the majority succeeded in inducing the Secretariat to issue a statement supporting India's stand on the McMahon Line. This statement declared: "Reports of the government of India show that the Chinese forces have crossed to the south of the McMahon Line and thus violated Indian territory, though the Chinese deny this. The Communist Party of India has always maintained that the McMahon Line is the border of India. Hence all necessary steps to defend it are justified."

A few days after this statement was issued fighting on the Indo–China border was intensified and the Chinese army crossed the McMahon Line. A clear-cut decision on the Indo–China question could no longer be shelved. The majority was in favour of condemning the Chinese outright, but the minority was not prepared to accept the view that China was intent on grabbing Indian territory. At one stage, Dange, who represented the majority view, made a distinction between aggression in the popular sense and aggression in the capitalist-imperialist sense and, in his polemics with the Chinese Communist Party, Dange had accused China of committing aggression only in the former and not in the latter sense. This distinction was later obliterated when a resolution of the Executive Committee of the party, which reflected the view of the majority, charged that the fact that the Chinese army had come to the foothills in NEFA showed that the Chinese were after the tea gardens and oil-fields of Assam.

The majority within the party believed, firstly, that China was the aggressor, secondly, that there could be no settlement except on a basis acceptable to India, and, finally, that for defending India military aid could be received even from the Western powers on a commercial basis. On all these three points the minority view was different. The minority could not believe that a socialist country could commit aggression, nor was it prepared to support a policy under which India would receive arms from the Western powers even though only on a commercial basis.

In the early stages the Soviet leaders were critical of the attitude of the "ruling circles" in India towards the Indo–China question. In an editorial in *Pravda's* issue dated 25 October 1962, apprehension was expressed that "even some progressively-minded people may succumb to nationalism and become jingoist." The editorial called upon the progressive forces in India not to forsake internationalism and to endeavour to settle the dispute with China through negotiations.

Later, the Soviet leaders changed their stand and broadly, though not entirely, supported the position of Government of India. The majority group headed by Dange, Adhikari, and others felt themselves vindicated by this shift in the Soviet position. Adhikari said: "We had no reason to regret it (that is, the earlier stand of the majority) either. Subsequently, it was the CPSU which had to change and had to do the same open criticism of the Chinese Party which we did earlier."

The disputes within the party had been attempted to be stilled by setting up a composite Secretariat as hereinbefore stated. But the tensions within the party were reflected in the functioning of the composite Secretariat. The meeting of the Central Secretariat held in the middle of October 1962 exposed these differences with Dange, the chairman, giving one interpretation and Namboodiripad, the general secretary, giving another, of a statement issued by the Secretariat on the Indo-China question. Three members of the Secretariat who supported Dange, namely, Yogindra Sharma, M. N. Govindan Nair, and Dr Ahmed jointly asked the general secretary to issue an explanation of the Secretariat statement on the lines indicated by them. This request was turned down by the general secretary. Thereafter Dange issued his statement explaining the Secretariat statement which conflicted directly with the interpretation given by the general secretary.

In November 1962 the National Council of the party passed a resolution, sponsored by the majority group, condemning the Chinese aggression. Later, a resolution of the Executive Committee of the party passed in December 1962 stated that the Chinese were after the tea gardens and oil-fields of Assam. The resolution of the National Council passed in November 1962 had marked the breaking point in the relationship between the majority and minority group inside the party. Three members of the Secretariat belonging to the minority group resigned. Whereas the majority considered the stand of the minority as pro–Chinese and anti-national, the minority view on the resolution of the National Council was this: "The consequences which followed the adoption of this resolution have been disastrous. The Party became in every sense of the term a tail of the Government of India—a tail of even such reactionary forces as the Jana Sangh and Swatantra Party. The type of jingoist propaganda that was let loose by the Party was not indulged in even by these reactionary parties."[67]

The split in the party which took place with the passing of the National Council resolution in November 1962 was formalized in 1964 when those opposed to Dange and his policies left the party. The *Current*, a Bombay weekly, had published on 7 March 1964, the text of certain letters alleged to have been written by Dange about forty years ago to the British government offering his services to that government when he was a prisoner after his conviction in the Cawnpore Conspiracy Case in 1924. Dange characterized these letters as forgeries. In a statement to the Press issued on 6 April 1964, nine members of the Central Executive Committee, namely, A. K. Gopalan, Jyoti Basu, P. Ramamurthy, M. Basavapunniah, P. Sundarayya, Promode Das Gupta, Jagjit Singh Lyallpuri, Harekrishna Konar, Harkishan Singh Surjeet, called for an examination of these letters which were lying at the National Archives at New Delhi, and they also took exception to the statement that had been issued by the Secretariat that they were trying to split the party. In a statement issued on 1 April 1964 the Secretariat had stated: "With the new line of open split of every Communist Party decided upon by the Chinese leadership and given expression to in their 4 February article, the supporters inside our own Party of the ideological positions of the Chinese leadership have evidently now decided to split the Indian party also."

In the circumstances, an emergent meeting of the Central Executive Committee of the party took place on 9 April 1964.

In the agenda placed before this meeting by the Secretariat, the first item was a proposed resolution on the disruptive and anti-party activities of certain leading members of the party, and the second item related to the discussion of the alleged Dange letters. Those who were opposed to Dange suggested that the first item in the agenda should be the Dange letters and that while this item was being considered, Dange, the chairman, should not occupy the chair. This suggestion was rejected as also the suggestion of Bhupesh Gupta that both items should be considered together, and the further suggestion of Jyoti Basu that the meeting may be adjourned to explore the possibility of arriving at an agreed agenda and procedure.

Thereupon E. M. S. Namboodiripad, A. K. Gopalan, P. Ramamurthy, M. R. Venkataraman, P. Sundarayya, M. Basavapunniah, Jyoti Basu, Harekrishna Konar, Promode Das Gupta, Harkishan Singh Surjeet, and Jagjit Singh Lyallpuri walked out of the meeting in protest against what they called "end of inner-party democracy" and they also issued an appeal calling upon the party members to repudiate Dange and his group and their "reformist political line."

The Executive Committee of the party then passed a resolution recommending to the National Council that seven members of the Committee, namely, Sundarayya, Basavapunniah, A. K. Gopalan, P. Ramamurthy, Promode Das Gupta, Harekrishna Konar, and Harkishan Singh Surjeet be expelled. The National Council of the party met on 19 April 1964. Here also the division between those who supported Dange and those who were against him was complete, final, and irrevocable. Some proposals for settlement that were mooted could not bring about a unity, and 32 members of the National Council walked out and issued a statement claiming that the letters in question were genuine. Thereafter the National Council passed a resolution stating that there was no *prima facie* case against Dange.

In July 1964 those who had left the party met at Tenali in Andhra and decided to form a separate party which was known as the Communist Party of India (Marxist). Many of the important leaders of the old undivided party, including A. K. Gopalan, E. M. S. Namboodiripad, P. Sundarayya, Jyoti Basu, Promode Das Gupta, B. T. Ranadive, M. Basavapunniah, and P. Ramamurthy belong to the CPI(M). The organizational report that was placed before the Congress of the official Communist party which took place in Bombay after the split stated that about 30 per cent of membership had gone with the "splitters." The CPI(M) claim that the percentage of members who left the official Communist Party and became members of the CPI(M) was much larger. In Kerala and Bengal the number of Marxist communists was undoubtedly greater than that of the official communists, but the official Communist Party is a stronger party on an all-India basis.

NOTES AND REFERENCES

1. Muzaffar Ahmed, *The Communist Party of India and its Formation Abroad*, Calcutta, 1962.
2. S. G. Sardesai, *India and the Russian Revolution* (Communist Party publication), August 1967, p. 17.
3. Ibid., p. 53.
4. *M. N. Roy's Memoirs*, 1964, pp. 499-500.
5. *National Liberation Movement in the East*, 1962, p. 254.
6. S. G. Sardesai, *India and the Russian Revolution* (Communist Party publication), pp. 49-50. See also "Lenin-Roy Controversy on Revolutionary Strategy," in *New Age*, 22 February 1970.
7. *Indian Annual Register*, 1925, II, p. 371.
8. Overstreet & Windmiller, *Communism in India*, 1960, p. 79.
9. R. P. Dutt, *Modern India*, p. 53.
10. Ibid., p. 77.
11. Ibid., p. 143.
12. Ibid., p. 144.
13. R. P. Dutt, *Modern India*, 1927, p. 17.
14. Ibid., p. 18.
15. *Legislative Assembly Debates*, Vol. 1, 1929, pp. 5-6.
16. *Meerut Communist Conspiracy Case*, Vol. 1, 1932, pp. 3-4.
17. *The Meerut Trial, Facts of the Case*, p. 10.
18. Ibid., pp. 10-11.
19. *Meerut Communist Conspiracy Case*, Vol. 1, 1932, pp. 312-13.
20. Ibid.
21. S. G. Sardesai, *India and the Russian Revolution*, 1967, pp. 62-63.
22. Ibid.
23. Ibid., pp. 60-61.
24. *The Communist*, Vol. 1, No. 12, September 1936, p. 2.
25. Ibid., pp. 10-11.
26. Jayaprakash Narayan, *Towards Struggle*, p. 131.

27. *The Communist,* Vol. 12, September 1936, p. 16.
28. M. R. Masani, *The Communist Party of India,* London, 1954, pp. 69-70.
29. Jayaprakash Narayan, *Towards Struggle,* p. 172.
30. Ibid., p. 179.
31. I. N. V. Rajkumar, ed., *The Background of India's Foreign Policy,* New Delhi, p. 85.
32. P. C. Joshi, *The Indian Communist Party,* pp. 12-13.
33. S. G. Sardesai, *India and the Russian Revolution* (Communist Party publication), 1967, pp. 99-100.
34. *Indian Annual Register,* 1945, Vol. 2, p. 122.
35. Ibid.
36. Ibid., pp. 119-20.
37. *The People's War,* 15 October 1944.
38. *The People's War,* 9 August 1942.
39. Sajjad Zaheer, *The Case for Congress—League Unity,* p. 20.
40. *National Herald,* 9 March 1946, p. 1.
41. R. P. Dutt in *Labour Monthly,* July 1947.
42. *People's Age,* 29 June 1947, pp. 6-7.
43. *Communist Violence in India,* Government of India publication, 1949, pp. 3-7.
44. Ibid., pp. 8-13.
45. Ibid., pp. 13-14.
46. *The Communist,* January 1950, pp. 108-9.
47. A. Dyakov, "The Situation in India," in *New Times,* 2 June 1948.
48. P. C. Joshi, *Problems of the Mass Movement,* pp. 37-38.
49. P. C. Joshi, *For a Mass Policy,* p. 15.
50. *Communist,* July–August, 1950, p. 1.
51. R. Palme Dutt, *Situation in India,* pp. 2-6.
52. *Programme of the Communist Party of India,* October 1951, p. 20.
53. *Election Manifesto of the Communist Party of India,* 1951, p. 29.
54. Ajoy Ghosh, "J. V. Stalin," in *New Age,* IV, 23 December 1956, p. 3.
55. "Resolution on the Congress Ministries," *The Communist,* July 1937, pp. 8-11.
56. *Constituent Assembly Debates, Official Report,* Vol. 1, pp. 45, 130-31.
57. Ibid., p. 80.
58. *Manifesto of the Central Committee of the Communist Party on the New Constitution,* Bombay, p. 8.
59. Lenin, *"Left Wing" Communism: An Infantile Disorder,* Moscow, 1950, pp. 81-82.
60. Hiren Mukherjee, *India and Parliament,* 1962, p. xiv.
61. Ibid., p. 130.
62. W. H. Morris-Jones, *Parliament in India,* pp. 330-31.
63. Hiren Mukherjee, *India and Parliament,* 1962, pp. 133-34.
64. W. H. Morris-Jones, *The Government and Politics of India,* 2nd ed., London, 1967, p. 210.

65. *Statement of Policy Adopted by the All India Conference of the Communist Party of India*, October 1951, pp. 3-4.
66. *Fourth Party Congress Document*, No. 2, pp. 3-8.
67. *Fight Against Revisionism: Political Organizational Report Adopted at the Seventh Congress of the Communist Party of India (Marxist), 31 October–7 November 1964*, Calcutta, December 1955, pp. 25-26.

CHAPTER NINE

The United Fronts of Bengal and Kerala

I. THE EMERGENCE OF THE UNITED FRONTS

The CPI(M) faced the fourth general elections in 1967 with the slogan that a united left front should be formed to destroy the Congress monopoly of power. To fight the Congress the CPI(M), unlike the CPI, was prepared to enter into electoral agreements and adjustments with all anti–Congress parties.[1] The CPI regarded the DMK, the Akalis, and the Muslim League as communal parties and was not agreeable to enter into any electoral adjustment with them. The CPI(M), on the other hand, argued that such a policy would only help the Congress to retain its monopoly of power and accordingly it entered into divers electoral arrangements. Referring to the attitude of the CPI, it said: "An attitude of 'touch-me-not' and keeping them at arm's length was considered to be a revolutionary virtue. These parties had come to be looked upon as embodiments of nothing but rank communalism, casteism, and disruption. They were left to be freely exploited by the bourgeois landlord Congress and its Government as and when needed by it and suited it."[2]

The CPI believed that the Congress consisted of two sections, one progressive and the other reactionary. The CPI considered that the right reactionary parties in the country were the Swatantra, Jana Sangh, DMK, Muslim League, and Akali party. The CPI wanted to concentrate the attack on these rightist parties and on that section of the Congress Party which was sympathetic to these rightist parties. The CPI(M), on the other hand, considered that the Congress Party as a whole was the main enemy and in fighting that enemy electoral alliances and adjustments could be made even with parties like the DMK, Akali party, and Muslim League.

The Congress suffered severe reverses in the 1967 general elections, and was reduced to a minority in eight states including UP and Bihar. The majority of the Congress Party in Parliament was greatly reduced. The Congress could secure a majority of only about 50 seats in Parliament. In Kerala the Congress secured only 9 out of 133 seats and in Madras only 49 out of 234 seats. Congress president Kamaraj was defeated, as also other leaders of the Congress High Command, such as S. K. Patil and Atulya Ghosh. The Congress, however, secured 40 per cent of the votes in the country.

The results of the fourth general elections were such that in many states no single party could form a government on its own. In these states coalition governments were inevitable. Both the CPI(M) and the CPI participated in some of these coalition and United Front governments. The CPI(M) taunted the CPI saying that before the elections the latter had refused to enter into electoral adjustments with many parties on the ground that they were rightist parties, but after the elections it had no compunction whatsoever in forming United Front governments with them.[3]

During the elections the CPI and the CPI(M) were ranged against each other. The CPI regarded the CPI(M) as pro–Chinese, and the CPI(M) denounced the CPI as revisionist. After the elections the CPI and the CPI(M) participated in the United Front governments in Kerala and West Bengal, but the tensions between these two parties were reflected in the functioning of these United Front governments and were partially responsible for the break-up and fall of the United Front government of Kerala in October 1969 and of the United Front government of West Bengal in March 1970.

The non–Congress governments that were formed immediately after the fourth general elections broadly fell under four different classes. The first class comprised the Kerala and West Bengal United Front governments in which both the CPI and CPI(M) participated, and the composition of which governments was predominantly leftist. In the second class fell the DMK government of Madras, which had an absolute majority and was not a coalition government. The third class consisted of the early coalition governments in Bihar and Punjab which included leftist parties as also the Jana Sangh. In the fourth class fell the early coalition governments formed in Orissa, Haryana, and UP where the Jana Sangh and Swatantra and other rightist parties were in a majority. The CPI(M) regarded that the DMK government was a "left radical bourgeois" government and was prepared to give conditional support to that government,[4] but so far as the early coalition governments in Orissa, UP, and Haryana were concerned, it said that "by no stretch of imagination can these Governments be characterized as more democratic or progressive than the earlier Congress Governments."[5]

In the fourth general elections in India in 1967 the CPI(M) secured a larger number of seats in the legislature in Bengal than the CPI. The CPI(M) secured 18.10 per cent of the total votes while the CPI secured 6.53 per cent. Eventually a United Front government was established in Bengal under the leadership of Ajoy Kumar Mukherji, the Bangla Congress leader, as Chief Minister, and Jyoti Basu, the CPI(M) leader, as the Deputy Chief Minister. The Bangla Congress, the CPI(M), the CPI, the Forward Bloc, and various other parties, opposed to the Congress, participated in the United Front government.

In November 1967 this United Front Ministry was dismissed by the Governor on the ground *inter alia* that it had lost its majority. The United Front started a resistance movement including a programme of civil disobedience against this dismissal. Eventually in February 1969 a mid-term poll took place in Bengal as also in certain other states, such as Uttar Pradesh, Bihar, and Punjab. In the mid-term polls in Bengal the United Front secured an absolute majority. Accordingly a United Front government was established in Bengal and the CPI(M), the CPI, the Bangla Congress, the Forward Bloc and various other anti-Congress parties again participated therein.

As a result of the mid-term polls, the CPI(M) emerged as the largest single party in the state legislature of Bengal. E. M. S. Namboodiripad and other communist leaders have claimed that the result of the mid-term polls in Bengal has shown at once the utility of leftist United Fronts as also the inevitability of the formation, in the future, of coalition governments in India. The successes of the CPI(M) in the elections generally, and particularly in Kerala and Bengal, strengthened the belief that parliamentary methods could, along with other extra-parliamentary methods, help the party to develop and to make itself the vanguard for bringing about a communist transformation of India.

The CPI(M) attached greater significance to the victory of the United Front in Bengal than in Kerala, because the former is industrially a more advanced state. The CPI(M) considered that the United Front in Bengal, born through a process of prolonged struggle, offered an example which the other states could follow. But though the CPI(M) holds that United Fronts are necessary in the present stage of the country's political development, it is equally emphatic that they should not degenerate into mere hotch-potch coalitions of opportunistic elements. In this connection they refer to the failure of the United Fronts in Bihar and Uttar Pradesh that were set up immediately after the fourth general elections in India.

In April 1969 the politbureau of the CPI(M) declared that the acid test of every genuine democratic party, group, and individual in the present context of political developments in the country was their attitude to the United Fronts in Bengal and Kerala and to the programmes they pursued against the Congress-dominated Centre. Though all leftist forces were called upon to support these two United Front governments, the CPI(M), however, made it clear that in the existing constitutional framework the United Front governments could do very little. In fact, in July 1967, Ranadive, a leading member of the CPI(M), made a statement in London that the task of the United Front governments in West Bengal and Kerala, in which the CPI(M) had a dominant voice, was to unleash the discontent of the people rather than to give relief. This statement was criticized by the Congress, the Swatantra, the Jana Sangh, and even by the CPI, though to a lesser extent. A. K. Gopalan and E. M. S. Namboodiripad, politbureau members of the CPI(M), however, supported Ranadive and asserted that real democracy and socialism could not be ushered in without a thorough change of the Constitution.[6] They explained that the CPI(M) believed that it would not be possible for a political party, functioning within the framework of the present Constitution, to bring into being a government of the toiling people. Therefore, the struggle for a thorough change of the Constitution was part of the struggle for the establishment of real democracy and socialism.[7]

In the context of these statements on 11 July 1969 at the meeting of the All-India Congress Committee held at Bangalore, a blistering attack was made on the communists, especially those who belonged to the CPI(M), for alleged subversion of democracy by democratic tools. Referring to Ranadive's statement, which had been supported by Gopalan and Namboodiripad, Nijalingappa, the Congress president, said: "We have to take serious note of the statement. It is a challenge to democracy and independence."[8]

Basavapunniah, a politbureau member of the CPI(M), however, pointed out that nothing had been stated by Ranadive, Gopalan, or Namboodiripad which had not been stated before in the documents and resolutions of the CPI(M), and, in particular, in the political report adopted by the Central Committee of the CPI(M) at its meeting in Calcutta in April 1967. That political report had said that the essence of state power lay in the army, police, bureaucracy, judiciary, and jails and all these machinery belonged to the "bourgeois landlord" state. "In class outlook, composition and in several other respects it is not an instrument that is suitable even for the implementation of a consistently democratic administration, let alone any class policies decisively directed against the vested interests."[9] A good and essential part of state power resided in the centre and whatever small share of power the state governments possessed under the provisions of the Constitution had to be exercised within the confines of this overall central power. Under these circumstances, to speak of real political power for the state governments, and that too of non–Congress or anti–Congress governments and composed of different opposition parties, "is unreal and devoid of substance."[10] It followed, therefore, that the United Front governments should "be treated and understood as instruments of struggle in the hands of our people, more than as governments that actually possess adequate power, that can materially and substantially give relief to the people. In clear class terms, our party's participation in such governments is one of specific form of struggle to win more and more people and more and more allies for the proletariat and its allies for the struggle for the cause of people's democracy and, at a later stage, for socialism."

Gopalan also declared that there was nothing new in the statement of Ranadive, inasmuch as the CPI(M) never held that the Constitution was something holy but had always openly stated that they would change it. The two tasks of participating in a government and of changing the Constitution were not incompatible, for, in 1937, even the Congress, which came to power in many states declaring allegiance to the Government of India Act of 1935, had pledged itself to a policy which would have entailed the abrogation of the 1935 Act. "What is wrong in our doing something like that now, though in a different historical context and with an altogether different approach and purpose?" asked Gopalan.[11] Gopalan felt that within the existing constitutional framework the United Front governments would not be able to solve the economic and political problems of the people completely, and these governments should, accordingly, be treated and understood as "instruments of struggle in the hands of the people."

On 12 July 1969 Y. B. Chavan, then Home Minister, referred to the challenge to the Constitution posed by those who spoke of wrecking it from within but claimed that the Constitution was an instrument of change and a weapon which could be used to solve social, economic, and other challenges.[12] Again on 24 July 1969, V. C. Shukla, Minister of State for Home Affairs, told the Lok Sabha that there was no doubt that the "wreck the Constitution from within" statement made by Namboodiripad and Gopalan raised serious issues for it was "against the basic principles of the Constitution of India" and that it put forward a theory that was the very negation of parliamentary democracy.[13]

While the debate as to whether a political party could legitimately pursue a policy of wrecking the Constitution was going on, the DMK leader and Tamil Nadu Chief Minister, M. Karunanidhi, stated that the DMK wanted only to mend the Constitution and not to break it.[14] Even during the anti–Hindi agitation in Tamil Nadu, the Kazhagam had burnt only the language chapter of the Constitution and not the whole of it. This was because what was desired was to get the Constitution amended by deleting its language chapter and not to reject the Constitution lock, stock, and barrel.

On 11 July 1969, S. A. Dange also criticized the joint statement of Namboodiripad and Gopalan though in a different way and to a lesser extent than other parties. Referring to the CPI(M) stand that a United Front government was an instrument of struggle and that the object of participating in such government was to take the revolutionary movement forward, Dange said: "We agree with a part of this position, but not with the whole." The CPI also wanted to promote the movement towards revolution, "but what is the point in saying the Constitution is capitalist-landlord bourgeois?" asked Dange.[15] The Constitution by itself was not "capitalist-landlord" but "those who worked in New Delhi were capitalists and landlords." The Constitution should, therefore, be used to strengthen the revolution and to overthrow the Congress government in Delhi.

But notwithstanding what Dange and others said, the CPI(M) stood firm by the statement made by Ranadive. In August 1969, while addressing the students of the Delhi School of Economics, Jyoti Basu reiterated the statement that the Constitution of India was a bourgeois constitution and that the "present Constitution will have to go lock, stock, and barrel."[16] The CPI, in its turn, also continued to criticize Ranadive's statement. In September 1969 Krishnan, a CPI leader, said that the CPI was more concerned about who had power at the centre than about the Constitution, for if a progressive government came to power many things in the present Constitution could be used in favour of the people.[17]

Though the CPI(M) wanted to change the Constitution lock, stock, and barrel, yet till the time that it could bring about such a change it asked that necessary amendments be made in the Constitution so that radical economic changes could be effected. For example, in September 1969 Harekrishna Konar, Land and Land Revenue Minister of West Bengal and a CPI(M) leader, said that certain constitutional amendments were immediately necessary because the present administrative machinery was "predominantly landlord-biased" and because the landlords were rushing to civil courts and the High Court and were obtaining *ex parte ad interim* orders against the government to frustrate the land reform policy of the government. To remedy all these Konar pleaded that necessary changes should be made in the Constitution to prevent the landlords from approaching the courts against radical land reform measures.[18]

Further, in April 1969 the Central Committee of the CPI(M) called upon the United Front governments in Bengal and Kerala to take up with Central government the demand that a radical and immediate change of Centre–state relations be effected, pending changes in the Constitution of India, to enable the state governments to fulfil their pledges to the people. It emphasized that the Industrial Security Forces, the CRP and the Border Security Forces should be handed over to the states, inasmuch as it was for the states to maintain law and order within the state. It asked that all Concurrent List subjects be transferred to the States' List, more constitutional powers be granted to the states, and, pending constitutional changes to effect this, 75 per cent of the central revenues be transferred to the states, all centrally-managed agricultural, industrial, educational, and social welfare departments be handed over to the states, and matters relating to the recruitment, service conditions, and disciplinary proceedings of the officers in the cadres of IAS, ICS and other all-India services be brought within the states' jurisdiction.

In spite of the pronounced differences that existed between the CPI and CPI(M), two important constituents of the United Front governments of Kerala and West Bengal, the leaders of these two parties met at Calcutta towards the end of May 1969 to discuss the question of unity. But even on the eve of these discussions these leaders, and particularly those of the CPI(M), stressed the ideological differences that separated the two parties. A. K. Gopalan, a leader of the CPI(M) group in the Indian Parliament, declared that the two parties differed on fundamental issues, such as the future class character of a government at the centre as also in their approach to other questions. The possibility of an immediate unity of the two parties was, therefore, ruled out.

On 19 April 1969 the CPI general secretary, Rajeswar Rao, wrote to the CPI(M) general secretary, P. Sundarayya, conveying to him three proposals made by CPI's National Council, namely, the setting up of an all-India co-ordination committee with representatives from both the parties, formation of a bloc of the two parties in Parliament and state legislatures, and unity of action in mass struggles. Gopalan said that while the last proposal could be considered, the first two were impractical, because the CPI still believed in the formation of a national democratic government at the centre consisting of the peasantry, the working class, and a section of the national bourgeoisie,

24

while the CPI(M) felt that this would be tantamount to a collaboration of the toiling classes with the exploiting classes.

The leaders of the CPI(M) and the CPI met at Calcutta in May 1969. Initially they discussed the CPI proposal for united action of the two parties at the national level and in mass fronts, but such talks did not bear fruit. The emergence of the CPI(M-L) was also discussed at some length at this summit meeting; the CPI(M) spokesmen complained that the CPI was directly or indirectly abetting the Naxalites, whereas the CPI representatives, denying such a charge, stated that though they had no political sympathy with the Naxalites they, unlike the CPI(M), would not brand the CPI(M-L) as representing anti-social elements or as CIA agents. After agreeing to disagree on divers issues, the leaders of the CPI and CPI(M) eventually found a common ground in holding that the United Front was the common tactical line for both the parties.

It was agreed that the United Fronts in Kerala and West Bengal should be safeguarded, strengthened and further activized as rallying points for the democratic forces throughout the country. For this purpose open hostility and polemics of one Communist Party against the other were to be eschewed. A joint communique issued[19] at the end of these meetings said that though on the problems confronting the United Front governments in Kerala and West Bengal and on certain other matters, differences continued to exist, both sides agreed that efforts must be continued for improving the relations between the two parties and that the United Front was the common tactical line for both parties. But within six months of the issue of this joint communique the United Front government of Kerala fell due to differences between the constituent units thereof and particularly between the CPI and CPI(M). Later, in March 1970 the United Front government in Bengal also fell due to differences amongst the constituent parties thereof and particularly between the CPI(M) and the Bangla Congress, which latter was supported by the CPI.

II. INTER-PARTY CLASHES

Though the relations between the divers constituent elements of the United Front in Bengal were not always harmonious, serious differences developed among the various constituents of the United Front in Kerala much earlier than in Bengal. The furore in Kerala arose out of Chief Minister Namboodiripad's decision to order a judicial probe into the allegations of corruption against the Finance Minister, P. K. Kunju of the Indian Socialist Party (ISP). The furore somewhat subsided when the earlier implied threat of the ISP to leave the United Front did not materialize. Later, the CPI gave a three-month ultimatum to the CPI(M) to implement the 13-point programme of the Kerala United Front or face the possible desertion of the CPI from the Front.

In June 1968 Sundarayya, general secretary of the CPI(M) and A. K. Gopalan, a CPI(M) leader, in a joint statement appealed to the CPI to put an end to the "maligning press and public campaign against our party Ministers and our party leaders and against the Chief Minister" before "we reach a point of no return."[20] The CPI(M) leaders charged that instead of continuing the bilateral and multilateral talks, started some time earlier, to iron out the persisting differences, the CPI had taken recourse to the press to pursue their maligning campaign against the CPI(M).

In spite of appeals for unity, with the passage of time the disputes increased rather than diminished. The United Front Coordination Committee in Kerala failed to patch up the differences among the eight members of the Front and the people of Kerala resigned themselves to the sight of coalition partners concentrating their energies on a paper warfare against each other.

One of the main issues which divided the constituents of the United Front in Kerala was the CPI(M) claim that the Chief Minister should have the right to inquire as to whether a *prima facie* allegation against a Minister had been made out. The CPI was not agreeable to concede this right to Namboodiripad on the ground that he was "not impartial." The CPI unit in West Bengal had, however, at a meeting of the United Front in June 1969 agreed to entrust the Chief Minister of West Bengal with the right to decide whether charges against his colleagues required to be taken notice of at all. The difference in policy in West Bengal, where the Ministry was headed by Ajoy Mukherji of the Bangla Congress, with whom the CPI had friendly relations, and in Kerala, where the Ministry was headed by a CPI(M) leader, was significant and revealed the deep suspicion and distrust that the CPI had of the CPI(M) which, of course, the latter reciprocated.

The crisis in the Kerala United Front came to a head when the CPI(M) Chief Minister declined to order an inquiry into the allegations of corruption against the CPI(M) Food Minister and the Health Minister of the Karshaga Thozhilali Party (KTP), a loyal ally of the CPI(M), on the ground that there was no *prima facie* case against them. The CPI, the Muslim League, and the Indian Socialist Party, all constituents of the ruling United Front in Kerala, denounced Namboodiripad's act in giving a clean bill to his Marxist colleague and the KTP Health Minister, and charged that this was inconsistent with Namboodiripad's previous action in ordering an inquiry into allegations against the Indian Socialist Party Finance Minister P. K. Kunju (who had since resigned). A. Sreedharan, MP and chairman of the Indian Socialist Party, criticized Namboodiripad and wondered whether the CPI(M) wanted the charges against the two Ministers to lie "in the outer space with no one to look into them."[21] N. Sreekantan Nair, MP and RSP leader, stated that his party also stood firmly committed to the demand for a judicial inquiry into charges of corruption against Ministers, including those against the CPI(M) Minister and the KTP Health Minister.

In June 1969 Namboodiripad warned that the United Front in Kerala was in grave danger and charged that the CPI was mainly responsible for some of the Front partners having ranged themselves against the CPI(M) and for engineering a polarization within the Front. He called upon the CPI to mend its ways, to abandon the path of slander, and to come round to bilateral and collective discussion of all controversial issues.[22]

The continuing feud between the CPI(M) and the CPI in Kerala led to the formation of an anti-CPI(M) front within the United Front, consisting of the CPI, the ISP, the RSP, and the Muslim League. In June 1969 the CPI(M) warned other constituents of the Front of the serious consequences of aligning themselves with the CPI against the CPI(M). But Govindan Nair, the CPI Minister, said that if the CPI(M) continued to pose as a "big party" and tried to dictate terms to others in the coalition, it would affect the smooth functioning of the government. He warned that the "reactionary and sectarian" attitude adopted by the CPI(M) with regard to the inquiry into corruption charges against ministers would spell disaster for the United Front. In July 1969 the Central Executive Committee of the CPI charged that Namboodiripad was functioning as the "captain of the CPI(M) ministerial team rather than as the head of the Council of Ministers." The Committee said: "The leadership of the CPI(M) has been following a policy of narrow partisan aggrandisement as well as of sectarianism.... The CPI(M) has been systematically using its strength and position not to sustain and strengthen the United Front or its Government, but to browbeat, weaken, if not eliminate, other partners in the Front."[23]

In October 1969 Namboodiripad decided to refer to a commission of inquiry the corruption charges against the CPI and ISP Ministers along with those against B. Wellingdon of the KTP, but he did not order any inquiry against the charges brought against CPI(M) Ministers. Protesting against this decision, ministers belonging to four parties, namely, the CPI, the Muslim League, the Indian Socialist Party, and the Revolutionary Socialist Party, resigned.

On 19 October 1969 these four parties, also described as the mini-front, declared that the continuance of the Namboodiripad ministry was against the mandate given by the people to the United Front and that the United Front "was wrecked by the sectarian big party bossism" of the CPI(M).[24] The four parties said that the CPI(M) Chief Minister had misused his powers and had adopted double standards with regard to the probe into corruption charges as was evident from the fact that when charges were made first against three ministers, one each of ISP, CPI(M), and KTP, the Chief Minister chose to order an inquiry into the charges against the ISP Minister only, and exonerated the CPI(M) Minister and the Minister belonging to the KTP party, which was loyal to the CPI(M). P. Ramamurthy of the CPI(M), on the other hand, accused the CPI of trying to break up the United Front in Kerala, and added: "Probably the CPI thinks that it can form a United Front with the Congress Party, as represented by Mrs Indira Gandhi, which, according to it, has become progressive."[25]

In the face of an impending collapse of the United Front government in Kerala, Z. A. Ahmed, member of the CPI Central

Executive, warned: "If the two Communist Parties and other left and democratic elements cannot pull together in a purposeful manner and give a stable and progressive government to a small State like Kerala, the prospect of Indian political life marching ahead is bleak indeed."[26] But events were moving inexorably towards a showdown between the CPI(M) and the CPI.

On 24 October 1969 a motion supported by the four parties of the mini-front calling for an inquiry against all the ministers charged with corruption was voted by a majority of 69 to 60. (The CPI(M) had a strength of 52 members in a house of 133.) Namboodiripad resigned and the 31–month old United Front ministry of Kerala came to an end. Neither the CPI(M) nor the CPI central leadership really wanted the United Front government in Kerala to fall, but the logic of events and the uncompromising attitude of the state units of the two parties led to the break-up of the United Front in Kerala, leaving behind a trail of charges and counter-charges: the CPI accusing the CPI(M) of bossism, of big brotherly attitude, and of using the administrative machinery to subserve the interests of the CPI(M), whereas the CPI(M) continued to charge the CPI of having conspired with the Congress to disrupt the United Front.

On 31 October 1969 a non-CPI(M) and non-Congress ministry was formed in Kerala with C. Achutha Menon of the CPI as the Chief Minister. Besides the CPI, the Muslim League, the Indian Socialist Party, and the rebel Kerala Congress, which the CPI likened to Bangla Congress, joined the ministry. The RSP supported the ministry but did not participate in it. The CPI(M) observed a "Betrayal Day" as the new Kerala ministry took over and Jyoti Basu dubbed the ministry as worse than a Congress government.[27]

The mini-front government that was set up in Kerala under the leadership of Achutha Menon in October 1969 had a brief existence. Finding that the majority that he enjoyed was not sufficient for the functioning of a stable government in Kerala, Achutha Menon advised dissolution of the Assembly and the holding of a mid-term poll, which was eventually held in September 1970.

The alignment of parties during this mid-term poll was significant. The CPI led a mini-front which contained, apart from the

CPI, the Muslim League, the RSP and the PSP. The other leftist front was led by the CPI(M) and its constituents included the SSP, the KTP and the KSP. It is noteworthy that the SSP, which in Bengal is hostile to the CPI(M), was a constituent of the CPI(M)-led front in the Kerala, whereas the RSP, which in Bengal is closely aligned with the CPI(M) was a constituent of the CPI-led front that was pledged to the task of electorally and politically containing the CPI(M).

Apart from the mini-front led by the CPI and the other front led by the CPI(M), there was yet another front in Kerala called the Democratic Front which was led by the Congress (o). This front included, amongst others, the Congress (o), the Kerala Congress, the ISP, the Jana Sangh and the Swatantra.

As a result of the mid-term poll in Kerala, the Congress (R) along with the CPI-led mini-front secured an absolute majority. In the 133-member Assembly this alliance secured 68 seats, the Congress (R) having 32 seats, the CPI 16, the Muslim League 11, the RSP 6 and the PSP 3. The Congress (R) emerged as the largest single party in the state. The CPI(M), which previously was the largest single party in the Kerala Assembly holding 52 seats, secured 28 seats in mid-term poll. In 1967 the undivided Congress had contested all the 133 seats and had secured only 9 seats, but in the mid-term election in 1970 the Congress (R) secured as many as 32 seats.

The results of this mid-term poll greatly encouraged the Congress (R). The Congress (o), on the other hand, failed to secure any seat at all. The position was likewise for two of its allies, namely, the Jana Sangh and the Swatantra. The results of the Kerala mid-term poll are given in the table on the next page.

The results of the Kerala mid-term poll were particularly gratifying for the Congress (R) inasmuch as it not only succeeded, on the basis of an electoral understanding with the CPI, in electorally containing the CPI(M) but it was also able to demonstrate its superior political appeal to the people vis-a-vis the Congress (o). Jagjivan Ram, the president of Congress (R), claimed that the electorate of Kerala had indicated their preference for the peaceful and democratic parties and Siddhartha Sankar Ray, a member of the Congress (R) Working Committee, claimed that the results demonstrated that the Congress (R) was the real Congress and, furthermore, that the CPI(M) was a paper tiger.

KERALA ASSEMBLY MID-TERM ELECTIONS: 1970

Total seats: 133

		Electorate	:	*10,170,038*
		Valid votes polled	:	*7,508,635*

Party	Seats contested	Seats won	Votes polled
Congress (R)	56	32	1,372,346
CPI (M)-led Front:			
CPI(M)	72	28	1,759,797
SSP	14	6	306,763
KTP	4	2	90,953
KSP	3	2	49,345
CPI-led Front:			
CPI	31	16	701,558
Muslim League	20	11	579,320
RSP	14	6	330,983
PSP	7	2	182,760
Congress (o)-led Democratic Front:			
Congress (o)	39	nil	261,057
Kerala Congress	31	12	443,232
ISP	11	3	244,205
Independents	92	12	1,098,733
Jana Sangh	8	nil	45,079
DMK	6	nil	19,309
Swatantra	2	nil	7,982
Revolutionary Communist Party	6	nil	5,127
Vettuva Mahasabha	4	nil	2,508
Kerala Karshaka Party	3	nil	5,048
RPI	1	nil	1,242
Socialist Unity Centre	1	nil	1,288

The success of the Congress (R) in Kerala was, however, a personal victory for Indira Gandhi because it was she who was in favour of the Congress (R) entering into an electoral understanding with the CPI. Jagjivan Ram and Fakhruddin Ali Ahmed openly and Chavan diplomatically had resisted an alliance or an understanding with the CPI-led front. They did not want the Congress to associate either with communists or the Muslim League. But in the course of her election campaign at Kerala Indira Gandhi declared that the pattern of the electoral understanding that was reached for the state of Kerala between the

Congress (R) and the CPI may, in future, develop into a national pattern for these parties. Such an electoral understanding or alliance at the national level was bound to have far-reaching consequences. All eyes were, therefore, turned to Kerala. The fact that such an understanding yielded substantial dividends for the Congress (R) in the mid-term poll at Kerala strengthened the hands of those inside the Congress who envisaged such an understanding or alliance at the national level.

But though the Congress (R) entered into an electoral understanding with the CPI, there were natural reservations on the part of Congress (R) in joining a government formed by the CPI-led front. The RSP made it known beforehand that it would not join a government of which the Congress (R) was a constituent. Within the state unit of the Congress (R) itself, and particularly among its younger section, there was also reluctance in joining a government formed by the CPI-led front. Association with a government of which the Muslim League was a part could also have adverse repercussions in the country, and particularly in northern India, so far as the Congress (R) was concerned. Eventually it was decided that the Congress (R) would support the CPI-led government but would not join it. This decision also facilitated the participation in the Achutha Menon government of the RSP, which had previously expressed its unwillingness to join a government of which the Congress (R) was a constituent.

But this decision of the state unit of the RSP to participate in the Achutha Menon government, which was dependent on Congress (R) support, precipitated a crisis in the RSP itself. The West Bengal and Kerala units of the RSP held diametrically opposite views in the matter. Whereas the West Bengal unit of the RSP is more or less aligned with CPI(M) and is anti–Congress (R), its Kerala unit is positively anti–CPI(M) and had fought the mid-term poll on the basis of an understanding with the Congress (R). Tridib Choudhury, the chairman of the party, was opposed to RSP's participation in the Achutha Menon government and the central leadership of the party threatened to suspend any of its members who joined such a government. The Kerala unit of the party defied this injunction issued by the central party organization and joined the Achutha Menon government.

Although political and other conditions in the two states of

Kerala and West Bengal were different, the United Front partners in West Bengal had been uneasy over the developments in Kerala long before the disruption of the United Front there in October 1969. Further, inter-party clashes in West Bengal had also developed at an early stage.

In fact, immediately after the mid-term elections in February 1969 there had developed a serious controversy within the United Front over who should hold the office of the Chief Minister. The CPI(M), the largest single party in the United Front, pressed its claim to that office. Though the CPI(M) eventually refrained from pressing its claim so far as to cause a split or to risk the chance of the United Front being unable to form a government, in accordance with the eventual compromise that was reached the CPI(M) obtained the important Home portfolio and divers other important portfolios. Ajoy Mukherji became the Chief Minister, but the preeminent position of the CPI(M) in the United Front government could not be ignored. In fact, representatives of business and trade chose Jyoti Basu, Deputy Chief Minister and CPI(M) leader, and not the Chief Minister, for their dialogue. In these circumstances Ajoy Mukherji allowed himself to be sidetracked on many important issues showing thereby that he was aware of the limitations within which he functioned. On law and order matters, in particular, he generally avoided comments till sometime in October 1969.

One of the causes of the differences among the members of the United Front in Bengal, in the early stages of its existence, was their approach to the policy of *gherao* (confinement). *Gherao* came into prominence when Subodh Bannerjee of the SUC was the Labour Minister of the first United Front government of Bengal in 1967. *Gherao* again became a controversial question after the United Front government was returned to power in February 1969 as a result of the mid-term elections. Congressmen condemned *gherao* altogether. Gulzarilal Nanda, Congress leader and the president of the Indian National Trade Union Congress, declared that the *gherao* was the ugliest form of violence and could not be tolerated. It was, he said, also inimical to the interests of the workers, for it gave rise to a law and order problem, and disturbed industrial peace so much so that the government, which had once encouraged this dangerous weapon, has now "itself fallen victim to it."[28] In saying that the government had fallen victim to *gherao*, Nanda was referring to the *gherao* of Sushil Dhara, Bangla Congress leader and Industries Minister in the West Bengal Cabinet, by some workers. Sushil Dhara even undertook a fast in protest against the policy of *gherao*. The Bangla Congress in general was opposed to the resort to *gherao*.

The CPI(M) regarded *gherao* as only one among numerous forms of struggle employed by workers to realize some of their day-to-day economic and other demands, and not as something which could be condemned outright. It was opposed to the Bangla Congress suggestion "of depriving the workers of this small right which they have come to avail under the United Front." In June 1969 a fairly authoritative enunciation of the CPI(M)'s view on the controversial subject of *gherao* was given by Basavapunniah. Basavapunniah stated that he was not oblivious of the fact that there were quite a few cases where the right to *gherao* had been improperly used and indiscreetly resorted to in certain essential services, like electric supply and hospitals, which are normally excluded even from the ambit of general strikes or *hartals*. "We now hear Ministers being *gheraoed* by their staff, teachers by their students, and parents by their children. It has now reached such ludicrous lengths."[29] Though these "abuses and excesses" had to be looked into, according to Basavapunniah, the real question before the United Front and the government is "not either to support the right of *gherao* in the abstract and upholding all *gheraos* or deny the right in principle and oppose it, as some tend to pose it." What was necessary was a case-by-case examination of *gheraos* by the government in order to find out whether this method of struggle was discreetly used or grossly abused. To Basavapunniah, *gherao* carried with it "a certain amount of moral pressure and coercion" but not violence.

But in June 1969 Ajoy Mukherji, the Bangla Congress leader and the United Front Chief Minister, said that if the existing trend of *gherao* continued it might affect fresh private investment to the extent of Rs 600 to 700 crores in the great petrochemical complex that was to grow near the proposed oil refinery at Haldia.[30] He suggested the formation of a tripartite body acceptable to both labour and management to stop *gheraos*, retrenchments, closures, and lay-offs. Ajoy Mukherji said that as a government "we must support the weaker party but not at the cost of the State's industrial development, which would weaken the employment potential."[31] He apprehended that gheraos would lead to flight of capital to other states, specially in a situation where other states, such as Gujarat and Maharashtra, were wooing industrialists in Bengal to make fresh investments there.

On 2 June 1969 the Bangla Congress Secretariat adopted a resolution stating that "gherao should not be allowed under any circumstances."[32] But though quite a number of United Front partners wanted to restrict gherao they were not in favour of banning it completely. The representatives of industry in Bengal, however, urged upon the United Front government to take steps to put an end to gheraos. At one of the meetings between the representatives of industry and labour, Krishnapada Ghosh, Labour Minister of the United Front government of Bengal, said that he would not comment on whether gherao was good or bad but he knew that its incidence could not be stopped by rifles and that gherao could be minimized only through successful negotiations.

Eventually in July 1969 the United Front Cabinet of West Bengal discussed gherao. The consensus reached at this meeting was that a total ban on gherao was neither desirable nor feasible.[33] Though the Bangla Congress Secretariat had passed a resolution that gherao should not be allowed under any circumstances, representatives of the Bangla Congress in the government acquiesced in the Cabinet decision in view of the overwhelming sentiment among the constituents of the United Front that gherao should not be banned altogether. Somnath Lahiri, the CPI leader, felt that gherao was only the symptom of a disease and the United Front should try to diagnose the disease and prescribe accordingly. The CPI(M) was also not agreeable to ban gheraos altogether. The RCPI considered that it was for the workers to choose how far they would employ gherao as a form of struggle. The Lok Sevak Sangh hoped that gherao could be systematized and conducted on peaceful lines. The PSP (Dissidents) felt that gheraos would continue in some form or other. The Marxist Forward Bloc opposed the adoption of a policy of gherao on minor issues or on flimsy grounds, but like most other parties, it was firmly against a total ban on *gheraos*.

The Congress and certain other parties condemned *gherao* in unmistakable terms. They pointed out that *gherao* is nothing but a form of wrongful restraint or confinement, and an offence under the law. As *gherao* had already been banned under the laws of the land, it was not open for the United Front government to consider whether or not it should be banned. The only question before the government was whether they would enforce the laws of the land which had already banned *gherao* or whether they would seek to place the government or executive above the laws of the land and by executive fiats paralyse or nullify those laws. The question raised the constitutional issue as to whether a government could pick and choose among the laws of the land and enforce some and not others, that is to say, whether by executive veto the rule of law could be subverted.

But even apart from the question of *gherao* there were various other matters on which the different constituent parties of the United Front in Bengal differed. In fact, from an early stage some of the parties had complained that the CPI(M), the largest single party in the government, had adopted an overbearing attitude towards the other constituents. On 15 June 1969 the CPI general secretary, Rajeswar Rao, urged the CPI(M) to give up its "dictatorial attitude" and to ensure proper functioning of the United Front governments. These governments had projected before the country a progressive and democratic path for the solution of economic, political, and other problems and the elimination of vested interests, such as the monopolists and landlords, who were "aided and abetted by the Central Congress Government." "But unfortunately," said Rajeswar Rao, "the CPI(M) leadership has been adopting a domineering attitude towards the other constituents, particularly towards the CPI. In fact, it has been adopting a hostile attitude towards us."[34]

Adverting to Rajeswar Rao's allegation that the CPI(M) had adopted a "domineering attitude," Promode Das Gupta, secretary of the West Bengal unit of the CPI(M) and a member of the party's politbureau, charged that the CPI was conducting a "disruptive vilification campaign" against the CPI(M).[35] In addition to the CPI, Promode Das Gupta attacked the Forward Bloc, SUC, and PSP. He criticized the Forward Bloc and SUC who had demanded the immediate resignation of the Food Minister, Sudhin Kumar (RCPI), from the Cabinet and he charged that these parties were playing to the tune of the reactionary forces which sought to disrupt the United Front. Referring to the CPI, Das Gupta said: "It must be clearly understood that communism and revisionism cannot go together. But we will continue talking with them, whenever they propose talks, as long as they are in the United Front. United action on specific issues is possible even with revisionists."[36] Replying to the CPI charge that the CPI(M) had adopted a domineering attitude, Das Gupta asserted that it was the CPI which wanted to dominate, although it did not have the necessary strength. The CPI(M) had emerged as the biggest party after the mid-term polls in Bengal in 1969, but the CPI at first not only objected to a CPI(M) nominee becoming the Chief Minister but also to the Home portfolio being given to the CPI(M).[37]

In order to resolve the differences between the different constituents of the United Front in Bengal, in June 1969 Promode Das Gupta prepared a note for consideration by the "Big Five" of the United Front. This note pointed out, firstly, that the United Front experiment was unprecedented and, therefore, its course could only be charted through trial and error and, secondly, that there was nothing unusual if all the partners sought to utilize the opportunity provided by the existence of a United Front government to further their interests politically and organizationally. But this did not mean that conflicts and clashes among the partners were inevitable or could not be averted. If the compelling force behind the formation of the United Front had been the desire to defeat the Congress, a determination to reverse the policies introduced by the previous Congress régimes could be the rallying point for the United Front as a whole, and the constituents could work together on the basis of a common programme relating to land, labour, food, and other matters in which the great mass of the people were concerned.[38]

Disputes between the constituent units of the United Front, however, continued. In June 1969 the CPI's West Bengal State Council adopted a political resolution which accused the CPI(M) of using the governmental machinery to further its own organizational interests.[39] In June 1969 the Samyukta Socialist Party (ssp) also asked Ajoy Mukherji, West Bengal's Chief Minister, "to exert his authority and influence in the United Front to prevent the cpi(m) from acting in a manner calculated to wreck people's unity achieved in the state."[40] George Fernandes, the ssp general secretary, referred to "the continued acts of assault and coercion perpetrated by cpi(m) workers against ssp workers in West Bengal."[41] After cataloguing the "excursions in violence by the cpi(m) in West Bengal" the ssp leader also warned that it might have repercussions everywhere "with the cpi(m) violence being met with similar acts of violence by others."[42]

In June 1969 the West Bengal unit of the psp charged the cpi(m) with "political hypocrisy in posing to run the administration democratically although not having faith in parliamentary democracy and thereby confusing the people and creating an acute crisis in the public life of the State." The Naxalites were clear in their stand inasmuch as they declared that they, as Maoists, did not believe in the parliamentary form of democracy. So in their case, unlike as in the case of the cpi(m), there was no cause for any confusion in the public mind. The political resolution passed by the West Bengal unit of the psp stated that the programme followed by the communists in West Bengal was an example of the phased movement of revolutionary tactics of classical communism and that although the communist bloc was vociferous in their criticism of the activities of the Naxalites, there was, in fact, no basic difference between the politics of the communists and the Naxalites. The resolution further stated that the people of Bengal had voted the United Front to power for solving the problems of the people through parliamentary democracy and for running the administration honestly and justly "and not for creating chaos by *gheraos,* anarchy, and suicidal activities."

In these criticisms made by the cpi, ssp, and psp, the cpi(m) discerned a sinister conspiracy. In June 1969 the West Bengal State Committee of the cpi(m) called upon the people to frustrate "a deep-laid conspiracy from within and without the Front" against the progressive measures of the United Front government. It said that the failure to fix priorities within the framework of the 32–point programme of the United Front of Bengal had led to the perfunctory functioning of the government, that primary attention should be given to problems relating to land, labour, and food, and that the "new conspiracies of jotedars and vested interests including the Congress and other reactionaries hatched in league with a certain section of the bureaucracy and the police" should be defeated by strengthening the leftist democratic movements.

The inter-party clashes between the constituents of the United Front in Bengal, on occasions, led to violence, assault, and even murder. Leaders of the "Big Five" of the United Front in Bengal, namely, the CPI(M), CPI, Bangla Congress, RSP, and Forward Bloc, had met towards the end of May 1969 and had considered concrete measures for stopping these clashes. During these meetings three important reasons as to why such clashes were taking place were suggested. First, since the mid-term elections of 1969 there had been an influx of anti-social elements, former Congress supporters, jotedars, hoarders and other vested interests, and of people having links with organizations like the CIA, into the ranks of almost all the Front constituents. These newcomers exploited the differences among the Front partners and sought to create trouble within the Front in an attempt to disrupt it. Secondly, sections of the bureaucracy and the police were deliberately trying to accentuate inter-party tensions either by overacting in certain situations in favour of one constituent or another or by remaining passive observers in other. The third cause that was suggested was that the concept of the United Front had not been fully appreciated by the rank and file of the constituent parties. It was felt that neither the newcomers nor the bureaucracy could act as they did had the concept of the United Front percolated down to the lower levels of the constituent parties. The crux of the issue was that at lower levels each Front constituent acted entirely on its own.

The fact that the "Big Five" had left out the other parties of the Front in their discussions created further dissensions within the front. On 13 July 1969, Nihar Mukherjee, secretary of the SUC, said that the five-party meeting on inter-party clashes had undermined the United Front's image before the people. Further, these five big parties had considered the issue in a very "superficial manner": they had failed to locate the major factor responsible for the clashes which, according to him, was that the CPI(M) was trying to emerge as the "only party" in West Bengal and to eliminate the other parties.[43] The SUC charged that the

CPI(M) was using the administration and the police in its party interests and that it sought to "intensify class struggles in the areas of influence of other parties" while coexisting "happily with class enemies in those areas where it has its own bases."

Disputes within the United Front were further accentuated when on 2 September 1969 the CPI stayed away from the West Bengal United Front meeting in protest against the alleged assault on some of its workers by CPI(M) workers in Baranagore on 30 August 1969. In a letter addressed to the United Front and circulated to its various constituents immediately before this meeting—which the CPI boycotted—Dr Ranen Sen, secretary of the West Bengal State Council of the CPI, detailed the circumstances in which the secretary of the party's Baranagore Local Committee, Sibapada Bhattacharyya, and two other workers had been brutally assaulted by a number of men armed with iron rods and lathis on 30 August 1969. Sibapada Bhattacharyya while lying in hospital in a critical condition made a statement to the police naming three men as his assailants. One of the alleged assailants was the secretary of the local unit of the CPI(M). It was stated in this letter that Somnath Lahiri, CPI Minister, had requested Jyoti Basu, CPI(M) Home Minister, to have the assailants arrested, but this was not done. "Several hours after the murderous assault on Mr Bhattacharyya, the alleged assailant," the letter continued, "together with some men armed with lathis and with the help of the police 'arrested' some four of our comrades who were kept in police custody till about 12 noon next day. The minimum that should have been done in the circumstances was to apprehend the assailants named by Mr Bhattacharyya, and then go through the necessary legal process. But this has not been done. The alleged assailant has been allowed to incite further violence openly and our people have been arrested at his instance."[44] Dr Ranen Sen stated that it was an intolerable situation and the CPI was, therefore, unable to attend United Front meetings to discuss normal business or to argue on paper proposals about stopping physical violence on comrades of the same front.

This boycott by the CPI of the United Front upset Jyoti Basu and he wondered whether the CPI wanted to break the United Front of Bengal. Jyoti Basu and Promode Das Gupta felt that the CPI had given a blow to the United Front at a time when

25

the different measures taken by the United Front government had encouraged an increasing number of farmers and workers to assert their rights, and when the jute, tea, and textile workers of the state had waged glorious struggles. Jyoti Basu charged that the CPI had all along been suffering from a fear complex in respect of the CPI(M): it appeared to wish for the growth of the United Front, but without any commensurate increase in the strength of the CPI(M).

In September 1969 the West Bengal State Council of the CPI decided to "expose" the role of the CPI(M) in the United Front in West Bengal and to draw the attention of the people to the "brankrupt opportunistic line" that it was pursuing.[45] The State CPI's secretary, Dr Ranen Sen, asserted that the CPI(M) was behaving in "an authoritarian manner" and that Jyoti Basu was misusing the police force to further the interests of the CPI(M). The West Bengal State Council of the CPI also referred to "the reign of terror" created by CPI(M) workers in Baranagore to silence possible witnesses in respect of the assaults on CPI workers on 30 August 1969.[46]

Leaders of the constituent partners of the United Front in West Bengal were uneasy about the manner in which the crisis within the United Front in West Bengal was developing on the lines it had previously developed in Kerala. In September 1969 a CPI(M) member of parliament, K. P. Subramaniam Menon, said that the CPI was repeating the same strategy in West Bengal which it had earlier followed in Kerala, that it was spreading the propaganda that its members were being beaten up by CPI(M) workers, that the CPI(M) was sheltering the assailants and preventing the police from taking action. Menon thought that the CPI was subject to internal pressures which had given rise to "their pro-unity resolutions and anti-unity misdeeds."[47]

A dramatic turn was given to the dissensions inside the United Front when early in October 1969 the Bangla Congress adopted a political resolution suggesting that almost every sphere of life has been disrupted during the seven months of United Front rule in West Bengal. The resolution, which read like a bill of indictment of the United Front, stated that inter-party clashes, gheraos, repressive measures in educational institutions, forcible occupation of land, police inaction, a general deterioration in the law and order situation, activities of anti-social elements protected by different political parties, indignities suffered by women and the indifference of the administration had combined to create a deep sense of insecurity and uncertainty among the people. The resolution said that peace in industries had not been maintained, *gheraos* and excessive and often unreasonable and unjustified demands which had been put forward, hampered production and had completely disrupted the economy. The resolution warned that "if such clashes and lawlessness were not stopped immediately, the Bangla Congress would be compelled to build up a resistance movement on Gandhian lines to end this intolerable situation."[48]

Jyoti Basu reacted sharply to the Bangla Congress resolution and said that the Bangla Congress allegation that during the seven months' rule of the United Front several hundred people had lost their lives "was absurd."[49] Mr Basu denied that as a result of *gheraos* or the demands of workers the economy had been disrupted. He claimed that there had only been seven or eight cases of forcible seizure of land, and said that such land had been restored to the owners. Further, Mr Basu charged that the Bangla Congress resolution had listed only "some negative features" and did not mention how the United Front rule had benefited the workers, landless agricultural workmen, teachers, and office employees.

. The Bangla Congress resolution which referred in special to police inaction was directed primarily against the CPI(M) for the Home portfolio was in the charge of Jyoti Basu of the CPI(M). Coming as it did in close succession to similar attacks on the CPI(M) by some other partners of the United Front, like the Forward Bloc and the CPI, the Bangla Congress's indictment assumed more than its usual importance and the question arose as to whether the Bangla Congress resolution was part of an attempt to isolate the CPI(M) within the Front or was part of a pressure tactics in order to contain the CPI(M). Some of the Front constituents had reacted sharply against the incidents of intimidation and harassment of their workers by persons allegedly belonging to the CPI(M) and the accompanying "police inaction." They said that they were disillusioned because the CPI(M) with "its domineering influence" was using the political and administrative machinery to strengthen and develop its party and to eliminate other parties and unless they resisted they may be "swallowed up" by the CPI(M).

The politbureau of the CPI(M) declared that the Bangla Congress resolution to the effect that law and order had broken down in West Bengal, hundreds had been killed, a severe crisis had been brought about in the industry because of *gheraos*, and that no action has been taken in murder cases, would only help the opponents of the United Front government and the vested interests.[50] The charges made by the Bangla Congress were the same as had been made "by the Congress Party and other enemies." According to Harekrishna Konar, the resolution proved to the hilt the correctness of the Marxian analysis that the vested interests in both industry and land were unhappy over the developments in West Bengal where the toiling people had, through their unity, made considerable headway, that as the Congress Party had suffered decline, these interests needed some forum in the United Front to reflect their views and the Bangla Congress resolution represented the views of these vested interests. "I do not like to call the Bangla Congress the agent of the vested interests, but it has lent itself, may be unknowingly, to be used by them."[51]

In protest against the deteriorating law and order situation in West Bengal the Bangla Congress, headed by the Chief Minister of the United Front government of West Bengal, launched a mass *satyagraha* accompanied by fasting from 1 December 1969. The spectacle of the Chief Minister fasting against the policy pursued by his own government was unprecedented. The *satyagraha* was directed against what the Bangla Congress called police inaction and police partisanship in favour of the CPI(M). When the second United Front government was formed in West Bengal in 1969, by agreement between the constituents of the Front, the Home portfolio was allotted to the CPI(M). Ajoy Mukherji argued that inasmuch as the Home portfolio had been allotted to the CPI(M) by agreement among the constituents of the United Front, he could not exercise the normal right of a Chief Minister to take over the Home portfolio or to reallocate work among the Ministers except in an emergency.[52]

Ajoy Mukherji, therefore, undertook a three days' fast along with many other Bangla Congress workers and supporters throughout Bengal from 1 December 1969. During this fast particularly, and also prior and subsequent thereto, Ajoy Mukherji denounced the law and order situation in West Bengal in unmistakable terms. He said: "The state must protect the life and property of the people, but unfortunately it is not being done in West Bengal. There is no precedent for this state of affairs in a civilized world. Not to speak of improvement in the law and order situation, murders, violent clashes, looting, *gheraos*, and forcible occupation of land have become the order of the day in West Bengal. There is no denying the fact that people, particularly in rural areas, have become panicky and in many places a sense of insecurity of life and property has gripped the population."[53]

Ajoy Mukherji was asked whether his criticism of the law and order situation in West Bengal was not tantamount to indictment of his own government and he replied: "You may think so. But a fact is a fact."[54] It was clear from the utterances of Ajoy Mukherji and Sushil Dhara, the general secretary of the Bangla Congress, that their real grievance was against the CPI(M), whom they characterized as pursuing an aggressive and sectarian policy.[55] As the *satyagraha* movement of the Bangla Congress developed Ajoy Mukherji's criticism of the law and order situation in West Bengal became increasingly strident. He said: "If the people of West Bengal think that the present state of lawlessness should continue we shall silently bid them farewell. We shall quit. We shall never be a party to the prevailing barbarism."[56] After his three days' fast, Ajoy Mukherji toured various parts of Bengal saying that arson, looting, and molestation of women by "youths with red scarves round their necks" were being carried on in the name of class struggle.[57]

Later, the SSP and the PSP (Dissidents) also joined the Bangla Congress in the mass *satyagraha* or fast in protest against police inaction. The Bangla Congress *satyagraha* movement created considerable tension within the United Front. On 2 December 1969 E. M. S. Namboodiripad, the CPI(M) leader from Kerala, said that the United Front in Bengal was on the verge of break-down because the Bangla Congress and certain other parties, particularly the CPI, were bent on splitting it. Such a charge was also made by Jyoti Basu who said that the Bangla Congress

was walking into the trap set up by the Congress to isolate the
CPI(M) from rest of the United Front.[58]

After Ajoy Mukherji had described the government in Bengal
as barbaric it was clear that the days of the United Front government in Bengal were numbered. He said that unless the law
and order situation improved he would resign and, eventually,
he set a date for his resignation. Various constituents within the
Front sought to dissuade him from resigning but without any
success. Ajoy Mukherji resigned on 16 March 1969. With his
resignation the United Front government came to an end in
Bengal and, as no alternative government could be formed,
President's rule was imposed on the state.

After the second United Front government in Bengal fell in
March 1970 with the resignation of Ajoy Mukherji the constituents of the old United Front were divided broadly into two
groups, one, led by the CPI(M), called the Six-Party Combination and the other comprising of the CPI, the Forward Bloc, the
SUC and others known as the Eight-Party Combination. The
Bangla Congress did not belong to either of these combinations:
it was anti–CPI(M) and, therefore, hostile to the Six-Party Combination, but it did not also feel at home with the Eight-Party
Combination having certain differences with it on the question
of law and order and on economic issues. As the Bangla Congress did not join the Eight-Party Combination, from time to
time discussions were held between the leaders of the Bangla
Congress and the Congress (R) so that some understanding
could be arrived at between these two parties.

The old United Front of Bengal which contained, amongst
others, the CPI(M), the CPI and the Bangla Congress, was hope-
lessly split when Ajoy Mukherji resigned in March 1970 and
the differences between the CPI and the CPI(M) increased rather
than diminished with the passage of time. So far as the Bangla
Congress is concerned it considered that the CPI(M) was
the greatest enemy of law and order in Bengal and it vowed
that it would never again make an alliance with the CPI(M) or
participate in any government with that party. The CPI(M), on
the other hand, has denounced the Bangla Congress as a reactionary party of the jotedars. The differences between the
CPI(M) and certain parties belonging to the Eight-Party Combination, such as the CPI, Forward Bloc and the SUC, are acute and

the same have on many occasions led to violent clashes. The differences between the CPI and the CPI(M) are the gravest, the CPI(M) claiming that the CPI, which had entered into an electoral understanding with the Congress (R) during the mid-term poll in Kerala in September 1970 in order to contain the CPI(M), has completely renounced Marxism, has become utterly revisionist and has begotten the "bastard child of Congress-Communism."[59]

The differences between the Six-Party Combination led by the CPI(M) and the Eight-Party Combination, led by the CPI, the Forward Bloc, the SUC and others are so acute and grave that the possibility of the formation of another United Front in Bengal which would contain all the previous constituents of the old United Front appears remote. The division of the leftist parties into two separate united fronts represented by the Eight-Party Combination and the Six-Party Combination have crystallized and there is no sign of such division disappearing. On the contrary, with the intensification of the differences between the two fronts that were begotten out of the old leftist United Front of Bengal the aversion to the Congress as such has somewhat diminished. The split inside the Congress into the Congress (R) and the Congress (O) also tended to lessen the antipathy that the leftist parties previously had towards that section within the Congress which eventually constituted the Congress (R). Furthermore, the fact that on many national issues the leftist parties in Parliament, such as the CPI and the PSP, have supported the Congress (R) and the fact that on these issues the Congress (R) was opposed by the Congress (O) along with certain rightist parties including the Jana Sangh and the Swatantra, diminished the gulf that separated the leftist parties, and particularly the CPI and the PSP, from the Congress (R).

In the mid-term poll in Kerala held in September 1970 the Congress (R) entered into an electoral understanding with the CPI. This understanding proved beneficial to the Congress (R) and the mini-front, led by the CPI, inasmuch as they taken together secured an absolute majority in the Kerala legislature. The results of this mid-term poll and the electoral understanding that had been entered into there between Congress (R) and the CPI had their inevitable repercussions in Bengal. The question arose in Bengal too as to whether an electoral understanding between the Congress (R) and the CPI should be arrived at. But among the left parties of Bengal the spirit of anti–Congressism was stronger than in Kerala. Accordingly, from time to time assurances were sought for by some of the allies of the CPI in the Eight-Party Combination in Bengal, namely, the Forward Bloc and the SUC, that the CPI would not enter into an electoral understanding with Congress (R). Such assurances were given.

But in October 1970 there was a significant shift in the policy of the CPI. In October 1970 the National Council of the CPI passed a resolution condemning "the obsolete concept of anti–Congressism" and giving a call for the formation of a broad anti–CPI(M) front in Bengal. This was to be achieved first by inducing the Bangla Congress to join the Eight-Party Combination and then this Nine-Party Combination was to enter into an electoral understanding with the Congress (R). The old United Front was, therefore, not to be revived but a new democratic front was to be formed against the CPI(M), which the CPI regarded as disruptionist, as also against the rightist forces represented by the Congress (O). But the suggestion made in the CPI resolution that there should be an understanding with the Congress (R) did not find favour with the Forward Bloc, SUC and other partners of the CPI in the Eight-Party Combination. The Patna session of the Congress, held soon after this resolution of the CPI, also refused to commit the Congress (R) beforehand to an alliance with the CPI at the national level and decided that the Congress should enter into local adjustments with such parties as may appear beneficial to it. Early in December 1970 Indira Gandhi too declared that there was no possibility of the Congress (R) entering into a Kerala-type electoral adjustment with the CPI at the national level.[60]

Though the CPI favoured an electoral adjustment with the Congress (R), the SSP remained wedded to its policy of unmitigated anti-Congressism.[61] It took part in an anti-Congress SVD ministry, first in Uttar Pradesh and later in Bihar in December 1970, which was an eventful month. On December 15, 1970 the Supreme Court, by a majority of 9 to 2, struck down the presidential order derecognizing the princes. Indira Gandhi reacted saying that the government was committed to abolishing the princely privileges lawfully, but some leftist parties, and particularly the CPI[62] and the CPI(M),[63] denounced this decision outright. Soon thereafter, on December 27, 1970 the Lok Sabha was dissolved and Indira Gandhi declared that in the mid-term elections that would follow she would seek a fresh mandate from the people for her policies of socialism and secularism. This dissolution came at a time when the differences between the Eight-Party Combination and the Six-Party Combination in Bengal were as grave as ever and it was clear that they would have to face the mid-term elections separately.

NOTES AND REFERENCES

1. *New Situation and Party's Tasks, Political Report Adopted by the Central Committee of Communist Party (Marxist), 10-16 April 1967,* Calcutta, pp. 32-33.
2. Ibid., p. 32.
3. Ibid., p. 34.
4. Ibid., pp. 71-72.
5. Ibid., p. 74.
6. *The Statesman,* 9 July 1969.
7. Ibid.
8. *The Statesman,* 13 July 1969.
9. *The Statesman,* 11 July 1969.
10. Ibid.
11. *The Statesman,* 12 July 1969.
12. *The Statesman,* 13 July 1969.
13. *The Statesman,* 25 July 1969.
14. *The Statesman,* 13 July 1969.
15. Ibid.
16. *The Indian Express,* 23 August 1969.
17. *The Statesman,* 3 September 1969.
18. *The Statesman,* 23 September 1969.
19. The joint communique was published in *New Age* and also in *People's Democracy,* 1 June 1969.
20. *The Statesman,* 9 June 1969.
21. *The Statesman,* 24 June 1969.
22. Ibid.
23. *The Statesman,* 28 June 1969.
24. *The Times of India,* 20 October 1969.
25. Ibid.
26. Ibid.
27. For the views of the cpi(m) see "History Will Never Forgive You, Sri Achutha Menon!" in *People's Democracy,* 11 January 1970.
28. *The Statesman,* 14 June 1969.

29. *The Statesman*, 12 June 1969.
30. *The Statesman*, 21 June 1969.
31. Ibid.
32. *The Statesman*, 11 June 1969.
33. *The Statesman*, 3 July 1969.
34. *The Statesman*, 16 June 1969.
35. *The Statesman*, 17 June 1969.
36. Ibid.
37. Ibid.
38. *The Statesman*, 19 June 1969.
39. *The Statesman*, 22 June 1969.
40. *The Statesman*, 21 June 1969.
41. Ibid.
42. Ibid.
43. *The Statesman*, 14 July 1969.
44. *The Statesman*, 3 September 1969.
45. *The Statesman*, 15 September 1969.
46. Ibid.
47. *The Statesman*, 5 September 1969.
48. *The Statesman*, 8 October 1969.
49. Ibid.
50. *The Statesman*, 9 October 1969.
51. *The Statesman*, 8 October 1969.
52. *The Statesman*, 30 November 1969.
53. *The Statesman*, 11 November 1969.
54. Ibid.
55. *The Statesman*, 16 November 1969.
56. *The Statesman*, 4 December 1969.
57. *The Statesman*, 19 December 1969.
58. For the views of the CPI(M) see "Revisionists are Shielding Bangla Congress Betrayal" in *People's Democracy*, 15 March 1970.
59. *People's Democracy*, 4 October 1970.
60. *The Statesman*, 14 December 1970.
61. Madhu Limaye, "Problems of Left Consolidation," *Amrita Bazar Patrika*, 26 December 1970.
62. "Assert People's Supremacy, Amend Constitution," *New Age*, 20 December 1970.
63. CPI(M) politbureau statement was published in *People's Democracy*, December 20, 1970.

CHAPTER TEN

The Ideology of the CPI

I. THE CPI ON MARXISM AND MAOISM

The communists believe that the destruction of capitalism and the establishment of socialism in its place is inevitable and in accordance with the laws of history. Another tenet of Marxist communism is that the working class, in alliance with the other toiling masses, is alone capable of bringing about the socialist revolution. "The main thing in the doctrine of Marx," wrote Lenin, "is that it brings out the historic role of the proletariat as the builder of a socialist society."

Socialism is achieved after the working class gains power and after the working people's state nationalizes the capitalist-owned means of production and turns them into public, socialist property. Though the working class is the most decisive force which brings about the socialist revolution, it does not act alone. Inasmuch as its interests coincide with those of all working people, the working class, as the leader of the revolution, can enter into alliances with other working people.

A bourgeois–democratic revolution or a national–liberation movement of an oppressed people or an anti-fascist, anti-imperialist struggle of liberation may eventually lead to a proletarian revolution. But it is the central tenet of Marxist communism that the task of leading the masses to a successful proletarian revolution can only be undertaken by the industrial workers or the proletariat. Hence the necessity of the dictatorship of the proletariat. It is through this dictatorship that the working people, led by the working class, build up socialism. It is this belief in the dictatorship of the proletariat which divides the Marxist-Leninists from the social–democrats. Lenin wrote: "Only he is a communist who extends the recognition of the class struggle to the recognition of the dictatorship of the proletariat. This is what constitutes the most profound difference between the Marxist and ordinary petty (as well as big) bourgeoisie. This is the touchstone on which the real understanding and recognition of Marxism is to be tested."

Proletarian dictatorship, according to the communists, takes the form of socialist democracy. "This system," claimed Lenin, "provides the maximum democracy for the workers and peasants, at the same time it marks a break with bourgeois democracy and the rise of a new type of democracy of world-historic importance, namely, proletarian democracy, or the dictatorship of the proletariat." This dictatorship is to be directed against the bourgeoisie for the establishment of socialism. During the dictatorship of the proletariat there is an alliance between the working class and all the working people pledged to the cause of socialism, but the special feature of such an alliance is that the working class has the guiding role or the leadership.

After socialism has been established through the dictatorship of the proletariat distribution takes place on the principle: "From each according to his ability, to each according to his work." But, later, when productive forces reach a higher level, and surplus product is available in sufficient quantities, distribution will be on the principle: "From each according to his ability, to each according to his needs." It is then that the highest stage of socialism, namely, communism is reached.

The dictatorship of the proletariat may, however, assume different forms. In the Soviet Union it assumed the form of Soviet power. There power was concentrated mainly in the hands of two classes, namely, the workers and the peasants. In China, the dictatorship of the proletariat took the form of what has been called a people's democracy. Under the people's democracy of China, unlike as in the Soviet Union, a multi-party system was retained. The people's democratic front included the working class, all strata of peasantry, the middle strata of urban population, a section of the intellectuals, and a part of the middle bourgeoisie.

There has been much debate within the Indian communist movement as to whether the Russian path or the Chinese path should be followed in effecting the Indian revolution or whether, relying on both the Russian and Chinese experiences, a new path

appropriate to Indian conditions should be evolved. In 1951 the
CPI decided that Indian communists should learn both from the
Russian and Chinese experiences but should follow a path of
revolution appropriate to Indian conditions.[1]

The communist movement has been an international movement. The communists believe in proletarian internationalism.
Does this mean that the communist parties the world over should
pursue the same tactics or identical forms of revolution? Lenin
had founded the Communist International which, at one time,
used to guide the international communist movement and to
indicate to different communist parties of the world the path
they should follow. The Communist International was dissolved
in 1943, and at the time of its dissolution it was asserted that
proletarian internationalism did not demand an international
organization and that the international communist movement
could be developed on the basis of bilateral and multilateral contacts and through world conferences.

The first communist revolution took place in Russia. In the
early years all communists looked to Russia for light. Later, communist revolutions took place in various other countries of the
world and the tactics followed by the revolutionaries in these
different countries were necessarily different. The Russians relied
on the general strike of industrial workers followed by country-
wide insurrection. The Chinese relied on partisan war of the
peasantry as the main weapon of the revolution. The revolution
in Cuba was different from the revolution either in Russia or
China. Many of the communist parties in Western Europe, such
as in Italy and France, actively participate in elections. The
Communist Party of Portugal works underground, and the
Communist Party of South Africa believes in armed violence.
During the period from 1948 to 1950 the Indian communists
sought to follow armed insurrectionary methods in Telengana on
the Chinese pattern. At the 1951 All India Party Conference, the
Indian communists, however, decided that they should not blindly
follow either the Russian path or the Chinese path but, relying
both on the Russian and Chinese experiences, they should evolve
a method of revolution appropriate to Indian conditions.[2] The
Indian communists have followed different modes of struggle;
they have participated in elections, organized strikes, demonstrations, *satyagraha* movements, *bandhs* and other divers forms

of mass movements. In the Indian communist movement a split took place in 1964 and the section that seceded from the party organized the CPI(M), a new party which sought to pursue a more leftist policy. In 1967 a section of the extremists left the CPI(M) and they sought to follow the Maoist path of armed insurrection in Naxalbari in Bengal and in Srikakulam and other parts of Andhra Pradesh.

The question as to what path the Indian communists should follow split the Indian communist movement in 1964. But before this split, the communist movement had been split first by Tito in Yugoslavia and then by Mao Tse-tung in China.

The split caused by China in the world communist movement was the most serious, and it developed rapidly after the startling disclosures about Stalin made by Khrushchev at the Twentieth Congress of the Communist Party of the Soviet Union in 1956. At this Congress Khrushchev made certain disclosures about the atrocities committed during Stalin's régime and he attacked the cult of personality. Certain formulations about the world socialist movement which were made at this Congress were later denounced by the Chinese communists as being revisionistic. The Twentieth Congress of the CPSU pointed attention to the change in the balance of world forces in favour of socialism. By the time this Congress was held socialistic systems had come to be established amongst a third of the world's population. The Congress referred to this as also to the growth of national liberation movements in the colonial countries, and urged the development of cooperation between the socialist world and the newly liberated countries for ensuring economic growth and safeguarding world peace.

A Conference of 12 communist and workers' parties of the world, including that of China, was held in Moscow in November 1957. This Conference declared that the main content of the epoch was the transition from capitalism to socialism. It pointed out that 950 millions of people lived under socialist systems, that 700 millions of colonial people had been liberated, that imperialism was declining, that class struggle was being intensified in imperialist countries and that the development of neo-colonial forms of domination by the USA was sharpening the contradictions between the imperialist countries.

In November 1960, 81 communist parties of the world, including that of China, attended a Conference at Moscow in which the 81 parties document, later denounced as revisionistic by the Chinese, was adopted. The 1960 Conference welcomed the resolutions passed at the Twentieth Congress of CPSU and defined the present epoch as one in which the balance of world forces had gone against imperialism and in which the world socialist forces were becoming the decisive factor. At this Conference the old Marxist–Leninist concept that war was inevitable so long as imperialism lasted was discarded.

When the old Marxist–Leninist concepts were evolved imperialism was strong and an all-embracing system, whereas the forces of socialism were weak. Because of the formation of the world socialist camp, the development of an international working class movement and the growth of the national liberation movements in colonial and semi-colonial countries, the power of imperialism had declined. Accordingly, the 1960 Moscow Conference resolved that war was not fatalistically inevitable. This formulation was later attacked by the Chinese communists, who asserted that so long as imperialism existed war could not be eliminated.

The 1960 Moscow Conference also evolved the concept of peaceful coexistence of countries with different socio-economic systems. The alternative to such coexistence was destructive war which could destroy civilization. This concept of peaceful coexistence was also later criticized by the Chinese communists. In an article in Peking's *People's Daily* published on 12 December 1963 it was stated: "Lenin's principle of peaceful coexistence was directed against imperialist war but Khrushchev has turned it into a policy of abject surrender to imperialism and of helping the imperialists in their agressive wars."

The Chinese communists claim that the Soviet leaders by formulating the concept of peaceful coexistence was following in the footsteps of the Kautsky and Bernstein. In 1914 Kautsky had said that the question was not whether a war was just or unjust because every war brought misfortune to all nations and all workers. But while Kautsky opposed war because it was harmful to everyone including the workers, the 1960 Moscow Conference spoke of peaceful coexistence not merely because war was harmful, but also because objective conditions had become ripe for averting war. This Conference asserted that because the world balance of forces had changed in favour of socialism, imperialist wars were no longer fatalistically inevitable. "In 1914 Bernstein advocated disarmament as an alternative to workers' revolt—as at that time there were no forces strong enough to prevent war. Is the world today," asks the CPI, "in the same position as in 1914? ... At a time when socialism has become a world system, when imperialism has been pushed into a defensive position, when so many of the countries in the world have become sovereign and anti-imperialist, when socialism is outstripping capitalism through economic competition, must it still be necessarily impossible to prevent and thwart the imperialist venture for a global war? Is there no power to force imperialism to agree to disarmament? Has history been frozen in 1914?"[3]

The 1960 Moscow Conference also approved of the concept of the peaceful transition to socialism and stated that in a number of capitalist countries it may be possible for the working class, headed by the communist party, and making a united front with other leftist and democratic forces, to win state power without going through a process of armed civil war. This concept had far-reaching consequences for the world communist movement but the Chinese communists rejected this concept altogether.

The Chinese communists cannot contemplate of a revolution except through armed struggle on the Chinese pattern. But the conditions in pre-revolutionary China and present-day India are vastly different. The CPI, therefore, claims that to conceive of a peaceful transition to socialism in India does not amount to renunciation of Marxism–Leninism, as the Maoists assert, but involves the creative application of Marxism–Leninism to the special conditions prevailing in India where universal franchise has been established and strong mass movements have developed. "It is possible," says the CPI, "that by developing a powerful mass revolutionary movement, by winning a stable majority in Parliament, backed by such a movement, the working class and its allies will be able to overcome the resistance of the forces of reaction and transform Parliament from an instrument serving the bourgeoisie into a genuine instrument of people's will for effecting a fundamental transformation in the social, economic, and state structure. It is possible in India to avoid the possibility of going through an armed civil war as the form of the revolutionary transformation. Such a possibility has been made real by the changed balance of forces in the world to the advantage of the forces struggling for revolutionary transformation of society and for socialism. This change has made the possibility of the imperialist export of counter-revolution far more difficult than in the past and it was precisely this export of counter-revolution which was one of the most important factors making armed civil war more or less inevitable and peaceful transition a very rare chance. Besides, in India, the class alliance for the national-democratic revolution is a very broad one and the forces opposing the revolution have a very narrow social base and can be isolated to a very considerable extent. Finally, in India the people through their struggle have won certain democratic rights and a parliamentary democratic form of state has been secured which offers certain scope to the democratic forces and whose potential can be increased through the extension of democracy. In the countries where the revolution succeeded through a bitter armed civil war, such rights and such a system did not exist."[4]

The CPI does not say that it is prepared to give up the path of armed struggle always and under all circumstances. The ruling class will not voluntarily surrender power and if they resort to violence, the CPI declares, the working class would also be entitled to resist violence with violence. Though communists should be prepared for all eventualities including armed civil war, in the conditions prevailing in India an attempt should be made to achieve power through peaceful means. "It is against all the tenets of Marxism–Leninism," says the CPI, "to equate violence and armed civil war with revolution, to make out that revolutionary power can only be born from the barrel of a gun. Communists do not make a fetish of either violence or non-violence. They work for revolution, if possible, in a peaceful form but, if necessary, through armed civil war."[5]

The Chinese view that there can be no peaceful transition to socialism and no peaceful coexistence of different socio-economic systems the CPI characterizes as being the product of an "infantile disorder."[6] China is following not the teachings of Lenin but those of Trotsky in seeking to export revolution.[7] Further, if China does not believe in peaceful coexistence and is pledged to wage war against all kinds of imperialism then the question naturally arises as to why China does not take steps to

liberate Taiwan or even Hong Kong, a part of Chinese main-
land, which is a British colony.

The CPI charges that China wants Russia to engage in a military war with the USA, and for not doing so Russia is being
denounced by China as an ally of the USA and as a revisionist
country that has abandoned Marxism. But it is the Maoists,
charge the CPI, who have renounced Marxism. "Anti-Sovietism
and discrediting the ideas of Communism under the pretext of
fighting the 'spearhead and fountainhead of world revisionism';
disruption of the national-liberation movement in the name of
its revolutionary championship, greater-power chauvinism and
hegemonism under the garb of spreading the gospel of the
Thoughts of Mao Tse-tung; placing great strains and stresses
upon the country's economy in the name of the 'great leap
forward'; poisoning the minds of youth and abandoning the
leadership of the working class and its party in the name of the
'proletarian cultural revolution'; and in all a gratuitous aid to
imperialism in the very name of fighting it to a finish," were,
declared the CPI, the ideological and political lines that the Maoist
leadership was following.[8]

The Maoist leadership in China formally dissolved the All-
China Trade Union Federation and the Young Communist
League. The supporters of the Great Proletarian Cultural Revolution physically disbanded party organs at all levels, right up
to the Central Committee of the Communist Party of China.
"Frenzied bands of young boys and girls, barely in their teens,"
lamented the CPI, "have been let loose in town and country to
invade factories, farms and residential areas, to enter private
houses for humiliating and physically molesting anybody and
everybody whom they consider to be guilty of revisionism and
'taking to the capitalist road'. Judged even by articles in the
Chinese press mass hysteria has led to hooliganism and anarchism
in a large number of places. Respected and veteran leaders and
heroes of the Communist Party of China have been publicly
humiliated and on occasions even physically liquidated."[9]

The CPI considers that the Chinese communists are pursuing
a policy of adventurism not only within the country but also in
matters relating to foreign affairs. It lamented that the "chauvinistic and bellicose attitude of the Mao group" towards the
newly-independent nations and their denunciation of all bour-

geois national leaders as stooges of American imperialism, had given a handle to anti-communist forces to arouse anti–Chinese and anti–communist sentiments, and had, thereby, helped the forces of imperialism.[10]

II. THE CPI CONCEPT OF NATIONAL DEMOCRACY

The CPI considers that the Chinese analysis is not based on the realities of the situation actually existing in the world today but suffers from left-sectarianism and adventurism. So far as India is concerned, the CPI also differs from the Chinese analysis to the effect that India is a semi-colonial country and that the stage of the Indian revolution is primarily anti-imperialist. On the contrary, the CPI holds that India is at the stage of the anti-imperialist, anti-feudal democratic revolution and the immediate task of the Indian communists is not the establishment of socialism but the establishment of the transitional stage of national democracy through a national democratic front. The national bourgeoisie would have a place in this national democratic front. This is because the national bourgeoisie in India has not yet exhausted its anti-feudal, anti-imperialist role.

In completing the unfinished anti-imperialist, anti-feudal revolution in India the national bourgeoisie has a part to play. This revolution is to be completed by the establishment of a national democratic government at the centre. For this purpose a national democratic front has to be formed. Such a front would be based on a broad cooperation of all national and democratic forces, namely, the working class, the peasantry, the progressive section of the national bourgeoisie and the national intelligentsia. In this broadbased front the working class would have no exclusive leadership but through this front the exclusive leadership of the bourgeoisie would also be ended. The CPI at its Patna Congress stated its position thus: "The national democratic state in the hands of the national democratic front will be a transitional stage, in which power will be jointly exercised by all those classes which are interested in eradicating imperialist interests, routing the semi-feudal elements and breaking the power of the monopolies. In this class alliance, the exclusive leadership of the bourgeoisie no longer exists. The leadership of this alliance belongs to firm anti-imperialist, anti-feudal, anti-monopoly forces."

All sections of the national bourgeoisie are not to be denounced or regarded as allies of imperialism. On the contrary, while the national democratic front should fight the imperialists, feudalists, and the monopoly bourgeoisie, it would seek the support of the other sections of the bourgeoisie and, particularly, of the non-big bourgeoisie. During the period of the freedom movement in India the CPI had often denounced the national bourgeoisie altogether as an ally of imperialism. This was a mistake and, in retrospect, the CPI admitted that it was a costly mistake. As G. Adhikari, a CPI leader, put it: "In the pre-independence period, the main mistake from which our party suffered most was the inadequate understanding of the specific and main task which faces us, namely, the national-liberation revolution movement, incorrect understanding and approach towards the national movement and its organ, the National Congress, that developed under the leadership of Mahatma Gandhi; incorrect understanding and inadequate concrete study of the role of the Indian national bourgeoisie in the revolution."[11]

It is in pursuance of this erroneous policy that the CPI took no part in the civil disobedience movements led by Gandhi saying that these were not revolutionary movements. Again, it is on the basis of this policy that the leftist tendencies of Nehru and Bose were denounced as the left-manoeuvring movements of the bourgeoisie and as being more dangerous than Gandhism. And, finally, it is this policy which made the CPI oppose the Quit India movement started by the Congress in 1942. All these arose, in the words of Adhikari, "from our dogmatic understanding of proletarian internationalism and sectarian attitude towards the national movement."[12]

In the course of the revolutionary struggle against imperialism, in communist theory there arises, first, the basic contradiction between imperialism and feudalism on the one hand and the entire people including the bourgeoisie on·the other, and a secondary contradiction between the vacillating national bourgeoisie and the revolutionary forces of the people. The error in tactics arises from regarding this secondary contradiction as being the primary contradiction and on that basis to assume during the national liberation movement that the bourgeoisie has gone over completely to the camp of imperialism and has become an enemy of revolution. To denounce the bourgeoisie as wholly counter-revolutionary when it still retains a vestigial anti-imperialist and anti-feudal role is to weaken the national democratic front.

This mistake of regarding the secondary contradiction as the primary one was made by the CPI during the stage of the national democratic revolution in the period from 1948 to 1951, when it pursued an extremist militant policy against the Indian government. The CPI states that such a mistake would not be repeated and asserts: "On this point, the CPI has been clear ever since the terrible fiasco of heavy damage caused by the 'left' sectarian line which it followed from 1948 to 1951. Forgetting the revolution, the CPI considered it as its main task to fight and overcome Indian capitalism as a whole. It completely missed the national-democratic character of our revolution. It made out that the national bourgeoisie as a whole, including the rich peasants, was the main enemy. It, therefore, isolated itself from its possible allies, its mass base began to shrink, the main enemy was missed and the Indian people could not develop much faith in the wisdom of the CPI, though the courage and self-sacrifice of its members was admired. The membership of the party came down from about a lakh to about 10,000 or so. Its organization was in shambles. Many of its fine leaders and cadres were physically liquidated and many more became disillusioned and demoralized. Its mass organizations like the trade unions, kisan sabhas, students' federations, etc. were totally smashed up. The entire movement was thrown back and the CPI lost a good chance of emerging as one of the leading forces of the nation at a time when the entire people were at the cross-roads. Thus, the CPI has learnt to its cost that simply indulging in ultra-revolutionary phrases does not help it or the revolution. To be a revolutionary one must make a scientific study of social reality, find out the stage of the revolution and the main and secondary contradictions."[13]

Though the CPI has learnt from the mistakes of the extremist militant policies pursued by it between 1948 and 1951, it also makes it clear that it has no illusions about the Congress Party and that it never believed that Nehru was building socialism. But it does not say, as it said during the early years of independence, that India did not attain political independence in 1947 or that India was some kind of a semi-colonial satellite country. The early communist characterization that the independence attained in 1947 was a fake independence sprang from dogmatism which, the communists later said, "isolates the communists not only from the reality but from the masses, from its allies and leads it to commit very serious political mistakes."[14]

It was a mistake to assert that the independence attained in 1947 was a fake independence or that no economic progress whatsoever had been made since independence. On the contrary, the CPI stated in 1968 that since independence, the national income "has risen by about 73 per cent; industrial production has increased by about 100 per cent and agricultural production by about 45 per cent. Basic industrial plants—steel, oil engineering, chemicals, etc.—have come up and India is now producing goods that were not produced at all some 15 years ago. . . . India succeeded in laying the foundations of a heavy machine-building industry and in considerably expanding iron and steel, machine tools, coal-mining and oil industries. New branches of industries and projects which emerged as a result of socialist aid go a long way in eliminating the legacy of the colonial past and reduce India's dependence on the capitalist world market for trained manpower, materials, and machinery. The state sector developed in the spheres of industry (especially heavy industry), finance and partly trade. This has contributed to the building of independent national economy and to the weakening of the grip of foreign monopoly capital and to a certain extent the Indian monopolies. As a result of the measure of industrialization that has taken place, the working class has not only expanded quantitatively but changed qualitatively with new skilled workers coming up in the heavy basic industries sector. This has not only added to the productive forces of the nation but strengthened one of the decisive elements of the democratic movement and the essential leader in the future transition to socialism. . . . In the field of agrarian relations as well, the Congress governments have substantially curbed feudal vested interests through various legislative measures. These have gone hand-in-hand with conscious efforts to develop and foster a class of rich peasants and capitalist landlords who could become the backbone of the new capitalist agrarian set-up"[15]

Despite the above views, the CPI asserts that the state in India is primarily an organ of class-rule of the national bourgeoisie which has strong links with the landlords. Because the bourgeoisie has a powerful influence over the Indian state, industrial development in India has resulted in the growth of monopoly houses. The monopoly commission report pointed out that 75 monopoly houses own assets worth Rs 2,605.95 crores, which comes to 46.9 per cent of the corporate capital of the private sector. A CPI publication of 1968 states: "Recent estimates have shown that Tatas (Rs 519 crores) and Birlas (460 crores) own officially declared capital assets of nearly 1,000 crores. Some of the other top monopoly houses are Martin Burn (Rs 154 crores), Mafatlal (Rs 107 crores), Bangur (Rs 88 crores), Thapar (Rs 85 crores), Walchand (Rs 83 crores), Sri Ram (Rs 73 crores), Sahu–Jain (Rs 66 crores), Scindia (Rs 64 crores). Twenty-two monopoly houses have assets worth Rs 2,268 crores and have an average rate of growth of 37.1 per cent. The reports of the Vivian Bose Enquiry into the Dalmia–Jain concerns and of Dr Hazari into the way the Birlas have gone in for licences have demonstrated the way in which India's monopolists constantly are on the lookout to retard or distort production in order to make profits."[16]

The CPI criticizes the policies of the Indian government because it has not prevented the growth of monopolies, "has contracted huge foreign loans amounting to Rs 4,005.05 crores on 31 July 1967, the bulk of which is owed to the USA,"[17] has permitted the preservation of semi-feudal relations in agriculture and has made provision for the giving of compensation to the landlords for the acquisition of land. It states that the state of the economy is such that "more than 60 per cent of our population has less than Rs 25 to spend for the purposes of consumption, while 33 per cent has only about Rs 15 per month. Some 80 per cent of our people live well below the minimum level of subsistence."[18] But in spite of all these criticisms, the CPI, unlike the Naxalites, does not regard that the Indian government is utterly anti-people or that it is in the nature of a fascist dictatorship.

Adult franchise and parliamentary democracy have conferred enormous power on the Indian people to bring about socio-economic changes. According to the CPI, political democracy in

India is limited and has been distorted by the economic power of the rich including the monopolists and feudalists, the emergency powers of the centre and the representation of vested interests in the composition of the administrative, judicial, and military services. But notwithstanding all these limitations the parliamentary democratic system has conferred some real power to the masses. The CPI has more faith in the parliamentary system than the CPI(M). It states: "Unlike the CPI(M), it [the CPI] does not hold to the view that, ... nothing has changed and that all the democratic institutions and rights won by the toilers through arduous struggles are nothing but a sham. The CPI believes that the parliamentary democratic system and the democratic rights are real, valuable and give the masses chance of advancing to their goal through sweeping struggles."[19]

The CPI complains that the CPI(M) has characterized the Indian state as being more reactionary than it actually is and this has led the CPI(M) to pursue a left-sectarian policy. The CPI(M) regards the Indian state as a bourgeois-landlord state in which the big bourgeoisie, increasingly collaborating with imperialism, exercises leadership. "The logical implication of this characterization," states the CPI, "is that Indian state is a state of right reaction, more or less corresponding to the state under Chiang Kai-shek's Kuomintang. It would be a neo-colonialist state, not very different from, say, that of South Korea, South Vietnam or Thailand. The ultras in the CPI(M) are perfectly correct when they state that this is the precise meaning of the formulation made in the CPI(M) Programme."[20]

The CPI, unlike the CPI(M), holds that the Indian state is the class rule of the entire Indian capitalist class—the monopoly bourgeoisie, the non-monopoly bourgeoisie, and the rural bourgeoisie. In this state the big monopoly bourgeoisie wields powerful influence and they have strong links with the landlords. But the CPI does not consider the Indian state to be as reactionary as does the CPI(M). Criticizing the CPI(M)'s analysis of the class-character of the Indian state, the CPI states: "It is utterly wrong to imagine that the more reactionary one makes out the Indian state to be, the more 'revolutionary' one is. If this were so, it would be best to call the Indian state a fascist dictatorship and then expect the 'revolution' to immediately break out."[21]

In order to effect the national democratic revolution the CPI pleads for a broadbased democratic front. The enemies of this front are the imperialists, the landlords, and Indian monopolists. Almost all other classes can be brought in as allies of this national democratic front. According to the CPI the classes who can be included in this front are: "First, the working class. This class is the most consistent fighter against not only imperialism, feudalism, and monopoly capitalism but against all forms of exploitation. It is a class which is not only interested in carrying out the national-democratic revolution but also in going forward from it to the socialist revolution. Second, the entire cultivating peasantry. The agricultural labourers and the poor peasantry will form the backbone of the national-democratic revolution in the countryside. . . . The other sections of the peasantry—the middle peasants and the rich peasants—have also to be united with. The middle peasants are interested in the thorough wiping out of feudalism. The rich peasants can also be won over to the side of the national-democratic revolution. While they are an exploiting stratum and have connections with the landlords and, thus, vacillate, they are also exploited by the monopoly manipulations of the power of the landlords. They would benefit from the break up of the landlord power. . . . Third, the rising class of the urban and rural intelligentsia. . . . Fourth, the non-monopoly section of the national bourgeoisie. This class is objectively interested, in terms of its own class interests, in the completion of the national-democratic revolution."[22]

Though the working class would be the most consistent fighter for bringing about a national democratic revolution, the CPI attaches great importance to drawing into this front all classes except the imperialists, feudalists, and monopolists. The CPI also attaches great importance to drawing not only the masses following the Congress Party but the progressive sections of that party itself inside the front.[23] The CPI had always envisaged that the intensification of mass movement would lead to a polarization inside the Congress and that the progressive section of that party would join the national democratic front. The CPI supported Indira Gandhi and her group against the "Syndicate," which latter it denounced as the representatives of right reaction, and welcomed the split that took place in the Congress Party in November 1969.

Though the CPI would welcome all democratic forces inside

the national-democratic front, it considers that the working class would be the initiator and prime builder of this front. The pivot of the front would be the alliance of the workers and the peasants, though the urban middle stratum and the intelligentsia would also take active part in the front, and even the non-monopoly section of the bourgeoisie would have a place in the front.

The CPI, however, does not consider that the working class would have exclusive leadership of the national democratic front. "It is this point," argues the CPI, "that has been seized upon by the leadership of the CPI(M) to advance the slander that the CPI has gone revisionist and does not 'want' that the national-democratic revolution be led by the working class. It is this point and this point alone that demarcates the CPI concept of national democracy from the CPI(M) concept of people's democracy. Both national democracy and people's democracy are forms of the completion of the anti-imperialist, anti-feudal, democratic revolution. Both in national democracy as also in people's democracy, there is a four-class alliance—workers, peasants, urban middle strata and intelligentsia, and the non-monopoly national bourgeoisie. There is also no difference with regard to the future —both national democracy and people's democracy are forms of transition to socialism."[24]

But sticking to the experience of China and the East European countries, the CPI(M) puts forward the concept of a people's democracy and asserts that the anti-imperialist, anti-feudal and democratic revolution cannot be completed in India without the leadership of the working class. The crucial difference between the CPI and the CPI(M) lies in the fact that the CPI(M) considers working-class leadership as the precondition for the building up of the united front. The CPI criticizes this approach of the CPI(M) saying that the CPI(M) has "not bothered to study either the changes in the world balance of forces or the specific situation in India. Today with the tremendous weakening of world imperialism, with the world socialist system and anti-imperialist forces increasingly determining the main trend of world developments, the anti-imperialist and anti-feudal, democratic potentialities of the various nonproletarian democratic classes have greatly increased. Their independent activity and role have also greatly increased as compared to some two decades ago. Thus not only can the working class more easily unite with these classes, but it has also to reckon with their greater potentialities and role."[25]

The CPI does not consider that the working class in all circumstances and in all countries should be the exclusive leader of the national democratic revolution. In pre-revolutionary China and in the Eastern European countries, before they joined the socialist bloc, the nonproletarian democratic classes, compared to their counterparts in present-day India, were relatively weak both economically and politically. Accordingly, in those countries the working class had no other contender for the leadership of the national democratic front, but inasmuch as the nonproletarian democratic classes are fairly well developed in India, the proletariat in India "has to treat with its allies on a far more equal footing."[26] The CPI states: "Thus it is not a question of subjective desire, a matter of 'wanting' the leadership of the working class. . . . Does or does not the CPI(M) agree that the world balance of class forces has radically altered compared to 1945 or 1949 when the East European and Chinese people's democratic revolutions took place? Does or does not the CPI(M) agree that the concrete relationship between the working class and the nonproletarian democratic classes in India is different from what it was in Eastern Europe and China? If so, then how will the building of the anti-imperialist, anti-feudal democratic united front differ in our country from that of the other above-mentioned countries? The CPI(M) leadership does not pose these questions to itself either out of ignorance or fear. Dogmatism offers them ready-made recipes from the revolutions made in other epochs and in other countries."[27]

The national democratic front, the CPI hopes, will place India on the noncapitalist path to socialism, so that India may attain socialism without passing through a fully developed capitalistic stage. A fully developed capitalistic economy has not yet been established in India. In fact, pre-capitalist relations of production, specially in the field of agriculture, occupy an important place in present-day Indian economy. In these circumstances, the CPI envisages that it may be possible so to reverse the gears of capitalist development that before India reaches the stage of full-blown capitalism she may be able to proceed to the road to socialism by going through the transitional non-capitalist stage. It is not obligatory that all the countries of Africa, Asia, and Latin America should traverse the same path that were taken by the USA and Western European countries. It may not be necessary for these countries to develop capitalism, then monopoly capitalism and in this manner prepare the objective and subjective conditions for the transition to socialism. "It is possible, in the new epoch, to prepare," asserts the CPI, "these preconditions in a new way, i.e. the non-capitalist way. The experience of Mongolia and the Central Asian Soviet Republics provided confirmation of this possibility in the past. The UAR, Syria, Algeria, Burma, Congo (Brazzaville), Guinea, etc., provide examples of the same possibility in the new epoch."[28]

The programme of pursuing the noncapitalist path of development to socialism through the national democratic front would involve, firstly, the elimination of foreign capital; secondly, the extension of the state sector in key and heavy industries with the nationalization of banks, general insurance, foreign trade, oil, coal, mines and plantations; thirdly, the breaking of Indian monopoly combines; fourthly, the destruction of the power of the landlords by the abolition of landlordism, imposition of ceilings on land holdings and distribution of surplus lands to agricultural labourers and poor peasants; and, fifthly, the provision of facilities for the development of non-monopolist private sector enterprises and small-scale industries. With the implementation of these measures the task of the national democratic revolution would be completed and the country would then be set firmly on to the road towards socialism.

NOTES AND REFERENCES

1. *Statement of Policy Adopted by the All India Conference of the Communist Party of India*, October 1951, Calcutta, pp. 3-4.
2. Ibid., p. 7.
3. *A Course of Party Education*, Second Stage (For Branch Secretaries), Communist Party publication, 1968, p. 136.
4. Ibid., p. 113.
5. Ibid., p. 114.
6. Ibid., p. 136.
7. Ibid., p. 138.

8. *Documents Adopted by Eighth Congress of the Communist Party of India*, 1968, Communist Party publication, pp. 241-42.

9. Ibid., p. 238.

10. Ibid.

11. *A Course of Party Education*, Second Stage (For Branch Secretaries). Communist Party publication, p. 75.

12. Ibid.

13. Ibid., pp. 77-78.

14. Ibid., p. 81.

15. Ibid., pp. 79-80.

16. Ibid., pp. 84-85.

17. Ibid., p. 82.

18. Ibid., p. 86.

19. Ibid., p. 90.

20. Ibid., p. 92.

21. Ibid., p. 93.

22. Ibid., pp. 101-2.

23. Ibid., p. 103.

24. Ibid., p. 106.

25. Ibid., pp. 106-7.

26. Ibid., p. 107.

27. Ibid., pp. 107-8.

28. Ibid., p. 109.

CHAPTER ELEVEN

The Ideology of the CPI(M)

I. THE CPI(M) CRITIQUE OF REVISIONISM

The CPI(M) claims that the CPI is a revisionist party which has completely deviated from Leninism and has renounced Marxism. It is to this renunciation by the CPI of Marxism and Leninism, and not to the differences arising out of the Chinese aggression on India, that the CPI(M) attributes the split in the Communist Party of India.[1]

The CPI(M) aims at establishing a people's democracy, whereas the goal of the CPI is the establishment of a national democratic state. The CPI(M) claims that for the complete fulfilment of the basic tasks of the Indian revolution in the present stage it is absolutely essential "to replace the present bourgeois–landlord state headed by the big bourgeoisie," by a people's democracy under the exclusive leadership of the working class.[2] The CPI, on the other hand, wants a national democratic state to be established through a national democratic front in which power will be jointly exercised by all classes which are interested in eradicating the power of the imperialists, feudalists, and monopolists but in which front the working class will share leadership with the bourgeoisie so that the exclusive leadership of the working class will not be established.

The difference between the aims of the CPI and CPI(M)—while the former seeks to establish a national democratic state and the latter a people's democracy—is not one of semantics only. The national democratic state of the CPI would not be under the exclusive leadership of the working class; it would be under a joint bourgeois and working-class leadership. This the CPI(M) characterizes as class collaboration and a strategy which would objectively lead to the sabotage and betrayal of the revolution, because it cannot be expected that the bourgeoisie would cooperate in the task of the complete liquidation of imperialism and feudalism and the freeing of the people from the grip of monopoly capital. "The offer of leadership to the bourgeoisie," claimed Ranadive, "can most certainly lead to nothing but the betrayal of the revolution. It is obvious that if this exploiting class, a class that has been taking a vacillating stand in the anti-imperialist struggle and compromising with feudalism, a class which is having ever-growing clashes with the working class and the peasantry, is kept in leadership, it will not stop at anything to achieve its claims and smash the demo-cratic revolution."[3]

Both the CPI and the CPI(M) consider that a section of the bourgeoisie may be won over as allies in the anti-feudal and anti-imperialist revolution. The non-big bourgeoisie, having no durable links with the monopolist bourgeoisie and foreign imperialists, may be won over as allies in the people's democratic front. But these non-big bourgeoisie will be vacillating allies, and the CPI(M) is not prepared to give them any part in the leadership of the front. According to the CPI(M), the working class alone can be the leader of the front. The CPI, on the other hand, considers that inasmuch as the nonproletarian democratic sections of the people in India are quite strong and numerous, they would, along with the working class, share the leadership of the national democratic front. The CPI proposal that the working class would not have exclusive leadership of the national democratic front is utterly abhorrent to the members of the CPI(M), and they ask: "What are these men to be called? Revo-lutionaries or the paid agents of the bourgeoisie?"[4]

The CPI(M) asserts that inasmuch as in the national demo-cratic front of the CPI the bourgeoisie would have a part in the leadership of the front, this bourgeois leadership would permit the national democratic revolution to go up to a stage only and not up to the point which would mean the liquidation of the bourgeoisie. "It will now be clear," wrote Ranadive, "why these men chose to split the Communist Party. When they realized that it was impossible any more to secure acceptance from the Party ranks of their treacherous outlook, straight they went in for splitting the party."[5]

There are crucial differences between the CPI and CPI(M) in

their analysis of the character of the Indian state. According to the CPI, the Indian state is controlled by the national bourgeoisie as a whole, but in the exercise of governmental power the big bourgeoisie wields considerable influence. The CPI(M) holds "that both the state and the Government belong to the bourgeois–landlord class, that they are led by the big bourgeoisie and that the big bourgeoisie are increasingly collaborating with imperialism."[6]

According to the CPI(M), the CPI does not wish to destroy the Indian state as it believes that the leadership of the state is mainly in the hands of the anti-imperialist section of the bourgeoisie and that the landlords, in alliance with the big bourgeoisie, do not control the state, but only influence it. With this analysis of the class character of the Indian state the CPI(M) does not agree. The CPI(M) asserts that the landlord class shares power in the government which is led by the big bourgeoisie and that it would be underestimating the role of the landlord class to say that the big bourgeoisie only yields some influence to that class.

The CPI(M) claims that instead of attacking the Indian government as a whole the CPI seeks to differentiate the progressive section from the reactionary section inside the government, and that is why it gave the slogan of first supporting the leftist Nehru against the rightist Patel and then of supporting Lal Bahadur Shastri against Morarji Desai. The CPI(M) asserts that instead of realizing that the Indian government was based on the alliance of the bourgeoisie with the landlords under the leadership of the big bourgeoisie, the CPI regarded the Indian government as a government of the national bourgeoisie. If the government was a government of the national bourgeoisie only and if it excluded the landlords then it was necessarily, to some extent, anti-feudal and anti-imperialist and, accordingly, it would not be desirable to oppose such a government altogether. Such an approach, the CPI(M) asserts, leads only to the pursuit of a policy of tailism behind the government.

The CPI(M) wants to destroy the Indian state completely and to establish a people's democracy. To attain this end it seeks to develop a people's democratic front. This front will be led by the working class. The chief allies of the working class would be the agricultural labourers and the poor peasants in the countryside. The middle peasants are regarded as firm allies and the rich peasants may also be brought within the front.[7] The urban and other sections of the petty bourgeoisie are also regarded as allies. The only enemies of this anti-feudal, anti-imperialist revolution are the monopolists, the big bourgeoisie and the imperialists.

There are great similarities between the analyses of the CPI and CPI(M) on the question as to which classes should be regarded as the allies and the enemies of the revolution. Both the CPI and CPI(M) maintain that the national democratic front and the people's democratic front respectively will be created out of people's struggles, that the working class will lead these fronts, that the mass movements of the peasantry will lend these fronts a broad national character and that the worker-peasant alliance will be the axis of these fronts. The classes that would participate in these fronts are the working class, the peasantry, the middle class, and some sections of the national bourgeoisie. The aim of these fronts would be the completion of the anti-imperialist, anti-feudal revolution.[8]

But in spite of all these similarities there are also crucial differences between the CPI and the CPI(M) as to the composition and functioning of these fronts. The first basic difference is that the CPI, unlike the CPI(M), does not consider that the working class should have exclusive leadership of the front. The second crucial difference concerns the question as to who should be regarded as vacillating allies. Ranadive stated: "For them [the CPI] poor peasants, the agricultural labourers and the rich peasants are all alike, all equally revolutionary. Unlike us, they do not worry about fixing the position of each of these strata, after making a proper class analysis. . . . The rich peasant has a place in this movement. But it will be very wrong to put him on par with the other sections and allow him to seize the leadership. . . . Marxists make a distinction between the vacillating class and the firm class precisely to understand the basic forces and the auxiliary forces. On that basis they decide which classes are to lead the revolution and which to support it. . . . In their Front all sections of the bourgeoisie, including the big bourgeoisie, have a place on an equal basis with the working class and the peasantry. Since they do not accept the need for a struggle for the establishment of the leadership of the working class, the leadership of the Front will remain with the bourgeoisie and that

27

precisely is their line. This Front, therefore, is not a Front for the democratic revolution, but a Front for class collaboration. ... [9]

The CPI(M) claim there are seven crucial differences between the national democratic front of the CPI and the people's democratic front of the CPI(M). These differences are, firstly, that the objective of the national democratic front, unlike that of the people's democratic front, is not the removal of the bourgeois–landlord government but only its cleaning and purification by the removal of the right reactionary forces. Secondly, the leadership of the national democratic front would not be exclusively with the working class. Thirdly, all classes including the rich peasants are treated alike in the front and no special importance is attached to the consistently revolutionary classes. Fourthly, not much distinction is made by the CPI between the working class and the bourgeoisie who are all treated alike. Fifthly, all sections of the bourgeoisie except the monopolists are given a place in the front. Sixthly, an illusion is created that all sections of the monopolists other than the bourgeoisie have already taken up an anti-imperialist position. And, finally, the vacillations of the bourgeoisie are not emphasized so that there may be no impediment in the path of the bourgeoisie in obtaining some share in the leadership of the front.

The CPI(M) also differs from the CPI in the assessment of the foreign policy of the government of India. In November 1964 the CPI stated: "Foreign policy pursued by the Government of India is, in the main, a policy of peace, nonalignment and anticolonialism. It conforms to the interests of the national bourgeoisie, meets the needs of India's economic development and reflects the sentiments of the mass of the people of India. It is sometimes vitiated by lapses and compromises, but, as a whole, the main character of the policy has been generally preserved." The CPI(M), on the other hand, regarded that this assessment stemmed from a revisionist approach and from the lack of a true understanding of the class character of the Indian state.

The CPI(M) considers that in making appreciative references to some aspects of the policy of the government of India and in giving the bourgeoisie some place in the national democratic front, the CPI departed from Lenin's teachings as also from the principles of proletarian internationalism and that, objectively, it stood for a policy of class collaboration in place of a policy of class struggle.[10] Ranadive summarized his criticisms of the CPI thus: "An opportunist analysis concerning the state; shameless propaganda to the effect that there is no sharing of power by feudalism in the state as also that it is not led by the big bourgeoisie; attempting in the name of the National Democratic Front to keep the working class and the peasantry under the leadership of the bourgeoisie, and in practice, advocating a programme for the encouragement of capitalism, opposition to the state of the People's Democracy; efforts to see that decisive power is not transferred to the hands of the workers, peasants and the middle classes; assigning the leading role for the bourgeoisie among the revolutionary forces; placing on par the vacillating as also the revolutionary strata in the countryside; occasionally labelling the capitalist path, which worsens our economic dependence, as the path of building an independent economy; refusal to see the growing danger of imperialism, in particular of US imperialism, and India's growing economic dependence on it; refusal to rouse the people against the policies of the Government in this regard; exonerating the Government by holding the monopolists responsible for the anti-people, anti-national policies of the Government, talking about opening their 'national front' not against the Government's policies but against the monopolists who are out to subvert the 'national' policies of the Government; attempting to enter into an alliance with the bourgeois–landlord Government and the Congress party, all in the name of opposing the reactionaries; supporting the drifting foreign policy and evading a struggle against US imperialist pressure—such are the broad features of their Programme. They are opposed to dislodging the Government led by the big bourgeoisie and replacing it by the People's Democratic Government led by the working class."[11]

II. THE CPI(M) CRITIQUE OF THE RUSSIAN COMMUNIST PARTY

The CPI was deeply split over the attitude that the Indian communists should take in respect of the Indo–China dispute. The rightists within the party led by Dange branded China as the aggressor, but the leftists were not prepared to accept that a socialist country like China could commit aggression on India. Eventually, the differences between the rightists and leftists on the question of the class character of the Indian state, the path to be pursued for completing the anti-imperialist and anti-feudal revolution, the approach to the question of China, the attitude towards the "Dange letters" and on certain other matters, brought about a split in the Communist Party of India in 1964. In the early years after the split the CPI was ideologically closer to the Russian communists and the CPI(M), which had seceded from it, to the Chinese communists, though in the course of time, and particularly after 1967, China also came to denounce the CPI(M) as a revisionist party.

From its very inception the CPI(M) characterized the CPI as a revisionist party. According to the CPI(M) on every crucial issue its views were diametrically opposed to those of the CPI. *The Draft for Ideological Discussion* prepared by the Central Committee of the CPI(M) in August 1967 stated: "To put it sharply, there is not one single basic question connected with the Indian revolution on which we and the revisionists [that is, the CPI] do not stand diametrically opposed to each other. Their class characterization of the post-independence Indian state and government, their assessment of the internal and external policies of the new government, their critique of the capitalist path of development and the advocacy of a noncapitalist path and National democracy, their study of the prevailing class contradictions in the country and their understanding of the present stage and strategy of our revolution, their estimation regarding the role of the nonmonopoly national bourgeoisie in the struggle against the capitalist path and for a noncapitalist path, their understanding of the Marxist-Leninist concept of the proletarian hegemony over the democratic revolution, their interpretation of the peaceful and nonpeaceful paths of development and their possibilities, their assessment of the role of foreign monopoly capital in the Indian economy on the one hand and the role and place of socialist aid in influencing the economic development of our country, their estimation of the state sector and its character and, above all, their assessment of Congress agrarian reforms have nothing in common with our Party's analysis and understanding. In this connection, it is very pertinent to note that the position taken by the leadership of the Communist Party of the

Soviet Union on all the fundamental questions connected with the Indian Communist movement, completely coincide with these of the Dangeite revisionists. . . . "[12]

The CPI(M) regard modern revisionism as the greatest danger to the world communist movement and attributes the growth of such revisionism mainly to the pursuit of revisionist theories by the leadership of the Communist Party of the Soviet Union (CPSU).[13] Khrushchev is denounced as the father of modern revisionism who had abandoned Lenin's theses on imperialism and war on the plea of applying Marxism–Leninism creatively to new conditions.[14] The CPI(M) calls upon the people to carry on a determined and principled fight against modern revisionism.

According to Marxism–Leninism, in the present era there exist four fundamental social contradictions, namely, the contradiction between the camps of world socialism and capitalism, the contradiction between the proletariat and the bourgeoisie in capitalist countries, the contradiction between the imperialist states and the oppressed countries, and the contradiction among the different imperialist states and among monopoly capitalist groups. Of these four contradictions Khrushchev had emphasized primarily the contradiction between the camps of world socialism and world capitalism. So far as the contradiction between the proletariat and the bourgeoisie is concerned he had envisaged a peaceful transition to socialism. This assessment the CPI(M) regards as "un–Marxian and opportunist."[15]

The CPI(M) considers that Khrushchev and modern revisionists have made four principal mistakes, namely, first, the assertion that the contradiction between the socialist and imperialist camps is the main contradiction of the era; secondly, the belief that the contradiction between proletariat and bourgeoisie may be resolved peacefully; thirdly, the assumption that international agreements among monopolists may mitigate or eliminate inter-imperialist contradictions; and, finally, that the contradiction between the socialist and the imperialist camps may be resolved through peaceful economic competition.

As a result of the change in the international balance of class forces and the establishment of socialism in a large number of countries of the world, Khrushchev came to the conclusion that imperialist wars were no longer inevitable. Accordingly, Khrushchev asserted that the Leninist theory as to the inevitability of wars was no longer appropriate or applicable to the modern world. Lenin had said that imperialist wars were absolutely inevitable under an economic system where there existed private property in the means of production. He also regarded national rebellions and wars and proletarian wars and rebellions against the bourgeoisie as inevitable. Khrushchev's thesis that, in the modern era, war was not fatalistically inevitable was denounced by the CPI(M) as revisionist and un–Marxian.

The new scientific and technological advances and the development of destructive nuclear weapons had induced Khrushchev to entertain the belief that modern wars would be so destructive that they had to be avoided by all means. Further, the strength of the socialist forces in the world had so increased that Khrushchev was convinced that it was now possible to avoid wars. The CPI(M), however, regards the inevitability of war as a fundamental tenet of Marxism and Leninism, and holds that neither technological advances nor the radically changed correlation of forces in the world in favour of socialism and against imperialism has made such a theory outmoded. The CPI(M) asserts that so long as imperialism exists, war cannot be avoided. It states: "But wars can be eliminated and lasting peace secured only when imperialism is eliminated; as long as imperialism exists, there will be soil for wars of aggression."[16]

The CPI(M) criticized Russian efforts to effect disarmament and denounced Russia for having signed the test ban treaty against the opposition of China. In such Russian efforts to achieve disarmament the CPI(M) discerned a pacifist, nonclass, and revisionist approach which could breed the illusion that imperialist wars would no longer take place and which would thereby undermine the strength of the anti-imperialist forces throughout the world. The CPI(M) considers that no sovereign nation, whose economy was viable, would reconcile itself to the idea of its independence being guaranteed by a nuclear umbrella either of the USA or the USSR. It asserts: "But the Soviet leaders, under the pretext of the struggle they are waging for disarmament, nonproliferation and banning of atomic weapons, tore off the agreement concluded with socialist China to provide it with atomic technical know-how, and thus sought to prevent People's China from acquiring atomic weapons. Further, the Soviet leaders in open conflict with and opposition to socialist China, concluded a test-ban treaty and is proceeding to conclude a so-called treaty of nonproliferation of nuclear weapons along with the US and British imperialists."[17]

Khrushchev and the leaders of Soviet Russia realized the grave peril to modern civilization that a thermo-nuclear warfare could cause, and, therefore, they were eager to reach an understanding with the USA to prevent such a war. But the CPI(M) criticized the Soviet leaders saying that instead of relying on the strength and unity of the socialist camp to prevent such a war the Soviet leaders were seeking to collaborate with the Anglo-American imperialists to secure world peace.[18]

The CPI(M) also criticized the Russian concept of peaceful coexistence between the capitalist and socialist states and pointed out that this concept was opposed to Lenin's analysis of war and imperialism. Lenin had said: "International imperialism . . . could not under any circumstances, on any conditions live side by side with the Soviet Republic both because of its objective position and because of the economic interests of the capitalist class. . . . In this sphere the conflict is inevitable. Therein lies the greatest difficulty of the Russian revolution, its greatest historical problem. . . . " Lenin was convinced that the existence of the Soviet Republic side by side with imperialist states for a long time was unthinkable. "One or the other must triumph in the end. And before that end supervenes, a series of frightful collisions between the Soviet Republic and the bourgeois states will be inevitable."

True, as early as 1916, Lenin had envisaged the possibility of accomplishing the socialist revolution in one or several countries while for a certain period capitalism existed in other countries, but he did not consider that socialist and capitalist states could live together side by side for all times to come. He said: "So long as capitalism and socialism remain, they cannot live at peace, in the long run either one or the other will be victorious, the funeral dirge will be sounded either over the Soviet Republic or over world capitalism. It will be a respite in the war." But Khrushchev and other Soviet leaders abandoned the Leninist theory that socialist and capitalistic states could not coexist for all times to come and in lieu thereof they evolved the concept of peaceful coexistence of socialist and capitalistic states. Such a concept was anathema to the CPI(M) which stated: "The

absurd limits to which this well-known revolutionary concept
of Lenin is reduced can be seen when the modern revisionists
who, in words, agree that US imperialism today has become 'the
biggest international exploiter', 'the chief bulwark of world
reaction', and 'international gendarme and the chief enemy of
the peoples of the world', in practice, treat the US Imperialist
rulers as those with whom real and lasting peaceful coexistence
is possible.... The interpretation of the concept of peaceful coexistence... between the socialist and imperialist states is reduced
by the revisionists to mean that the chief struggle between the
two systems is in the main peaceful economic competition and
thus conceal the truth that the struggle between the two systems
comprises every field of economic, political, ideological, and
military nature... it seems to conceal the constant imperialist
aggression and to appease the aggressor, and it disarms the revolutionary proletariat of the world in its uncompromising fight
against imperialism—economic, political, ideological, and military."[19]

The CPI(M) subjected the theory of peaceful transition to
socialism propounded by Khrushchev and other Russian leaders
to a similar criticism and characterized this concept as a deviation from Leninist principles. Though Lenin had rejected the
theory that armed uprising as a form of struggle was obligatory
under all circumstances, and had visualized the possibility of
some small country, in the neighbourhood of a big socialist
country, being able to effect a peaceful transition to socialism,
he had yet asserted that generally such transition to socialism
could not be achieved peacefully. But the development of the
forces of socialism and the growth of parliamentary institutions
in divers countries of the world had emboldened Khrushchev
and other Soviet leaders to cherish the belief that a peaceful
transition to socialism was possible. The CPI(M) did not subscribe to this belief, and attacked the concept of peaceful transition to socialism, saying: "But the modern revisionists maintain
that in view of the changed correlation of forces on an international scale as well as in each country in favour of the proletariat
and its cause of socialism, and in view of the ever-increasing
grip of the ideas of socialism on the minds of wide masses of
the people, the universal law of violent revolution as propounded
by Marx, Engels, Lenin, and Stalin, forced on the proletariat by

the bourgeoisie, and as universally accepted by all the Marxist–Leninists has become outmoded and hence to be discarded. In its place, they argue, the law of peaceful transition and parliamentary path is to be substituted; they even expound the thesis that socialist transformation can be effected by a state of so-called National Democracy where the bourgeoisie and the proletariat hold joint hegemony of the National Democratic Revolution and the National Democratic state; . . . "[20]

Marx was not oblivious of the mighty power of the franchise and, in fact, in the 1870s both Marx and Engels had considered that Britain and the USA, where parliamentary institutions had developed, could be regarded as exceptions to the theory of the inevitability of revolution as the only means of effecting a transition to socialism. But the CPI(M) believed that with the change of circumstances, these exceptions to the general rule no longer held good and that it was precisely because of this that "Lenin after studying the development of capitalism to the stage of monopoly capitalism and imperialism asserted that the above exceptions conceived by Marx and Engels in 1870 to the USA and Britain would no more hold valid. . . . "[21] The CPI(M) regards that the thesis of peaceful transition to socialism would only ideologically disarm the proletariat and dampen their revolutionary ardour.

The CPI(M) asserts that the Russian theory of national democracy and the noncapitalist path as a transitional form for socialist revolution is nothing but opportunistic. At the Second Congress of the Comintern held in 1920, the question was considered whether the colonial countries must inevitably pass through a capitalist stage or whether they could advance to communism without passing through the intermediary capitalist stage. Lenin urged that it might be possible, in some cases, for backward countries to skip this intermediate capitalist stage and establish communism provided that such a country obtained powerful assistance from the proletariat of the advanced countries and from Soviet Russia. The CPI(M) argued that this concept of Lenin was distorted and vulgarized by the revisionist Soviet leaders and that their concept of the noncapitalist path of development, in effect, negatived the concept of proletarian hegemony and substituted in its place the concept of the joint hegemony of the proletariat along with the bourgeoisie.[22]

The CPI(M) unreservedly criticized all the three concepts of peaceful coexistence, peaceful economic competition, and peaceful transition that were propounded by Khrushchev at the Twentieth Congress of the CPSU. Though the CPI(M) did not accept the Chinese Communist Party's characterization that the Soviet Union had become an ally of US imperialism and was working with the USA to share world hegemony, the CPI(M) yet considered that the application of the afore-mentioned three concepts would only lead the Soviet Union to pursue "a line of class conciliation and collaboration on a global plane."[23] The CPI(M) did not place the Soviet Union outside the socialist camp, in the manner that the Chinese Communist Party did, but it praised China for having exposed the revisionist character of Soviet policy. "Modern revisionism led by Khrushchev and pursued by the present CPSU leaders," declared the CPI(M), "has done the greatest damage to the cause of the working class and Communist movement in the world. It should be said that the Communist Party of China has rendered yeoman service to the world working class and Communist movement in fighting against this menace of modern revisionism and in defence of Marxism–Leninism."[24]

At the Twenty-second Congress of the Communist Party of the Soviet Union the concept of the people's state was evolved and it was said that the working class of the Soviet Union had transformed the state of proletarian dictatorship into a state of the whole people. The CPI(M) regards this concept of the people's state and the idea of the ending of the dictatorship of the proletariat as being wholly repugnant to Marxist–Leninist ideas. In Marxist–Leninist terminology, the state is a special organization of force or violence which exists for the suppression of some class. According to this terminology every state is a class state, and there can be no nonclass state. According to Lenin, so long as classes remain, the dictatorship of the proletariat would be necessary, but when classes disappear altogether then the dictatorship of the proletariat would also disappear. In Marxist–Leninist terminology the proletarian state would disappear when its class task of bringing about socialism and communism has been completed. The task of building socialism and communism has not yet been completed in Russia. Accordingly the CPI(M) is opposed to the concept of a people's state and it asserts that "to indulge in the talk of transforming the dictatorship of the proletariat into a state of the whole people or in other words the abolition of the proletarian state, would be a betrayal of Marxism–Leninism and treachery to the working class."[25]

The nonclass concept of a people's state so propounded at the Twenty-second Congress of the Communist Party of the Soviet Union was criticized by the CPI(M) in the same manner as another concept formulated at this Congress, namely, the characterization of the Communist Party of the Soviet Union as the party of the whole people. If the dictatorship of the proletariat was to remain then the party of the proletariat had to remain. Accordingly the CPI(M) could not envisage with equanimity the proposal of the Communist Party giving up its class character and converting itself into an amorphous nonclass party of the whole people.[26]

The attempt of the Soviet leaders to revive economic incentives in the Soviet Union for the purpose of augmenting production was similarly criticized by the CPI(M), who said that this would mould the working-class consciousness on the bourgeois ideal of securing personal profit. The CPI(M) asserted that "capitalist incentives and ideas of personal profit, in the final analysis, pave the way for the restoration of a new type of capitalism, and harms the cause of socialism and communism."[27]

Another crucial difference between the CPI(M) and the CPSU centred round the latter's criticism of Stalin and the pursuit of the de-Stalinization policy in Russia. This policy started with the submission of the secret report of Khrushchev at the Twentieth Congress of the CPSU in 1956 in which Khrushchev had spoken of the many atrocities committed during Stalin's régime. The CPI(M) considered that in making these criticisms of Stalin without reference to the divers, communist parties of the world, the CPSU had sought to treat Stalin as its personal property forgetting that thirty years of the history of the world communist movement were intimately associated with Stalin and the policies that he had pursued. About Khrushchev's startling disclosures regarding Stalin, the CPI(M) said: "The biggest fact of history—that he [Stalin] was destined to act as the spokesman of the CPSU and the Communist International for decades following the death of Lenin, to defend Marxism–Leninism from the attacks of right and left opportunist trends, to head the building of socialism in the Soviet Union and transform it into a mighty world power, to lead the historic anti-fascist war to victory, to rebuild rapidly the war-ravaged economy and industrial might of the Soviet Union, and to lead the formation and functioning of the world socialist camp was sought to be simply ignored, and a one-sided, distorted and subjective assessment was made."[28]

The CPI(M) discerned further revisionistic tendencies on the part of the leaders of the Soviet Union in their failure to expose the revisionism of the Yugoslav Party. The Yugoslav Party had refused to accept the 1957 Moscow declaration of the Communist Parties of the world. Later, the 1960 Moscow Conference of the 81 Communist Parties of the world had condemned Yugoslav revisionism thus: "The Communist Parties have unanimously condemned the Yugoslav variety of international opportunism, a variety of modern revisionist 'theories' in concentrated form. After betraying Marxism–Leninism, which they termed obsolete, the leaders of the League of Communists of Yugoslavia opposed their anti–Leninist, revisionist programme to the Declaration of 1957; they set the League of Communists of Yugoslavia against the international Communist movement as a whole, severed their country from the socialist camp, made it dependent on so-called 'aid' from the US and other imperialists, and thereby exposed the Yugoslav people to the danger of losing the revolutionary gains achieved through heroic struggle. The Yugoslav revisionists carry on subversive work against the socialist camp and the world Communist movement." But in spite of all these, the Soviet leaders, the CPI(M) laments, were underestimating the menace of Yugoslav revisionism.

Though the CPI(M) did not carry its criticism of the Communist Party of the Soviet Union to the length that the Chinese party did, and though the CPI(M) did not place the Soviet Union as a country outside the socialist camp altogether, the CPI(M)'s criticisms of the Soviet leaders were fundamental and far-reaching. As between the Soviet Union and China, the sympathies of the CPI(M) were with China. It stated: "The high-handed manner in which the leadership of the CPSU revised a series of Marxist–Leninist propositions at the 20th Congress and sought to arbitrarily impose its understanding on fraternal parties, the open denunciation of the Chinese Communist Party by Khrushchev at Bucharest in 1960 after it expressed its serious ideological differences with the CPSU, the blatant violations of fraternal socialist relations by the Soviet leaders through the stoppage of aid, annulling agreements mutually entered into, and sudden withdrawal of the Soviet technicians from China, the unashamed backing out from the Sino–Soviet agreement to share the technical know-how of atomic weapons, the test-ban treaty that was signed and the proposed treaty of non-proliferation to be signed by the Soviet leaders with the USA and Britain bypassing China and in the teeth of its opposition, the Soviet leaders' refusal to help China to acquire the latest military techniques and to develop its military capability to meet the American atomic and rocket menace, the most vicious international campaign organized by the Soviet Party and Government to isolate it and pressurize it into submission, and a host of similar steps and actions deliberately perpetrated by them to damn the Chinese Communists as war-mongers and traitors to the cause of socialism, cannot be wiped out with the stroke of a pen by issuing the slogan, let us unite in action against US aggression."[29]

Nearly a decade after the Moscow Conference of 1960, a large number of communist parties of the world again met at Moscow in 1969 and issued a policy statement. By 1969 the split in the world communist movement had been complete and the Communist Party of China, one of the two big communist parties of the world, did not participate in this Conference. The Albanian party, which had supported China in its ideological warfare with Russia, also did not attend. The Communist Party of Cuba attended as an observer but made its independent stand clear. The Communist Party of Vietnam and the Korean Party of Labour also did not attend.

From India, only the representatives of the CPI attended the Conference. The CPI(M) characterized the statement issued by the Conference as revisionist and utterly opposed to the principles of Marxism–Leninism.[30] The CPI(M) lamented that instead of being a conference for joint anti-imperialist action, it degenerated, to a certain extent, into a forum for denouncing the Communist Party of China.

The 1969 Moscow Conference placed great emphasis on the struggle for peace. Acknowledging that the preservation of peace was one of the main tasks that faced the anti-imperialist movement of the world, the Moscow Conference declared: "The main link of united action of the anti-imperialist forces remains the struggle against the war danger ... and the fight for world peace. ... The defence of peace is inseparably linked with the struggle to compel the imperialists to accept peaceful coexistence of states with different social systems." The Conference recognized that there were certain sections in the ruling circles of imperialist countries who took a more realistic approach to international problems and attempted to solve them in a spirit of peaceful coexistence between states with different systems. The Conference welcomed this and emphasized that the most urgent task facing the world was to take steps to prevent the spread of nuclear weapons and to enforce nuclear nonproliferation treaty.

The Moscow Conference was silent on the question of the Soviet intervention in Czechoslovakia. This Soviet intervention had given rise to serious misgivings among various communist parties of the world and particularly among those in Western Europe. Some of these Western European communist parties had criticized the Soviet intervention in Czechoslovakia. The CPI(M), on the other hand, had fully supported the Soviet intervention in Czechoslovakia saying that such an intervention had become necessary to stamp out counter-revolutionary tendencies in Czechoslovakia. The CPI(M) was, therefore, unhappy that the Moscow Conference was silent on this question.[31]

The CPI(M) charged that the anti-imperialist struggle that the Chinese people were waging had been completely ignored by the 1969 Moscow Conference but that, on the other hand, Yugoslavia, which had been branded as a revisionist country by the 1960 Moscow Conference, was treated as part of the socialist camp at the 1969 Moscow Conference.[32]

The support to the doctrine of peaceful coexistence and peaceful transition to socialism given by the 1969 Moscow Conference was also similarly criticized by the CPI(M) and it particularly referred to the fact that the warning clause of the 1960 document which declared: "Leninism teaches, and experience confirms, that the ruling classes never relinquish power voluntarily" had been deleted from the 1969 Moscow Conference statement.[33] The CPI(M) felt that the 1969 Moscow

Conference had discarded the Marxist–Leninist doctrine of war and revolution and that by envisaging peaceful transition to socialism it would encourage the growth of parliamentary illusions among the proletariat. The Central Committee of the CPI(M) stated: "The document [issued by the 1969 Moscow Conference] sustains the illusion that far-reaching social changes can take place in newly liberated countries, and these countries can even develop a socialist orientation without an organized party of the working class based on Marxism–Leninism and without the leading role of the working class. In effect, it means that the democratic anti-feudal anti-imperialist revolution can be completed without the leadership of the working class and its party."[34]

The CPI was well represented at this Moscow Conference of 1969. The CPI welcomed the 1969 Moscow Conference to the effect that in the newly-liberated countries transition to socialism might take place peacefully. The CPI(M) had serious reservations about this policy which it considered to be revisionist and it had nothing but scorn for the part played by the CPI at the 1969 Moscow Conference. "The revisionist leaders of the Right CP," declared the Central Committee of the CPI(M), "who were given an honoured place at the conference, utilized the opportunity to toe faithfully the opportunist revisionist line."[35]

III. THE CPI(M) CRITIQUE OF THE CHINESE COMMUNIST PARTY

After the communist split in India in 1964 the CPI(M) had often made appreciative observations as to the fight initiated by the Chinese Communist Party (CPC) against modern revisionism. But by 1967 the CPC had commenced to refer to the CPI(M) as a revisionist party and the CPI(M), in its turn, charged that the later formulations of the CPC showed that it had got "derailed into dogmatism and sectarianism."

By 1967 the CPC ceased to regard the CPI(M) as a genuine communist party and it began to denounce the CPI(M) publicly and through the press and radio as a reformist and revisionist party. The Naxalites, who had broken away from the CPI(M), were now considered by the CPC as the real revolutionaries. The CPI(M) took note of these developments, and in August 1967

the Central Committee of the party adopted a resolution at
Madurai regarding the divergent views of the CPI(M) and the
CPC on certain fundamental issues relating to programme and
policy.[36]

There were three basic differences between the CPI(M) and
CPC. The first difference related to the programmatic aspect,
namely, the class character of the Indian state and the role of
different sections of the Indian bourgeoisie in relation to imperialism. The second difference concerned the assessment of the
economic and political situation in the country and the tactics
and forms of struggle to be adopted. The third difference was
about political and organizational matters and about what should
be the relationship between the different communist parties of
the world.

The programmatic difference inside the communist movement
itself had, to a considerable extent, been responsible for the split
in the Communist Party of India in 1964. The rightists inside
the party believed that Nehru represented the aspirations of the
anti-imperialist and anti-feudal sections of the Indian bourgeoisie
and that the hands of Nehru in his encounter against the pro-
imperialist and pro-feudal sections should be strengthened. P. C.
Joshi was the most pronounced champion of this point of view.
The view of the CPC was diametrically opposite to this.

The Chinese view was stated in two published documents,
namely, "Nehru's Philosophy" and "Once More on Nehru's
Philosophy" and in divers editorials in the *People's Daily* and in
the broadcasts over Peking Radio. According to the Chinese,
the Indian big bourgeoisie was a parasitic class. It represented
the comprador, bureaucratic capital in India and was being
fostered by British imperialism. It is this bourgeoisie which
controlled the Congress government. According to this view,
though for some time after independence Nehru acted on behalf
of the noncomprador, nonbureaucratic, and nonmonopoly sections, later he went over completely to imperialism and became
a mouthpiece of imperialism in the same manner as Chiang
Kai-shek had been since 1927. Accordingly, the stage of the
Indian revolution was principally anti-imperialist.

The CPI(M) naturally could not accept the CPC analysis that
the stage of the Indian revolution is principally anti-imperialist,
or that the situation in India in 1967 was the same as in China in

1927. There has been considerable capitalistic development in India, and, accordingly, the capitalists in India were in a far stronger position than their counterparts in pre-revolutionary China. Again, it is the industrial big bourgeoisie and not the comprador bourgeoisie, unlike in China, which emerged as a powerful force in India. The position in India, where the industrial big bourgeoisie were seeking to expand industries, was quite different from that of pre-revolutionary China where four big families of Soong, Keng, Chang, and Lin, acting as the representatives of comprador bourgeoisie in alliance with feudalism and imperialism, served as retarding forces in the development of the national economy.

In view of these crucial differences between the Chinese and Indian situation, the CPI(M) did not accept the CPC thesis that the stage of the Indian revolution was principally anti-imperialist. According to the CPI(M) the Indian government was a bourgeois–landlord government which was led by the big bourgeoisie though it was compromising and collaborating with foreign monopoly capital. It was clear that the Indian government had a far wider social base than the pre-revolutionary Chinese government. Accordingly, the CPI(M), differing from the CPC, asserts: "Hence, we do not find any valid reason for the present Indian government, which has a ... wider social base when compared to most of its counterparts in several countries and which does not face the imminent threat of class revolution at home, opting to play the role of 'puppet', 'stooge' and 'lackey' of imperialism."[37]

The assessment of the CPC that the Indian government was a puppet government, which was serving mainly the interests of the foreign imperialists, could only lead to the conclusion that a national liberation struggle would have to be waged against the foreign imperialists and not that a class struggle should be waged against the big bourgeoisie and landlords who, according to the CPI(M), controlled the Indian government. If the Chinese premise was to be accepted then, asserts the CPI(M), "the national liberation aspect of our revolution stands in the forefront, the edge of the revolution will have to be directed against the foreign imperialists, the contradiction between alien imperialists and the nation as a whole assumes the principal role, and a corresponding strategy of general national united front will have to be substituted in place of the present class strategy incorporated in our Programme. The concept of concentrating the main fire against the bourgeois–landlord state power with the agrarian revolution as its axis will have to be given up."[38]

On the basis of the analysis that India is a semi-feudal, semi-colonial country where the principal struggle should be against imperialism, the CPC relied on armed struggle as the main weapon of revolution and, therefore, supported the militant Naxalites and condemned not only the CPI but also the CPI(M), who participated in non–Congress United Front governments, as revisionists. In an editorial in the *People's Daily* on 5 July 1967 it was stated: "The so-called 'non–Congress Government' in West Bengal openly sided with the reactionary Indian Government in its bloody suppression of the revolutionary peasants in Darjeeling. This gives added proof that these renegades and revisionists are running dogs of US imperialism and Soviet revisionism and the lackeys of the big Indian landlords and bourgeoisie. What they call the 'non–Congress government' is only a tool of these landlords and bourgeoisie." In a comment in the *People's Daily* on 11 July 1967 it was similarly stated: "In India today, the rule of the Congress clique has become so discredited that the Indian reactionaries have had to try some new tricks such as bringing some scabs and renegades in some states to establish a so-called 'non-Congress Government' in order to deceive the people."

The CPI(M) could not accept the Chinese view that no advance whatsoever can be made through the parliamentary method or by the utilization of the power of the franchise. The parliamentary path opened up certain opportunities for developing the class struggle. The programme adopted by the CPI(M) in October–November 1964 at its Seventh Congress stated: "However, universal adult franchise and parliamentary and state legislature can serve as instruments of the people in the struggle for democracy, for defence of their interests. Although a form of class rule of the bourgeoisie, India's present parliamentary system also embodies an advance for the people. It affords certain opportunities to them to defend their interests, intervene in the affairs of the state to a certain extent, and mobilize them to carry forward the struggle for peace, democracy, and social progress."[39]

This programme of the CPI(M), adopted at its Seventh Congress, stated that the threat to the parliamentary system and to democracy came not from the working people but from the exploiting classes, who sought to undermine the parliamentary system in order to repress the toiling masses. "When the people begin to use parliamentary institutions for advancing their cause and they fall away from the influence of the reactionary bourgeoisie and landlords, these classes," the programme stated, "do not hesitate to trample underfoot parliamentary democracy as was done in Kerala in 1959. When their interest demands they do not hesitate to replace parliamentary democracy by military dictatorship. It will be a serious error and dangerous illusion to imagine that our country is free from all such threats. It is of the utmost importance that parliamentary and democratic institutions are defended in the interest of the people against such threats, and that such institutions are skilfully utilized in combination with extra-parliamentary activities."[40]

The CPI(M) places reliance primarily on extra-parliamentary activities but does not shun the parliamentary path altogether. It seeks to pursue the Leninist method of combining parliamentary with nonparliamentary activities and admonishes the Naxalites who would have nothing to do with parliamentary activities. It also criticizes the Chinese party for interference with the Indian communist movement and for describing the Naxalites as the real revolutionaries of India.[41]

The Central Committee of the CPI(M) at its session at Madurai in August 1967 formulated its policy towards the Naxalites and characterized them as being guilty of left-sectarianism and left-opportunism.[42] The Naxalites regard the Indian government as a stooge government and the Indian state as a neo-colonial state which has to be subverted by armed revolution. Their programme stated: "In this situation, fearing revolution, the big bourgeoisie (representing the monopoly and big capitalists) of the country established Congress rule in 1947 on the basis of collaboration with imperialism so as to preserve intact the interest of imperialism and to exploit jointly with imperialism Indian labour and resources." Such an assessment of the nature of the Indian state could only lead to the pursuit of a policy of armed insurrection for subverting the Indian state. The CPI(M) rejected such an analysis which "leads to left-sectarian and adventurist errors. ... What is the implication of stooge government, a neo-colonial state? ... It implies that the state government is already completely isolated, universally hated and armed struggle is the only form (of struggle) left to the people. ... "[43]

Believing that the Indian state was a neo-colonial state headed by a stooge government, the Naxalites gave a call for the boycott of the legislatures. The Naxalites rejected the path of parliamentarianism altogether and denounced the United Front governments formed after the fourth general elections by the leftist parties. They asked the people to follow Mao's teachings that power could grow only out of the barrel of a gun. But was not such a theory, which rejected parliamentary methods even as an auxiliary form of struggle, opposed to the teachings of Lenin? asked the CPI(M). "You say that parliament is an instrument with the aid of which the bourgeoisie deceive the masses. But this argument," said Lenin, "should be turned against you, and it does turn against your theses. How will you reveal the true character of parliament to the really backward masses, who are deceived by the bourgeoisie? How will you expose the various parliamentary manoeuvres, or the positions of the various parties, if you are not in parliament, if you remain outside parliament? If you are Marxists, you must admit that, in capitalist society, there is a close link between the relations of classes and the relations of parties. How, I repeat, will you show all this if you are not members of parliament, and if you renounce parliamentary action? The history of the Russian revolution has clearly shown that the mass of the working class, the peasantry, and petty office employees could not have been convinced by any arguments, unless their own experience had convinced them.

"It has been claimed here that it is a waste of time to participate in the parliamentary struggle. Can one conceive of any other institution in which all classes are as interested as they are in parliament? ... If all classes are drawn into the parliamentary struggle, it is because the class interests and conflicts are reflected in parliament. If it were possible everywhere and immediately to bring about, let us say, a decisive general strike so as to overthrow capitalism at a single stroke, the revolution would have already taken place in a number of countries. But we must reckon with the facts, and parliament is a scene of the class struggle."[44]

The CPI(M) regard the Naxalite policy of the boycott of the legislatures as anti–Leninist and considers that Mao's doctrine that political power grows only out of the barrel of a gun has no universal application and that the Indian revolution need not necessarily take the Chinese path. The CPI(M) believes in the Leninist policy of a skilful combination of parliamentary and extra-parliamentary activities for bringing about the Indian revolution.

NOTES AND REFERENCES

1. B. T. Ranadive, *The Two Programmes—Marxist and Revisionist,* Calcutta, December 1966.
2. *Programme of the Communist Party of India Adopted by the Seventh Congress of the Communist Party of India,* Calcutta, 31 October to 7 November 1964, p. 45.
3. B. T. Ranadive, op. cit., p. 5.
4. Ibid., p. 8.
5. Ibid., p. 9.
6. Ibid., p. 14.
7. Ibid., p. 34.
8. Ibid., p. 35.
9. Ibid., pp. 37-40.
10. Ibid., p. 143.
11. Ibid., p. 144.
12. *Central Committee Draft for Ideological Discussion Adopted by the Central Committee of the Communist Party of India (Marxist),* Madurai, 18 to 27 August 1967, pp. 3-4.
13. Ibid., p. 6.
14. Ibid., p. 8.
15. Ibid., p. 10.
16. Ibid., p. 17.
17. Ibid., pp. 19-20.
18. Ibid., pp. 20-21.
19. Ibid., pp. 23-24.
20. Ibid., pp. 27-28.
21. Ibid., p. 29.
22. Ibid., pp. 31-32.
23. Ibid., p. 33.
24. Ibid., p. 35.
25. Ibid., p. 37.
26. Ibid., p. 38.
27. Ibid., p. 39.

28. Ibid., pp. 40-41; see also B. T. Ranadive's article, "In Memory of Stalin," in *People's Democracy*, 21 December 1969.
29. *Central Committee Draft For Ideological Discussion Adopted by the* CPI(M), Madurai, 18 to 27 August 1967, pp. 3-4.
30. *Central Committee Statement on Moscow Conference Adopted by the Central Committee of the Communist Party of India (Marxist) at its Session in Calcutta, 15-20 July 1969*, Calcutta, 1969.
31. Ibid., p. 9.
32. Ibid., p. 11.
33. Ibid., p. 7.
34. Ibid., p. 8.
35. Ibid., p. 13.
36. *Central Committee Resolutions Adopted by the Central Committee of the Communist Party of India (Marxist), Madurai, 18 to 27 August 1967.*
37. Ibid., p. 9.
38. Ibid., p. 10.
39. *Programme of the Communist Party of India Adopted by the Seventh Congress of the Communist Party of India, Calcutta, 31 October–7 November 1964*, Calcutta, 1966, p. 30.
40. Ibid., pp. 30-31.
41. *Central Committee Resolutions Adopted by the Central Committee of the* CPI(M), *Madurai, 18 to 27 August 1967, Calcutta*, p. 22.
42. *On the Left Deviation, Resolution of the Central Committee, Communist Party of India (Marxist), Madurai, 18 to 27 August 1967, and Other Information Documents*, Calcutta, p. 4.
43. Ibid., p. 5.
44. Lenin, *Collected Works*, Vol. 31, pp. 255-56.

CHAPTER TWELVE

Maoism and the Naxalites

When in 1964, the CPI(M) was formed, the CPI was ideologically and otherwise closer to the Russian communists, whereas the CPI(M) was closer to the Chinese communists. There were basic ideological differences between the CPI and the CPI(M). These two parties gave different answers to the three questions which are important for the purpose of communist strategy, namely, first, at what stage is the revolution, secondly, who are its enemies, and, finally, who are its allies.

The CPI considers that the Indian state is an organ of the class rule of the national bourgeoisie, which upholds and develops capitalism and capitalist relations of production, distribution and exchange, and that in the Indian state the big bourgeoisie or the monopolists exert considerable influence. According to the CPI the revolution in India is at the national–democratic stage, that is, at the stage where it is anti-imperialist and anti-feudal. For completing this revolution the classes interested are the working class, the cultivating peasants, including not only the agricultural labourers but the rich peasants, the urban and rural intelligentsia, and the national bourgeoisie. The enemies are the imperialists, the landlords, the big monopolists, and the right reactionaries. The CPI believes in the development of a national democratic front as a multiclass and multiparty platform. In this class alliance the exclusive leadership of the working class is not established, though the exclusive leadership of the bourgeoisie no longer exists. The national democratic front, in which the CPI would have an important role to play, would establish a national democratic government at the centre. Later, with the development of the socialistic consciousness of the people, the CPI hopes, that the communists would succeed in winning a majority in parliament. With such a majority parliament would be transformed into an instrument of the people's will for the socialistic reconstruction of society.

The CPI(M) assessment of the situation is somewhat different.[1] According to the CPI(M), the present Indian state is not the organ of the national bourgeoisie as the CPI asserts. It is the organ of the class-rule of the bourgeoisie and landlords headed by the big bourgeoisie, who are collaborating with foreign finance capital. This state has to be replaced and overthrown by a people's democracy and not by a national democratic government as envisaged by the CPI. Further, the people's democratic front would be led by the working class, unlike the national democratic front of the CPI, where the working class would not have exclusive leadership. The allies of this people's democratic front, led by the working class, would be the peasants, the lower middle classes and probably a section of the national bourgeoisie, but this latter section would in all probability be a vacillating ally. The enemies are the big bourgeoisie, feudal landlords, the foreign monopoly capitalists, and right reactionary forces. One of the main tasks of the people's democratic revolution would be to effect an agrarian revolution, which the "bourgeois–landlord state" have sought to prevent. To effect this revolution a people's democratic front under the leadership of the working class and its political party, the CPI(M), would have to be formed. Though this people's democratic front, with the support of the working class and the peasantry, would seek first to establish a people's democracy and then to effect a socialist transformation of society by peaceful means, the CPI(M) asserts that the people would have to remain vigilant and they would have to adopt violent means if the forces of reaction, by resorting to violence, force it upon them.

The Naxalites, who consider even the CPI(M) as a revisionist party, has no faith in parliamentarianism or in any method other than the method of armed struggle. Accordingly, they gave a call for the boycott of the mid-term polls held in Bengal in February 1969, though without any success. During this time efforts were made to organize the Naxalites into a separate communist party. Towards the end of February 1969, the All-India Coordination Committee of the communist revolutionaries, comprising Naxalites and other extremist elements from different states, held a secret conference for this purpose. At this conference a resolution was passed which declared: "A stage has now been reached when the formation of the Communist Party brooks no further delay. The party should immediately be formed, with, as the core, those revolutionaries who are building up and conducting revolutionary class struggles." This party, which was to be Maoist in outlook, would seek to unite with "our class brethren who are waging heroic struggles in Burma, Thailand, Malaya, Indonesia, and various other countries of the world, and to forge that great bond of internationalism which has been given noble expression by Chairman Mao in the great proletarian cultural revolution." Such a party was necessary to develop the agrarian struggle going on in different parts of the country. The resolution also criticized "all the parties of the ruling classes, including the various revisionist parties, which are feverishly trying to strengthen parliamentary illusions." Such a party was also to carry on intensive propaganda to expose "the hollowness of parliamentarianism and the counter-revolutionary character of the revisionist and neo-revisionist parties."

A leading article published in the Naxalite weekly *Deshabrati* said that the installation of the United Front government in Bengal had opened up opportunities for communist revolutionaries to work with renewed vigour among the people so that the revisionists may be exposed and the class struggle intensified. The article said: "We are not of the same opinion as those who hold that our call to boycott the elections has not been effective. The correctness of the slogan cannot be verified by one election only. This is only the beginning and the slogan's political impact can be realized from the reactions it has evoked in the bourgeois and revisionist circles."

Though efforts were made to form a third and more militant communist party composed of those who are generally called Naxalites, there persisted differences among the Naxalites themselves as to the policy that they should pursue. Besides West Bengal, the two major bastions of the Naxalite movement in the country are in Andhra Pradesh and Kerala, but most of the Maoist followers in these states have serious differences with the tactical approach approved by the West Bengal Naxalites.

In 1968 about eight thousand Naxalites in Andhra Pradesh broke away from the cpi(m). But the vast majority of these Naxalites led by Nagi Reddy were disaffiliated from the All-

India Coordination Committee because of their alleged divergent stand on the tactical line adopted by the Central Committee,[2] though it was stated that the relationship between the Committee and the Andhra unit will be a "nonantagonistic one."[3] Nagi Reddy and his followers were not entirely enthusiastic about the need to boycott all elections, and they were in favour of a limited participation in parliamentary elections. Nagi Reddy and his group were also not inclined to support the attack on Tellicherry and Pulpalli police stations by the Naxalite group of Kunnikal Narayanan, and in adopting this attitude they defied the stand taken by the All-India Coordination Committee. Another criticism that the Coordination Committee made of Nagi Reddy and his group was that this group had not given their wholehearted support to the Girijan tribal revolt in Sirkakulam district of Andhra Pradesh.[4] So far as the various Naxalite groups in Kerala are concerned, they also follow a line almost identical to that of Nagi Reddy and, as such, they are not viewed with favour by the militant Naxalites of Bengal.

The Naxalites, in spite of their internal dissensions, have been active in the political field and have engaged in various violent activities in Bengal, Andhra Pradesh, and Kerala. In Srikakulam and surrounding areas the Naxalite-led tribals have participated in open revolt, attacking landlords, confiscating grains, and otherwise taking the law in their own hands. The Naxalites seek to follow Maoist methods and are generally supported by Peking Radio. In various parts of Bengal, Andhra Pradesh, Kerala, and even Tamil Nadu, Mao posters continue to appear from time to time.

The Naxalites characterized the leftist United Front government of Bengal as a revisionist government and as "the answer of the reactionary ruling class to the challenge thrown by the people." The participants in these governments were described as "lackeys of imperialism."[5] The United Front government of Bengal, on the other hand, while regarding the Naxalites as misguided extremists, ordered the release, early in 1969, of all the Naxalite prisoners including Kanu Sanyal, the Naxalite leader of Bengal.

After his release from prison, Kanu Sanyal declared on 1 May 1969 at a May Day rally at Calcutta that a new communist party called Communst Party of India (Marxist–Leninist) had been formed on 22 April 1969. Kanu Sanyal claimed that a revolutionary situation existed in the country and that such a situation called for a revolutionary party, the formation of which had been obstructed in the past by "revisionists" within the communist movement. He urged the people to shun "petty-bourgeois revolution-mongering" and asked them to regard the Naxalbari movement as an illustration of the successful application of Mao's teachings to a specific case. He welcomed the "fire" that had spread to Srikakulam in Andhra Pradesh[6] and in several other places in different parts of India, and emphasized the importance of armed peasants' struggles in a "semi-colonial, semi-feudal" country like India.

At this May Day rally[7] a resolution was passed emphasizing the need to defend communist China, the "great fortress of the international communist movement" and to carry forward the Indian revolution "which had already begun." Kanu Sanyal also recalled the revolutionary struggles of the Indian people in the past and attributed the setbacks that they had suffered to the lack of any revolutionary party worth the name. He asserted that the credit for launching the Naxalbari movement belonged to the peasants of the area and to Charu Mazumdar, the theoretician of the CPI(M–L), this third communist party, and he warned the people against the attempts of "revisionists and neo-revisionists" to misdirect their revolutionary urge into the "blind alley" of parliamentary democracy.

The CPI(M–L) called upon its hard core of youth and students to go to the villages and to work there amongst the peasants as wholetime workers. The basic task, according to this new party, was to liberate the rural areas through armed agrarian revolution and then to encircle the cities and, finally, to liberate them. This new party has pledged itself to the task of bringing about an agrarian revolution in the light of Mao's teachings. For completing the revolution, four principal enemies have to be defeated by armed force. They are: US imperialism, Soviet social imperialism, the comprador–bureaucrat big bourgeoisie, and the feudal landlords. This new party places the USA and the Soviet Union in the same category and claims that in the name of giving economic aid "US imperialism and Soviet social–imperialism have reduced India into a neo-colony and are carrying on their cruel neo-colonial exploitation and rule."[8]

As regards the CPI and the CPI(M) and divers leftist forces in India, this new party has nothing but scorn. All these parties are only serving the reactionary classes. They are counter-revolutionaries. They have kept their movements within the bounds of the law, which was "based on exploitation," and have indulged merely in a programme of economism, reformism, and parliamentarianism. "We must reject," declares this new party, "the hoax of parliamentarianism and accomplish the People's Democratic Revolution through revolutionary people's war by uniting the fighting masses in a revolutionary way under the leadership of the Communist Party and the working class and on the firm basis of workers–peasants alliance."

The CPI(M–L) emphasizes the need for internationalizing the national liberation movements in different countries under the leadership of Chairman Mao. World history, according to it, has entered into the new era of Maoism,[9] and the task of all revolutionaries in this era is to take "the pledge of uniting with the great people of China, establishing unity with the liberation movements in different countries, to develop a revolutionary united front for destroying imperialism and its main collaborator, modern revisionism." According to this new party the communist movement in India during the last 40 years had betrayed the cause of the revolution and had suffered because the communist parties of India had not taken into account the role of the peasantry. The new party would seek to mobilize the peasants for launching guerrilla wars and for bringing about an armed agrarian revolution.[10]

In April 1970 this new party, which had so far operated primarily in different rural pockets in West Bengal and had concentrated on the annihilation of jotedars and other "class enemies," decided to extend its programme and field of operation to industrial areas. This change of programme was necessitated because, it was felt, that conventional weapons, such as hartals and strikes, had become largely "blunted against organized capitalist attacks in the form of lock-out, lay-off and closures." The struggle had, therefore, to "take the form of a *gherao*, clashes with the police and the capitalists, barricade fights, and annihilation of class enemies and their agents." But urban struggles were, however, to remain only secondary and the industrial workers, who had been initiated in Maoist philosophy, were to go to the countryside to join the battle of the peasants engaged in the armed seizure of the countryside. In spite of the criticism of the Nagi Reddy group that this new party was seeking to follow the path of terrorism and a Ché Guevara line in politics in the name of Maoism, this new party did not rule out resort to terroristic methods either in the countryside or in industrial areas. In April 1970 bands of young men, believed to be Naxalites, raided various educational institutions and libraries in Calcutta, raised slogans in support of Maoism and burned portraits of Gandhi as also books by or on Gandhi.

After Kanu Sanyal had announced on 1 May 1969 that a new communist party wedded to a policy of armed seizure of power had been formed, Y. B. Chavan, Home Minister of India, declared that he was considering what changes in the law were necessary to meet the insurrectionary challenge of the Naxalites. To discuss this question Chavan invited leaders of various political parties. Individuals were liable under the existing law for sedition and for acts of violence, but there was no law under which activities of organizations advocating armed revolution and taking steps in pursuance of that objective could be curbed, and, therefore, thought Chavan, legislative action might be necessary to meet the challenge posed by extremist Maoist groups in the country.

Certain Swatantra leaders met Chavan in this connection and urged him to introduce legislation to outlaw not only the Naxalites but also the communists. The Swatantra leaders made no distinction between the Naxalites and the other communists. They charged that the communists have no faith in democracy and lamented that "communists were given respectability" since Nehru's time. They urged Chavan to follow the example of UAR and certain other countries in banning the communist parties altogether.[11]

The CPI did not accept Chavan's invitation to discuss the threat to law and order posed by the Naxalites, and they pointed out that there were communal and other anti-social elements in the country against whom action should be taken first. Ajoy Mukherji, then United Front Chief Minister of West Bengal, declared in May 1969 that the Naxalites did not yet pose a serious threat to the law and order situation in Bengal,[12] and Jyoti Basu, CPI(M) leader, declared that the United Front government of Bengal considered the Naxalite movement as basically a peasants' movement, but that if the Naxalites indulged in anti-social activities they would be arrested.[13]

From time to time violent clashes have taken place between the Naxalites and the supporters of the United Front in Bengal. Such clashes also took place during the May demonstrations at Calcutta in 1969 and, as a result, more than a hundred people were injured. Denouncing the activities of the Naxalites, Jyoti Basu claimed that they were the "agents of the Congress" and asserted that the government could, if it so desired, "finish the Naxalites in a day."[14] Referring to the violent activities of the Naxalites, Jyoti Basu asked: "Is this politics? Is this revolution to attack the representatives of democratic people with bombs, beat up journalists and engage in anti-social activities by carrying the portrait of the great leader Mao Tse-tung?"

The Naxalites attacked the supporters of the United Front in Bengal saying that the exploiting classes had two fronts: one, the Congress and, the other, the United Front. They claimed that through elections the people could never be liberated, only the personnel of those who exploited them could be changed. They raised the slogan that a people was powerless without a people's army or without guns and rifles. They filled up the walls of the city of Calcutta with these slogans and with the portraits of Mao Tse-tung. They declared that China's Chairman was India's Chairman and that the Indian people could attain liberation only by pursuing Maoist methods.

After the United Front government of Bengal fell in March 1970 and President's rule was imposed the virulence of Naxalite activities increased. Since April 1970 the Naxalites began to burn Gandhi's portraits and books. They desecrated the statues of Gandhi, C. R. Das and other political leaders as also those of religious and social reformers, such as Swami Vivekananda, Iswar Chandra Vidyasagar, and Acharya P. C. Ray. They attacked educational institutions and examination centres, threw bombs at or set fire to libraries and laboratories, and denounced the present educational system and the prevailing cultural values as being utterly bourgeois and wholly reactionary. Resort was also had to individual terroristic activities in order to intimidate businessmen and government officials, some of whom were assassinated. A large number of police constables and officials

were also wounded as a result of attacks with knives or bombs
and some of them succumbed to the injuries.

Faced with all these the administration and police authorities
in Bengal clamoured for greater and more stringent powers in
order to stamp out the widespread and evergrowing violent
activities. In particular, the authorities in Bengal desired the
enactment of a Preventive Detention Act. Eventually, in November 1970 the West Bengal Prevention of Violent Activities Act
received the Presidential assent. This Act armed the authorities
with powers similar to those conferred by the Preventive Deten-
tive Acts. But almost all the leftist parties of Bengal vehemently
denounced this Act and organized a *bandh* throughout Bengal
on 8 December 1970 in protest against this Act and what were
claimed to be the excesses of the police and particularly of the
CRP.

The Naxalites of Bengal have organized themselves under
the CPI(M–L). Other Naxalite and Maoist sections, particularly
in Andhra Pradesh, who have not joined the CPI(M–L), have also
taken some concrete steps for the formation of a new centre,
short of a party, to coordinate their movements. The most
prominent figure in these efforts is Nagi Reddy.

In May 1969 Nagi Reddy is reported to have produced a
secret blueprint for the formation of a new Maoist party or a
centre wedded to the concept of violent overthrow of the
established government. The immediate programme envisaged by
Nagi Reddy follows faithfully the Maoist strategy of starting
a revolution in the mountains, gradually coming down to the
plains and ending with the encirclement of the major towns and
their capture. The first priority in this programme is the launching of a movement for the forcible occupation of lands belonging to big landlords and for the distribution thereof among the
landless. This movement of forcible seizure of land is to start
in the forest-covered mountains and contiguous areas. Later, as
the people's revolt would gather momentum, this movement
would extend to the plains, and then to the towns, leading to the
ultimate overthrow of the "existing big bourgeoisie landlord
rule" in the country. The programme of the proposed new party
also includes the taking over of all foreign investments and the
investments of those Indian capitalists who collaborate with
foreign capitalists, the provision of higher wages for the working

class, the securing of full employment for the middle class, the replacement of the existing army by a "people's army," the promise of the right of self-determination to the different "nationalities" in the country, the scrapping of all unequal treaties, and the immediate withdrawal of India from the Commonwealth. Another significant objective of the Andhra Naxalites is the radical reorientation of India's foreign policy so that India would range herself against "international imperialism in general, and against American and British imperialism and the collaborating Soviet revisionist gang in particular," that is to say, India would take steps for the formation of a Sino–Indian front against the world's major powers.[15]

The party contemplated by these Andhra Naxalites would organize a united front for carrying out the programme of a new people's democratic revolution. This party would dissociate itself from "the revisionist parties who have washed their hands of the Indian revolution," and would support not merely the revolutionary Girijan tribals, now being sustained by the Calcutta Naxalite group[16] in the Srikakulam area, but other revolutionary groups also. There are pockets in Andhra Pradesh and the adjoining areas—in the dense forests of Warangal, East Godavari, and Visakhapatnam, Karimnagar, Adilbad, as also in Bastar—where, in the opinion of the Nagi Reddy group, conditions are ideal for starting revolutionary activities.

Nagi Reddy and his emissaries toured different parts of the country, including Calcutta, and held secret discussions with like-minded groups for the formation of a "centre" which will be less than a rigidly disciplined party but yet more than a loose coordinating committee. The centre will have power to enforce a minimum code of discipline, bearing in mind the three fundamental aspects of Maoism: a well-organized party based on Marxism–Leninism, an organized army under the party's political control, and the successful implementation of the programme of a united front of all revolutionary classes. This centre will have nothing to do with the CPI(M–L). In fact, the Nagi Reddy group fears that the CPI(M–L) with its methods and style of work is likely to degenerate into petty-bourgeois romanticism, sectarianism, and terrorism so that the party would tend more towards the Ché Guevara line than Maoism. It is noteworthy that even a section of the Bengal Naxalites have charged Charu

Mazumdar, secretary of the CPI(M–L), as being arrogant, and they bitterly criticized Kanu Sanyal, Naxalite leader of Bengal, for having compared Mazumdar with Mao. This section also charged that Mazumdar had neglected work among the masses and sought to rely only on the formation of secretive armed guerrilla units.[17]

In Andhra Pradesh violent communist revolutionary bands have been quite active from the salwood forests of Srikakulam to the scattered mountains of Telengana. There have been raids on houses of landlords and the ambushing of police patrols as part of a violent guerrilla struggle for a "proletarian revolution." The Naxalite activities in Andhra Pradesh are not perpetrated by a few isolated and militant revolutionaries. There is more than one band or group of Naxalites which operates in the state, with activities that are almost identical and progressing on parallel lines. The two most important groups, one affiliated to the newly formed CPI(M–L) and the other led by the former CPI(M) leader Nagi Reddy, have both engaged themselves in collecting arms and money in preparation for the "coming revolution."[18]

In Srikakulam district the Naxalites are well organized and have a considerable sway over the 80,000 Girijan tribals of the district. Through a number of raids the Naxalites have also been able to create an arsenal of guns in addition to spears, axes, bows, and arrows. Further, Naxalite activity is now no longer confined to the tribal belt of Srikakulam but has spread to divers other places including Visakhapatnam, east and west Godavari, Krishna, Guntur, Nellore, Anantapur, and Khammam districts. These rebel bands have conducted numerous raids in order to secure arms and money, and the raids have been mainly directed against landlords known to possess licensed arms and cash money. As a result of these raids the financial troubles of these rebels have also been eased. Governmental efforts in stamping out these raids and Naxalite violence have not been entirely successful. The Naxalites have perfected their underground hideouts and there are several safe houses in the coastal belt used by these extremists as venues for conferences, resting places for couriers, and indoctrination centres for new recruits.

The Naxalites, whether belonging to the CPI(M–L) or not, differ fundamentally both from the CPI and the CPI(M). Accord-

29

ing to CPI(M–L), India is a semi-colonial and semi-feudal country and the immediate task before it is to effect the kind of agrarian people's democratic revolution that was effected in China. The enemies of this revolution are the imperialists of the USA and USSR and the comprador–bureaucratic capitalists and feudalists. The allies of this revolution are the workers, landless peasants, middle peasants, revolutionary intelligentsia, and other toiling people. The CPI(M–L) hails the revolutionary path taken by China and relies on the experience gained in armed resistance in Naxalbari. "Naxalbari represents," wrote Charu Mazumdar, "the first ever application of Mao Tse-tung thought on the soil of India."[19]

The CPI(M–L) does not believe that revolutionary advance is possible through the parliamentary road or by the adoption of peaceful means. The ultimate truth is contained in Mao's saying —political power grows out of the barrel of a gun. To effect the Indian revolution, revolutionary bases or pockets would have to be established in rural areas. From these rural areas the peasants' revolutionary or guerrilla forces would eventually encircle the cities and capture them.

The path for this revolution was foreshadowed in Naxalbari and the neighbouring districts of Darjeeling in 1967 when the extreme communists, now members of the CPI(M–L), led the landless or land-poor peasants to mount attacks on landlords, the plantation owners and the governmental authorities; seized land, arms, and grain, organized people's courts to punish "local tyrants" and to defend by armed violence the fruits of this agrarian revolution. The power of the feudal landlords and plantation owners was shattered as also the law and order which protected their power.

According to the CPI(M–L) India is a neo-colonial country where, under the formal facade of independence, foreign impe-rialists and Indian feudalists wield absolute power. The Indian government, therefore, cannot give relief to the people or do anything worthwhile. On the contrary, by subserving the inter-ests of the imperialists and feudalists it can only accentuate the economic crisis of the country and increasingly isolate itself from the people. The only way of destroying a government attached to the apron strings of the imperialists and feudalists is armed struggle. Accordingly, Mao's teaching that the seizure of power through armed force is the highest form of revolution is the only teaching worth following and the only path towards revolution.[20]

The CPI(M–L) charges that both the CPI and the CPI(M) harbour the illusion that a socialist transformation of society would be possible without resort to violence. The CPI(M–L) rules out such a possibility altogether. According to it, violence must necessarily accompany revolution, and power can never be seized except through the barrel of the gun. The CPI(M–L) not only believes in violence; it also considers that India is now ready for a violent revolution. In fact, it does not regard the situation in India as any different from that which existed in pre-revolutionary Russia or China.

The communists have always been inspired by the model of the Russian revolution and, prior to the Russian revolution, by the experience of the Paris Commune. Later, the history of the Chinese revolution, the struggle of the Cuban revolutionaries, and the fight of the Vietnamese guerrillas inspired them. In all these revolutions, force had been used. Could there be any revolution without force and violence? Did the history of the Paris Commune, or the revolution in Russia, or the struggle of the Chinese communists, or the activities of the Cuban revolutionaries, or the war waged by the Vietnamese people, warrant any conclusion that a revolution could be attained without violence? It is this question which the CPI(M–L) considers the most fundamental and as one which cannot but be answered in the negative.

But is the condition of India the same as that of pre-revolutionary Tsarist Russia or feudal, warlord-ridden China? Does not the existence of parliamentary democracy, the introduction of universal franchise, and other democratic rights make Indian conditions fundamentally different from those which existed in Russia under the despotism of the Tsars, and in China under the domination of feudal warlords? It is this fundamental and crucial difference in the Indian situation that the CPI(M–L) refuses to recognize.

The CPI(M–L) regards the franchise only as a means for the deception of the masses and, accordingly, it gave a call for boycotting the elections. But if the franchise was only a means for deceiving the people and if the ruling class, through the ruling

29A

SOCIALISM AND COMMUNISM IN INDIA

Congress Party, could never be displaced, then how could the ruling Congress Party lose so many states in the fourth general elections in India in 1967, and how could leftist united fronts capture state power in West Bengal and Kerala? Here again the CPI(M–L) chooses to ignore the great power which adult franchise and other democratic rights have given to the people.

Marx had recognized the mighty power that the common man could exercise by wielding the franchise in a country where universal franchise had been introduced. In one of his letters, Marx said: "If the working class in England and the United States should win a majority in parliament, in Congress, it could legally abolish those laws and institutions which obstruct its development."[21] Again, writing in the *New York Daily Tribune* of 25 August 1852, Marx declared: "Universal suffrage is the equivalent of political power for the working class of England, where the proletariat forms the large majority of the population, where, in a long, though underground, civil war, it has gained a clear consciousness of its position as a class, and where even the rural districts know no longer any peasants, but only land-lords, industrial capitalists (farmers) and hired labourers. The carrying of universal suffrage in England would, therefore, be a far more socialistic measure than anything which has been honoured with that name on the continent. Its inevitable result, here, is the political supremacy of the working class."[22]

India is not a semi-colony but a parliamentary democracy with a system of adult franchise. It has also a centralized political machinery and an all-India army. Is revolution through old-style street fighting with barricades, or revolution of the classical Chinese communist style either necessary or feasible in the conditions prevailing in India? Behind the armed raiders in Telengana or Naxalbari, the Indian police or the army did not see the "people" but only rebels. Further, there are formidable difficulties in the way of developing pockets of resistance throughout India in the manner of Telengana or Naxalbari. The communist movement in India is not one organized movement. It has been split among the CPI, the CPI(M), and the CPI(M–L), leaving aside other minor splinter parties or groups. The CPI and CPI(M), to some extent, are prepared to tread the parliamentary path, though they do not rule out the possibility of resorting to nonparliamentary and violent methods, if need be. But it is unlikely that either the CPI or the CPI(M) would cooperate with the CPI(M–L) to bring about an armed revolution. Again, India is a vast country with a federal political structure, and communist influence is not uniform throughout the country. Moreover, there is an underlying hostility between certain socialist parties, such as the SSP and the PSP, and communist parties of India. The other parties opposed to the communist parties are the two Congress parties and, even more vehemently, the Jana Sangh and Swatantra, which latter are opposed not merely to communism but also to socialism. In the face of the great diversities of India and her varied political parties, and also in view of the existence of a unified Indian state, having emergency powers, and which can rely on the support of an all-India army, the task that the CPI(M–L) has set before itself of bringing about an armed revolution through peasant guerrillas is hazardous in the extreme.

NOTES AND REFERENCES

1. See B. T. Ranadive, *The Two Programmes Marxist and Revisionist*, CPI(Marxist) publication, Calcutta, 1966.
2. See the article, "Politics of Nagi Reddy," in *Liberation*, October 1969, Vol. 2, No. 12, pp. 37-45.
3. *Liberation*, March 1969.
4. See the article, "Srikakulam—Going the Way Predicted by Charu Mazumdar," in *Liberation*, September 1969, Vol. II, No. 11, pp. 66-85.
5. "Political Resolution of the Communist Party of India (Marxist-Leninist)," in *Liberation*, May 1969.
6. After visiting Srikakulam in March 1969, Charu Mazumdar wrote an article, "Srikakulam—Will it be the Yenan of India?" in *Liberation*, Vol. 2, No. 5.
7. A detailed report of the speeches at the rally was given in *The Statesman* on 2 May 1969.
8. See the article, "Soviet Revisionist New Tsars' Use 'Aid' to Stretch Their Claws into Asia, Africa and Latin America," in *Liberation*, October 1969, Vol. 2, No. 12, pp. 76-83.
9. *Liberation*, October 1969, Vol. 2, No. 12, pp. 13-14.
10. *Liberation*, September 1969, Vol. 2, No. 11, pp. 81-82.
11. *The Statesman*, 12 May 1969.
12. Ibid.
13. *The Statesman*, 10 May 1969.

14. *The Statesman*, 2 May 1969.

15. The CPI(M–L) also holds similar views. See Charu Mazumdar's article, "Develop Revolutionary War to Eliminate War of Aggression Against China," in *Liberation*, Vol. 2, October 1969, pp. 5-6.

16. See the article, "Flames of Guerrilla Struggle Burn Brightly in Srikakulam," in *Liberation*, October 1969, Vol. 2, No. 12, pp. 46-49.

17. *The Statesman*, 9 July 1969.

18. *The Statesman*, 5 July 1969.

19. See the artcle, "Fight Against the Concrete Manifestation of Revisionism," in *Liberation*, September 1969, Vol. 2, No. 11, p. 8.

20. *Liberation*, September 1969, Vol. 2, No. 11, pp. 75, 81-82.

21. *Letters to Bebel, Liebknecht, Kautsky and Andere*, Moscow, 1935, pp. 516-17.

22. Karl Marx, *Selected Writings in Sociology and Social Philospohy* (ed. Bottomore and Rubel), London, 1956, p. 138.

Bibliography

PRIMARY AUTHORITIES

A. Books, Pamphlets, Speeches and Miscellaneous Writings •

ADHIKARI, G. M., *From Peace Front to People's War*, 2nd ed., Bombay, 1944.

——*Pakistan and Indian National Unity*, Bombay, 1944.

AHMAD, MUZAFFAR, *The Communist Party of India and Its Formation Abroad*, Calcutta, 1962.

——*S. A. Dange and the National Archives*, Calcutta, 1964.

BHINGA, THE RAJA OF, *Democracy Not Suited to India*, Allahabad, 1888.

BHAVE, VINOBA, *Revolutionary Sarvodaya*, Bharatiya Vidya Bhavan, 1964.

——*Bhoodan Yagna*, Ahmedabad, 1957.

——*Swaraj Sastra*, Kashi, 1959.

BOSE, SUBHAS, *The Indian Struggle, 1920-34*, Calcutta, 1948.

——*The Indian Struggle, 1935-42*, Calcutta, 1952.

——*Important Speeches and Writings of Subhas Bose*, ed. J. S. Bright, 1945

——*Selected Speeches of Subhas Chandra Bose*, Publications Division, Government of India, 1962.

——*Crossroads : Being the Works of Subhas Chandra Bose*, Netaji Research Bureau, Calcutta.

DAS, BHAGAWAN, *Ancient Versus Modern Scientific Socialism*, Madras, 1934.

DEVA, ACHARYA NARENDRA, *Socialism and the National Revolution*, Bombay, 1946.

DANGE, S. A., *For Anti-Imperialist Unity, Democratic Consolidation*, Speech at the International Conference of Communist and Workers' Parties, October 1969.

——*On the Indian Trade Union Movement*, Bombay, 1952.

——*Mahatma Gandhi and History*, New Delhi, 1969.

——*Gandhi Versus Lenin*, Bombay, 1921.

——*India: From Primitive Communism to Slavery*, 4th ed., 1961.

DUTT, R. P., *Modern India*, London, 1927.

——*India Today*, London, 1940.

——*Situation in India*, Bombay, 1950.

——*India Today and Tomorrow*, Delhi, 1955.

DYAKOV, A. M., *Crisis in the Colonial System*, Bombay, 1951.

——*A New Stage in India's Liberation Struggle*, 1947.

——"The Situation in India," in *New Times*, 28 February 1947.

GANDHI, M. K., *Hind Swaraj*, Madras, 1921.
——*An Autobiography*, Ahmedabad, 1959.
——*Mahatma Gandhi : His Life, Writings and Speeches*, Madras, 1918.
——*Socialism of My Conception*, Bharatiya Vidya Bhavan, 1957.
——*The Essential Gandhi : An Anthology*, ed. Louis Fischer, London, 1963.
——*Towards Lasting Peace*, ed. A. T. Hingorani, Bharatiya Vidya Bhavan, 1966.
——*To· The Students*, Ahmedabad, 1958.
——*Economic and Industrial Life and Relations*, Ahmedabad, 1957-59.
GLADING, PERCI, *India Under British Terror*, London, 1931.
GHOSH, AJOY, *On the Work of the Third Congress of the Communist Party of India*, Delhi.
——*Articles and Speeches*, Moscow, 1962.
——*Towards a Mass Communist Party*, New Delhi, 1958.
GOPALAN, A. K., & HIREN MUKERJEE, *Communists in Parliament*, New Delhi, 1957.
GOVERNMENT OF INDIA, *Communist Violence in India*, New Delhi, 1949.
HUTCHINSON, L., *Conspiracy at Meerut*, London, 1935.
JOSHI, P. C., *Indian Communist Party : Its Policy and Work in the War of Liberation*, Introduction by Harry Pollitt, Communist Party of Great Britain, 1942.
——*For the Final Bid for Power : The Communist Plan Explained*, Bombay, 1946.
——*Communist Reply to Congress Working Committee's Charges*, Bombay, 1945.
——*For a Mass Policy*, Allahabad, 1951.
KRIPALANI, J. B., *Sarvodaya*, New Delhi, 1951.
LIMAYE, MADHU, *Evolution of Socialist Policy*, Hyderabad, 1952.
LENIN, V. I., *Selected Works*, 12 Vols.
——*Complete Works*, 18 Vols.
LOHIA, RAM MANOHAR, *Marx, Gandhi and Socialism*, Hyderabad, 1963.
——*The Third Camp in World Politics*, Bombay, 1951.
MASANI, M. R., *Socialism Reconsidered*, Bombay, 1944.
——*Congress Misrule and the Swatantra Alternative*, Bombay, 1966.
MARX, KARL, *Articles on India*, Bombay, 1943.
——*Selected Works*, 2 Vols, Moscow, 1955.
Meerut Conspiracy Case, London, 1933.
Meerut Trial : Facts of the Case, London, 1929.
MEHTA, ASOKA, *Democratic Socialism*, Bharatiya Vidya Bhavan, 1959.
——*Studies in Asian Socialism*, Bombay, 1959.
MUKERJEE, HIREN, *India and Parliament*, New Delhi, 1962.
NARAYAN, JAYAPRAKASH, *Why Socialism*, Benaras, 1936.
——*Towards Struggle*, Bombay, 1946.
——*From Socialism to Sarvodaya*, 1959.
——*Socialism, Sarvodaya and Democracy*, ed. Bimla Prasad, 1964.

NAMBOODIRIPAD, E. M. S., *Economics and Politics of India's Socialist Pattern*, New Delhi, 1966.
——*The Programme Explained*, December, 1966.
——*The Mahatma and the Ism*, New Delhi, 1959.
NAOROJI, DADABHAI, *Poverty and Un-British Rule in India*, London, 1901.
——*Speeches and Writings*, Natesan, Madras, 1910.
NEHRU, JAWAHARLAL, *Whither India*, Allahabad, 2nd ed., 1933.
——*Autobiography*, 1936.
——*India and the World*, London, 1936.
——*Recent Essays and Writings*, Allahabad, 1937.
——*Eighteen Months in India*, Allahabad, 1938.
——*The Unity of India*, 1944.
——*The Discovery of India*, 2nd ed., London, 1947.
——*A Bunch of Old Letters*, 2nd ed., 1960.
——*Nehru on Socialism: Selected Speeches and Writings*, Delhi, 1964.
——*Selected Writings of Jawaharlal Nehru (1915-50)*, ed. J. S. Bright, New Delhi.
——*Conversations with Nehru*, ed. Tiber Mende, 1956.
——*Soviet Russia*, Bombay, 1929.
——*Jawaharlal Nehru's Speeches, 1935-57*, Publications Division, Government of India, New Delhi, 1958.
——*Quintessence of Nehru*, selected and with an introduction by K. T. Narasimha Char, London, 1961.
PAI, M. R. (ed.), *Socialism in India: A Commentary*, a collection of Forum of Free Enterprise Publications, Bombay, 1967.
PAL, B. C., *Nationality and British Empire*, Calcutta, 1916.
——*The World Situation and Ourselves*, Calcutta, 1919.
RAI, LAJPAT, *The Political Future of India*, New York, 1919.
——*India's Will to Freedom*, Madras, 1921.
RANADE, M. G., *Essays on Indian Economics*, Bombay, 1899.
RANADIVE, B. T., *The Two Programmes—Marxist and Revisionist*, Calcutta, December 1966.
——*On People's Democracy*.
RANGA, N. G., *Kisans and Communists*, Bombay.
RAO, C. RAJESWAR, BHOWANI SEN & Y. V. KRISHNA RAO, *Problems of India's Agrarian Sector*, New Delhi.
RAO, M. B. (ed.), *The Mahatma: A Marxist Symposium*, New Delhi, 1969.
ROY, M. N., *India in Transition*, Geneva, 1922.
——*One Year of Non-Cooperation*, Calcutta, 1923.
——*The Future of Indian Politics*, London, 1926.
——*The Aftermath of Non-Cooperation*, London, 1926.
——*The Alternative*, Bombay, 1940.
——*Nationalism and Democracy*, 1942.
——*War and Revolution*, 1942.
——*The Communist International*, 1943.
——*Jawaharlal Nehru*, Delhi, 1945.
——*Revolution and Counter-Revolution in China*, Calcutta, 1946.

——*New Humanism: A Manifesto*, Calcutta, 1947.
——*Materialism: An Outline of the History of Scientific Thought*, Calcutta, 1951.
——*Radical Humanism*, 1952.
——*Reason, Romanticism and Revolution*, Calcutta, 1952.
——*National Government or People's Government*, Delhi, 1956.
——*Fragments of a Prisoner's Diary*, Calcutta, 2nd ed., 1957.
——*Politics, Power and Parties*, Calcutta, 1960.
——*Memoirs*, 1964.
SARDESAI, S. G., *India and the Russian Revolution*, Communist Party publication, New Delhi, 1967.
SAUNDERS, R., *A Glance at India's Aristocracy, or Should there be a House of Lords for India?*, Manchester, 1890.
SPRATT, PHILIP, *Blowing Up India*, Calcutta, 1955.
SEN, MOHIT, *Communism and the New Left*, 2nd ed., New Delhi.
STALIN, J., *Problems of Leninism*, Moscow, 1947.
TAGORE, RABINDRANATH, *Letters From Russia*, Calcutta, 1960.
——*Nationalism*, London, 1917.
TAGORE, SOUMENDRA NATH, *Historical Development of the Communist Movement in India*, Calcutta, 1944.
TELANG, K. T., *Selected Writings and Speeches*, ed. V. V. Thakur, Bombay, 1916.
TSE-TUNG, MAO, *New Democracy and Other Articles*, National Book Agency, Calcutta, 1966.
——*Selected Writings*, National Book Agency, Calcutta, 1967.
ZAHEER, SAZZAD, *A Case for Congress-League Unity*, Bombay, 1944.
ZHDANOV, A., *The International Situation*, Moscow, 1947.

B. PARTY REPORTS, STATEMENTS, RESOLUTIONS AND OTHER DOCUMENTS

Indian National Congress, Annual Reports.
Congress Presidential Addresses, First Series, Madras, 1915.
Congress Presidential Addresses, Second Series, Madras, 1934.
Report of the First Conference of the Congress Socialist Party, 1934.
Platform of the Party, Adopted at the First Conference of the Congress Socialist Party, 1934.
Report of the Faizpur Conference of the Congress Socialist Party, 1936.
Socialist Unity, Congress Socialist Party, 1938.
War Circulars Nos. 1 to 3, 1939-40, Congress Socialist Party.
Correspondence between Mahatma Gandhi and P. C. Joshi, Bombay, 1945.
For the Final Assault: Tasks of the Indian People in the Present Phase of Indian Revolution, Communist Party of India, Bombay, 1946.
Declaration of Independence: Communist Party Resolution for the Constituent Assembly, Bombay, 1946.

Resolutions on Foreign Policy 1947-1957, Indian National Congress, All India Congress Committee, New Delhi.

Communist Statement of Policy : For the Struggle for Full Independence and People's Democracy, Resolution Passed by the Central Executive Committee of the Communist Party of India Held in Bombay 'on December 7-16, 1947, Bombay, 1947.

Resolutions Passed at the Sixth Annual Conference of the Socialist Party Held at Nasik, March, 1948, Bombay, 1948.

Political Thesis of the Communist Party of India Adopted at the Second Congress Held in Calcutta from February 2 to March 6, 1948, Bombay, 1948.

The Leninist Way, Revolutionary Socialist Party, 1950.

We Build for Socialism : Platform of the Socialist Party, Bombay, 1951.

Election Manifesto of the Communist Party of India, Central Election Board of the Communist Party of India, Calcutta, 1951.

Draft Programme of the Communist Party of India, issued by CPI Politbureau, April, 1951.

Statement of Policy Adopted by the All India Conference of the Communist Party of India, October 1951, Calcutta.

Socialist Party Policy Statement, Bombay, 1951.

Election Manifesto of the All India Forward Bloc (Subhasist), Calcutta, 1951.

Election Manifesto of the All India Forward Bloc (Marxist), 1951.

Election Manifesto, Revolutionary Socialist Party, Calcutta, 1951.

Election Manifesto : What Congress Stands For, All India Congress Committee, New Delhi, 1951.

Manifesto of the Kisan Mazdoor Praja Party, New Delhi, 1951.

The Merger : How and Why, Praja Socialist Party, Bombay, 1952.

Nehru–Jayaprakash Talks, Praja Socialist Party, Bombay, 1953.

Programme of the Communist Party of India Adopted by the Third Party Congress, Madurai, December 27, 1953 to January 4, 1954, New Delhi, 1954.

Communist Conspiracy at Madurai, Documents on the III Congress of the CPI, Democratic Research Service, Bombay, 1954.

Policy Statement Adopted by the Second National Conference of the Praja Socialist Party Held in Gaya from December 26 to 30, 1956, New Delhi, 1956.

Political Resolution Adopted at the Fourth Congress of the Communist Party of India Held in Palghat from April 19 to 29, 1956, New Delhi, 1956.

Indian National Congress, Election Manifesto, New Delhi, 1957.

Socialist Party, Election Manifesto, Praja Socialist Party, New Delhi, 1957.

Constitution of the Communist Party of India Adopted at the Extraordinary Party Congress, Amritsar, April 1958, New Delhi, 1958.

Resolutions of the Communist Party of India Adopted at the Extraordi-

nary Party Congress, Held in Amritsar in April 1958, Communist Party of India, New Delhi, 1958.

Resolution of the Meeting of the Communist and Workers' Parties of Socialist Countries (1957) and Statement of the Conference of the 81 Communist and Workers' Parties (1960), National Book Agency, Calcutta, 1960.

A Proposal Concerning the General Line of the International Communist Movement, Letter Dated June 14, 1963 of the CPC *Central Committee to the Central Committee of the* CPSU, National Book Agency, Calcutta.

Fight against Revisionism: Political Organizational Report Adopted at the Seventh Congress of the Communist Party of India (Marxist), 31 October to 7 November 1964, Calcutta, December 1955.

Resolutions Adopted at the Seventh Congress 31 October to 7 November 1964, Calcutta, Communist Party publication.

Programme of the Communist Party of India Adopted by the Seventh Congress of the Communist Party of India, Calcutta, 31 October to 7 November 1964.

Resolutions of the Seventh Congress of the CPI, *Resolutions of the Central Committee of the Communist Party of India (Marxist), Tenali, 12 to 19 June 1966.*

Election Manifestos of the Indian National Congress, CPI, CPI(M), PSP *and* SSP *for the Fourth General Elections. These* are set out in *General Election In India,* ed. M. Pattabhiram, New Delhi, 1967.

Central Committee Draft for Ideological Discussion Adopted by the Central Committee of the Communist Party of India (Marxist) Madurai 18 to 27 August 1967, Calcutta.

Central Committee Resolutions Adopted by the Central Committee of the Communist Party of India (Marxist), Madurai, 18 to 27 August 1967, Calcutta.

On the Left Deviation, Resolution of the Central Committee, Communist Party of India (Marxist), Madurai, 18 to 27 August 1967 and Other Information Documents, Calcutta.

Full Text of the Alternative Ideological Draft of the Andhra Comrades Placed at the Burdwan Plenum of the CPI(M) *1968.*

Ideological Resolution Adopted by the Central Plenum, Burdwan, 5 to 12 April 1968, Communist Party of India (Marxist).

National Integration: Note Submitted by the CPI(M) *to the National Integration Council meeting in Srinagar from 20 June 1968.*

Political Organizational Report of the Central Committee to the Eighth Congress of the Communist Party of India (Marxist), Cochin, 23 to 29 December 1968.

Political Resolution Adopted by the Eighth Congress, Cochin, 23 to 29 December 1968, Communist Party of India (Marxist).

Constitution Adopted by the Eighth Congress, Cochin, 23 to 29 December 1968, Communist Party of India (Marxist).

*Tasks on the Trade Union Front, Resolution of the Central Committee of
the Communist Party of India (Marxist)*, National Book Agency, 3rd
ed., July 1968.

A Course of Party Education, Second Stage (For Branch Secretaries),
Communist Party publication, 1968.

*Documents Adopted by Eighth Congress of the Communist Party of
India, 1968*, Communist Party publication.

*Central Committee Statement on Moscow Conference Adopted by the
Central Committee of the Communist Party of India (Marxist) at its
Session in Calcutta, 15 to 20 July 1969*, Calcutta, 1969.

*Tasks on the Kisan Front, Resolution of the Central Committee, Communist
Party of India (Marxist)*, 3rd ed., May 1968.

*19th Session, All India Kisan Sabha, Madurai, 26–28 January 1968, Decision
and Resolutions*, AIKS publication, New Delhi.

On the Agrarian Question : A Collection, National Book Agency, August
1969.

*Forward to Unity and Struggle, Proceedings and Documents of the All-
India Trade Union Conference, Calcutta, 28 to 31 May 1970*, CITU
publication, Calcutta, 1970.

All India Kisan Sabha, Report of the 20th Session, Barasat, AIKS publication, 1970.

*Struggle for Land Surges Forward, Proceedings and Resolutions of the
Central Kisan Council 24 to 25 April 1970, All India Kisan Sabha.*

*Resolutions and Report of the National Council of the Communist Party
of India, New Delhi, 8 to 13 May 1970.*

Previous Splits in the AITUC, CPI(M) publication, Calcutta, 1970.

C. PERIODICALS, JOURNALS AND NEWSPAPERS

Communist International
Congress Socialist
Harijan
Labour Monthly
Liberation
Modern Review
New Age
People's Democracy
People's War
People's Age
Radical Humanist
The Indian Annual Register
The Masses of India
Young India
The Statesman
The Times of India
The Tribune

The Hindu
The Hindustan Times
National Herald

SECONDARY AUTHORITIES

AIYAR, S. P., & R. SRINIVASAN, *Studies in Indian Democracy*, Bombay, 1961.
AUSTIN, GRANVILLE, *The Indian Constitution: Cornerstone of a Nation*, London, 1966.
AZAD, MAULANA ABUL KALAM, *India Wins Freedom*, Delhi, 1959.
BHARGAVA, G. S., *Leaders of the Left*, Bombay, 1951.
BALABUSHEVICH, V. V., & BIMLA PRASAD, *India and the Soviet Union: A Symposium*, New Delhi, 1969.
BALABUSHEVICH, V. V., & A. M. DYAKOV (ed.), *A Contemporary History of India*, Delhi, 1964.
BANDYOPADHYAYA, JAYANTANUJA, *Indian Nationalism Versus Internatoinal Communism*, Calcutta, 1966.
BARY, WM. THEODORE DE, & OTHERS (ed.), *Sources of Indian Tradition*, New York, 1958.
BEAUCHAMP, JOHN, *British Imperialism in India*, 1935.
BOSE, NIRMAL, *Studies in Gandhism*, Calcutta, 1947.
BRECHER, MICHAEL, *Nehru: A Political Biography*, London, 1961.
BUCHANAN, D. H., *The Development of Capitalist Enterprise in India*, 1934.
CHAND, GYAN, *Socialist Transformation of Indian Economy*, New Delhi, 1965.
CHAND, TARA, *History of the Freedom Movement in India*, Publications Division, Government of India, 1961.
DESAI, A. R., *Social Background of Indian Nationalism*, Bombay, 4th ed., 1966.
DRUHE, DAVID N., *Soviet Russia and Indian Communism*, New York, 1959.
DUTT, ROMESH, *The Economic History of India under Early British Rule*, 2 Vols, Publications Division, Government of India.
FIC, VICTOR M., *Peaceful Transition to Communism in India, Strategy of the Communist Party*, Bombay, 1969.
FISCHER, LOUIS, *The Life of Mahatma Gandhi*, 2 Vols, Bharatiya Vidya Bhavan, 1965.
GADGIL, D. R., *Indian Planning and the Planning Commission*, Ahmedabad, 1958.
GHOSE, SANKAR, *The Renaissance to Militant Nationalism in India*, Calcutta, 1969.
GOYAL, O. P., *Contemporary Indian Political Thought*, Allahabad, 1965.
GRIFFITHS, SIR PERCIVAL, *Modern India*, 4th ed., London, 1965.
HANGEN, WELLES, *After Nehru, Who?*, London, 1965.
HARRISON, S. S., *India: The Most Dangerous Decades*, Madras, 1965.

KARNIK, V. B., *The Left-groups in India*, Calcutta.

KAUSHIK, P. D., *The Congress Ideology and Programme 1920-47*, Bombay, 1964.

KAUTSKY, JOHN H., *Moscow and the Communist Party of India*, New York, 1946.

KAYE, SIR CECIL, *Communism in India*, 1926.

LAKHANPAL, P. L., *History of the Congress Socialist Party*, Lahore, 1946.

LIMAYE, MADHU, *Communist Party : Facts and Fiction*, Hyderabad, 1951.

——*Indian Communism Today*, Bombay, 1954.

MAJUMDAR, R. C., *History of the Freedom Movement in India*, 3 Vols, Calcutta, 1963.

MAJUMDAR, R. C. (ed.), *The History and Culture of the Indian People : Struggle for Freedom*, Bombay, 1969.

MASANI, M. R., *A Short History of the Communist Party of India*, London, 1954.

MASHRUWALA, K. G., *Gandhi and Marx*, Ahmedabad, 1954.

MEHERALLY, YUSUF, *Leaders of India*, 2 Vols, Bombay, 1942.

MORRIS-JONES, W. H., *Parliament in India*, London, 1957.

——*The Government and Politics of India*, London, 2nd ed., 1967.

MORAES, FRANK, *Jawaharlal Nehru*, Bombay, 1959.

MUKERJEE, HIREN, *Gandhi : A Study*, 2nd ed., 1960.

——*The Gentle Colossus : A Study of Jawaharlal Nehru*, Calcutta, 1964.

OVERSTREET, GENE D., & MARSHALL WINDMILLER, *Communism in India*, Bombay, 1960.

PALMER, N. D., *Indian Political System*, 1961.

PANNIKKAR, K. B., *An Outline of the History of the AITUC*, 1959.

PANIKKAR, K. M., *Asia and Western Dominance*, London, 1965.

PARK, R. L., & IRENE TINKER, *Leadership and Political Institutions in India*, Princeton, 1959.

PATTABHIRAM, M. (ed.), *General Election in India*, 1967.

PHILIPS, C. H. (ed.), *Evolution of India and Pakistan, 1885-1947, Select Documents*, London, 1962.

RAM, MOHAN, *Indian Communism : Split within a Split*, New Delhi, 1969.

RANGA, N. G., *Kisans and Communists*, Bombay.

RIENCOURT, AMAURY DE, *The Soul of India*, London, 1961.

SHAH, A. B., *Planning for Democracy and Other Essays*, Bombay, 1967.

SHARMA, B. S., *The Political Philosophy of M. N. Roy*, Delhi, 1965.

SHARMA, G. K., *Labour Movement in India*, 1963.

SHELVANKAR, K. S., *The Problem of India*, 1943.

SINHA, L. P., *The Left-Wing in India (1919-47)*, Muzaffarpur, 1965.

SOCIALIST UNION, *Twentieth Century Socialism : The Economy of To-morrow*, Indian edition, 1970.

SPRATT, PHILIP, *Communism in India*, New Delhi, 1952.

SITARAMAYYA, P., *The History of the Indian National Congress*, 1946-47..

TENDULKAR, D. G., *The Mahatma : The Life of Mohandas Karamchand Gandhi*, 8 Vols, Publications Division, Government of India, Revised edition, 1960.

TINKER, HUGH, *India and Pakistan: A Political Analysis*, London, 2nd ed., 1967.

TOYE, HUGH, *The Springing Tiger*, London, 1959.

VARMA, V. P., *Modern Indian Political Thought*, Agra, 3rd ed., 1967.

WEINER, MYRON, *Party Politics in India, Princeton*, 1957.

Index

Adhikari, G. M., 160
Ahmed, Fakhruddin Ali, 225
Ahmed, Muzaffar, 293, 322
Ahmed, Z. A., 85
Ali, Sadiq, 232
Allison, G., 154
Anandamath, 46
Association, British Indian, 75, 78, 79
Ayyanger, Gopalaswami, 68
Azad, Maulana Abul Kalam, 163

Balabushevich, 131, 320
Balwantrai, Mehta, 86-87
Banerjee, Surendranath, 173
Banerjee, Sasipada, 47
Banerjee, Subodh, 286, 378
Basavapunniah, 251, 366
Basu, Jyoti, 322, 385-87, 446
Bengalee, S. S., 50
Bhakta, Satya, 297
Bhave, Vinoba, 83, 86-87, 101, 113-14
Bose, Mrinal Kanti, 71
Bose, Subhas Chandra, 16, 19, 29, 60, 82, 129, 195-202, 203, 264
Bradley, B. F., 155
Brayne, F. L., 86
Bulganin, 131

Cawnpore Conspiracy Case, 162, 357
Champaran Agitation, 80
Chatterjee, Bankim Chandra, 46
Chatterjee, Ramananda, 10
Chattopadhyaya, Virendranath, 144

Chauri Chaura incident, 121, 148
Chavan, Y. B., 151, 166, 219, 239, 367, 445-46
Chettiar, Singaravelu, 297
Chowdhury, Tridib, 377
Citrine, Walter, 60
Comintern, 123-24, 128, 144, 148, 150, 151, 156, 158-69, 301, 304-08
Communist and Workers Party, 138, 347
Communist International, 15, 31, 126, 140, 299-309
Communist Party, British, 152, 154, 297, 329
Communist University of Toilers of the East, 145
Congress of Oppressed Nationalities, 155
Cornwallis, Lord, 37
Curzon, Lord, 80

Dalhousie, Lord, 38-39
Dange, S. A., 88, 136-37, 155, 293, 322, 329, 331, 351, 354, 355, 367
Das, Bhagawan, 25-27
Das, C. R., 18-19, 56, 58, 105, 147, 148, 149, 197
Dasgupta, Promode, 222, 251, 381-82, 385
David, Sassoon, 52
Desai, Mahadev, 107
Desai, Morarji, 216, 219, 225, 226-27, 228-29, 232, 237, 238, 240
Deshmukh, C. D., 229
Deva, Narendra, 210, 263, 268-69, 282

466

Dhara, Sushil, 379
Digby, William, 3
Dutt, R. P., 17, 61, 97, 121, 125, 128, 130, 153-54, 159, 297, 298, 299, 310-11, 320, 330, 331-32
Dutt-Bradley thesis, 128
Dutt, Romesh, 3, 4
Dyakov, A. M., 130, 131, 132, 320, 321, 324, 327

Fernandes, George, 383

Gadgil, D. R., 208
Gandhi, Indira, 185, 216, 217, 218, 219-20, 223, 224-48, 392
Gandhi, Mahatma, 19-20, 22, 28, 29, 54, 70, 80-81, 86-92, 93-94, 95, 96, 97, 98, 99, 100, 101, 102, 104, 105, 106, 108-15, 117, 119, 120-39, 146, 187, 218, 267, 269
Gangapadhaya, Dwarakanath, 46, 47
Ghate, S. V., 58
Ghose, Ajoy, 137, 324, 329, 334, 353
Ghose, Atulya, 242
Ghose, Aurobindo, 6
Ginwala, F. J., 56
Giri, V. V., 55, 56, 222, 232
Godwin, William, 101
Gokhale, Gopal Krishna, 107, 173
Gopalan, A. K., 365, 366
Goray, N. G., 288
Gupta, Bhupesh, 88, 353

Hardie, Keir, 2, 52
Hardinge, Lord, 40
Horniman, B. G., 10
Hyndman, 1, 2

Indian Communists, 16, 17, 20, 22, 23, 30, 31-32, 58, 59, 60, 61-62, 63, 67, 127-28, 129, 133, 135, 136,

137, 138, 154-55, 202, 293-359
Indian Communist Party, 24, 31, 67, 70, 125-26, 135, 136, 297, 310-11, 312, 313, 317-20, 324-59
Indian Labour, 15, 19, 45-73
Indian National Congress, 16, 18, 55, 56, 61, 62, 63, 65, 79, 82, 117, 148, 161, 164, 201, 205, 209, 216-25, 260, 261, 276, 284, 366, 381
Indian Socialists, 19, 23-24, 260-90
Iqbal, 13, 14, 28-29
Irwin, Lord, 301

Jinnah, M. A., 19
Joshi, N. M., 56
Joshi, P. C., 129, 317, 321, 322, 325, 328, 331, 353

Kamath, H. V., 238
Kamaraj, 223, 225, 231, 235, 237, 246
Kardelji, E., 321
Karunanidhi, M., 229, 367
Kerala mid-term poll, 375, 391
Khan, Syed Ahmed, 77
Kishan Sabha, 81, 82, 85
Konar, Harekrishna, 85, 368
Kripalani, J. B., 185, 238, 283, 284
Kripalani, Sucheta, 223
Krishnamachari, T. T., 247
Krishnan, N., 250
Kumar, Sudhin, 282
Kundu, Nishith Nath, 288
Kuusinen, Otto, 132

Lahiri, Somnath, 335, 385
Lal, Dewan Chaman, 56
Laski, Harold, 60
Lenin, 20-22, 23, 53, 112, 145, 295
Limaye, Madhu, 88, 284
Liu Shao-Chi, 327-28
Lohia, Ram Manohar, 282, 284, 285
Lokhandy, N. M., 51
Lytton, Lord, 75

MacDonald, Ramsay, 52
Madhok, B., 220, 227
Mahatab, Harekrishna, 239
Malaviya, K. D., 229
Marx, Karl, 2, 4, 452
Masani, M. R., 170, 223, 229, 267, 279-81, 313
Mazumdar, Charu, 443, 450
Mehta, Asoka, 3, 275, 285
Menon, Achutha, 256, 351, 374
Menon, K. P. Subramaniam, 386
Menon, V. K. Krishna, 217-18
Meerut Conspiracy Case, 60, 293, 301-04
Mill, J. S., 4
Minto, Lord, 77-78
Misra, S. N., 245
Mitra, Krishna Kumar, 47
Mohini, Hazarat, Maulana, 31, 151
Montagu-Chelmsford Report, 40-41
Montagu, 79
Moore, Major, 49, 50
Moplah rebellion, 81
Morley, 39-40
Mukerjee, Hiren, 133-34
Mukherjee, Ajoy, 252, 379, 383, 388, 389, 390
Mukherjee, Biswanath, 252
Munro, Thomas, 37-38
Munshi, K. M., 117, 208

Nair, M. N. Govindan, 352
Nair, N. Sreekantan, 372
Namboodiripad, E. M. S., 131, 133, 134, 135, 170, 249, 354, 365, 371, 372, 389
Nanda, Gulzari Lal, 64-65, 378
Narain, Raj, 88
Naoroji, Dadabhai, 1, 2, 3, 4, 173
Narayan, Jayaprakash, 24-25, 67, 68, 87, 114, 115, 116, 164, 170, 238, 261, 262, 263, 266, 273, 276, 277-79, 284, 285, 313, 316-17, 322
Nehru, Jawaharlal, 9, 14, 29, 82, 100, 101, 117, 118, 119, 120, 131, 132,
155, 181-213, 218, 260, 302-03, 319-20, 322-23
Nijalingappa, 217, 219, 220, 225, 231, 232, 238, 239, 242, 243, 244

Osmani, Shaukat, 293
Owen, Robert, 1, 2, 49

Pal, Bepin, 6, 7-8, 27, 75
Pal, Kristo Das, 77
Pant, G. B., 201
Patel, Vallabhbhai, 81, 185, 203, 216, 218
Patil, S. K., 218, 224-25, 240
Petit, J. B., 53
Piatnitsky, O., 155-56
Pillai, Pattom Thanu, 284
Plekhanov, 294
POLITICAL PARTIES :
  Bangla Congress 261, 380, 386-87, 387-88, 388-89
  C. P. I., 70, 221-22, 229, 230, 248-57, 347, 362, 371-72, 382, 392, 395-412
  C. P. I.(M), 31, 70, 77, 84-85, 138, 222, 248, 249-50, 257-359, 362-63, 368-69, 370, 379 383-84, 388, 414-37
  C. P. I.(M-L), 84, 85, 138-39, 439-44, 446-49, 450, 451-52
  Congress (O), 245, 246
  Congress (R), 247-48, 257, 376
  C. S. P., 61, 70, 128, 197, 264, 277, 283, 311, 313
  Forward Bloc, 285-86
  Jana Sangh, 114
  Lok Tantrik Dal, 289
  Lok Sevak Sangha, 380
  Marxist Forward Bloc, 380
  Muslim League, 19
  Peasants and Workers Party, 289
  Poona Sarvajanik Sabha, 50
  P. S. P., 255, 283, 284, 285, 288, 383
  R. C. P. I., 380
  R. S. P., 285, 286, 377

s. s. p., 254, 285, 287, 382
s. u. c., 253-54, 286
Swarajya Party, 153, 261
Swatantra Party, 111, 116-17
Prasad, Rajendra, 106, 185

Rai, Lajpat, 6, 7, 8,14-15, 55, 56
Rajagopalachari, C., 116,117, 185
Ramamurthy, P., 227
Ram, Jagjivan, 246, 247, 375
Ranade, M. G., 4, 7, 173
Randive, B. T., 126, 251, 317-18, 320-24, 325-26, 328, 365
Ranga, N. G., 65, 81, 82, 117
Rao, Rajeswar, 255, 328, 331, 369, 381
Rao, Shiva, 59
Ray, Siddhartha Sankar, 242, 375
Roy, Ellen, 120, 121
Roy, Kiran Sankar, 322
Roy, M. N., 23, 31, 97, 120, 124, 135, 139, 143-67, 169-79, 278-79, 294-95, 296
Roy, Rammohan, 1
Reddy, Nagi, 441, 447, 448
Reddy, N. Sanjiva, 225
Rosmer, Alfred, 296

Saklatwala, S., 58-59, 61, 122
Sanyal, Kanu, 442
Saraswati, Swami Sahajananda, 82
Sardesai, S. G., 20, 124
Saunders, R. C., 76
Sen, P. C., 242
Sen, Ranen, 385, 386
Shastri, Pandit Shivnath, 46, 47
Shastri, Lal Bahadur, 216, 219
Shekhar, Chandra, 216, 218
Shukla, V. C., 367
Singaravelu, 31
Singh, Charan, 239
Singh, Ram Subhag, 243
Sinha,Tarakeshwari, 237
Sitaramayya, Pattabhi, 201
Spratt, Philip, 135, 154, 155

Strikes, 6, 51, 52, 53, 54, 58, 59, 64, 67-68, 145
Subramaniam, 242, 244, 246, 247
Succaram, Rughabe, 51
Sundaryya, P., 249, 369, 372
Sun-Yat-sen, 23
Swaraj, 17, 147

Tagore, Rabindranath, 10-13, 107, 110, 111
Tagore, Soumendranath, 155, 156
Telang, K. T., 1, 4, 113
Tilak, 6, 53, 295
Tolstoy, 9
TRADE UNIONS :
   a.i.t.u.c., 14, 15, 55, 56, 57-58, 60-61, 63, 67, 68, 69, 70
   All India Red Trade Union Congress, 70
   c.i.t.u., 72
   Girni Kamgar Union, 59
   h.m.p., 70
   h.m.s. 71
   h.m.s.s., 65
   International Federation of Trade Unions, 57
   i.l.o., 55
   International Labour Union, 57
   i.n.t.u.c., 65, 70, 71, 72
   Red International Trade Union, 57
   u.t.u.c., 71-72
Trotsky, 24, 257

United Fronts, 361-92

Vajpayee, A. B., 222-23
Valia, 127
Vivekananda, 11, 30, 120, 197

Wadia, B. P., 54-55, 57

Zaheer, Sajjad, 319
Zhadnov, 321
Zhukov, 131, 320, 326